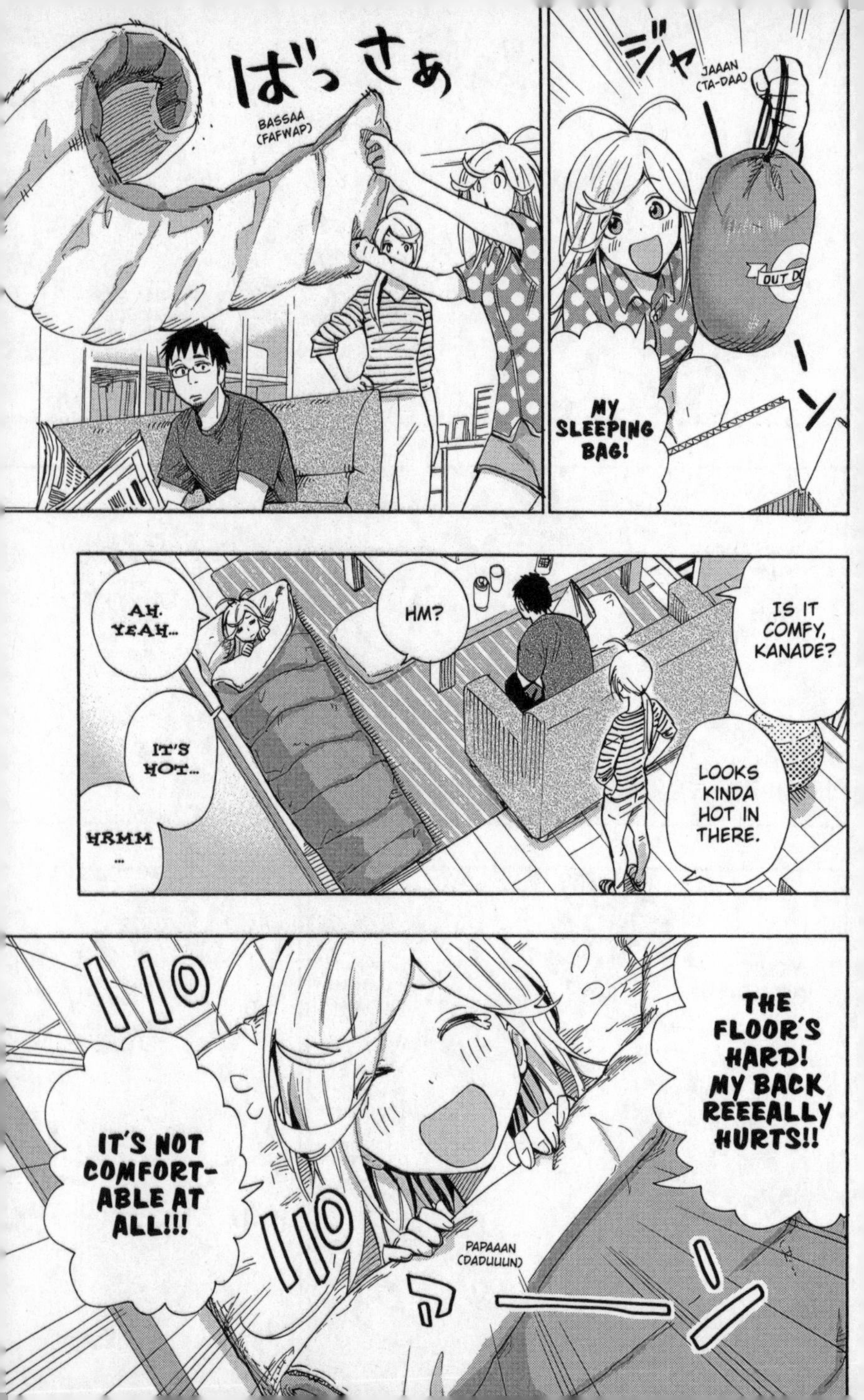
ジャーン
JAAAN (TA-DAA)
MY SLEEPING BAG!
ばっさぁ
BASSAA (FAFWAP)
IS IT COMFY, KANADE?
LOOKS KINDA HOT IN THERE.
HM?
AH. YEAH...
IT'S HOT...
HRMM ...
THE FLOOR'S HARD! MY BACK REEEALLY HURTS!!
PAPAAAN (DADUUUN)
IT'S NOT COMFORT-ABLE AT ALL!!!

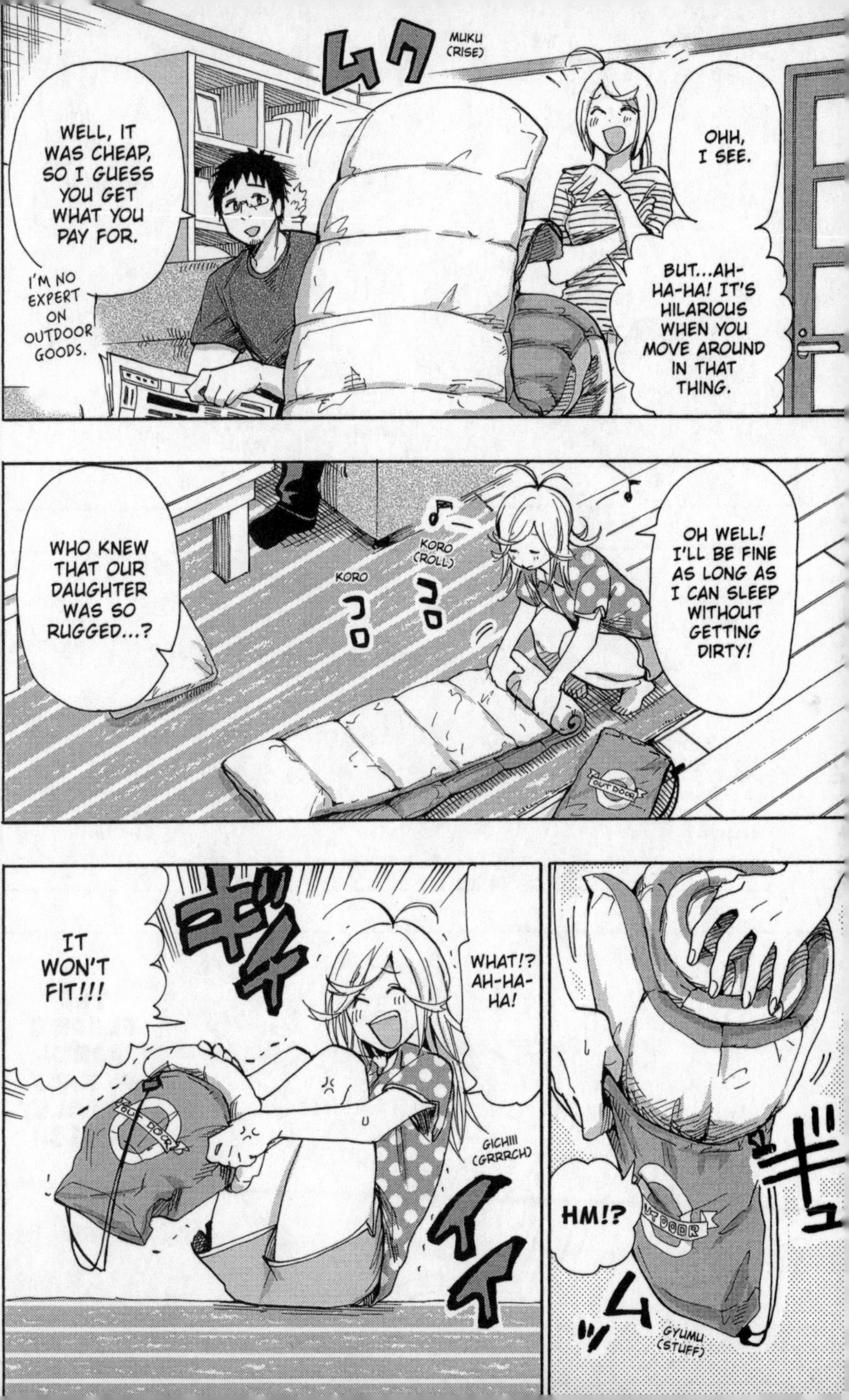
OHH, I SEE.
BUT...AH-HA-HA! IT'S HILARIOUS WHEN YOU MOVE AROUND IN THAT THING.
MUKU (RISE)
WELL, IT WAS CHEAP, SO I GUESS YOU GET WHAT YOU PAY FOR.
I'M NO EXPERT ON OUTDOOR GOODS.
OH WELL! I'LL BE FINE AS LONG AS I CAN SLEEP WITHOUT GETTING DIRTY!
KORO (ROLL)
KORO
WHO KNEW THAT OUR DAUGHTER WAS SO RUGGED...?
HM!?
GYUMU (STUFF)
WHAT!? AH-HA-HA!
GICHIII (GRRRCH)
IT WON'T FIT!!!

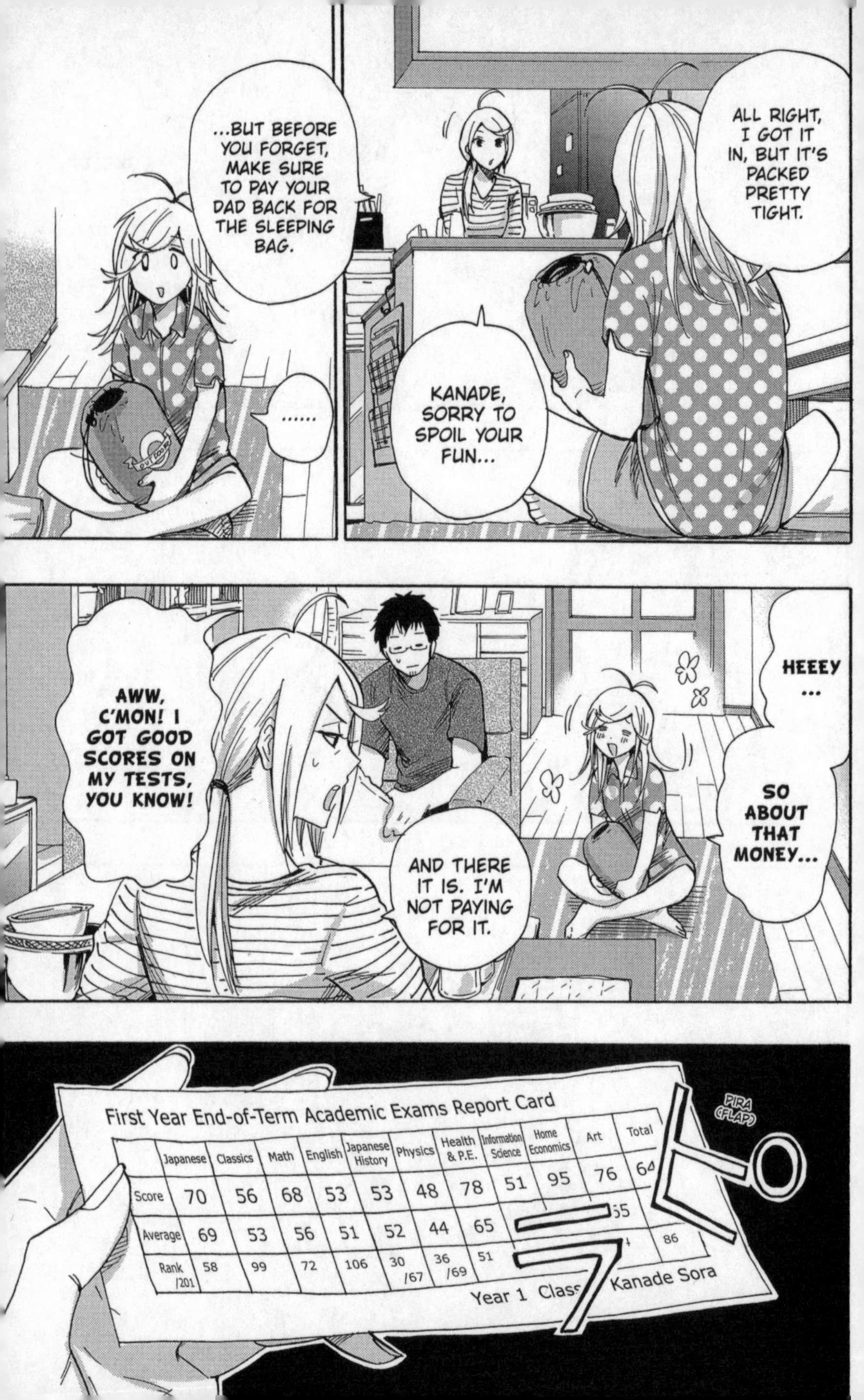
ALL RIGHT, I GOT IT IN, BUT IT'S PACKED PRETTY TIGHT.
KANADE, SORRY TO SPOIL YOUR FUN...
...BUT BEFORE YOU FORGET, MAKE SURE TO PAY YOUR DAD BACK FOR THE SLEEPING BAG.
......
OUTDOOR
HEEEY ... SO ABOUT THAT MONEY...
AND THERE IT IS. I'M NOT PAYING FOR IT.
AWW, C'MON! I GOT GOOD SCORES ON MY TESTS, YOU KNOW!
PIRA (FLAP)
First Year End-of-Term Academic Exams Report Card
Japanese Classics Math English Japanese History Physics Health & P.E. Information Science Home Economics Art Total
Score 70 56 68 53 53 48 78 51 95 76 64
Average 69 53 56 51 52 44 65
Rank /201 58 99 72 106 30 /67 36 /69 51 86
Year 1 Class
Kanade Sora

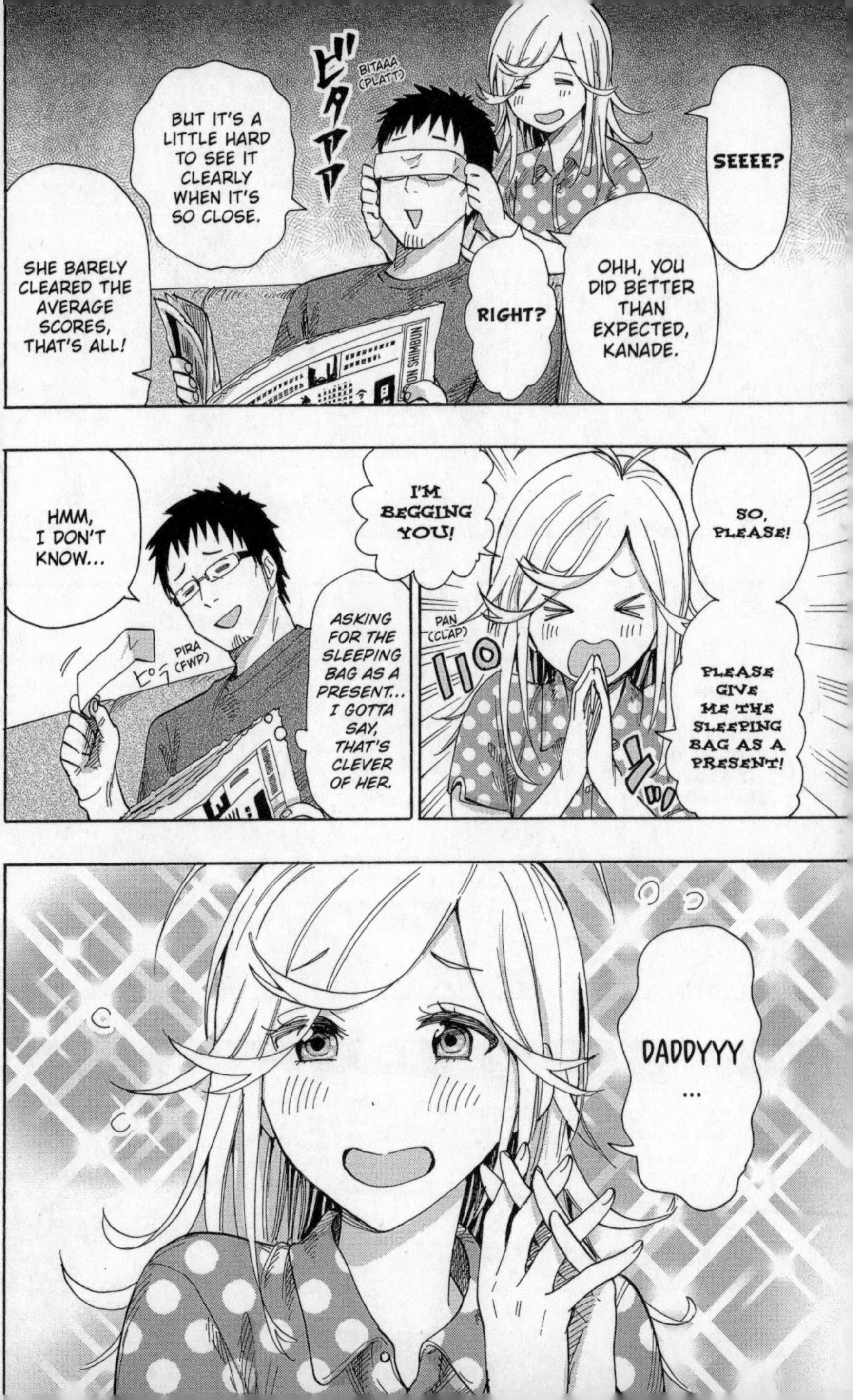
SEEEE?
OHH, YOU DID BETTER THAN EXPECTED, KANADE.
RIGHT?
BITAAA (PLATT)
BUT IT'S A LITTLE HARD TO SEE IT CLEARLY WHEN IT'S SO CLOSE.
SHE BARELY CLEARED THE AVERAGE SCORES, THAT'S ALL!
SO, PLEASE!
I'M BEGGING YOU!
PAN (CLAP)
PLEASE GIVE ME THE SLEEPING BAG AS A PRESENT!
ASKING FOR THE SLEEPING BAG AS A PRESENT... I GOTTA SAY, THAT'S CLEVER OF HER.
HMM, I DON'T KNOW...
PIRA (FWP)
DADDYYY
...

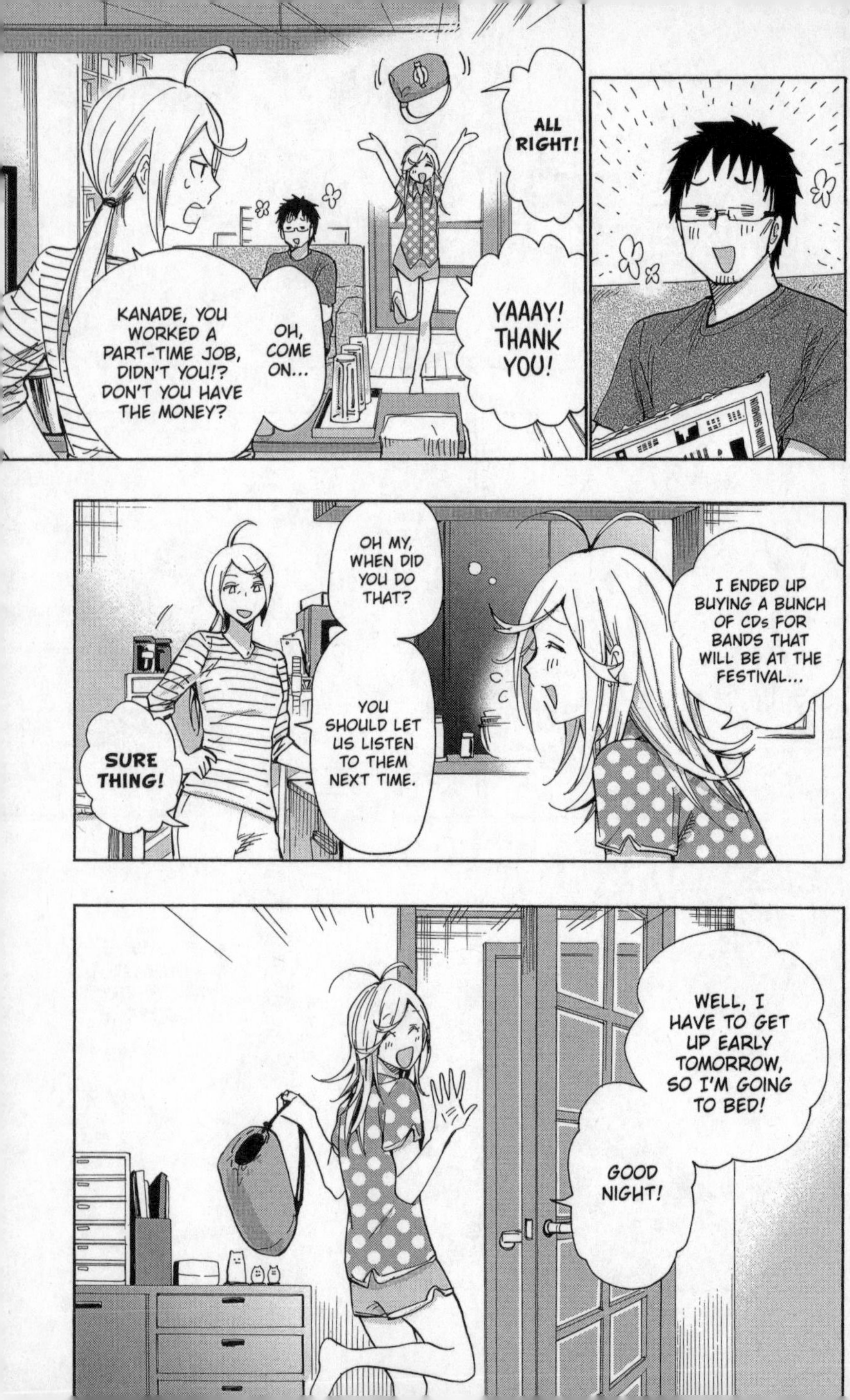
ALL RIGHT!
YAAAY! THANK YOU!
OH, COME ON...
KANADE, YOU WORKED A PART-TIME JOB, DIDN'T YOU!? DON'T YOU HAVE THE MONEY?
I ENDED UP BUYING A BUNCH OF CDs FOR BANDS THAT WILL BE AT THE FESTIVAL...
OH MY, WHEN DID YOU DO THAT?
YOU SHOULD LET US LISTEN TO THEM NEXT TIME.
SURE THING!
WELL, I HAVE TO GET UP EARLY TOMORROW, SO I'M GOING TO BED!
GOOD NIGHT!

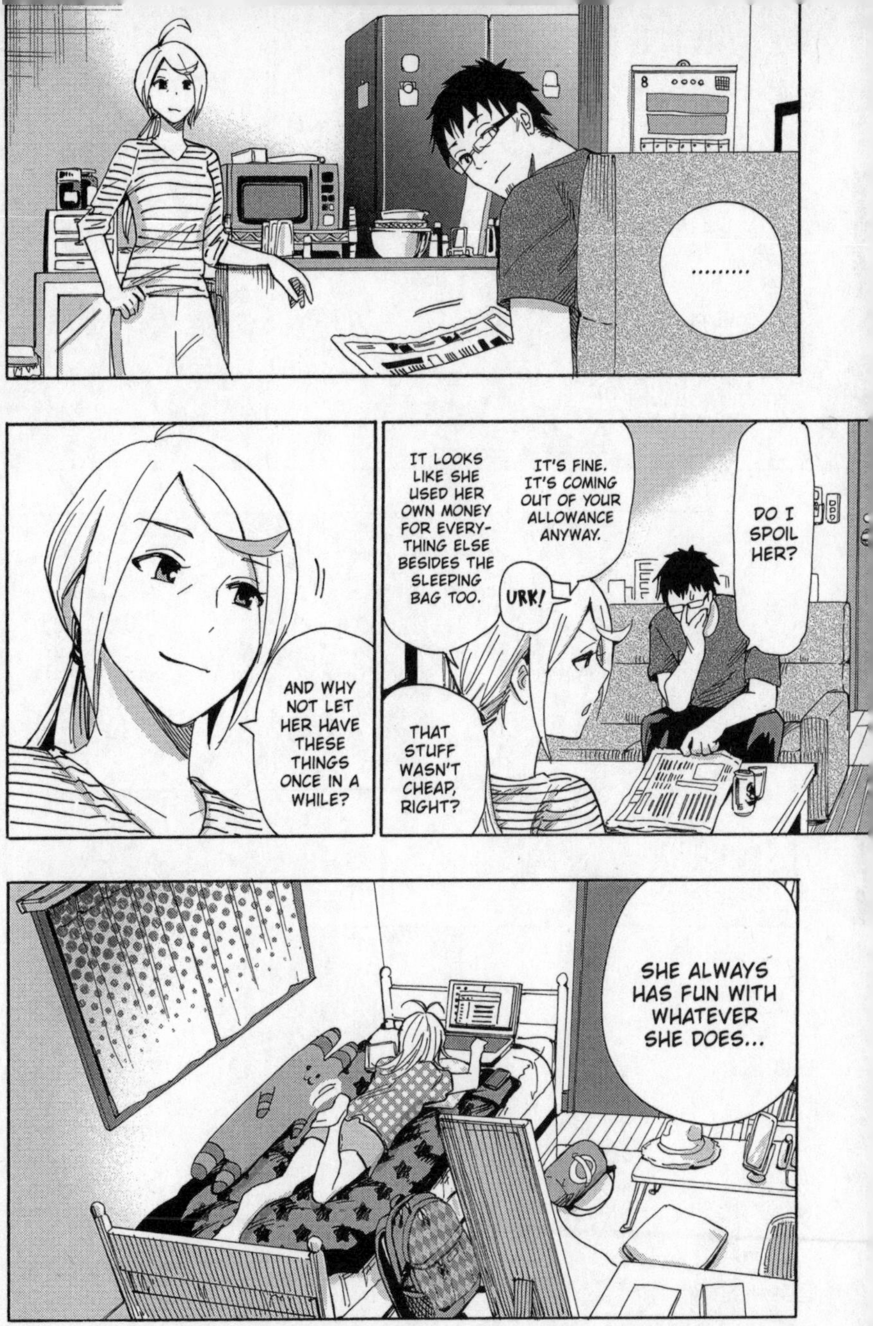
....
DO I SPOIL HER?
IT'S FINE. IT'S COMING OUT OF YOUR ALLOWANCE ANYWAY.
IT LOOKS LIKE SHE USED HER OWN MONEY FOR EVERY-THING ELSE BESIDES THE SLEEPING BAG TOO.
URK!
THAT STUFF WASN'T CHEAP, RIGHT?
AND WHY NOT LET HER HAVE THESE THINGS ONCE IN A WHILE?
SHE ALWAYS HAS FUN WITH WHATEVER SHE DOES...

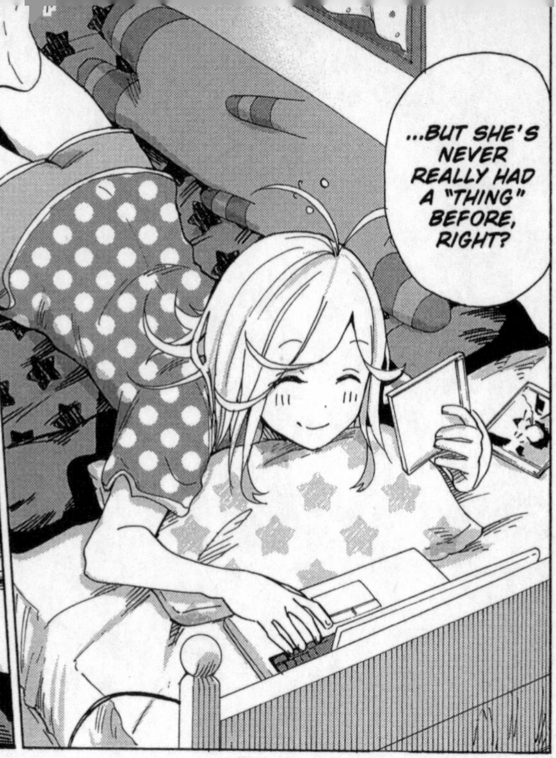
...BUT SHE'S NEVER REALLY HAD A "THING" BEFORE, RIGHT?

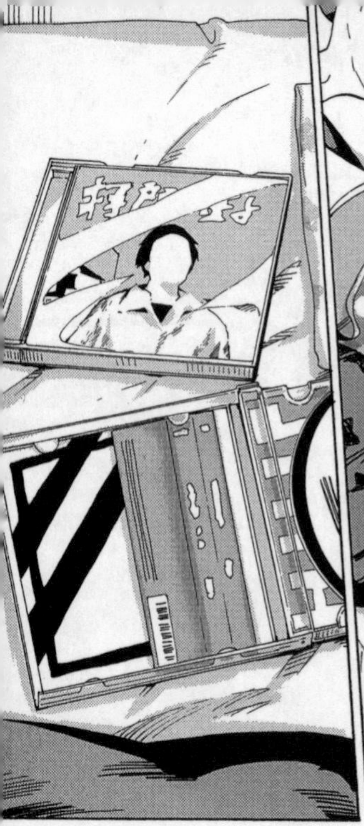

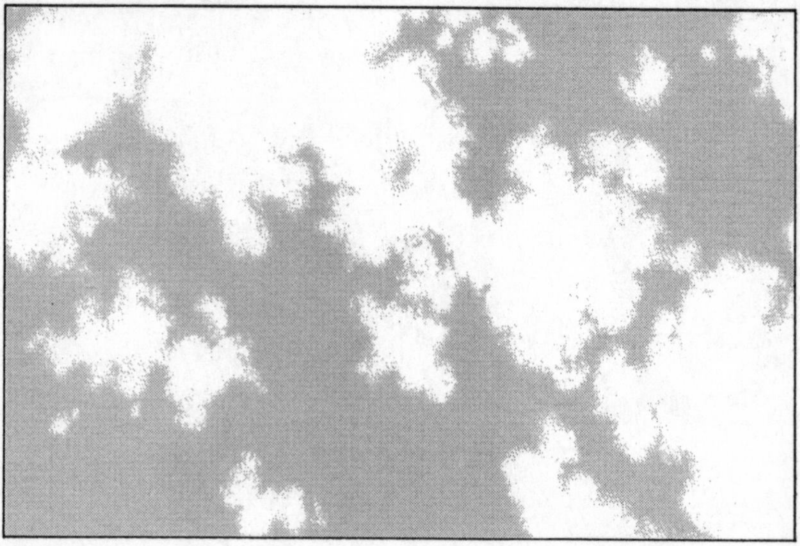

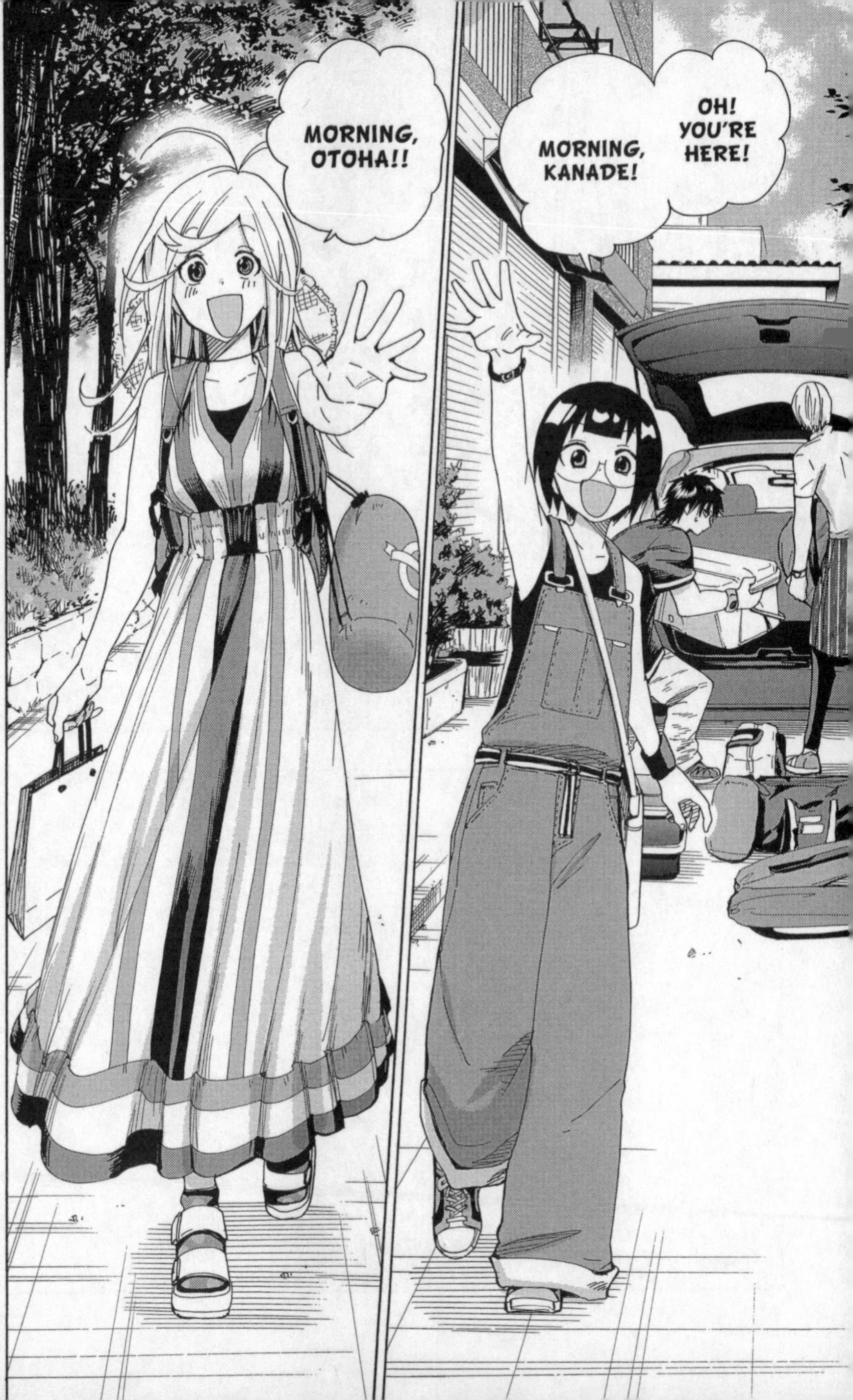
OH! YOU'RE HERE!
MORNING, KANADE!
MORNING, OTOHA!!

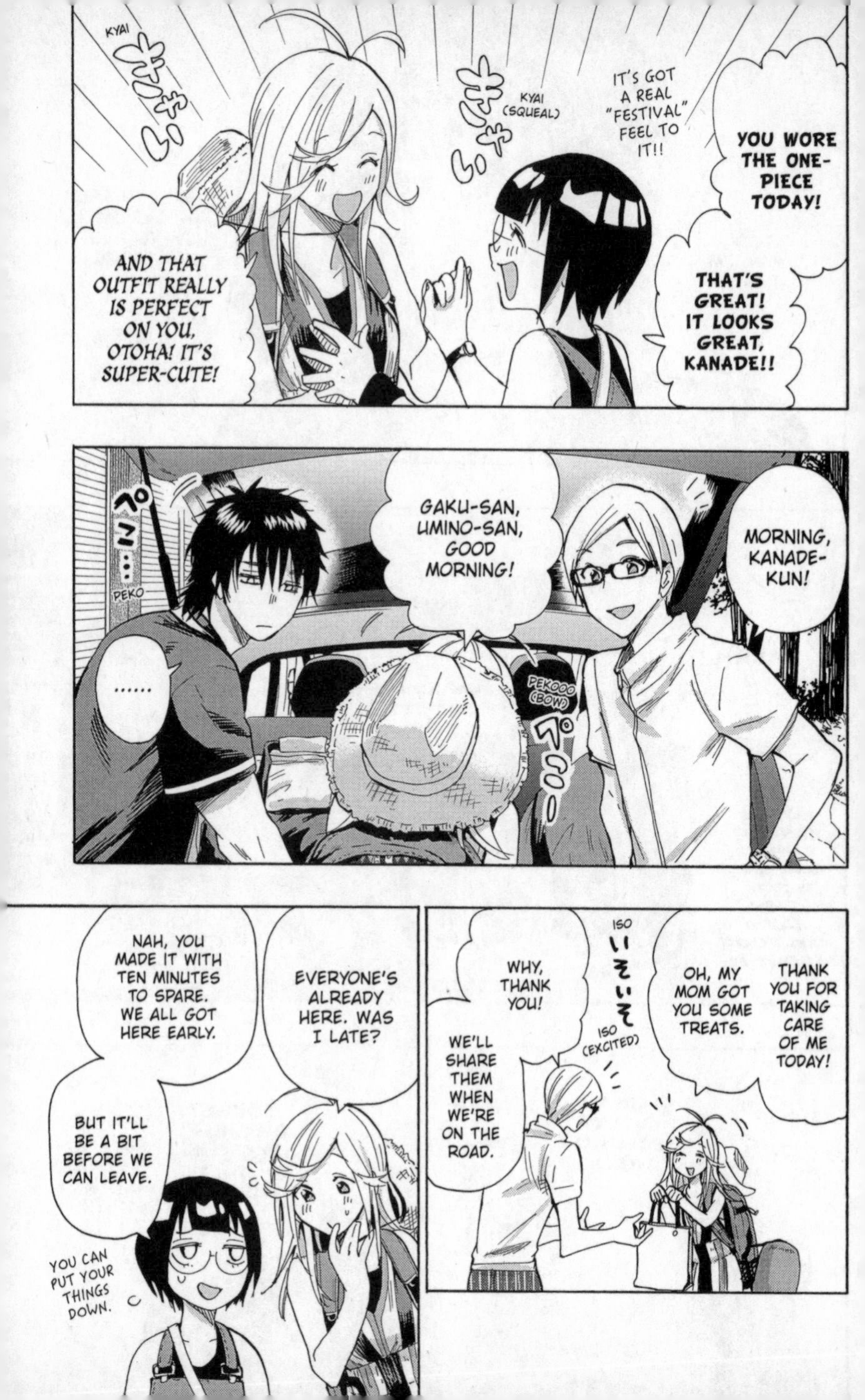
YOU WORE THE ONE-PIECE TODAY!
IT'S GOT A REAL "FESTIVAL" FEEL TO IT!!
THAT'S GREAT! IT LOOKS GREAT, KANADE!!
KYAI (SQUEAL)
KYAI
AND THAT OUTFIT REALLY IS PERFECT ON YOU, OTOHA! IT'S SUPER-CUTE!
MORNING, KANADE-KUN!
GAKU-SAN, UMINO-SAN, GOOD MORNING!
PEKOOO (BOW)
PEKO
......
THANK YOU FOR TAKING CARE OF ME TODAY!
OH, MY MOM GOT YOU SOME TREATS.
ISO
ISO (EXCITED)
WHY, THANK YOU!
WE'LL SHARE THEM WHEN WE'RE ON THE ROAD.
EVERYONE'S ALREADY HERE. WAS I LATE?
NAH, YOU MADE IT WITH TEN MINUTES TO SPARE. WE ALL GOT HERE EARLY.
BUT IT'LL BE A BIT BEFORE WE CAN LEAVE.
YOU CAN PUT YOUR THINGS DOWN.

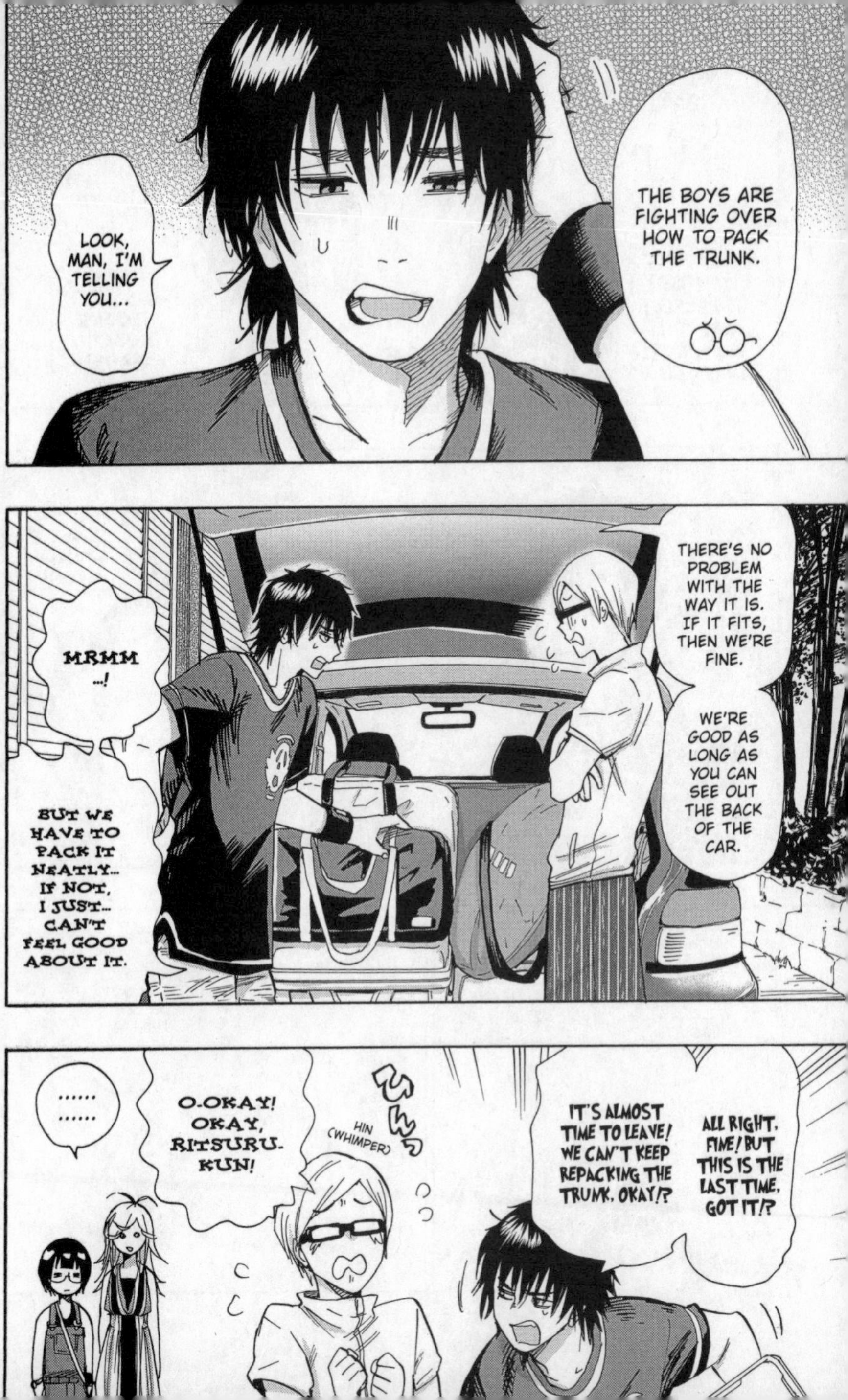
THE BOYS ARE FIGHTING OVER HOW TO PACK THE TRUNK.
LOOK, MAN, I'M TELLING YOU...
THERE'S NO PROBLEM WITH THE WAY IT IS. IF IT FITS, THEN WE'RE FINE.
WE'RE GOOD AS LONG AS YOU CAN SEE OUT THE BACK OF THE CAR.
MRMM ...!
BUT WE HAVE TO PACK IT NEATLY... IF NOT, I JUST... CAN'T FEEL GOOD ABOUT IT.
ALL RIGHT. FINE! BUT THIS IS THE LAST TIME. GOT IT!?
IT'S ALMOST TIME TO LEAVE! WE CAN'T KEEP REPACKING THE TRUNK, OKAY!?
HIN (WHIMPER)
O-OKAY! OKAY, RITSURU-KUN!
....

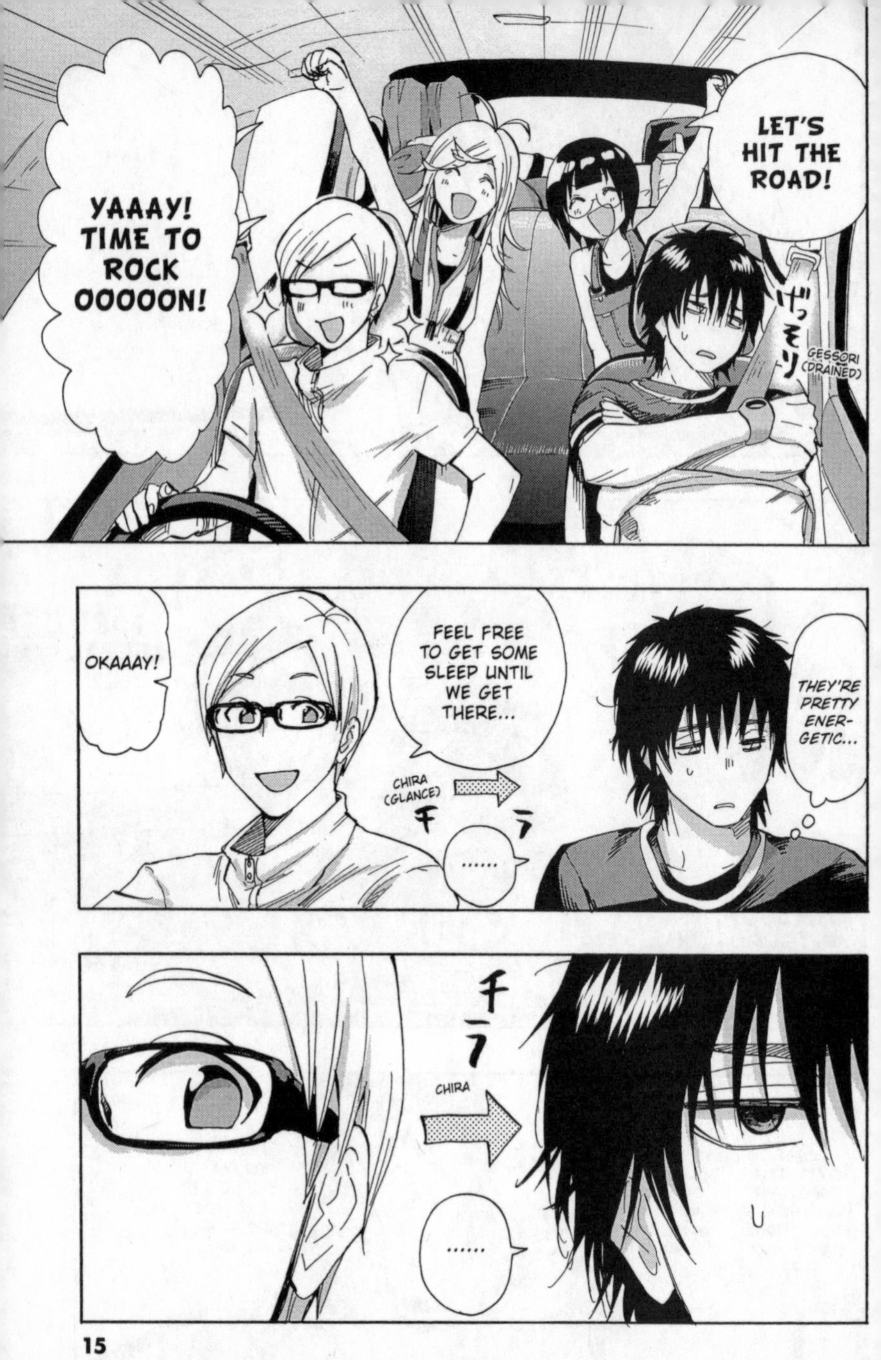
LET'S HIT THE ROAD!
げっそり
GESSORI (DRAINED)
YAAAY! TIME TO ROCK OOOOON!
THEY'RE PRETTY ENER-GETIC...
FEEL FREE TO GET SOME SLEEP UNTIL WE GET THERE...
OKAAAY!
......
チラ
CHIRA (GLANCE)
チラ
CHIRA
......

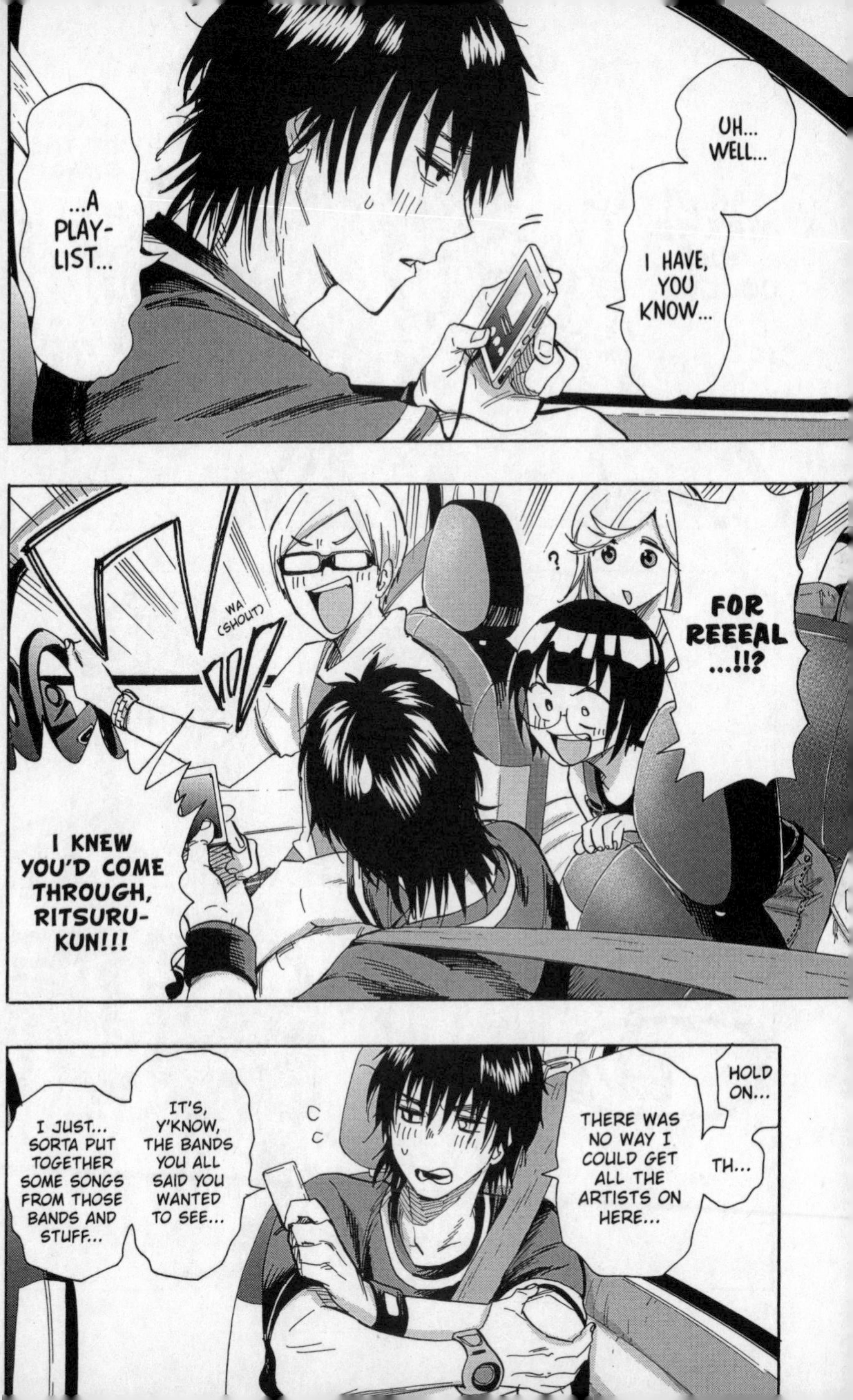
UH... WELL...
I HAVE, YOU KNOW...
...A PLAY-LIST...
FOR REEEAL...!!?
WA (SHOUT)
I KNEW YOU'D COME THROUGH, RITSURU-KUN!!!
HOLD ON...
TH...
THERE WAS NO WAY I COULD GET ALL THE ARTISTS ON HERE...
IT'S, Y'KNOW, THE BANDS YOU ALL SAID YOU WANTED TO SEE...
I JUST... SORTA PUT TOGETHER SOME SONGS FROM THOSE BANDS AND STUFF...

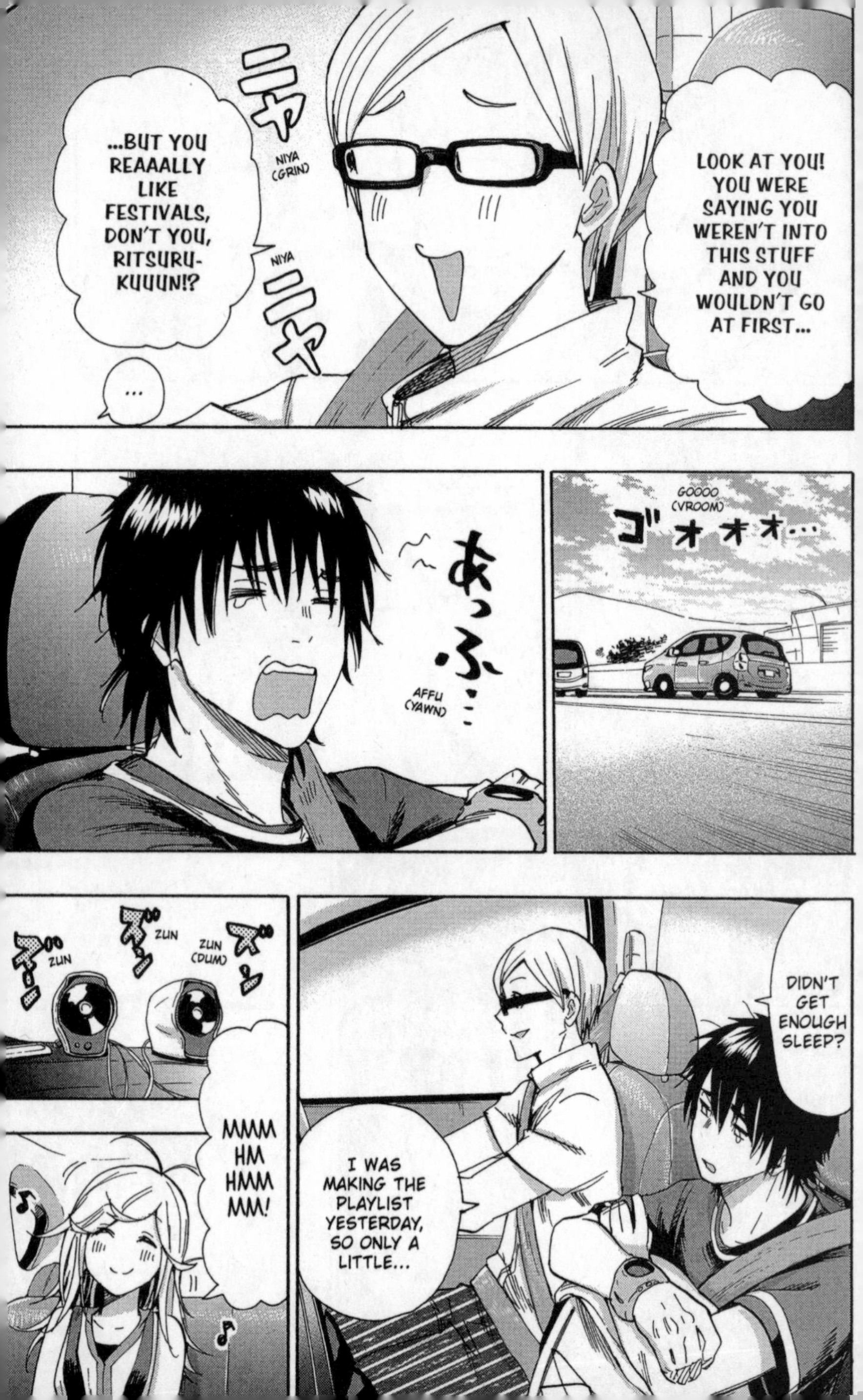
LOOK AT YOU! YOU WERE SAYING YOU WEREN'T INTO THIS STUFF AND YOU WOULDN'T GO AT FIRST...
NIYA (GRIN)
...BUT YOU REAAALLY LIKE FESTIVALS, DON'T YOU, RITSURU-KUUUN!?
NIYA
...
GOOOO (VROOM)
AFFU (YAWN)
DIDN'T GET ENOUGH SLEEP?
I WAS MAKING THE PLAYLIST YESTERDAY, SO ONLY A LITTLE...
ZUN (DUM)
ZUN
ZUN
MMMM HM HMM MM!

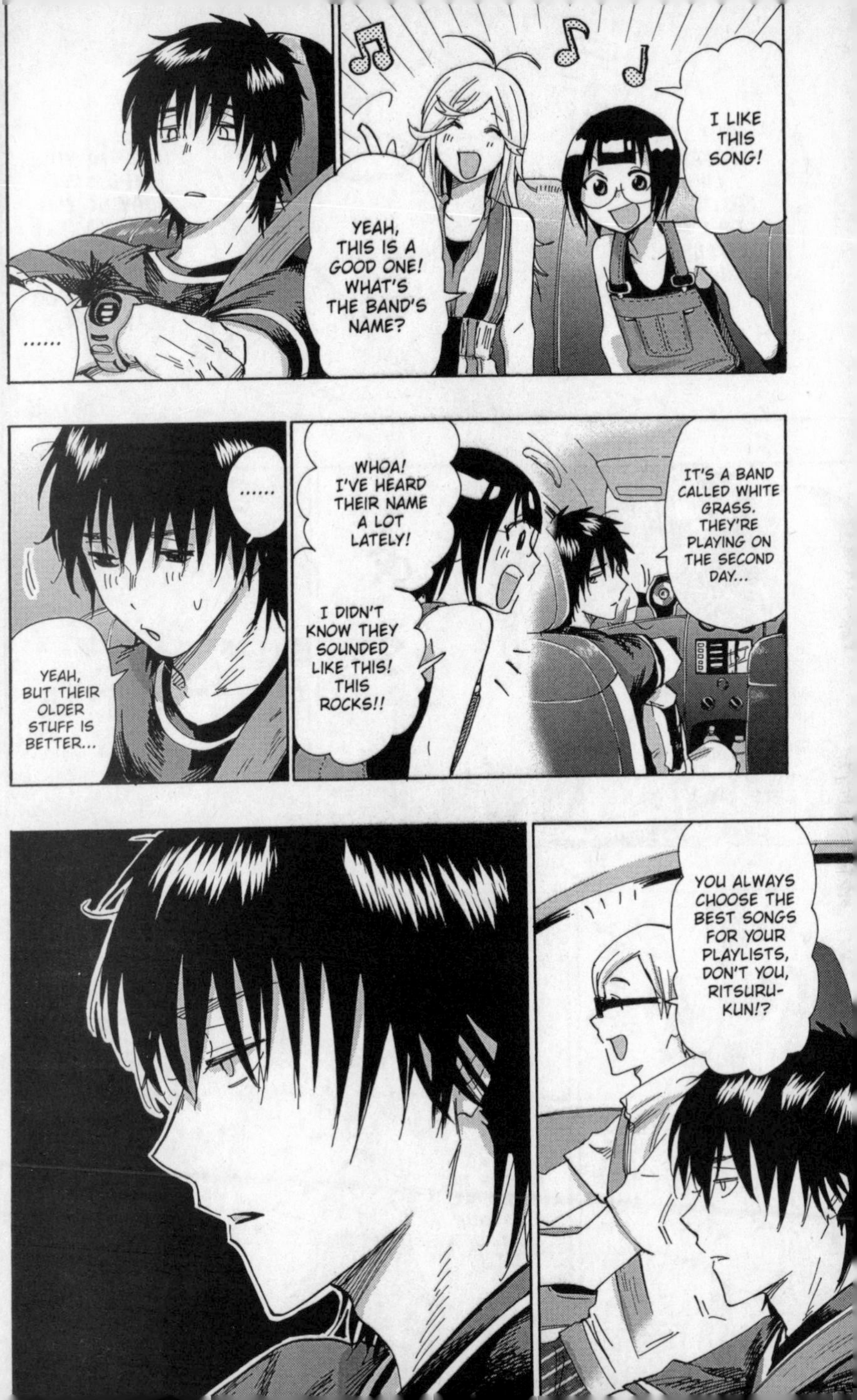
I LIKE THIS SONG!
YEAH, THIS IS A GOOD ONE! WHAT'S THE BAND'S NAME?
......
IT'S A BAND CALLED WHITE GRASS. THEY'RE PLAYING ON THE SECOND DAY...
WHOA! I'VE HEARD THEIR NAME A LOT LATELY!
I DIDN'T KNOW THEY SOUNDED LIKE THIS! THIS ROCKS!!
......
YEAH, BUT THEIR OLDER STUFF IS BETTER...
YOU ALWAYS CHOOSE THE BEST SONGS FOR YOUR PLAYLISTS, DON'T YOU, RITSURU-KUN!?

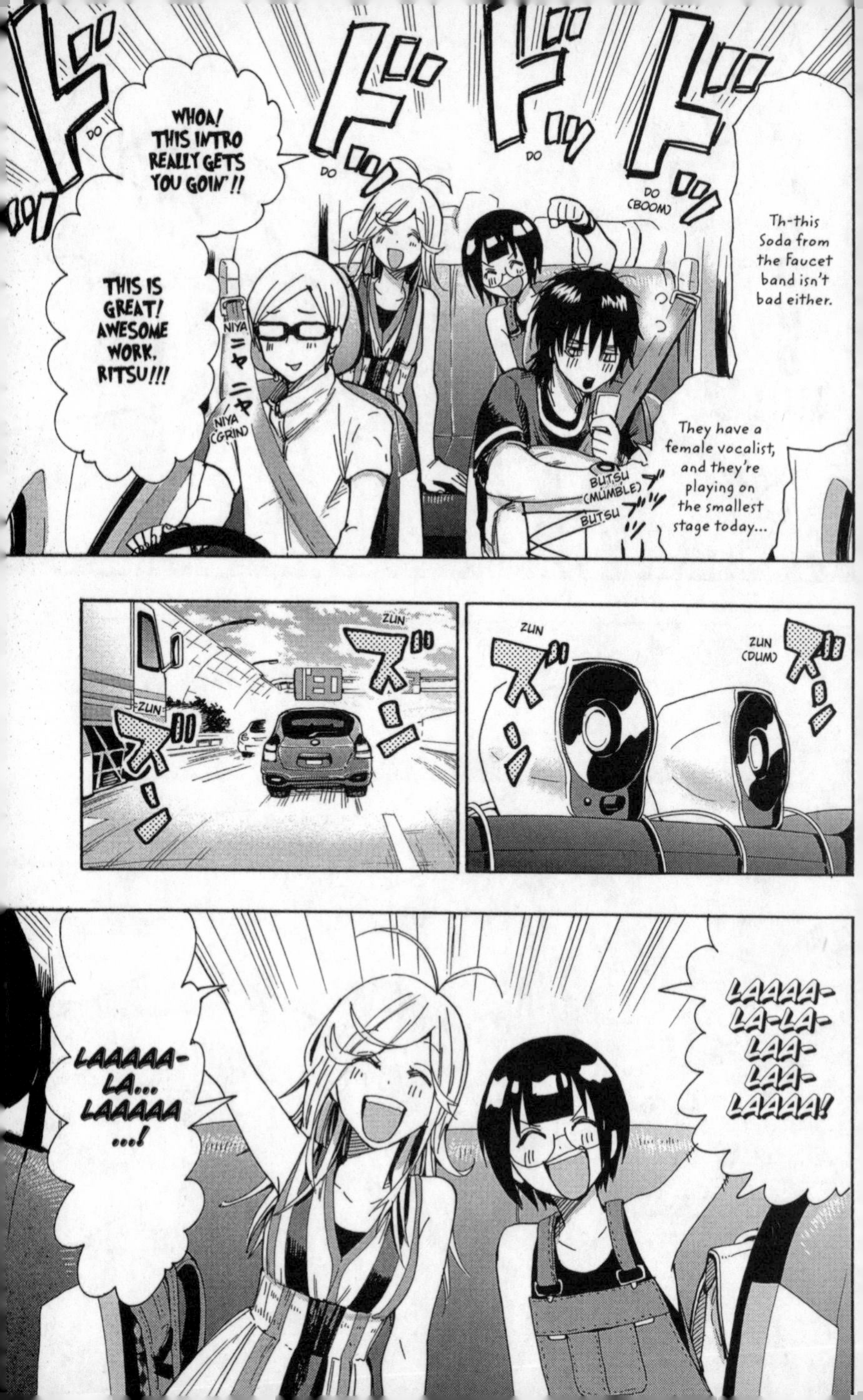
DO
DO (BOOM)
DO
DO
Th-this Soda from the Faucet band isn't bad either.
They have a female vocalist, and they're playing on the smallest stage today...
BUTSU (MUMBLE)
BUTSU
NIYA ニヤ
ニヤ NIYA (GRIN)
WHOA! THIS INTRO REALLY GETS YOU GOIN'!!
THIS IS GREAT! AWESOME WORK, RITSU!!!
ZUN (DUM)
ZUN
ZUN
ZUN
LAAAA-LA-LA-LAA-LAA-LAAAA!
LAAAAA-LA... LAAAAA ...!

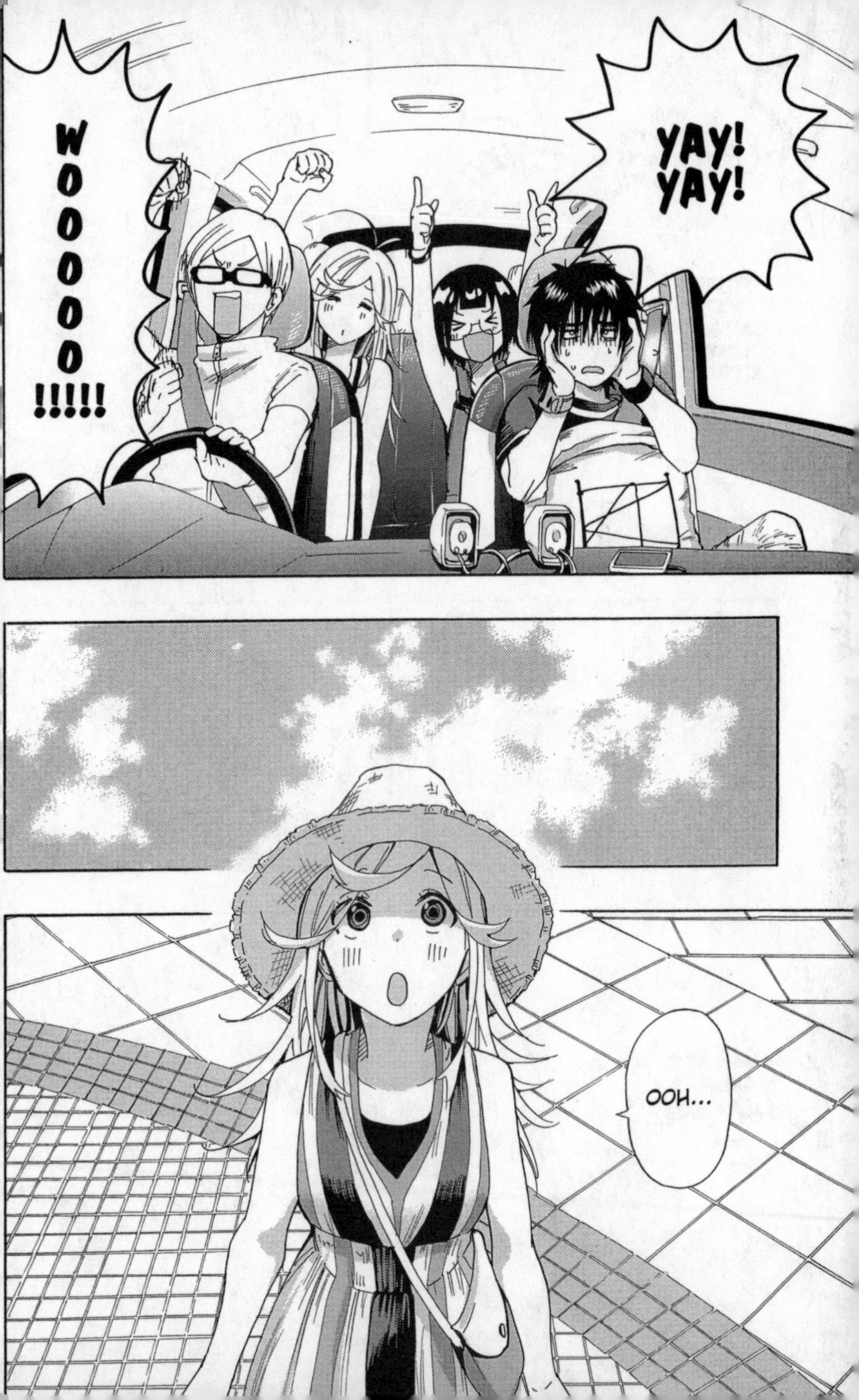
YAY! YAY!
WOOOOOO!!!!!
OOH...

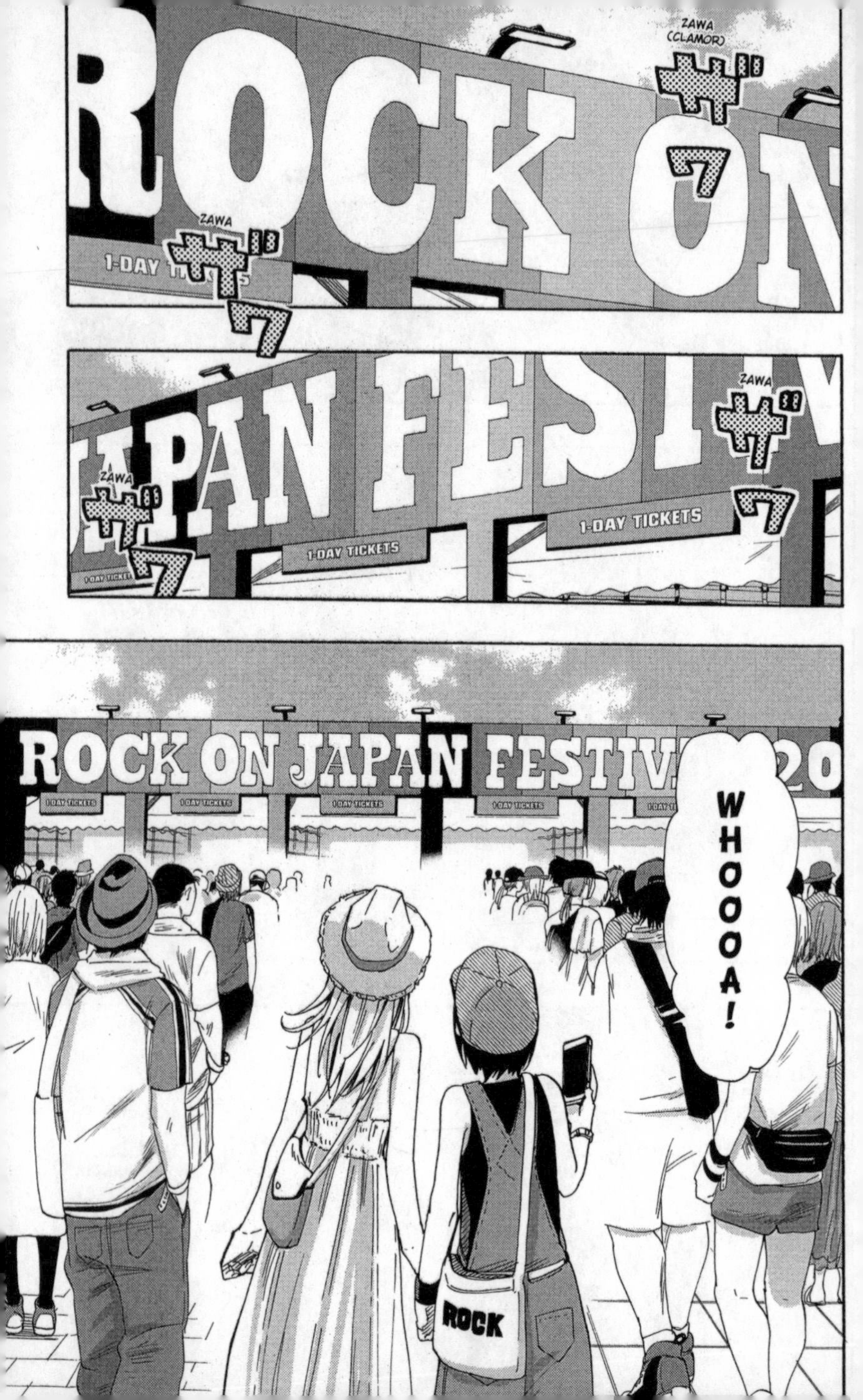
ZAWA (CLAMOR)
ROCK ON
ZAWA
1-DAY TI
ZAWA
1-DAY TICKETS
1-DAY TICKETS
JAPAN FESTI
ZAWA
1-DAY TICKET
ROCK ON JAPAN FESTIV 20
1-DAY TICKETS
1-DAY TICKETS
1-DAY TICKETS
1-DAY TICKETS
WHOOOOA!
ROCK

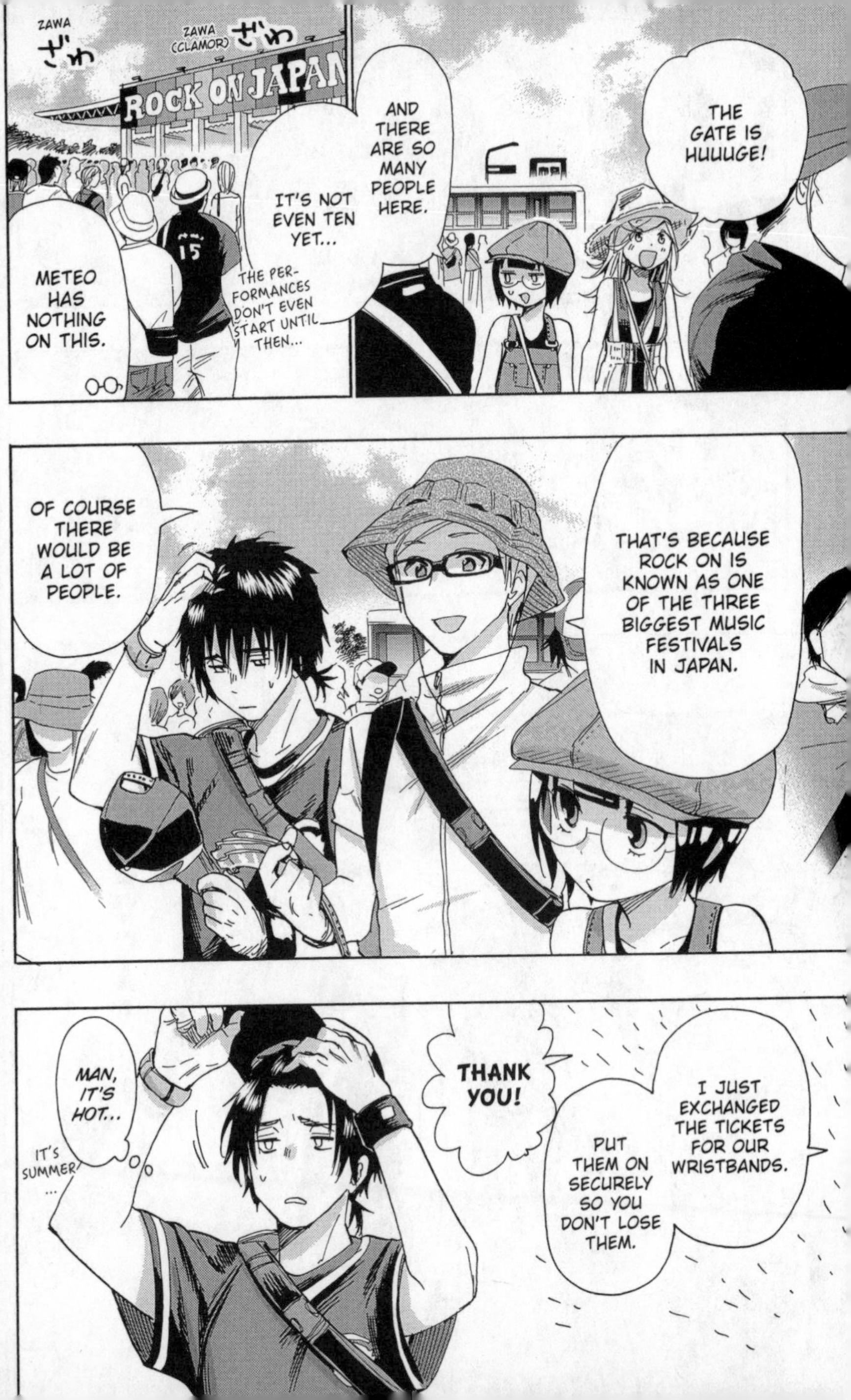
THE GATE IS HUUUGE!
AND THERE ARE SO MANY PEOPLE HERE.
IT'S NOT EVEN TEN YET...
THE PERFORMANCES DON'T EVEN START UNTIL THEN...
ROCK ON JAPAN
ZAWA (CLAMOR) ざわ
ZAWA ざわ
METEO HAS NOTHING ON THIS.
THAT'S BECAUSE ROCK ON IS KNOWN AS ONE OF THE THREE BIGGEST MUSIC FESTIVALS IN JAPAN.
OF COURSE THERE WOULD BE A LOT OF PEOPLE.
I JUST EXCHANGED THE TICKETS FOR OUR WRISTBANDS.
PUT THEM ON SECURELY SO YOU DON'T LOSE THEM.
THANK YOU!
MAN, IT'S HOT...
IT'S SUMMER...

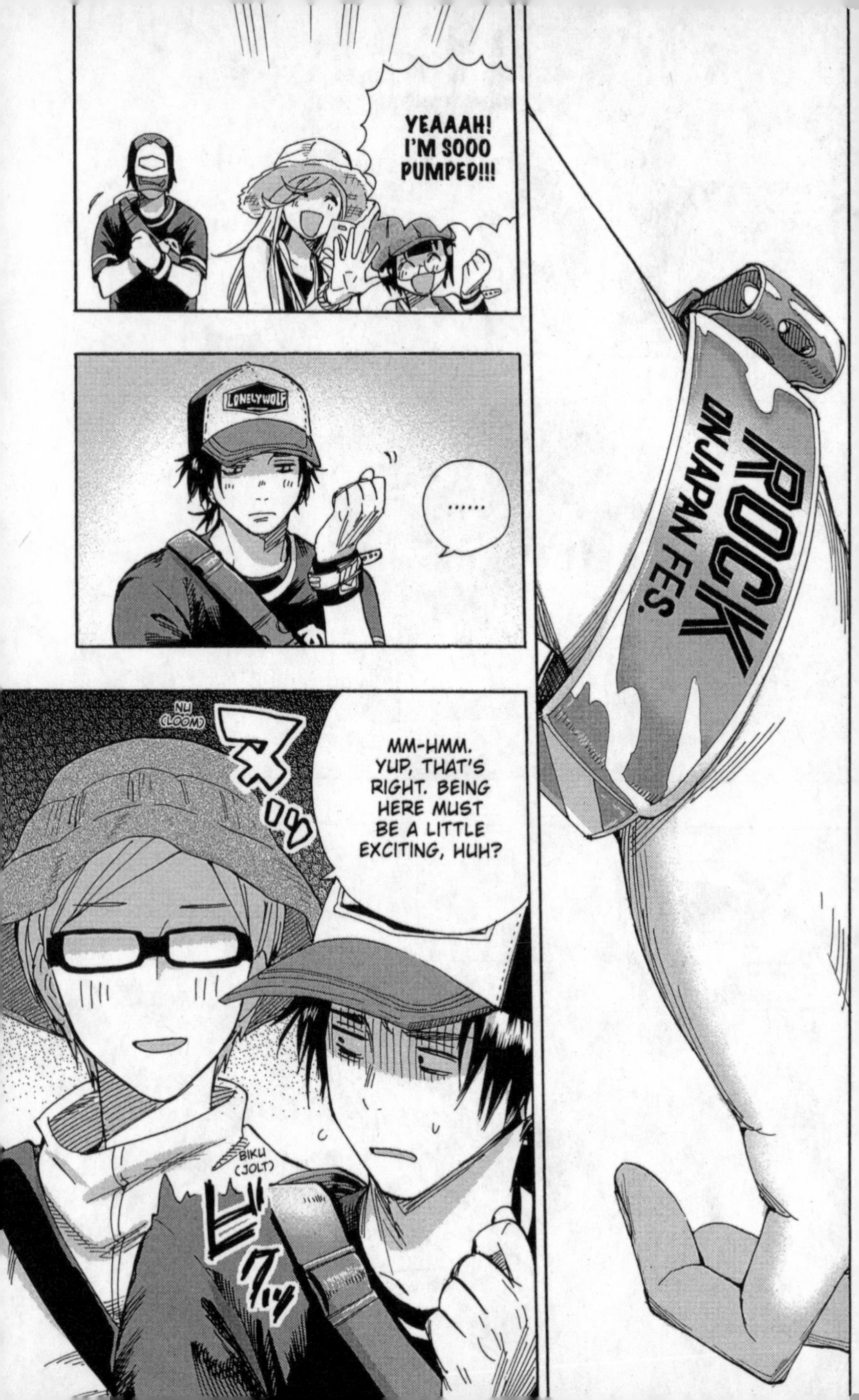
ROCK IN JAPAN FES.
YEAAAH! I'M SOOO PUMPED!!!
......
MM-HMM. YUP, THAT'S RIGHT. BEING HERE MUST BE A LITTLE EXCITING, HUH?
NU (LOOM)
BIKU (JOLT)

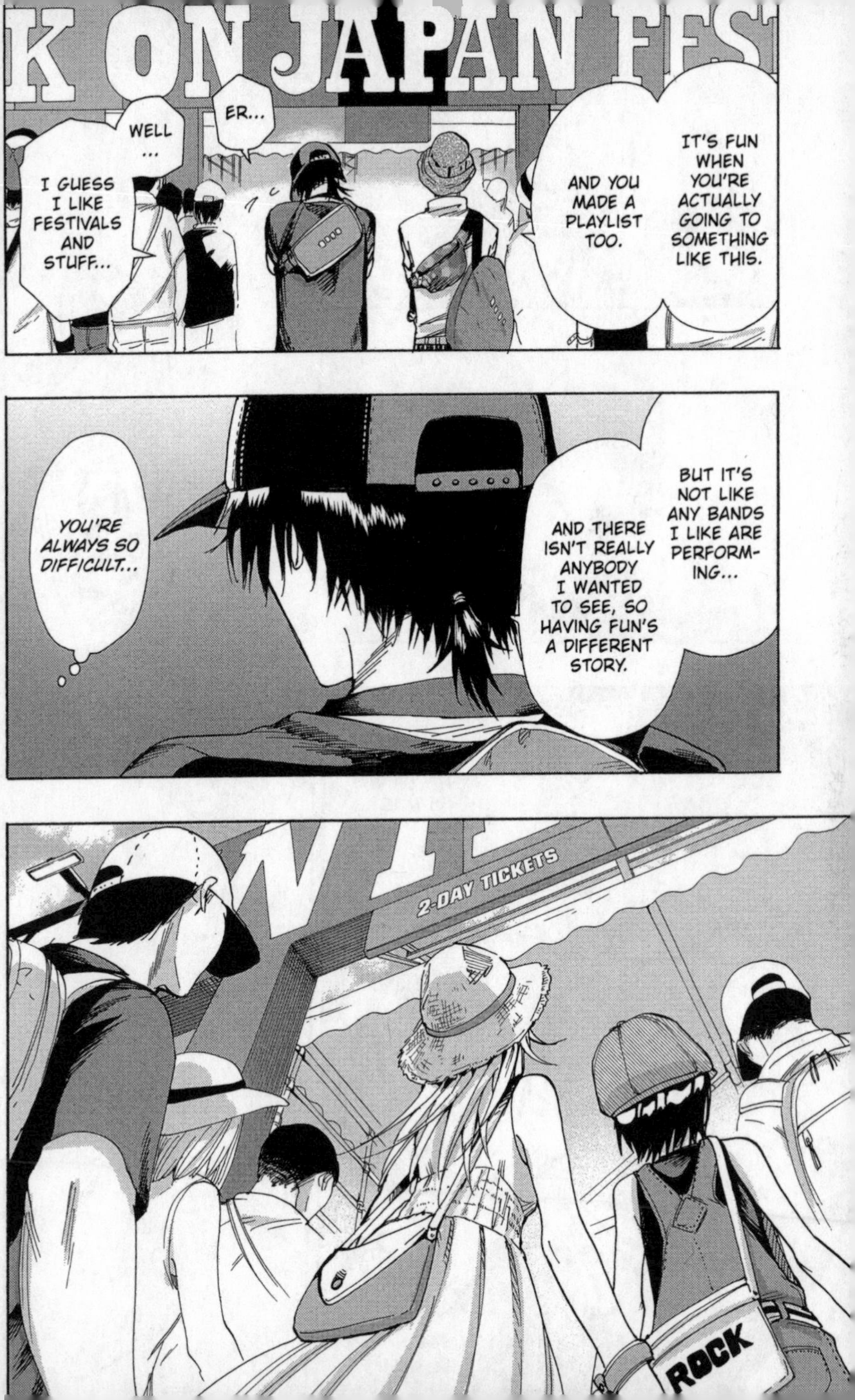
K ON JAPAN FES
IT'S FUN WHEN YOU'RE ACTUALLY GOING TO SOMETHING LIKE THIS.
AND YOU MADE A PLAYLIST TOO.
ER...
WELL ...
I GUESS I LIKE FESTIVALS AND STUFF...
BUT IT'S NOT LIKE ANY BANDS I LIKE ARE PERFORMING...
AND THERE ISN'T REALLY ANYBODY I WANTED TO SEE, SO HAVING FUN'S A DIFFERENT STORY.
YOU'RE ALWAYS SO DIFFICULT...
2-DAY TICKETS
ROCK

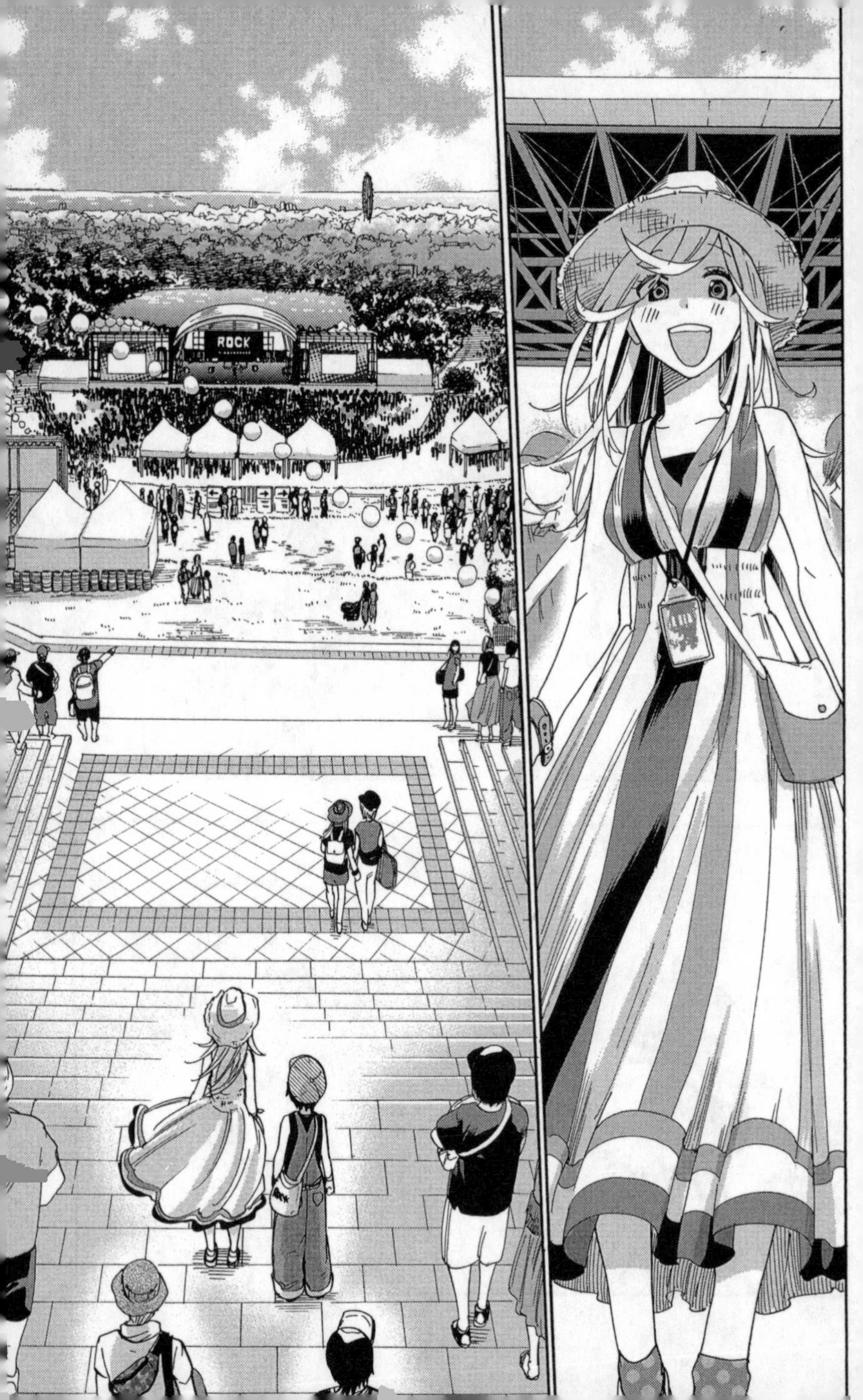
ROCK

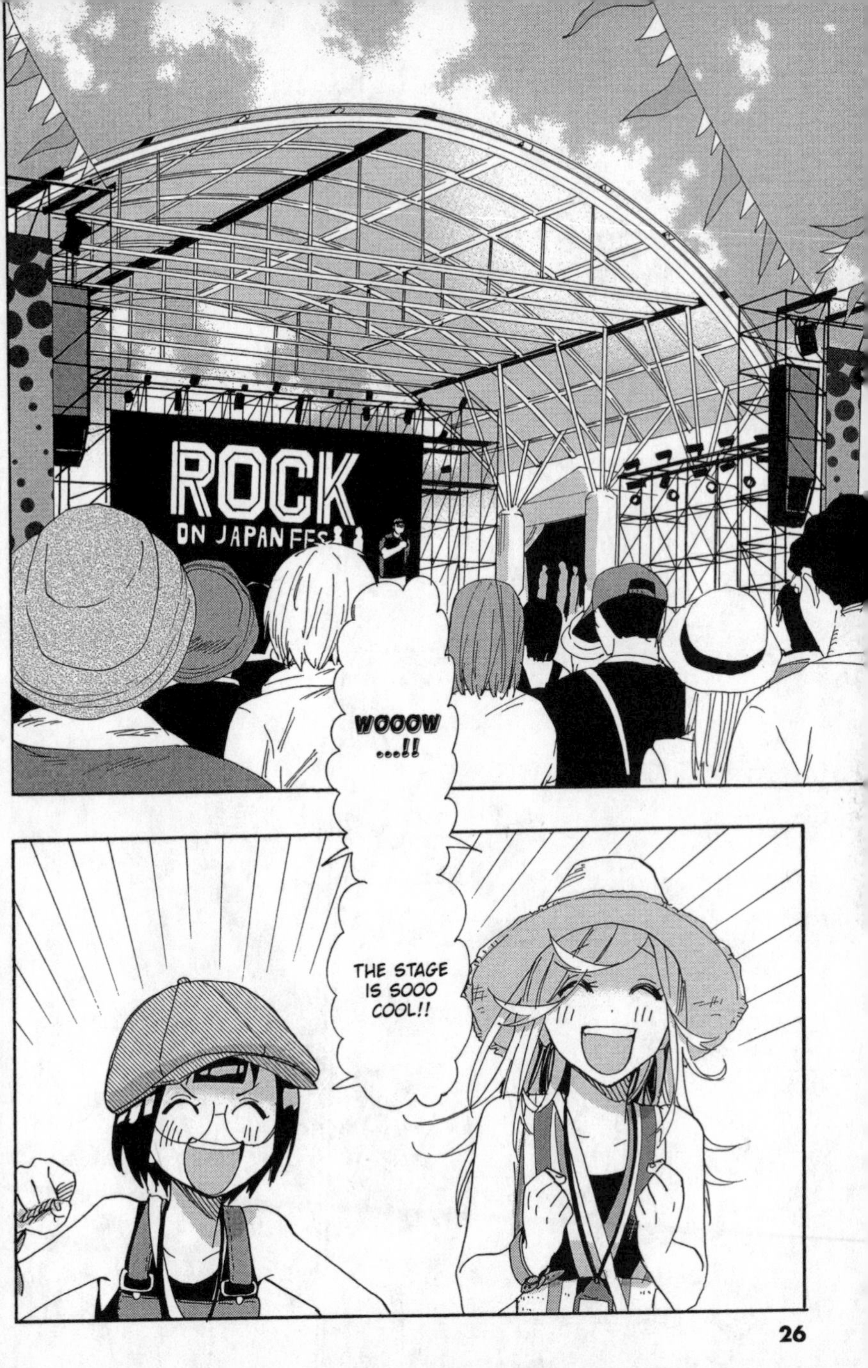
ROCK
ON JAPAN FES
WOOOW ...!!
THE STAGE IS SOOO COOL!!

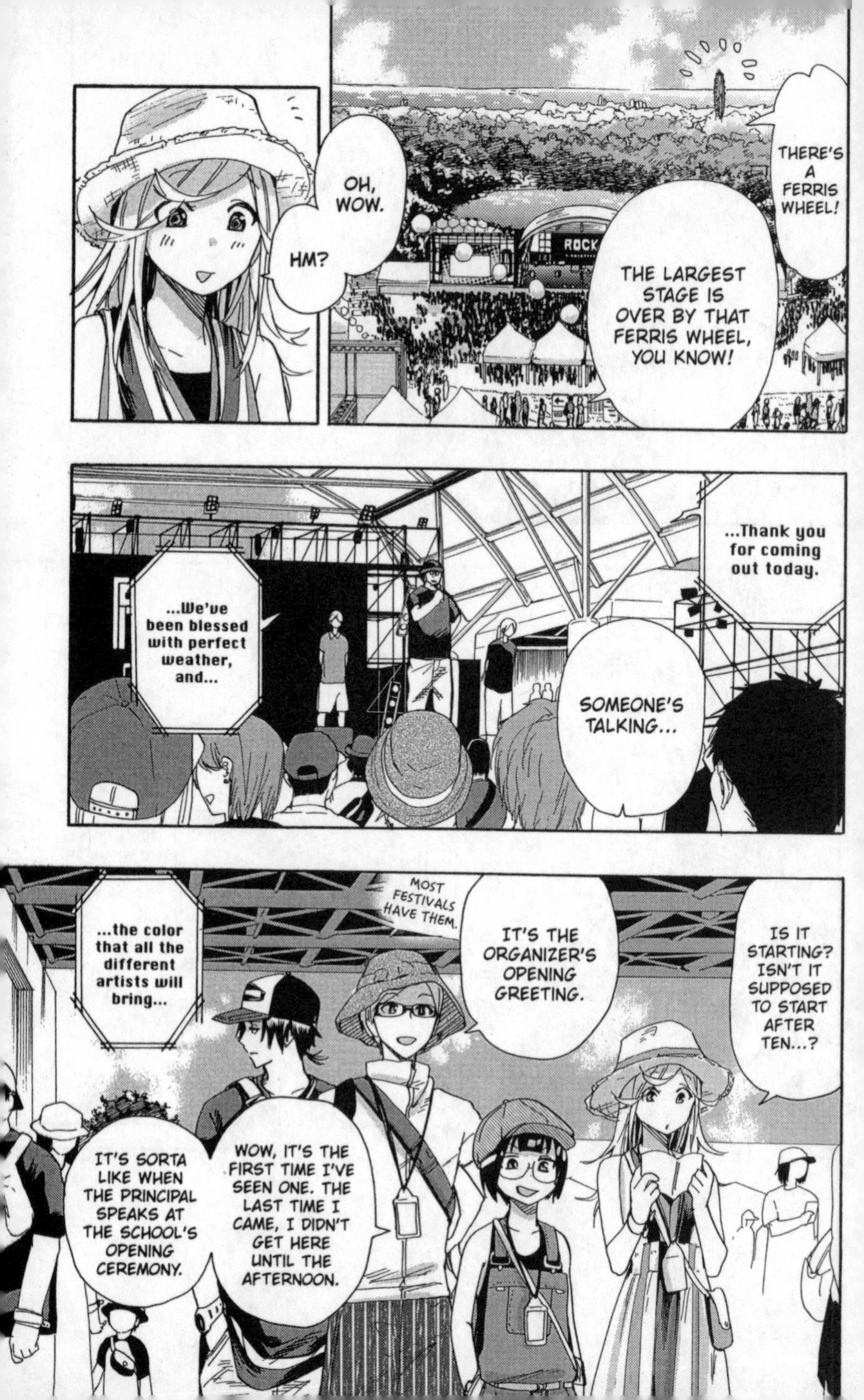
THERE'S A FERRIS WHEEL!
THE LARGEST STAGE IS OVER BY THAT FERRIS WHEEL, YOU KNOW!
ROCK
OH, WOW.
HM?
...Thank you for coming out today.
SOMEONE'S TALKING...
...We've been blessed with perfect weather, and...
IS IT STARTING? ISN'T IT SUPPOSED TO START AFTER TEN...?
IT'S THE ORGANIZER'S OPENING GREETING.
MOST FESTIVALS HAVE THEM.
...the color that all the different artists will bring...
WOW, IT'S THE FIRST TIME I'VE SEEN ONE. THE LAST TIME I CAME, I DIDN'T GET HERE UNTIL THE AFTERNOON.
IT'S SORTA LIKE WHEN THE PRINCIPAL SPEAKS AT THE SCHOOL'S OPENING CEREMONY.

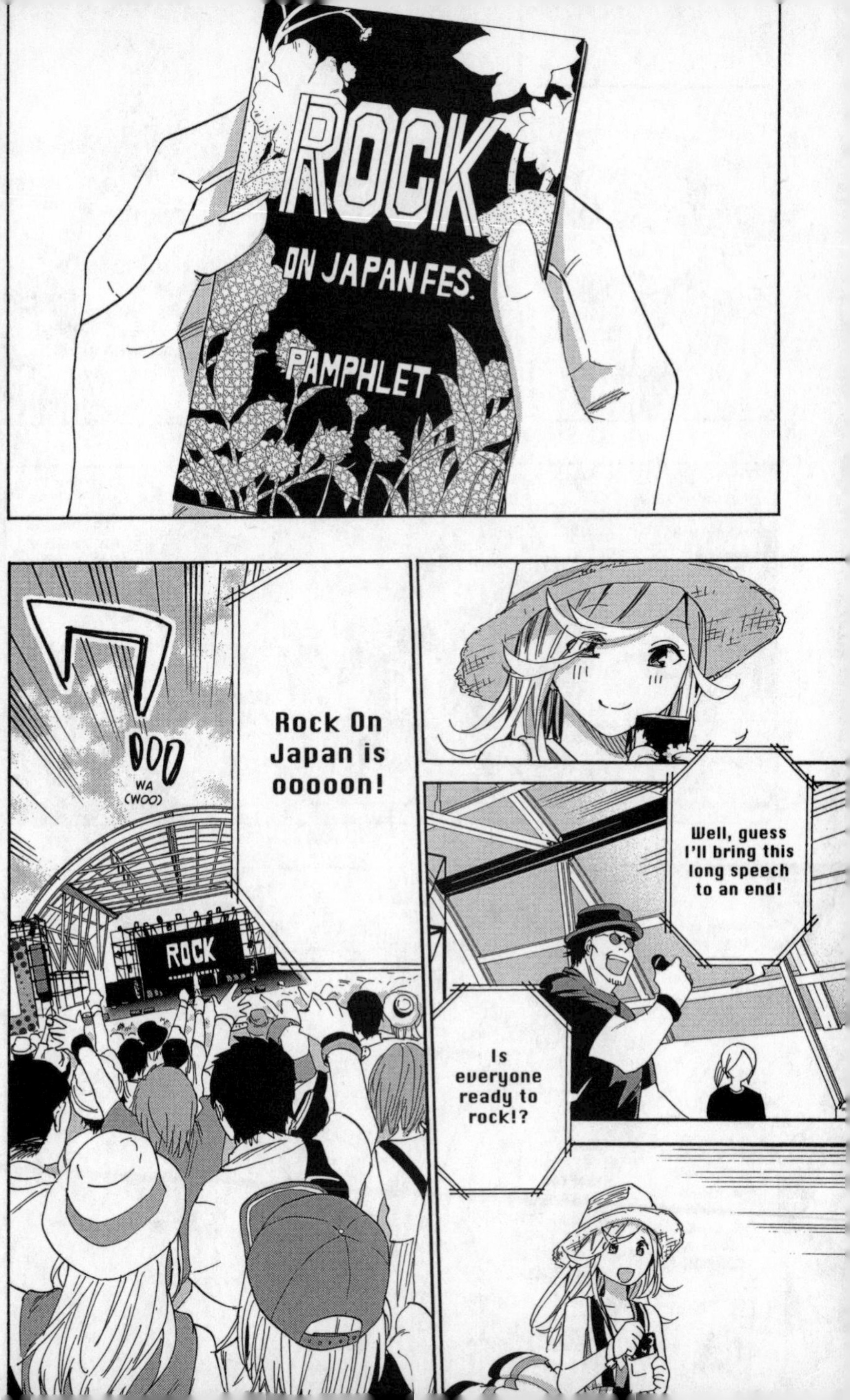
ROCK
ON JAPAN FES.
PAMPHLET
Well, guess I'll bring this long speech to an end!
Is everyone ready to rock!?
Rock On Japan is oooooon!
WA (WOO)
ROCK

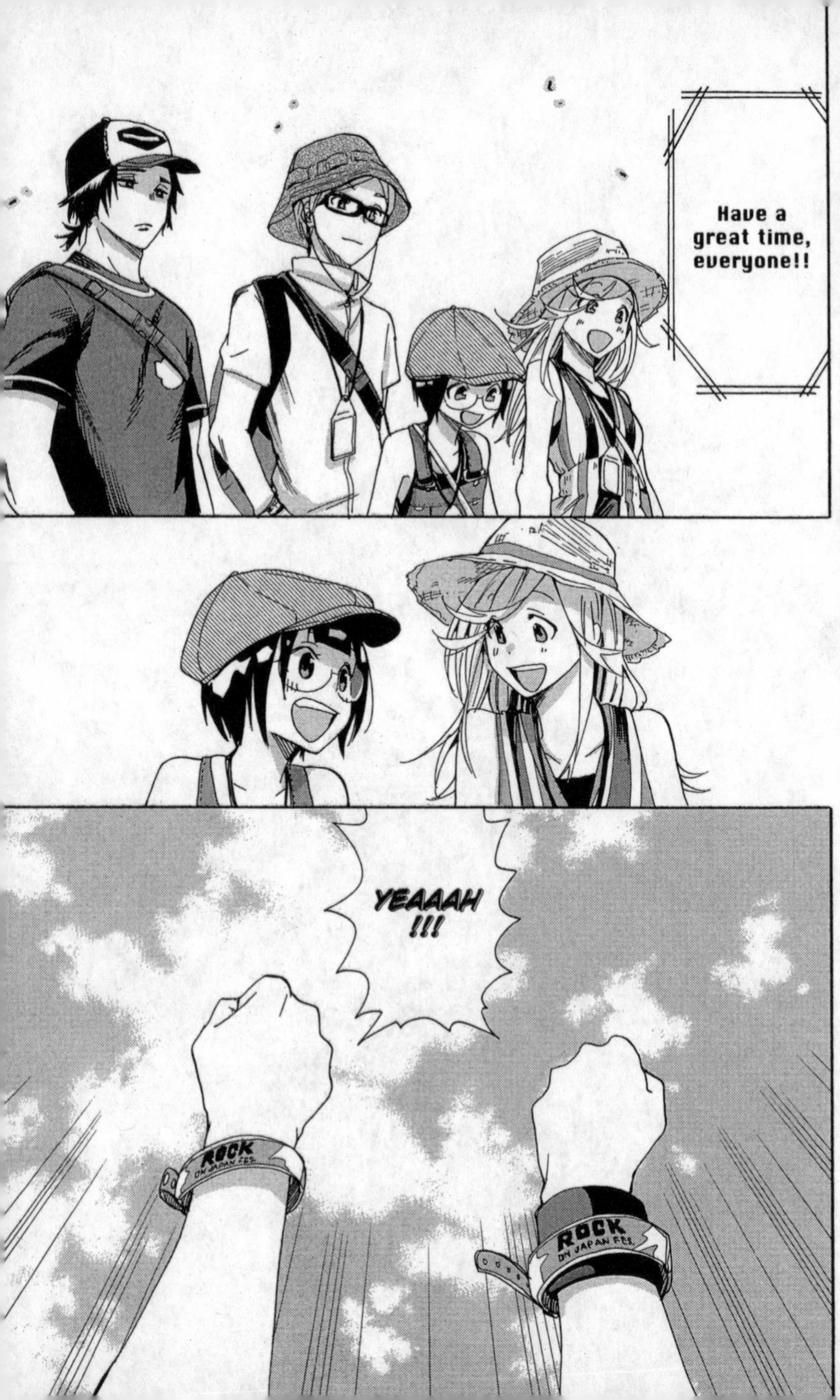
Have a great time, everyone!!
YEAAAH !!!
ROCK ON JAPAN FES.
ROCK ON JAPAN FES.

Days on Fes

FES 6.5

EVERYONE'S EVENING BEFORE THE FESTIVAL <RITSURU>

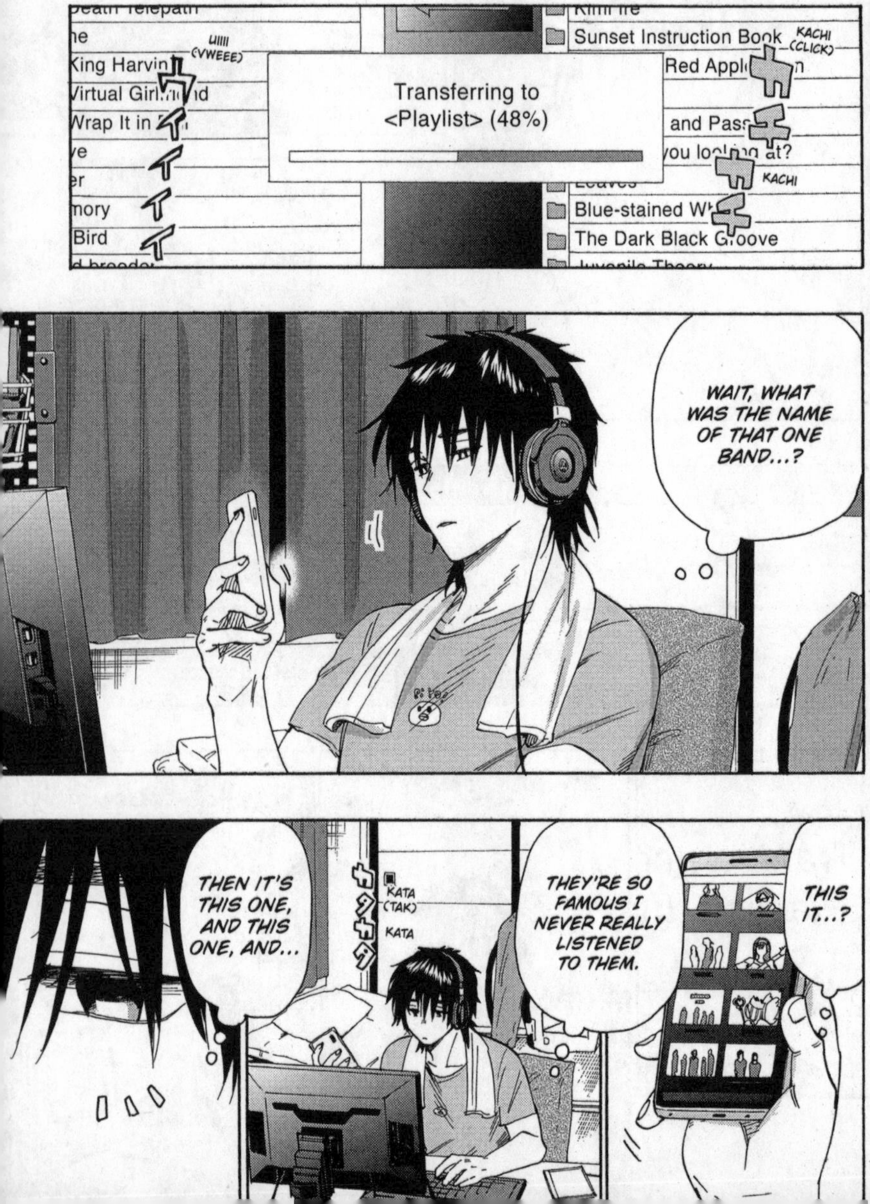
KACHI (CLICK)
KACHI
Sunset Instruction Book
The Dark Black Groove
Transferring to
<Playlist> (48%)
UIIII (VWEEE)
WAIT, WHAT WAS THE NAME OF THAT ONE BAND...?
THIS IT...?
THEY'RE SO FAMOUS I NEVER REALLY LISTENED TO THEM.
KATA (TAK) KATA
THEN IT'S THIS ONE, AND THIS ONE, AND...

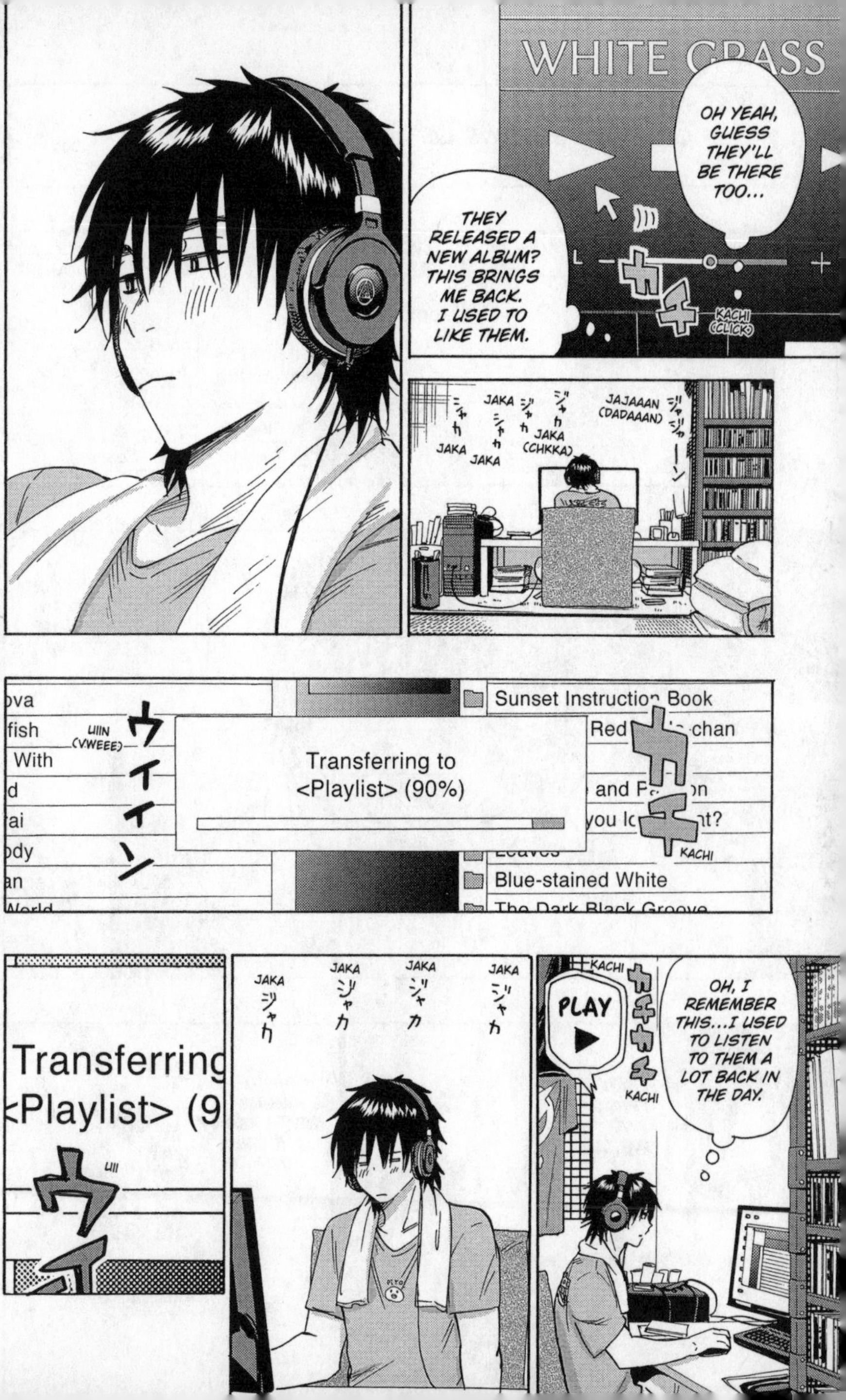

WHITE GRASS
OH YEAH, GUESS THEY'LL BE THERE TOO...
THEY RELEASED A NEW ALBUM? THIS BRINGS ME BACK. I USED TO LIKE THEM.
KACHI (CLICK)
JAJAAAN (DADAAAN)
JAKA (CHKKA)
JAKA
JAKA
JAKA
Sunset Instruction Book
KACHI
Blue-stained White
Transferring to <Playlist> (90%)
UIIN (V.WEEE)
KACHI
PLAY
OH, I REMEMBER THIS...I USED TO LISTEN TO THEM A LOT BACK IN THE DAY.
KACHI
JAKA
JAKA
JAKA
JAKA
Transferring
<Playlist> (9
UII

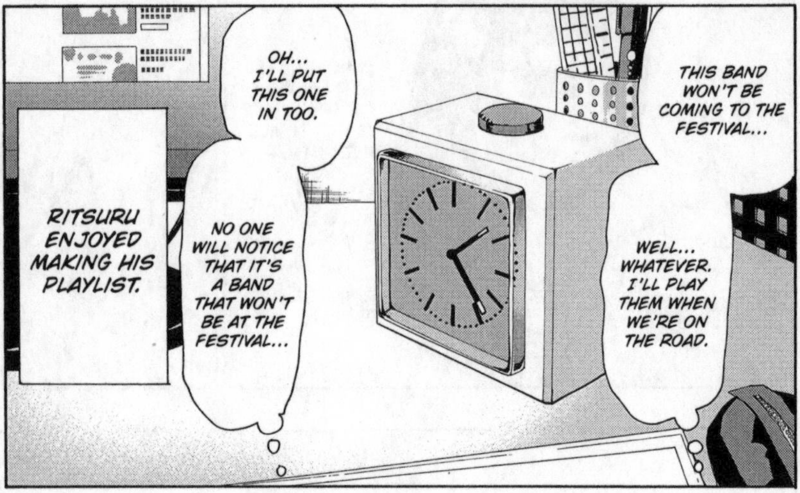
THIS BAND WON'T BE COMING TO THE FESTIVAL...
WELL... WHATEVER. I'LL PLAY THEM WHEN WE'RE ON THE ROAD.
OH... I'LL PUT THIS ONE IN TOO.
NO ONE WILL NOTICE THAT IT'S A BAND THAT WON'T BE AT THE FESTIVAL...
RITSURU ENJOYED MAKING HIS PLAYLIST.

EVERYONE'S EVENING BEFORE THE FESTIVAL <OTOHA>

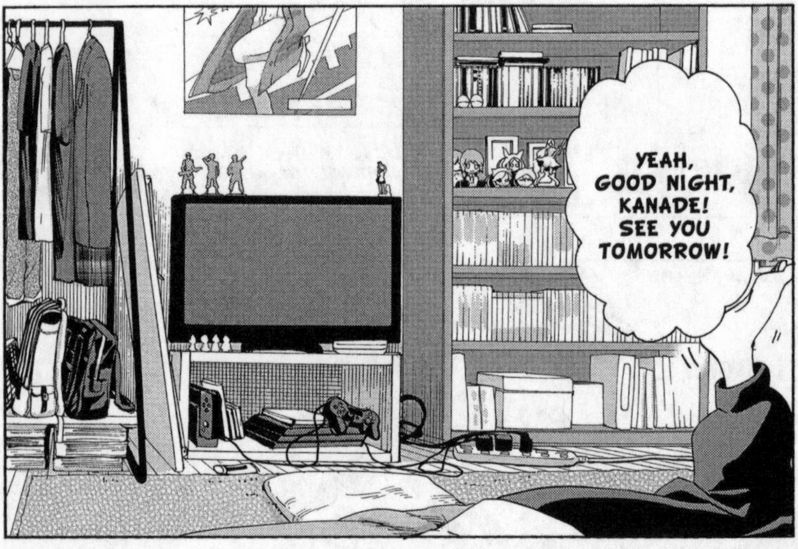
YEAH, GOOD NIGHT, KANADE! SEE YOU TOMORROW!

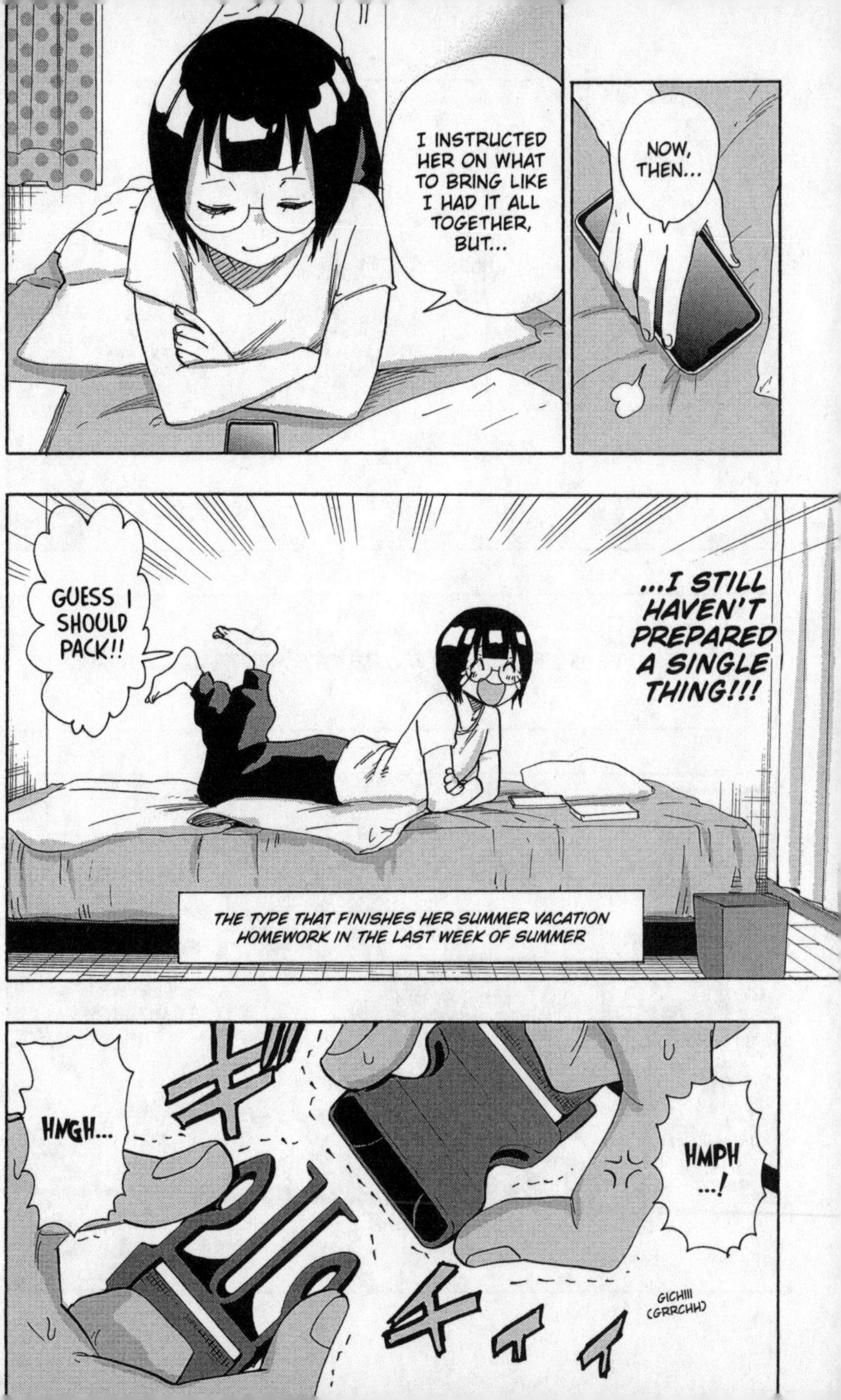
NOW, THEN...
I INSTRUCTED HER ON WHAT TO BRING LIKE I HAD IT ALL TOGETHER, BUT...
...I STILL HAVEN'T PREPARED A SINGLE THING!!!
GUESS I SHOULD PACK!!
THE TYPE THAT FINISHES HER SUMMER VACATION HOMEWORK IN THE LAST WEEK OF SUMMER
HMPH ...!
GICHIII (GRRCHH)
HNGH...

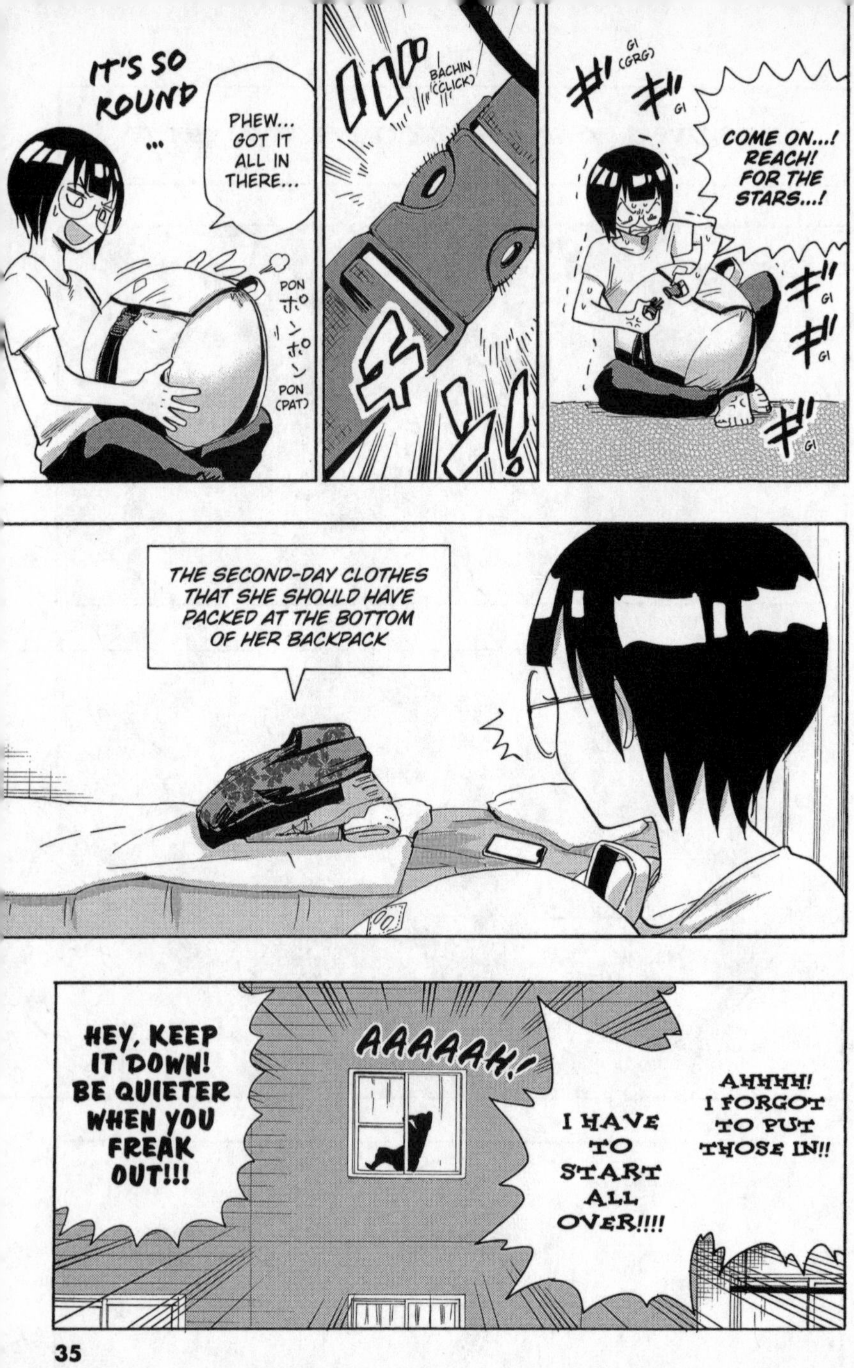
GI (GRG)
GI
COME ON...! REACH! FOR THE STARS...!
GI
GI
GI
BACHIN (CLICK)
IT'S SO ROUND...
PHEW... GOT IT ALL IN THERE...
PON ポンリンポン PON (PAT)
THE SECOND-DAY CLOTHES THAT SHE SHOULD HAVE PACKED AT THE BOTTOM OF HER BACKPACK
AHHHH! I FORGOT TO PUT THOSE IN!!
I HAVE TO START ALL OVER!!!!
AAAAAH!
HEY, KEEP IT DOWN! BE QUIETER WHEN YOU FREAK OUT!!!

EVERYONE'S EVENING BEFORE THE FESTIVAL <GAKU>

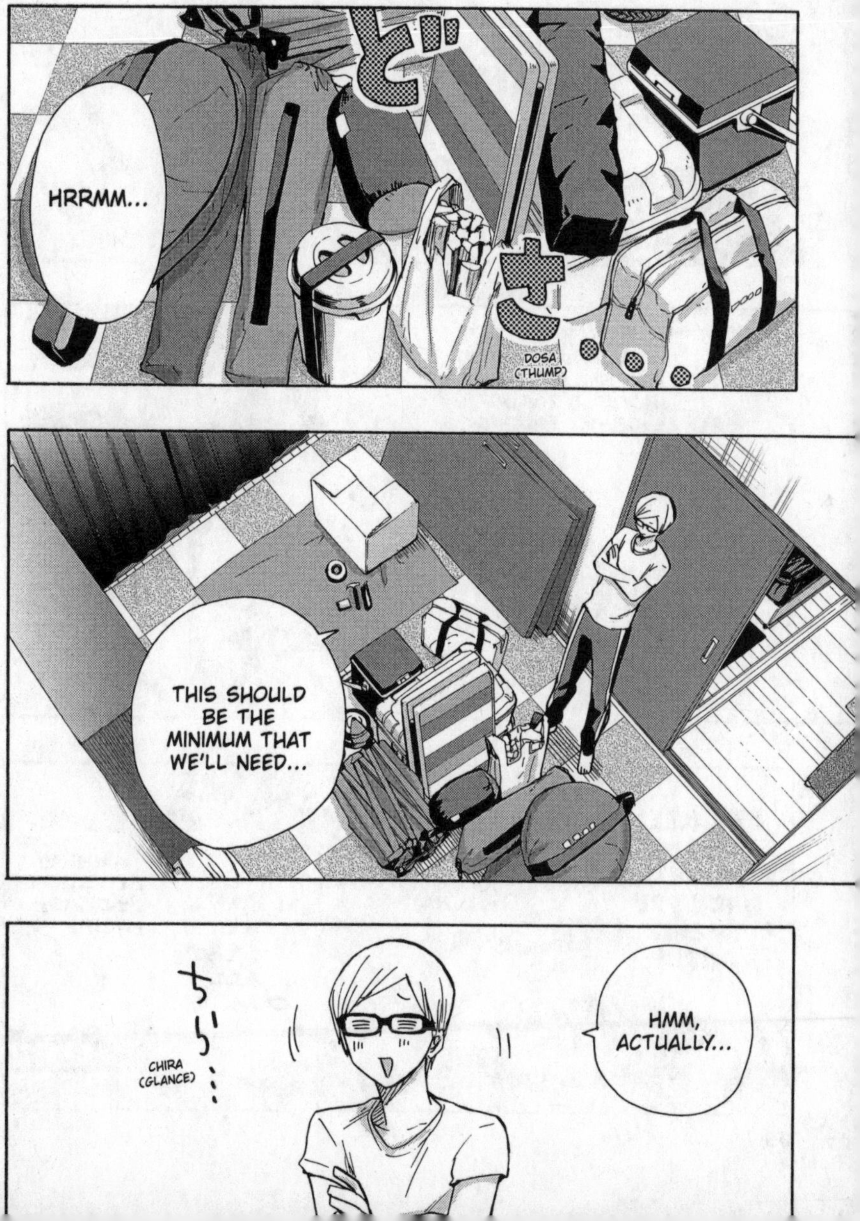
DOSA (THUMP)
HRRMM...
THIS SHOULD BE THE MINIMUM THAT WE'LL NEED...
HMM, ACTUALLY...
CHIRA (GLANCE)

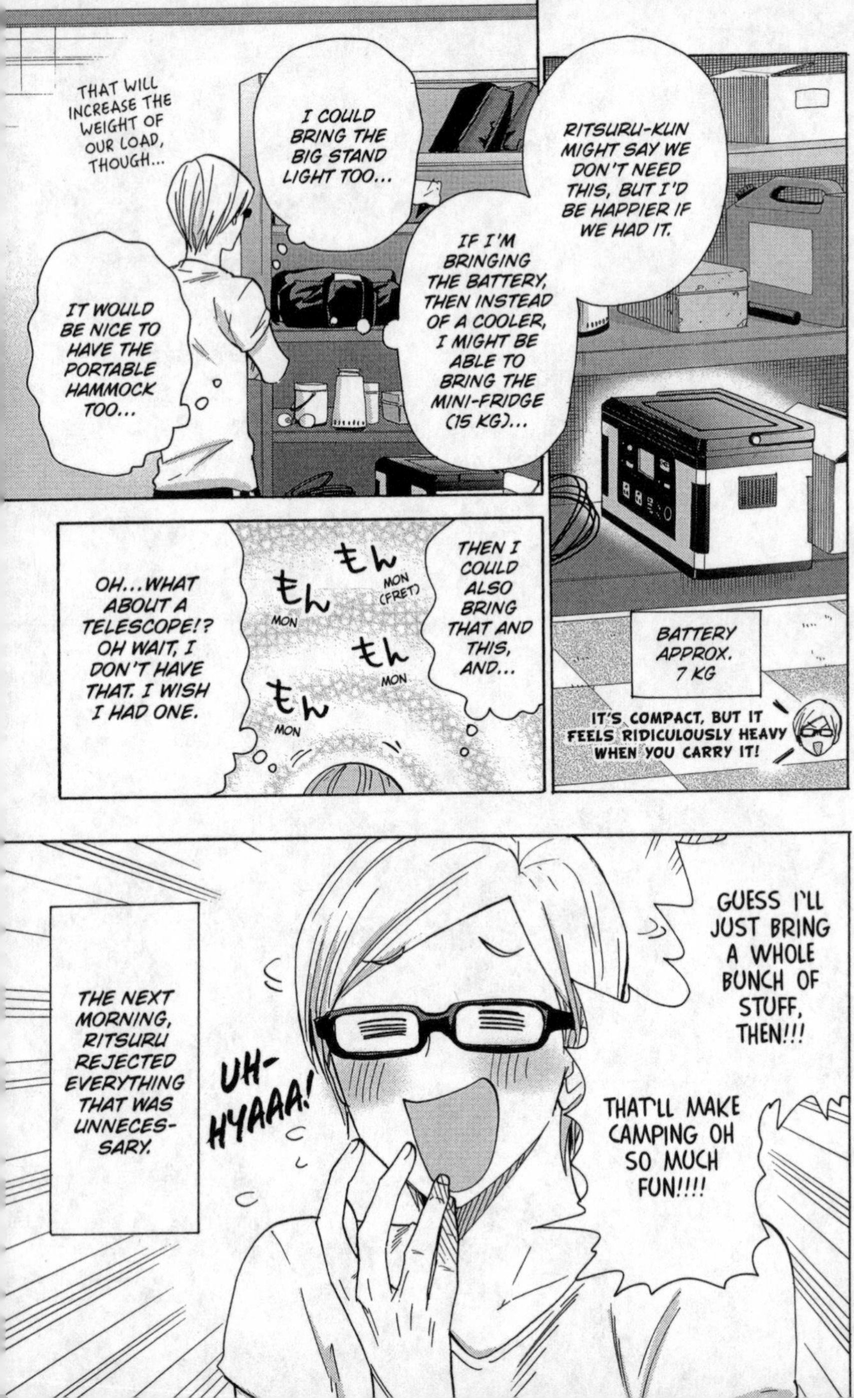
RITSURU-KUN MIGHT SAY WE DON'T NEED THIS, BUT I'D BE HAPPIER IF WE HAD IT.
BATTERY APPROX. 7 KG
IT'S COMPACT, BUT IT FEELS RIDICULOUSLY HEAVY WHEN YOU CARRY IT!
IF I'M BRINGING THE BATTERY, THEN INSTEAD OF A COOLER, I MIGHT BE ABLE TO BRING THE MINI-FRIDGE (15 KG)...
I COULD BRING THE BIG STAND LIGHT TOO...
THAT WILL INCREASE THE WEIGHT OF OUR LOAD, THOUGH...
IT WOULD BE NICE TO HAVE THE PORTABLE HAMMOCK TOO...
THEN I COULD ALSO BRING THAT AND THIS, AND...
もん MON (FRET)
もん MON
もん MON
もん MON
OH...WHAT ABOUT A TELESCOPE!? OH WAIT, I DON'T HAVE THAT. I WISH I HAD ONE.
GUESS I'LL JUST BRING A WHOLE BUNCH OF STUFF, THEN!!!
THAT'LL MAKE CAMPING OH SO MUCH FUN!!!!
UH-HYAAA!
THE NEXT MORNING, RITSURU REJECTED EVERYTHING THAT WAS UNNECES-SARY.

Days on Fes

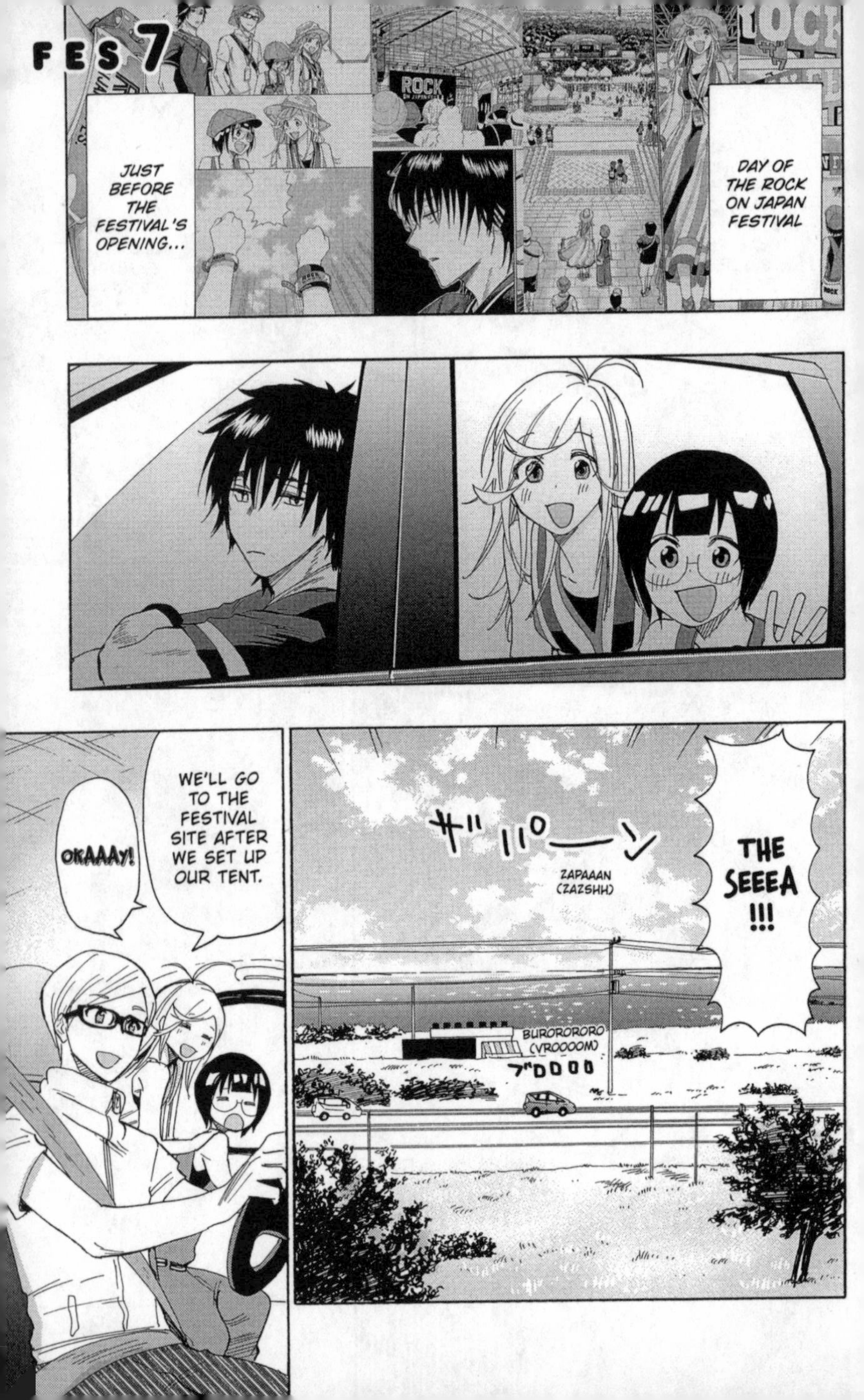
FES 7
DAY OF THE ROCK ON JAPAN FESTIVAL
JUST BEFORE THE FESTIVAL'S OPENING...
THE SEEEA!!!
ZAPAAAN (ZAZSHH)
BURORORORO (VROOOOM)
WE'LL GO TO THE FESTIVAL SITE AFTER WE SET UP OUR TENT.
OKAAAY!

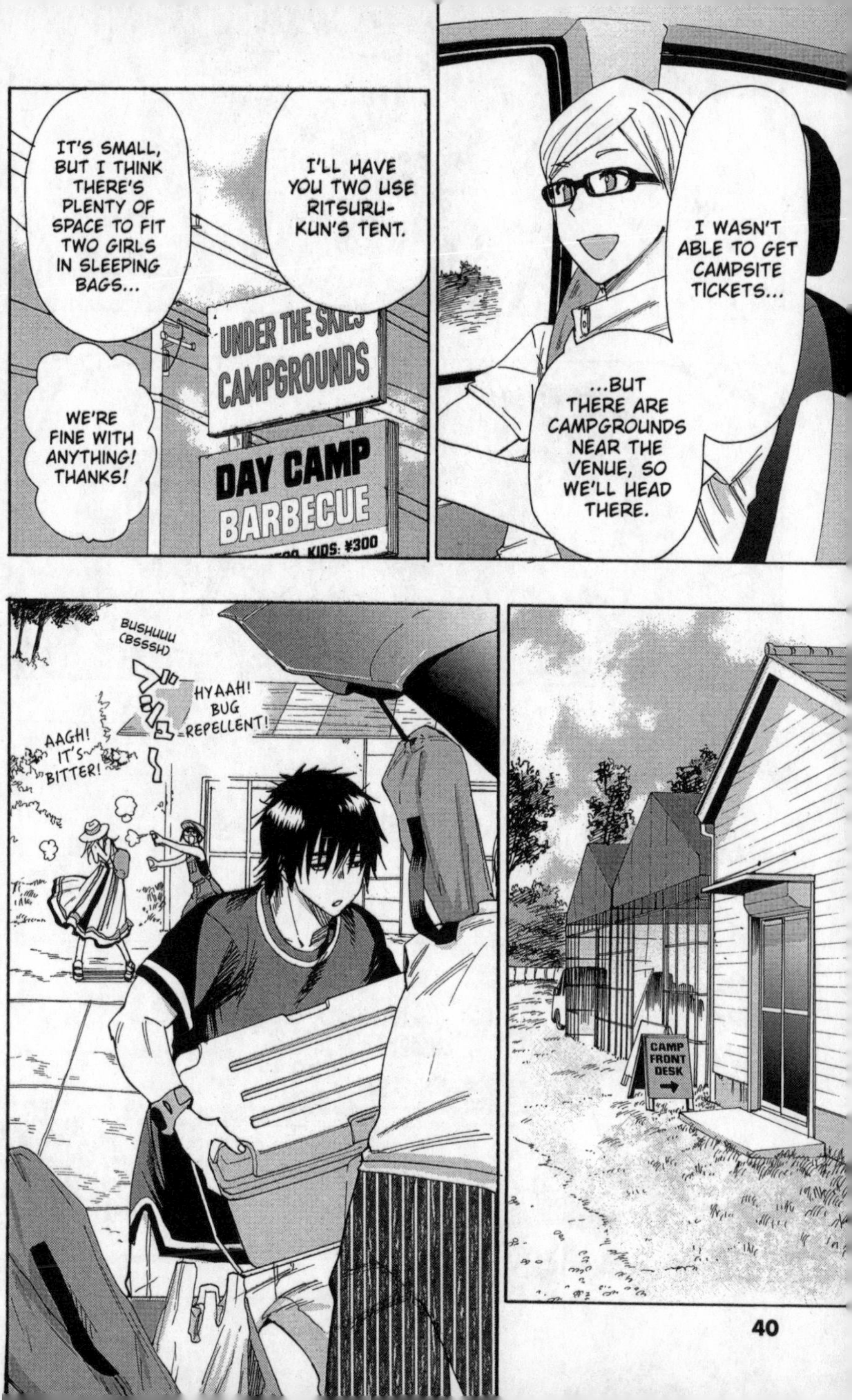
I WASN'T ABLE TO GET CAMPSITE TICKETS...
...BUT THERE ARE CAMPGROUNDS NEAR THE VENUE, SO WE'LL HEAD THERE.
I'LL HAVE YOU TWO USE RITSURU-KUN'S TENT.
IT'S SMALL, BUT I THINK THERE'S PLENTY OF SPACE TO FIT TWO GIRLS IN SLEEPING BAGS...
UNDER THE SKIES CAMPGROUNDS
DAY CAMP
BARBECUE
KIDS: ¥300
WE'RE FINE WITH ANYTHING! THANKS!
CAMP FRONT DESK
BUSHUUU (BSSSH)
HYAAH! BUG REPELLENT!
AAGH! IT'S BITTER!

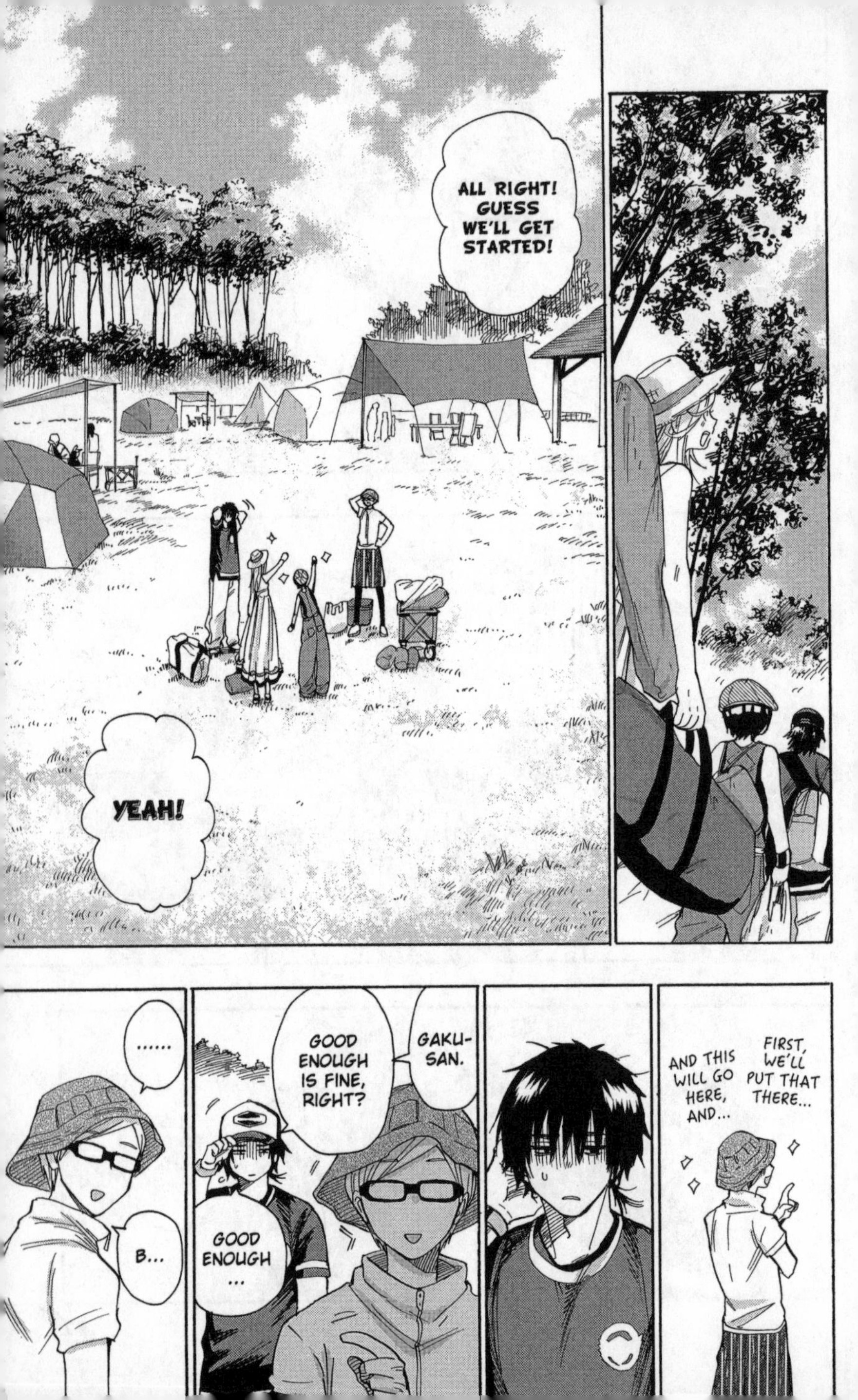
ALL RIGHT! GUESS WE'LL GET STARTED!
YEAH!
FIRST, WE'LL PUT THAT THERE...
AND THIS WILL GO HERE, AND...
GAKU-SAN.
GOOD ENOUGH IS FINE, RIGHT?
GOOD ENOUGH ...
......
B...

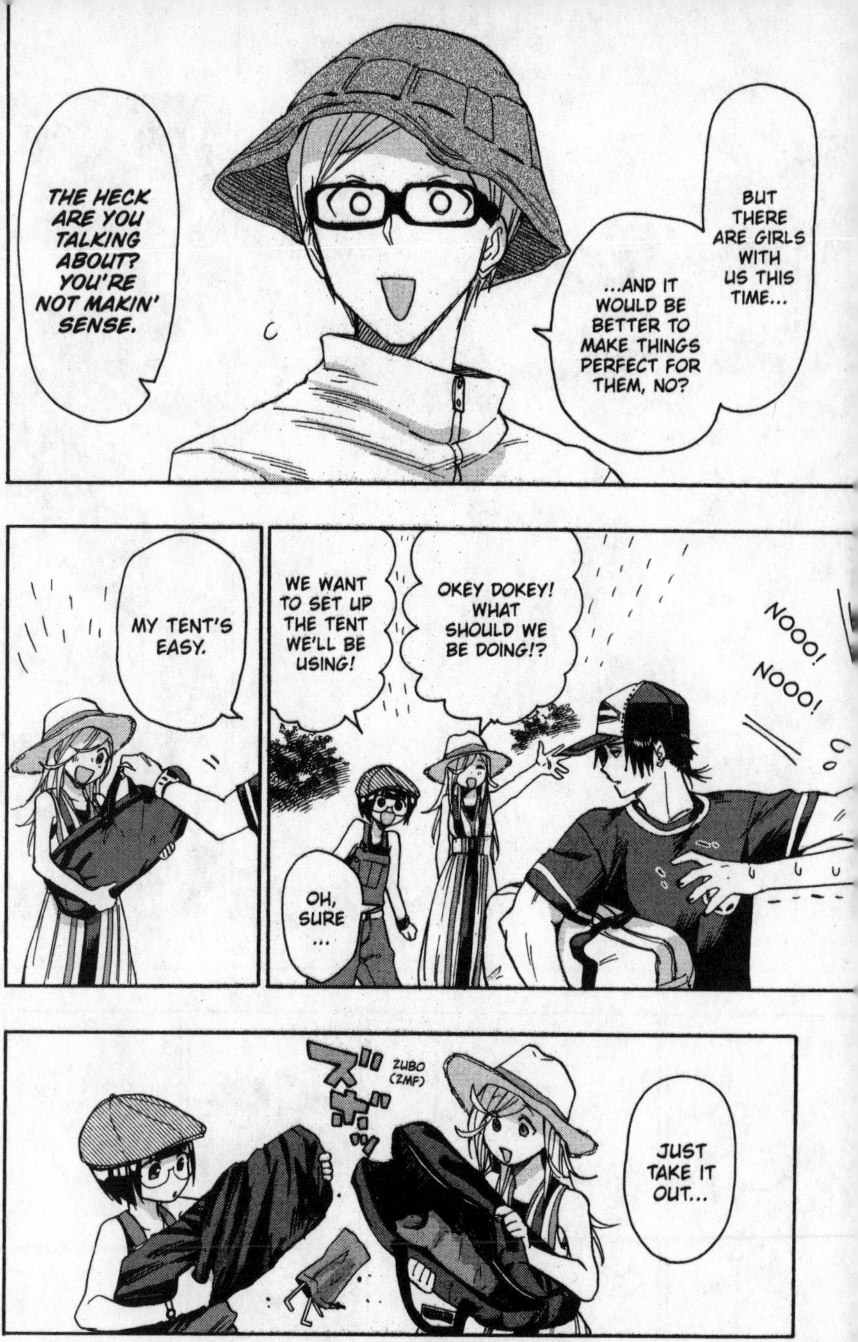
BUT THERE ARE GIRLS WITH US THIS TIME...
...AND IT WOULD BE BETTER TO MAKE THINGS PERFECT FOR THEM, NO?
THE HECK ARE YOU TALKING ABOUT? YOU'RE NOT MAKIN' SENSE.
NOOO! NOOO!
OKEY DOKEY! WHAT SHOULD WE BE DOING!?
WE WANT TO SET UP THE TENT WE'LL BE USING!
OH, SURE ...
MY TENT'S EASY.
JUST TAKE IT OUT...
ZUBO (ZMF)

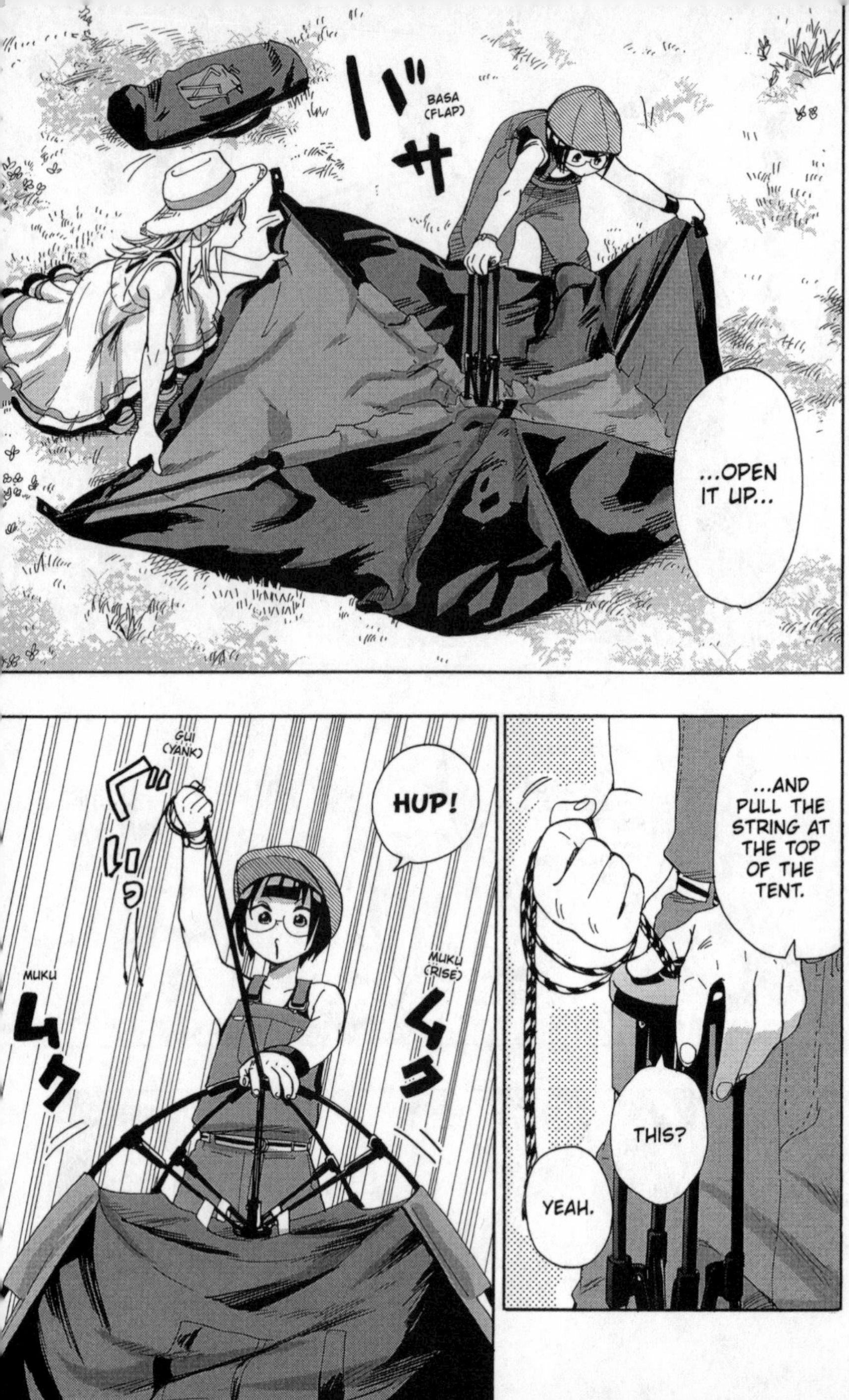
バサ
BASA (FLAP)
...OPEN IT UP...
...AND PULL THE STRING AT THE TOP OF THE TENT.
THIS?
YEAH.
HUP!
MUKU (RISE)
ムク
GUI (YANK)
グイッ
MUKU
ムク

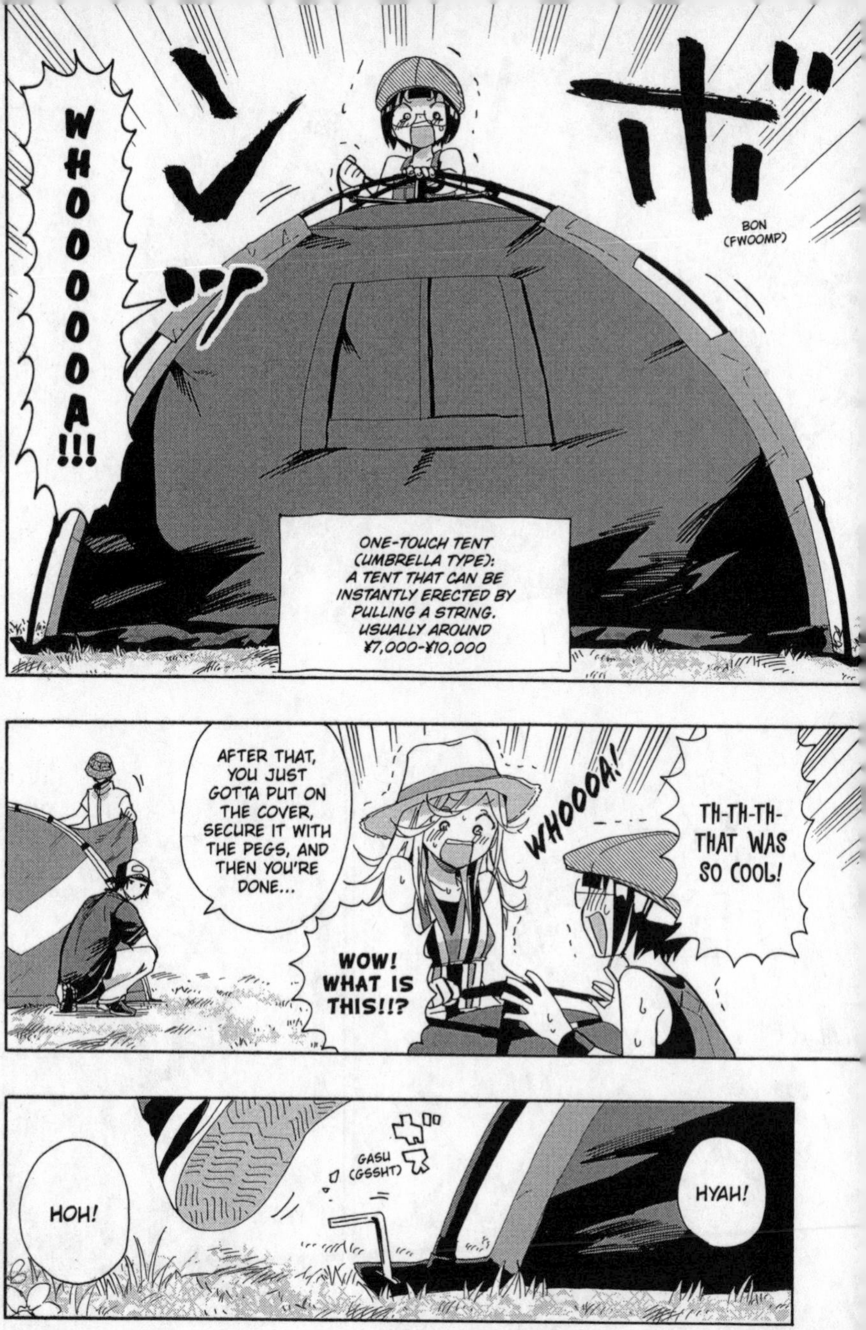
BON (FWOOMP)
WHOOOOOOA!!!
ONE-TOUCH TENT (UMBRELLA TYPE): A TENT THAT CAN BE INSTANTLY ERECTED BY PULLING A STRING. USUALLY AROUND ¥7,000-¥10,000
TH-TH-TH-THAT WAS SO COOL!
WHOOOA!
AFTER THAT, YOU JUST GOTTA PUT ON THE COVER, SECURE IT WITH THE PEGS, AND THEN YOU'RE DONE...
WOW! WHAT IS THIS!!?
HYAH!
GASU (GSSHT)
HOH!

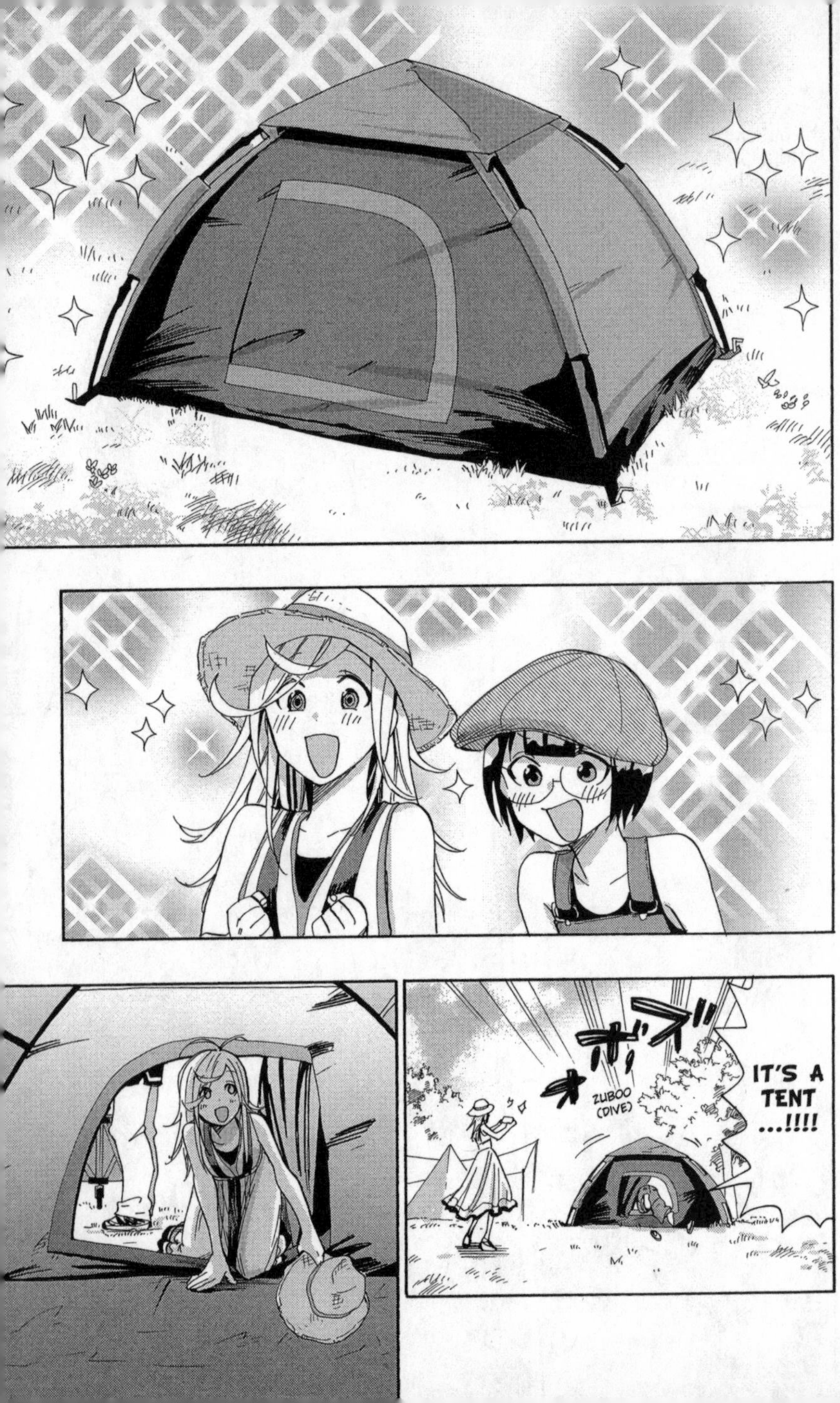
ZUBOO
(DIVE)
IT'S A TENT ...!!!!

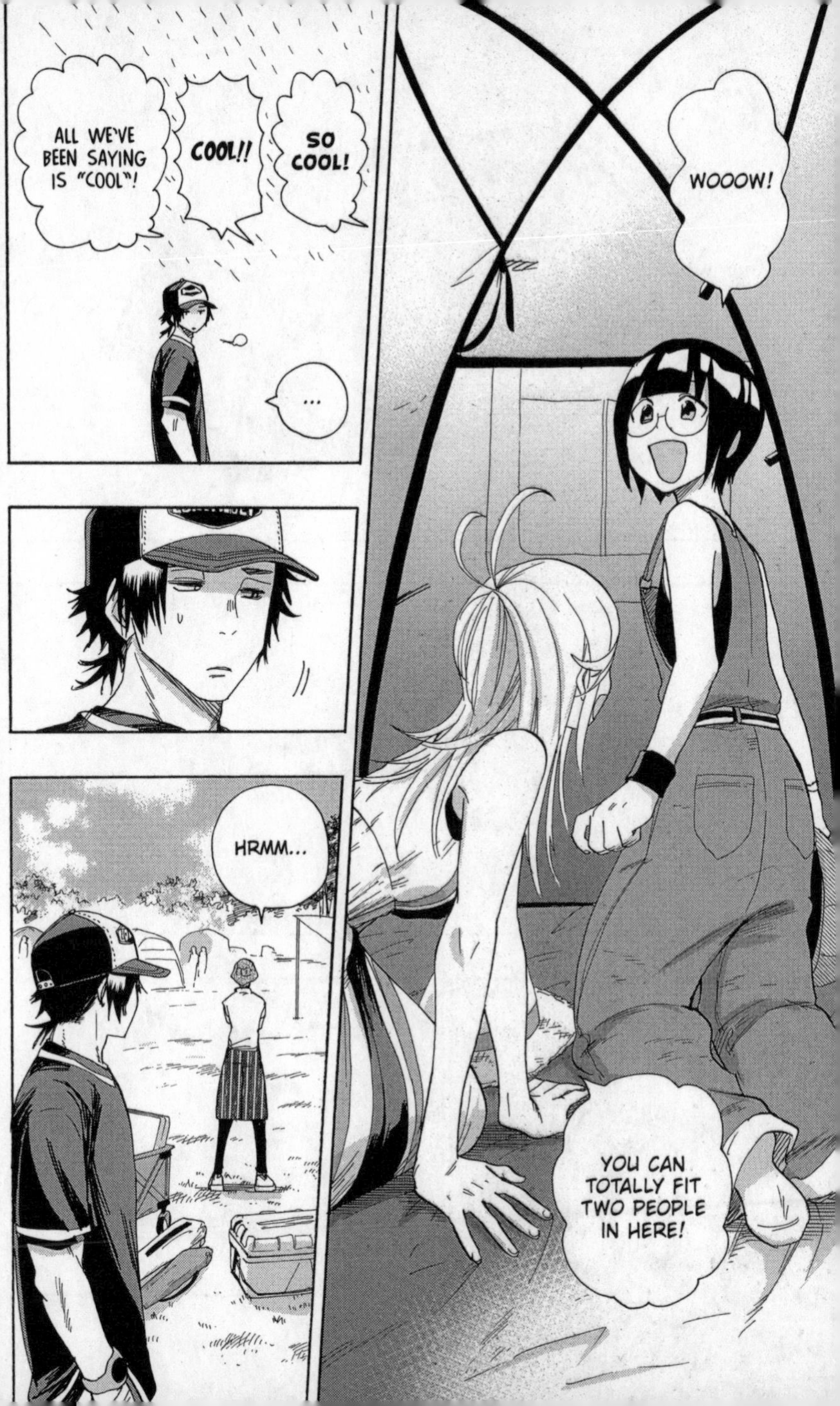
WOOOW!
YOU CAN TOTALLY FIT TWO PEOPLE IN HERE!
SO COOL!
COOL!!
ALL WE'VE BEEN SAYING IS "COOL"!
...
HRMM...

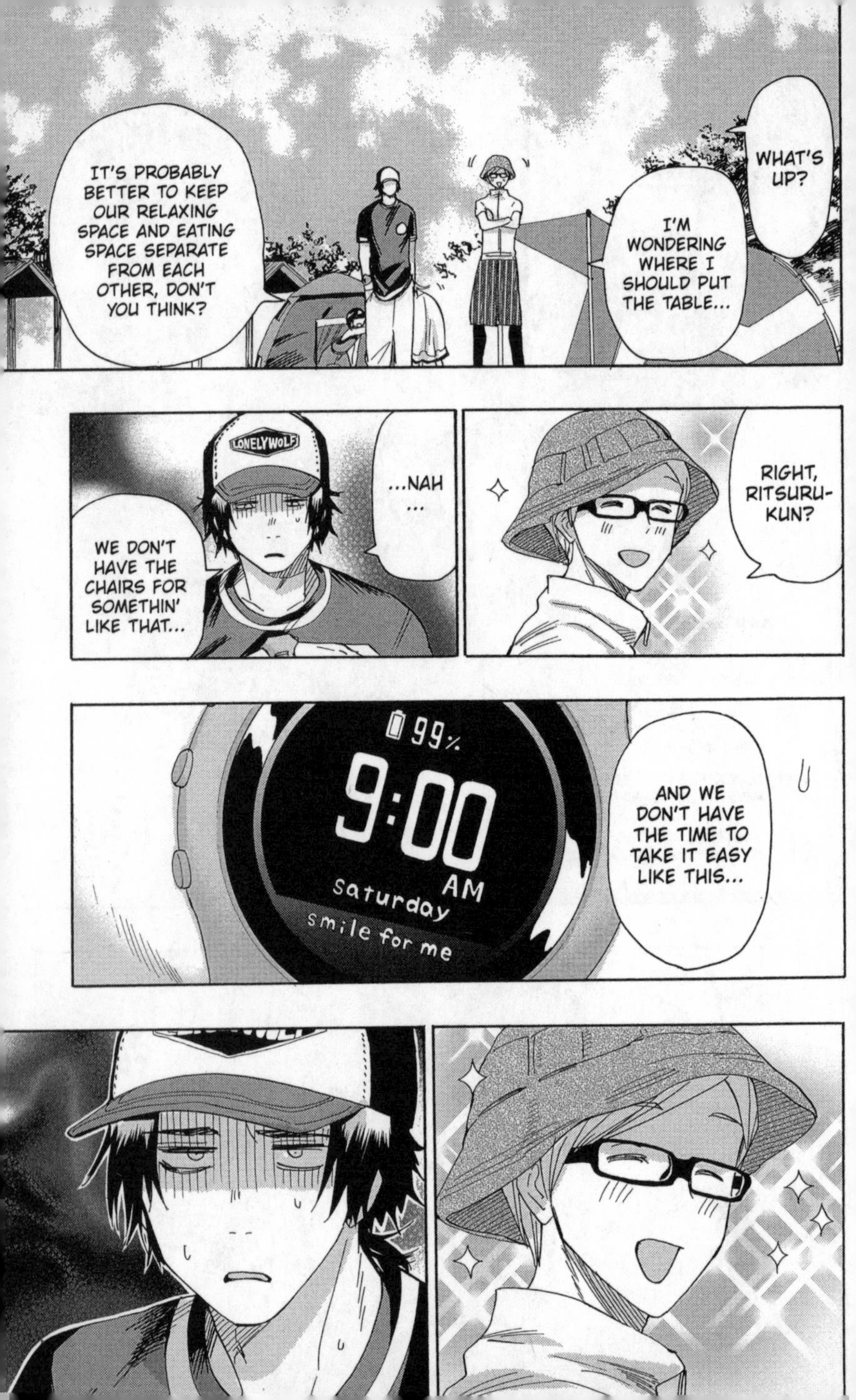
WHAT'S UP?
I'M WONDERING WHERE I SHOULD PUT THE TABLE...
IT'S PROBABLY BETTER TO KEEP OUR RELAXING SPACE AND EATING SPACE SEPARATE FROM EACH OTHER, DON'T YOU THINK?
RIGHT, RITSURU-KUN?
LONELYWOLF
...NAH ...
WE DON'T HAVE THE CHAIRS FOR SOMETHIN' LIKE THAT...
AND WE DON'T HAVE THE TIME TO TAKE IT EASY LIKE THIS...
99%
9:00
AM
saturday
smile for me

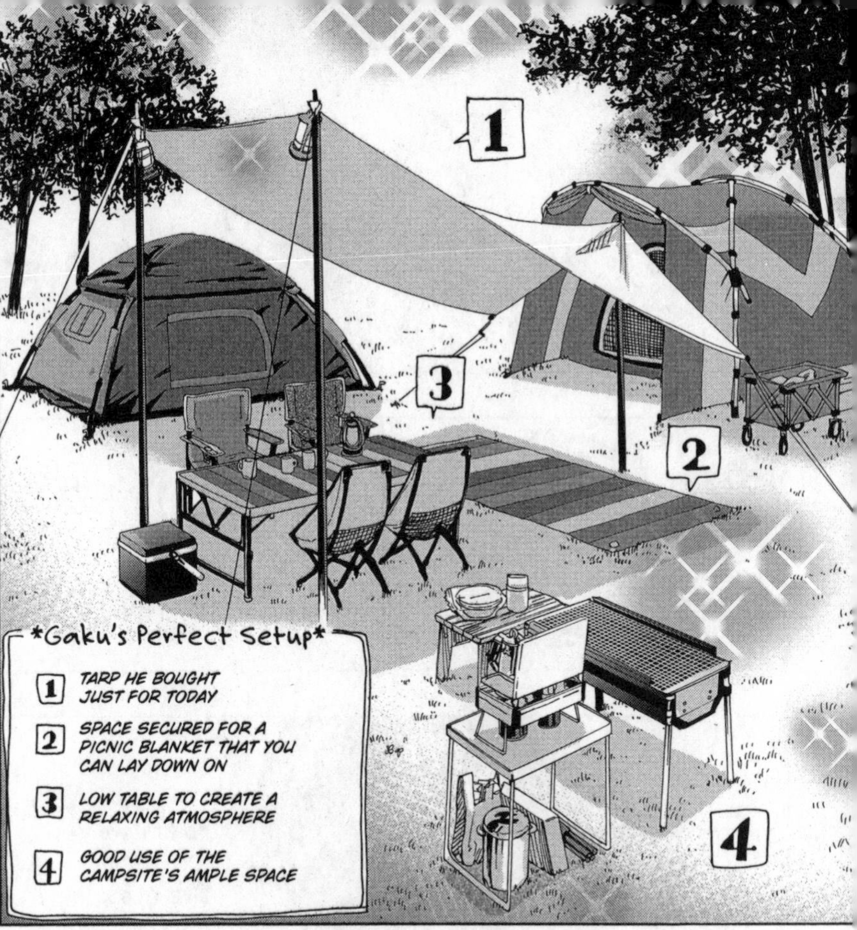
1
3
2
4
Gaku's Perfect Setup
1 TARP HE BOUGHT JUST FOR TODAY
2 SPACE SECURED FOR A PICNIC BLANKET THAT YOU CAN LAY DOWN ON
3 LOW TABLE TO CREATE A RELAXING ATMOSPHERE
4 GOOD USE OF THE CAMPSITE'S AMPLE SPACE

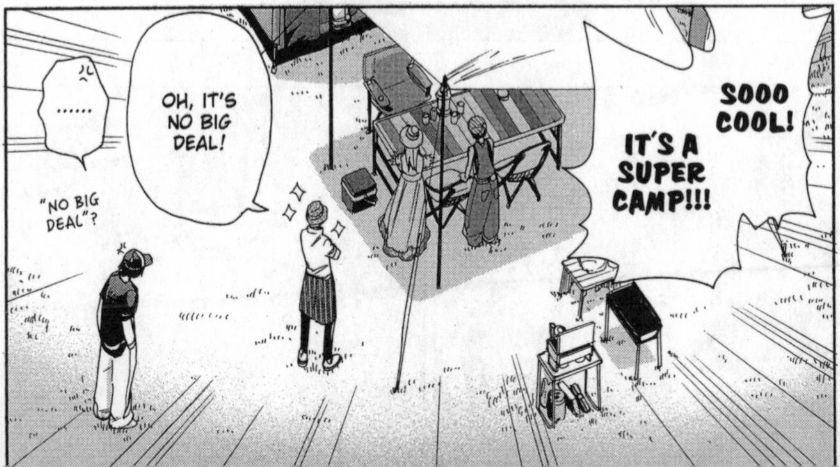
SOOO COOL!
IT'S A SUPER CAMP!!!
OH, IT'S NO BIG DEAL!
......
"NO BIG DEAL"?

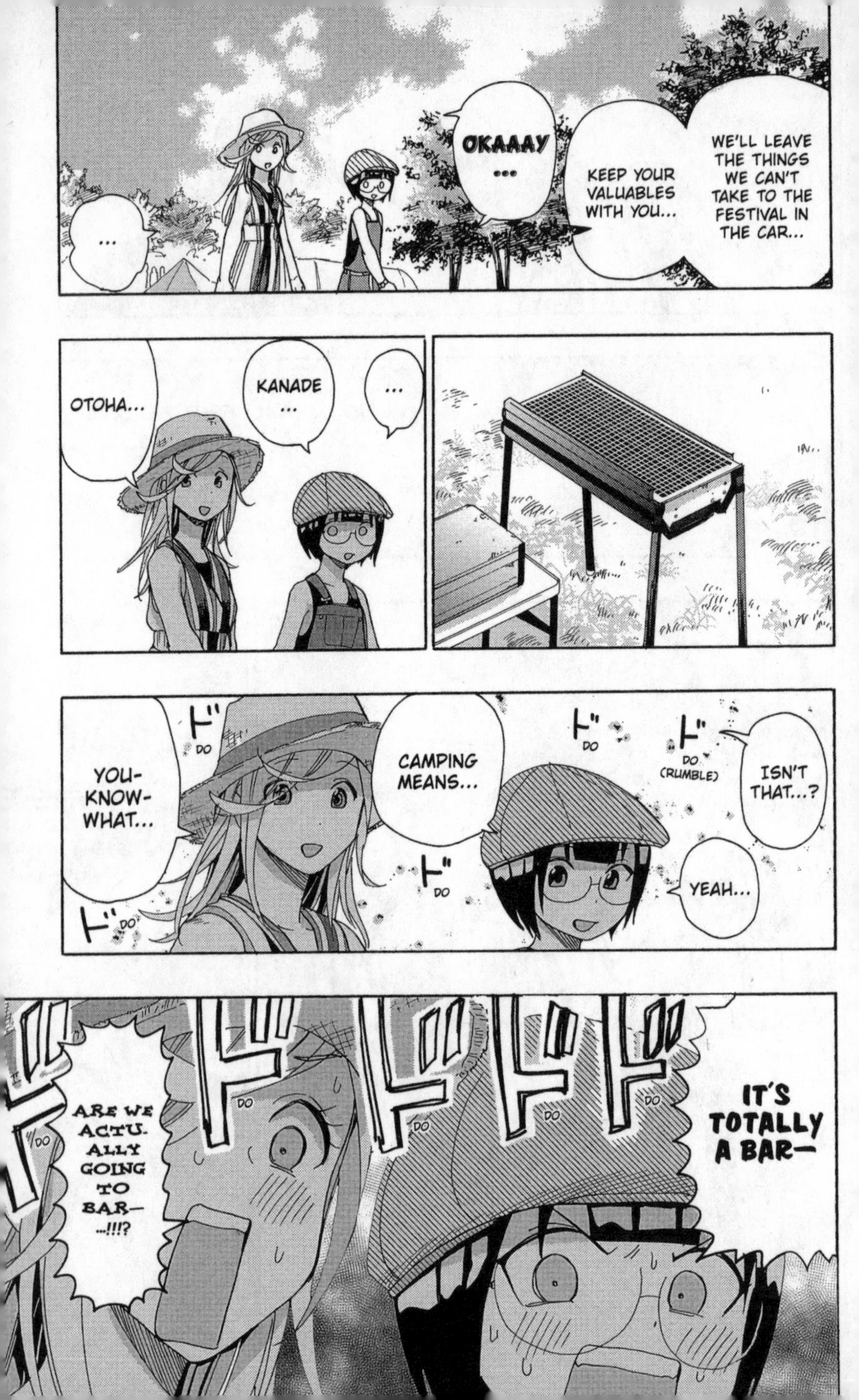
WE'LL LEAVE THE THINGS WE CAN'T TAKE TO THE FESTIVAL IN THE CAR...
KEEP YOUR VALUABLES WITH YOU...
OKAAAY ...
...
...
KANADE ...
OTOHA...
ISN'T THAT...?
ド DO (RUMBLE)
ド DO
YEAH...
CAMPING MEANS...
ド DO
ド DO
YOU-KNOW-WHAT...
ド DO
IT'S TOTALLY A BAR—
ド DO
ド DO
ド DO
ド DO
ド DO
ARE WE ACTU-ALLY GOING TO BAR—...!!!?

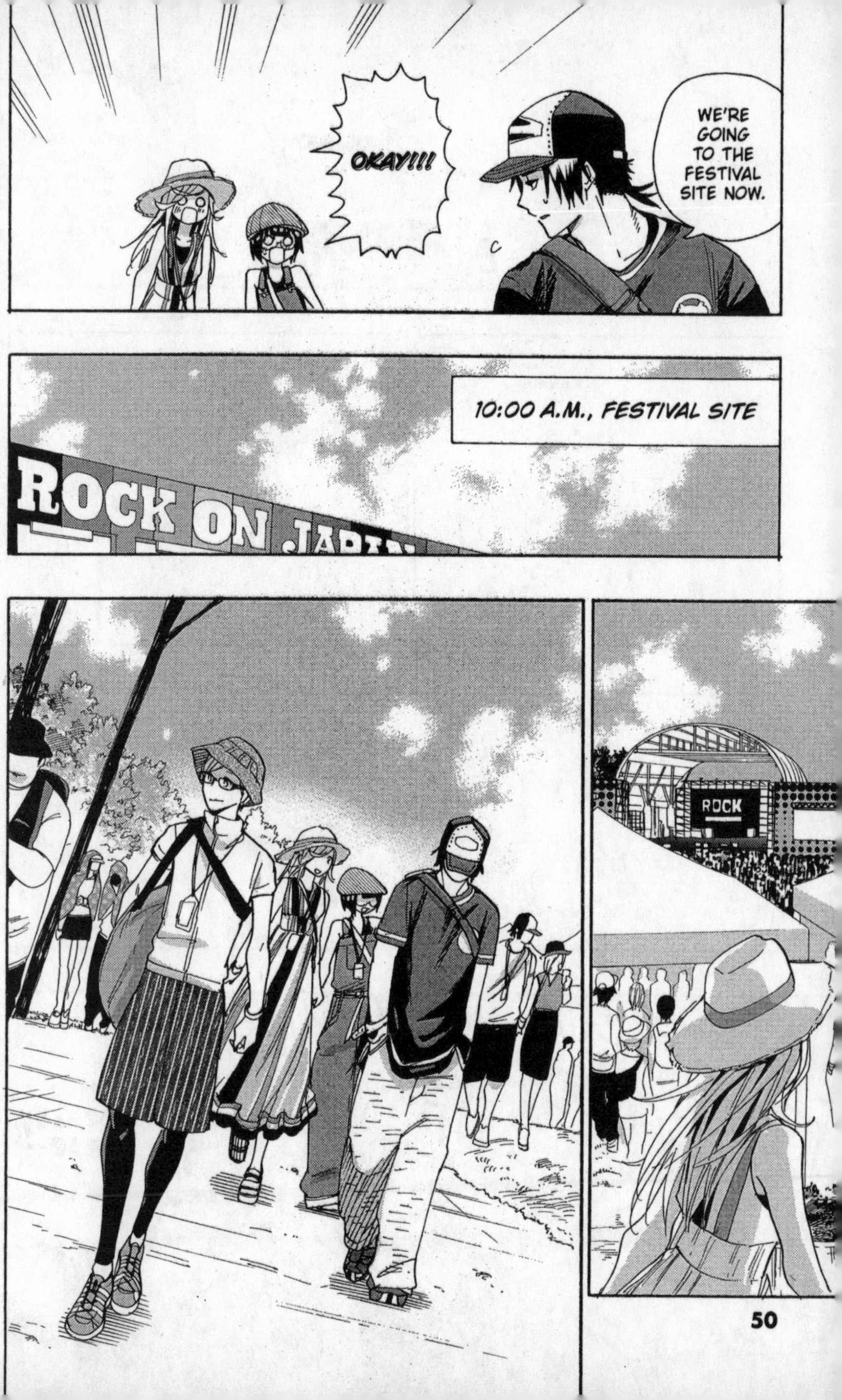
WE'RE GOING TO THE FESTIVAL SITE NOW.
OKAY!!!
10:00 A.M., FESTIVAL SITE
ROCK ON JAPAN
ROCK

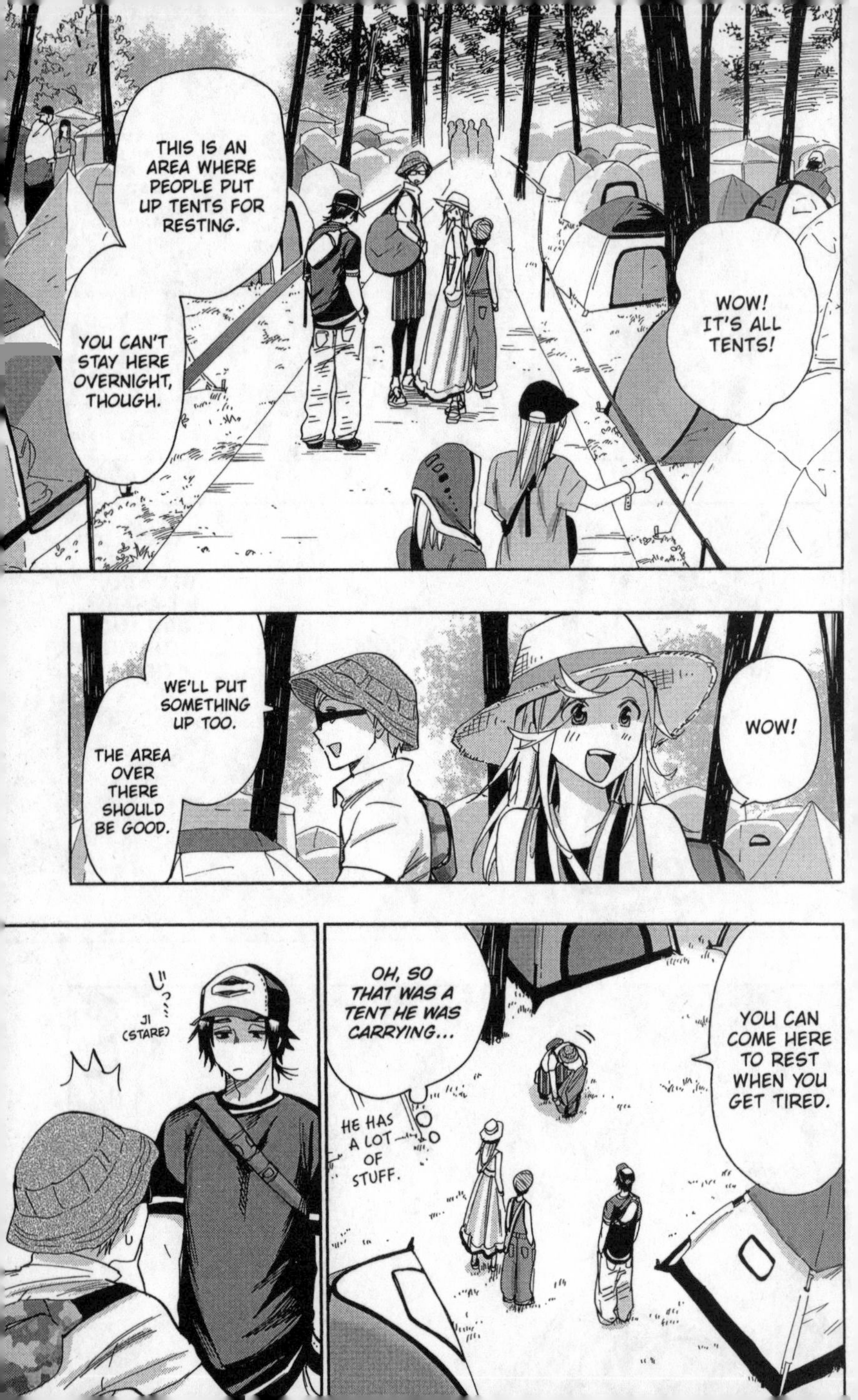
WOW! IT'S ALL TENTS!
THIS IS AN AREA WHERE PEOPLE PUT UP TENTS FOR RESTING.
YOU CAN'T STAY HERE OVERNIGHT, THOUGH.
WOW!
WE'LL PUT SOMETHING UP TOO.
THE AREA OVER THERE SHOULD BE GOOD.
YOU CAN COME HERE TO REST WHEN YOU GET TIRED.
OH, SO THAT WAS A TENT HE WAS CARRYING...
HE HAS A LOT OF STUFF.
JI (STARE)

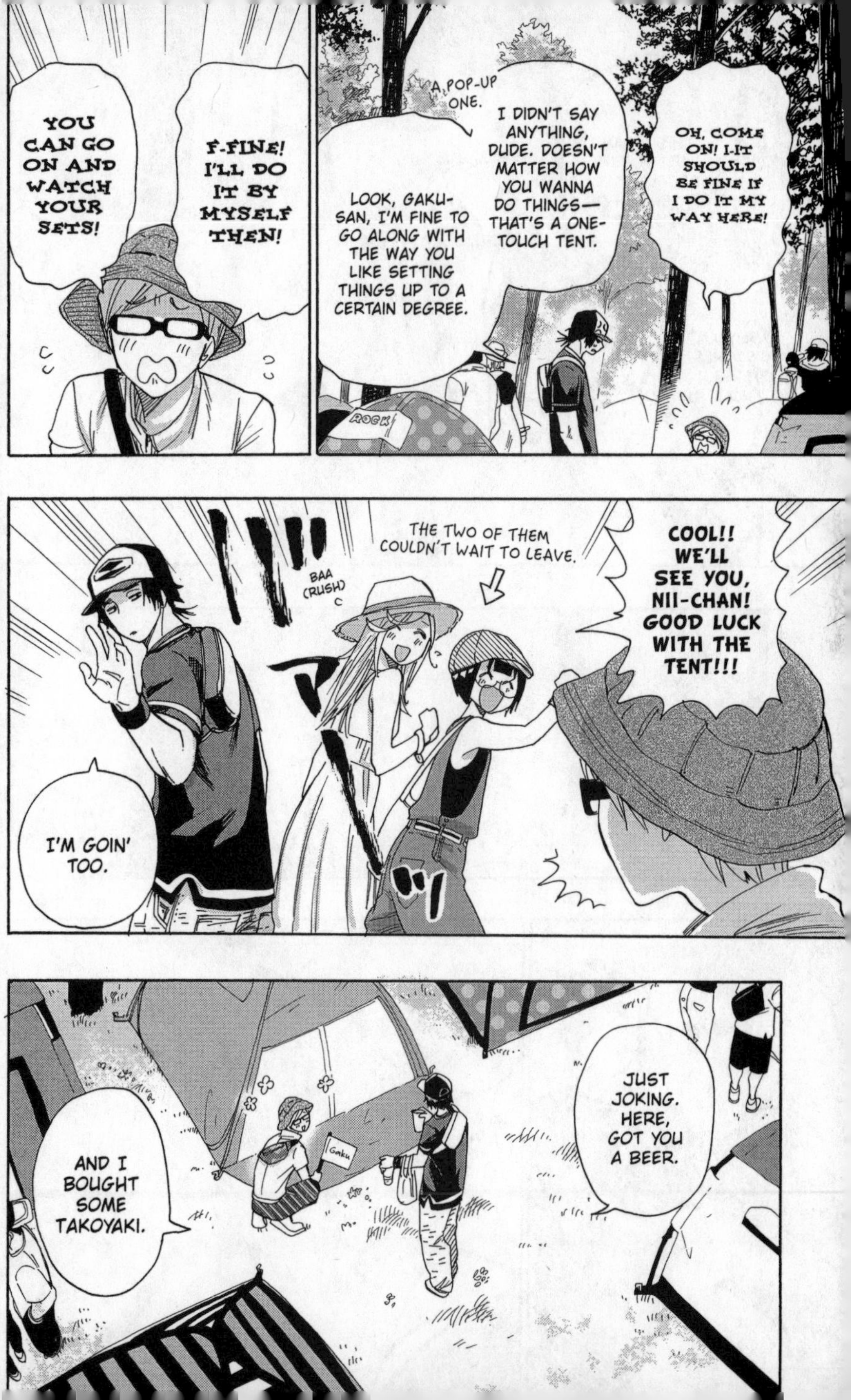
OH, COME ON! I-IT SHOULD BE FINE IF I DO IT MY WAY HERE!
I DIDN'T SAY ANYTHING, DUDE. DOESN'T MATTER HOW YOU WANNA DO THINGS—THAT'S A ONE-TOUCH TENT.
A POP-UP ONE.
LOOK, GAKU-SAN, I'M FINE TO GO ALONG WITH THE WAY YOU LIKE SETTING THINGS UP TO A CERTAIN DEGREE.
ROCK
F-FINE! I'LL DO IT BY MYSELF THEN!
YOU CAN GO ON AND WATCH YOUR SETS!
COOL!! WE'LL SEE YOU, NII-CHAN! GOOD LUCK WITH THE TENT!!!
THE TWO OF THEM COULDN'T WAIT TO LEAVE.
BAA (RUSH)
I'M GOIN' TOO.
JUST JOKING. HERE, GOT YOU A BEER.
Gaku
AND I BOUGHT SOME TAKOYAKI.

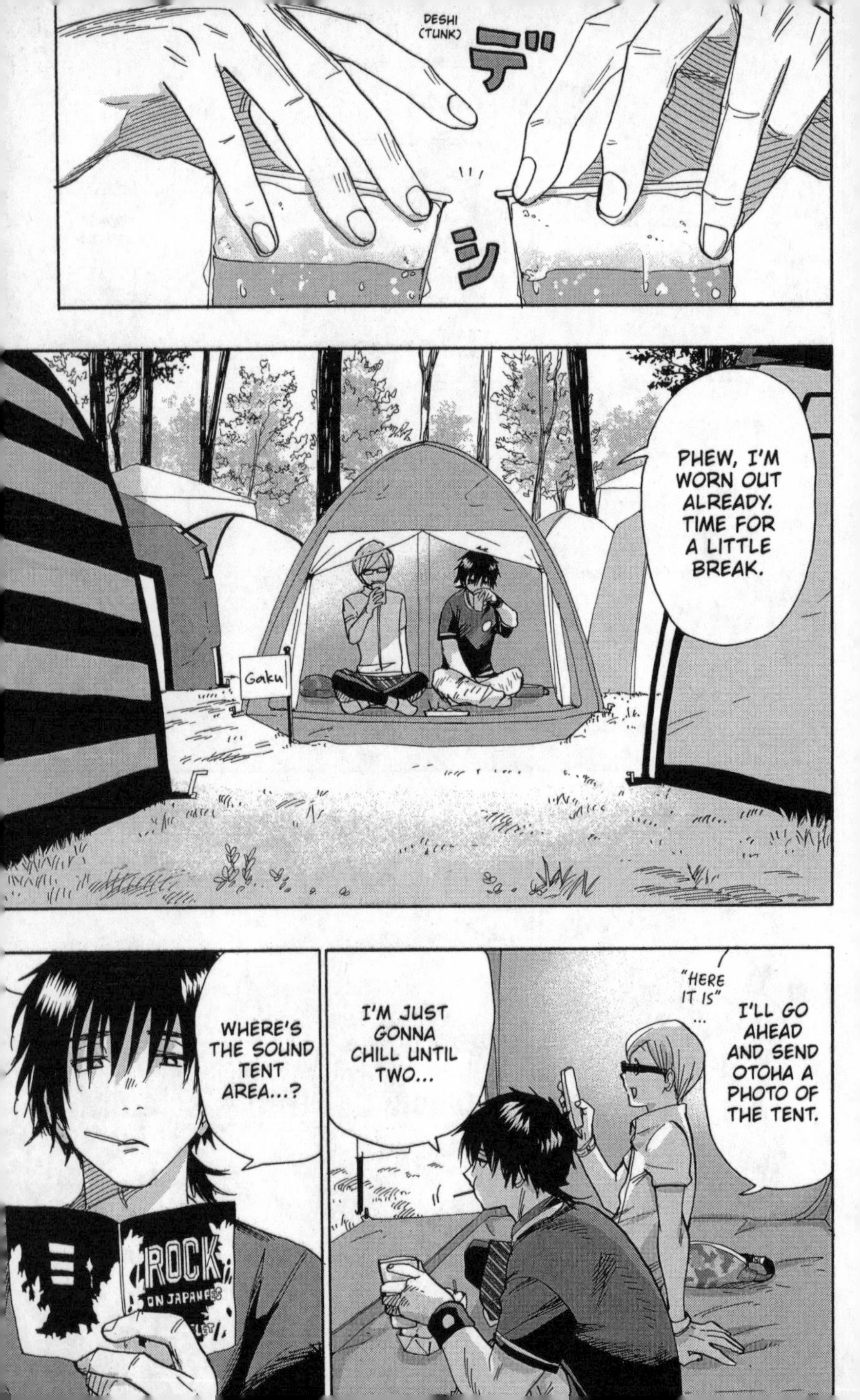

DESHI (TUNK)
デシ
PHEW, I'M WORN OUT ALREADY. TIME FOR A LITTLE BREAK.
Gaku
I'LL GO AHEAD AND SEND OTOHA A PHOTO OF THE TENT.
"HERE IT IS" ...
I'M JUST GONNA CHILL UNTIL TWO...
WHERE'S THE SOUND TENT AREA...?
ROCK
ON JAPANESE

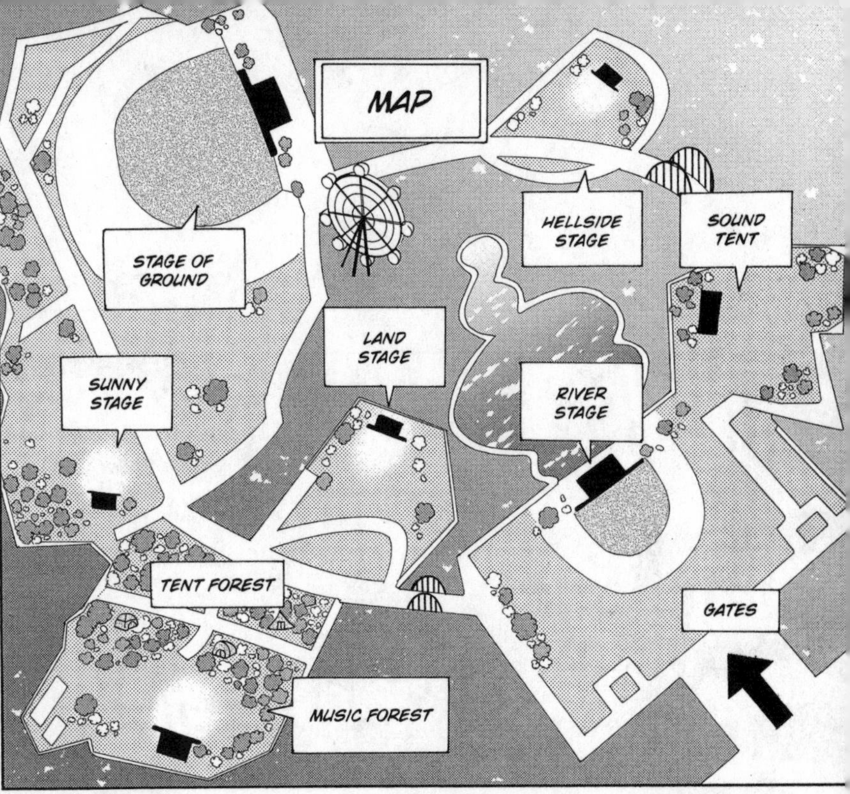
MAP
HELLSIDE STAGE
SOUND TENT
STAGE OF GROUND
LAND STAGE
RIVER STAGE
SUNNY STAGE
TENT FOREST
GATES
MUSIC FOREST

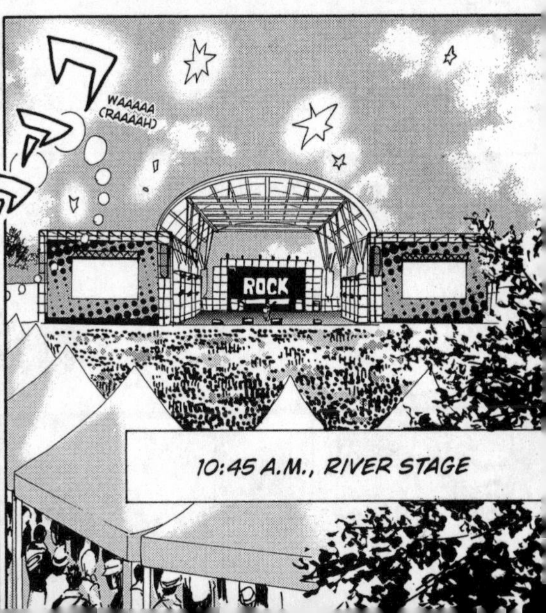
WAAAAA (RAAAAAH)
ROCK
10:45 A.M., RIVER STAGE

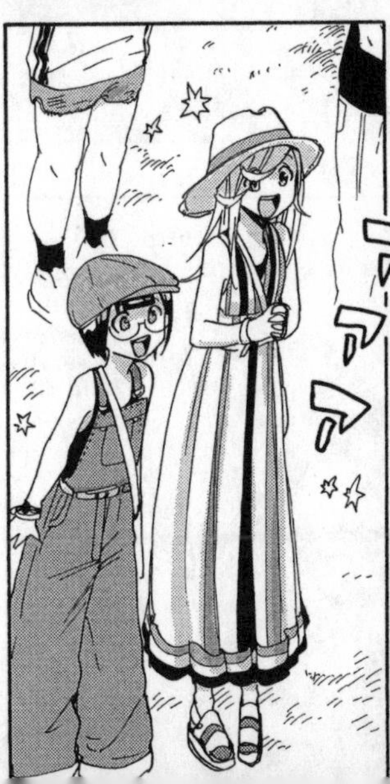

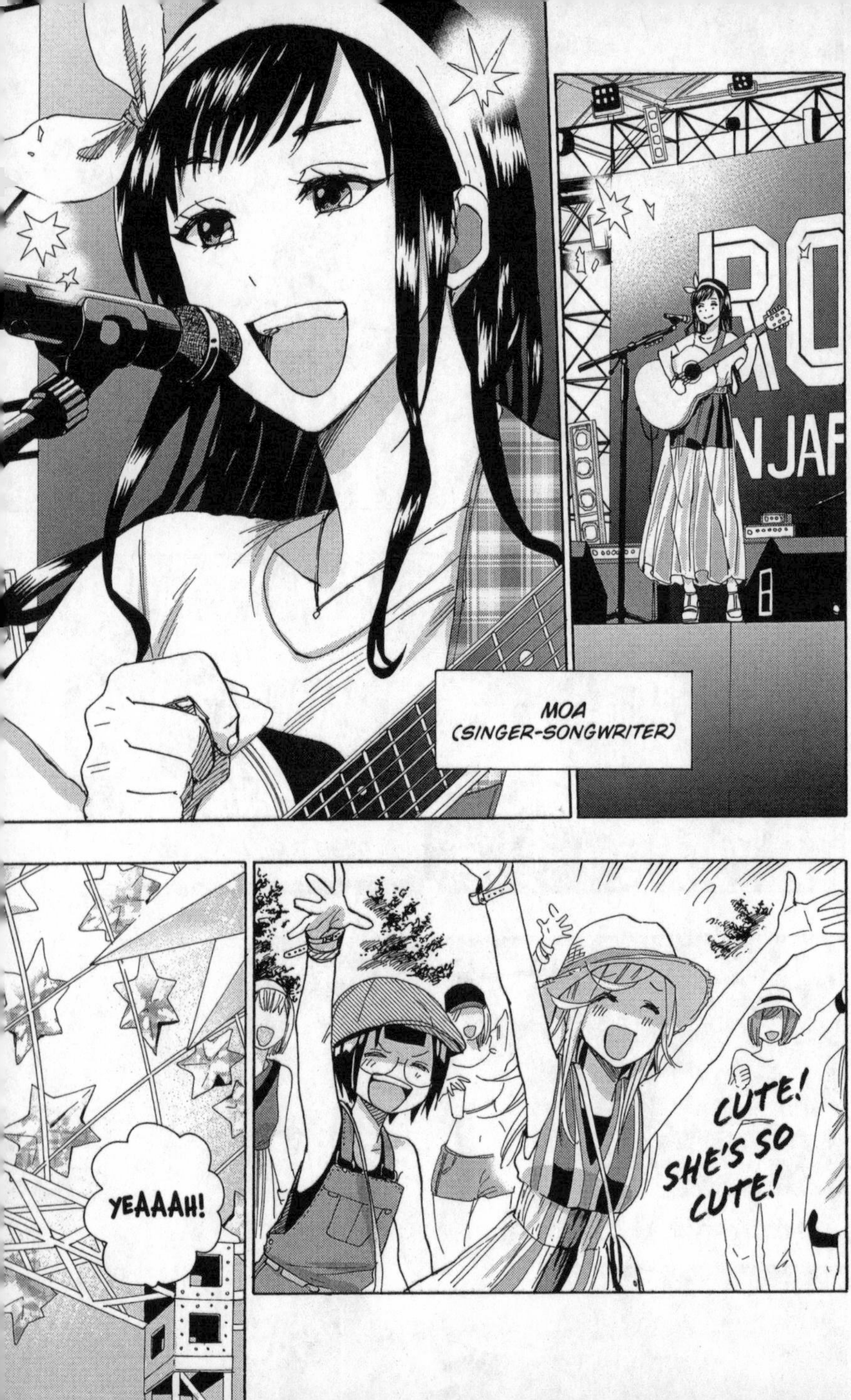
MOA
(SINGER-SONGWRITER)
CUTE! SHE'S SO CUTE!
YEAAAH!

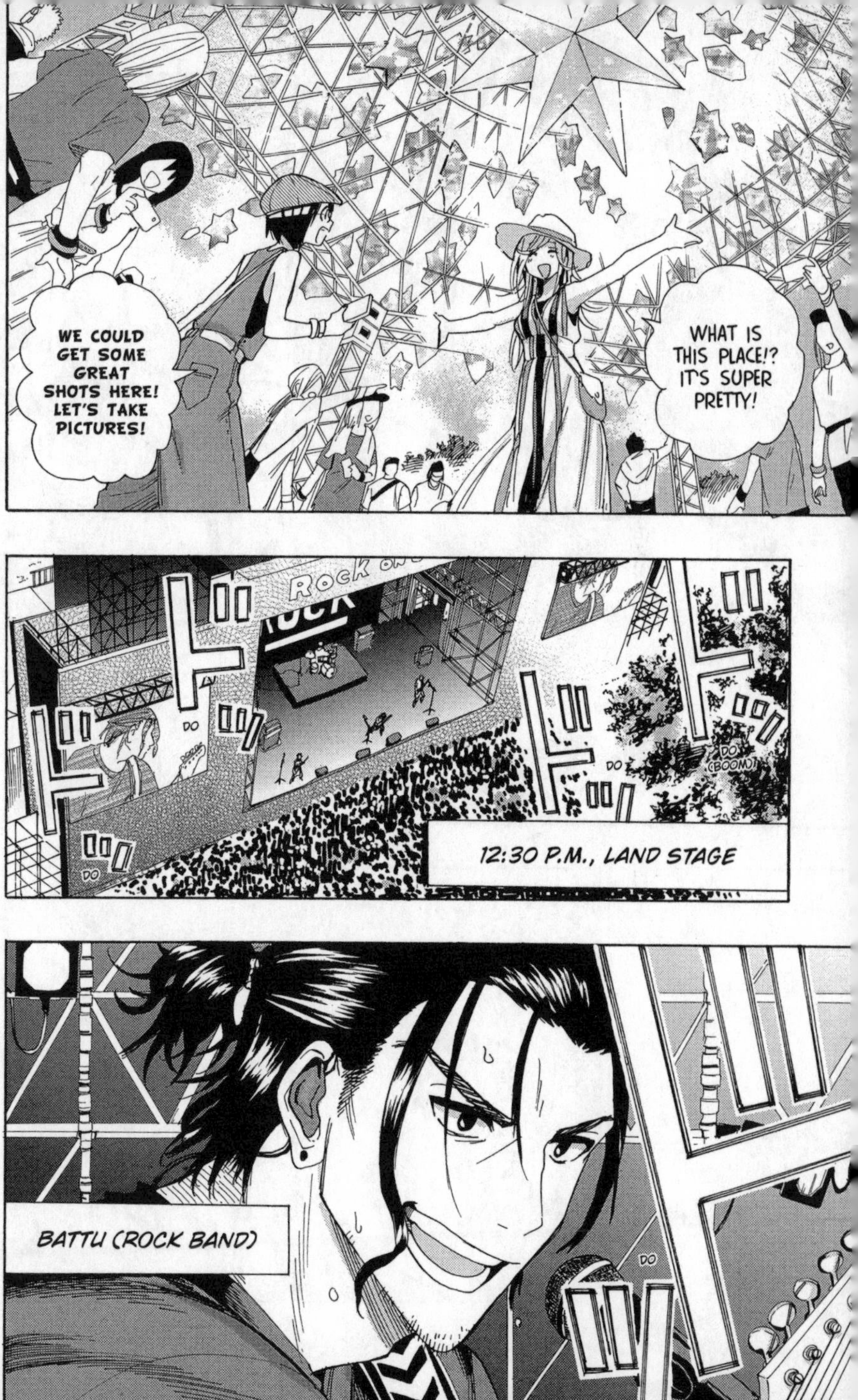
WHAT IS THIS PLACE!? IT'S SUPER PRETTY!
WE COULD GET SOME GREAT SHOTS HERE! LET'S TAKE PICTURES!
DO (BOOM)
DO
DO
DO
12:30 P.M., LAND STAGE
DO
BATTU (ROCK BAND)

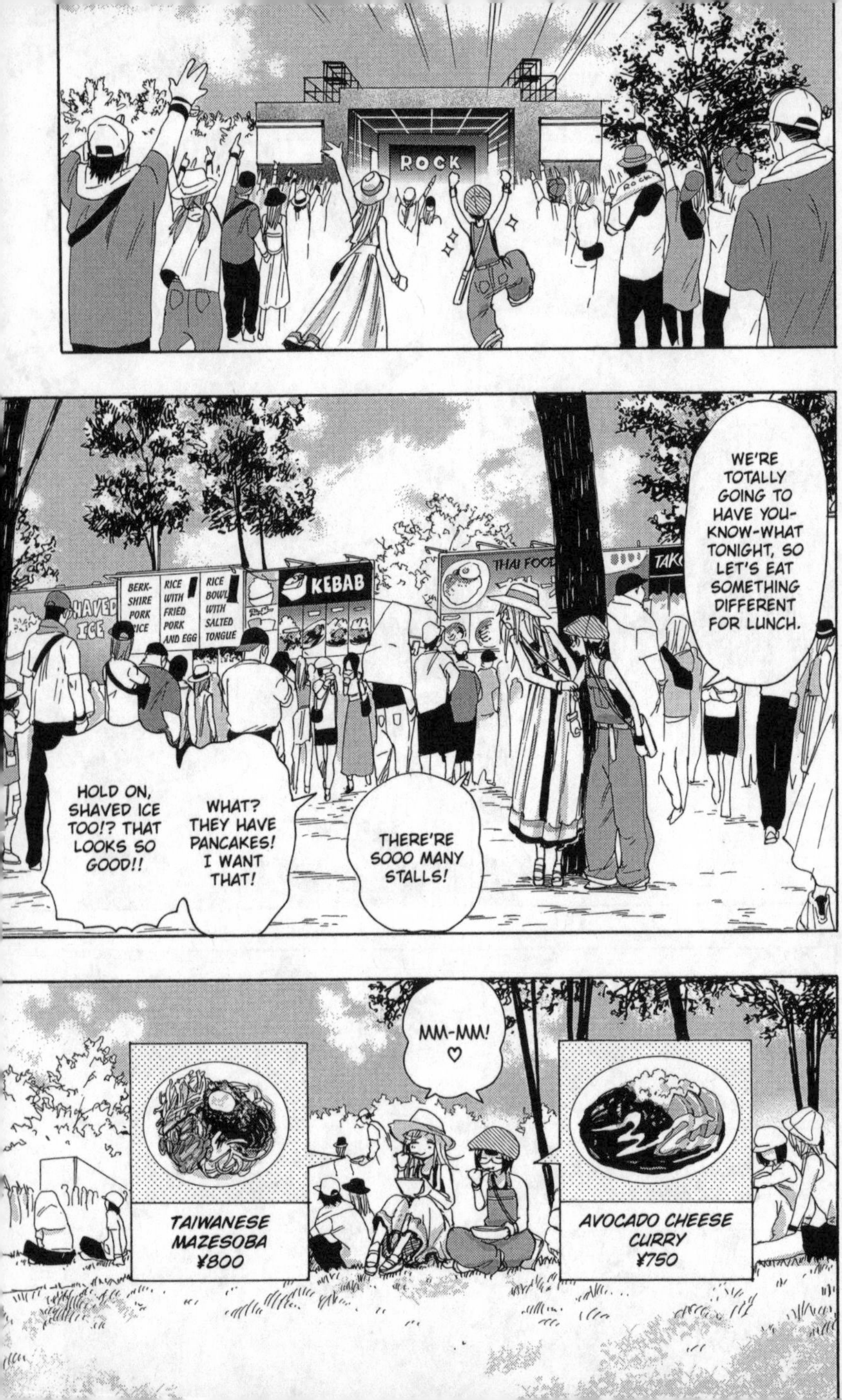
ROCK
WE'RE TOTALLY GOING TO HAVE YOU-KNOW-WHAT TONIGHT, SO LET'S EAT SOMETHING DIFFERENT FOR LUNCH.
THAI FOOD
KEBAB
RICE BOWL WITH SALTED TONGUE
RICE WITH FRIED PORK AND EGG
BERK-SHIRE PORK RICE
SHAVED ICE
THERE'RE SOOO MANY STALLS!
WHAT? THEY HAVE PANCAKES! I WANT THAT!
HOLD ON, SHAVED ICE TOO!? THAT LOOKS SO GOOD!!
AVOCADO CHEESE CURRY ¥750
MM-MM! ♡
TAIWANESE MAZESOBA ¥800

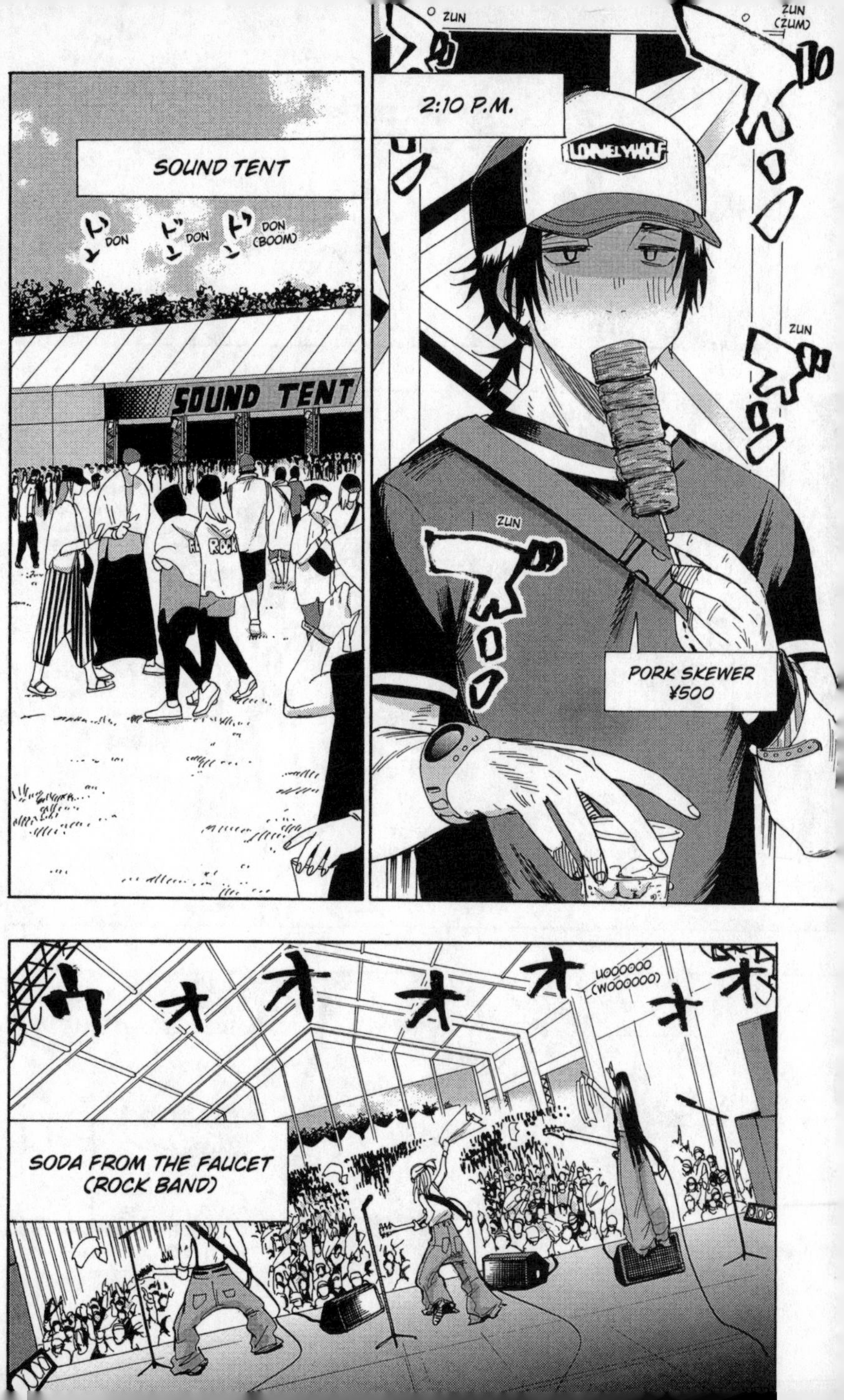
ZUN
ZUN (ZUM)
2:10 P.M.
ZUN
ZUN
PORK SKEWER ¥500
SOUND TENT
DON
DON
DON (BOOM)
SOUND TENT
ROCK
UOOOOOO (WOOOOOO)
SODA FROM THE FAUCET (ROCK BAND)

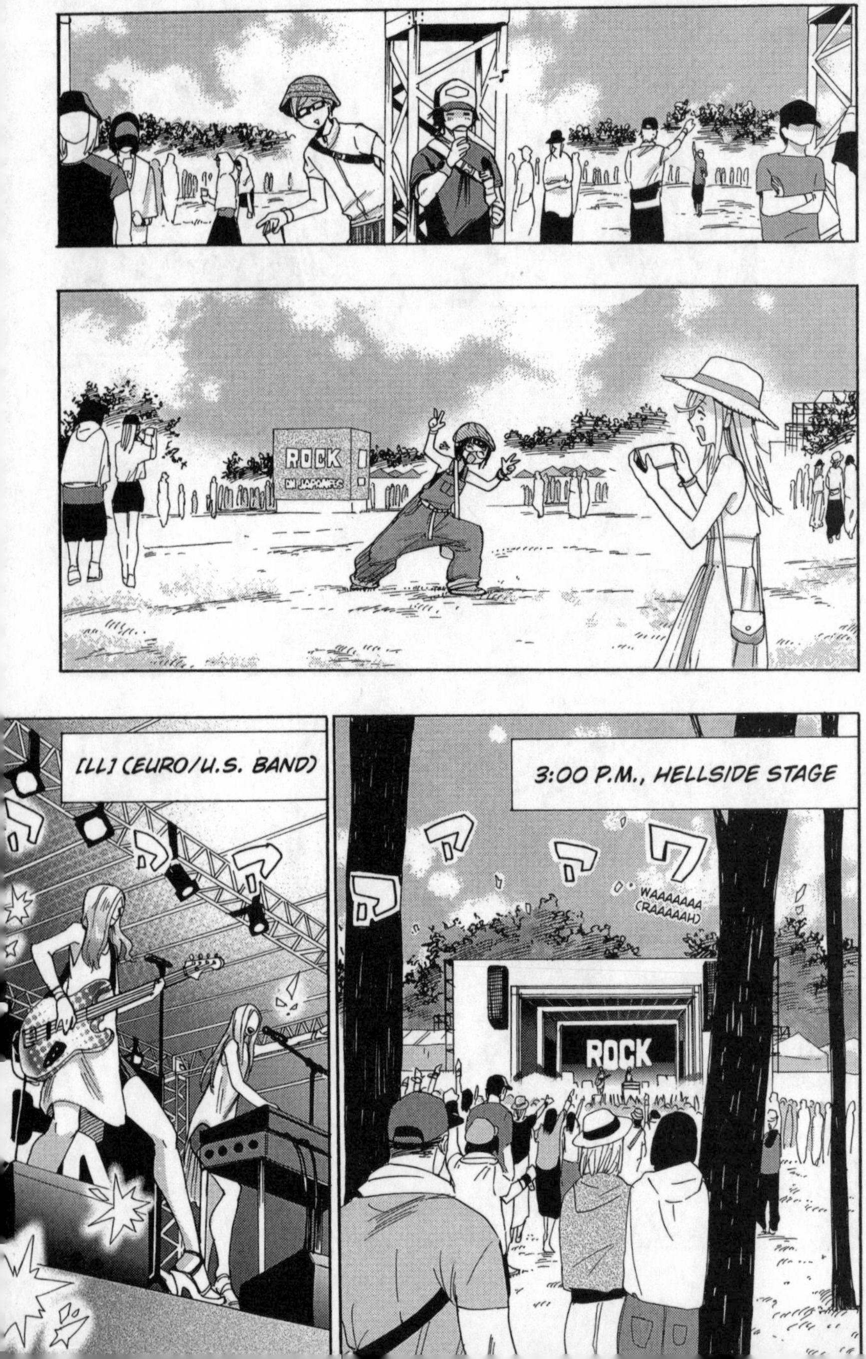
3:00 P.M., HELLSIDE STAGE
WAAAAAAA
(RAAAAAH)
[LL] (EURO/U.S. BAND)

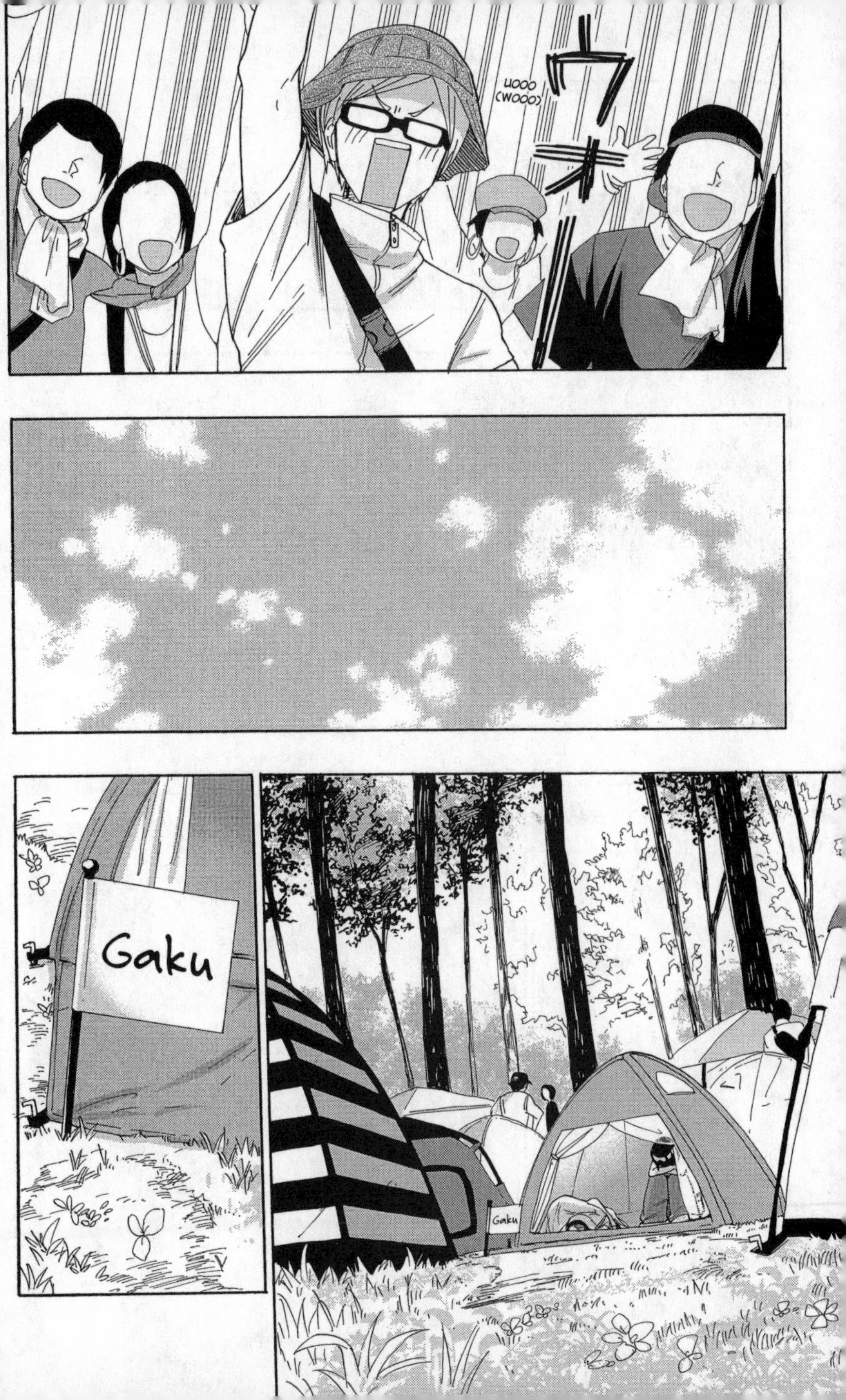
UOOO
(WOOO)
Gaku
Gaku

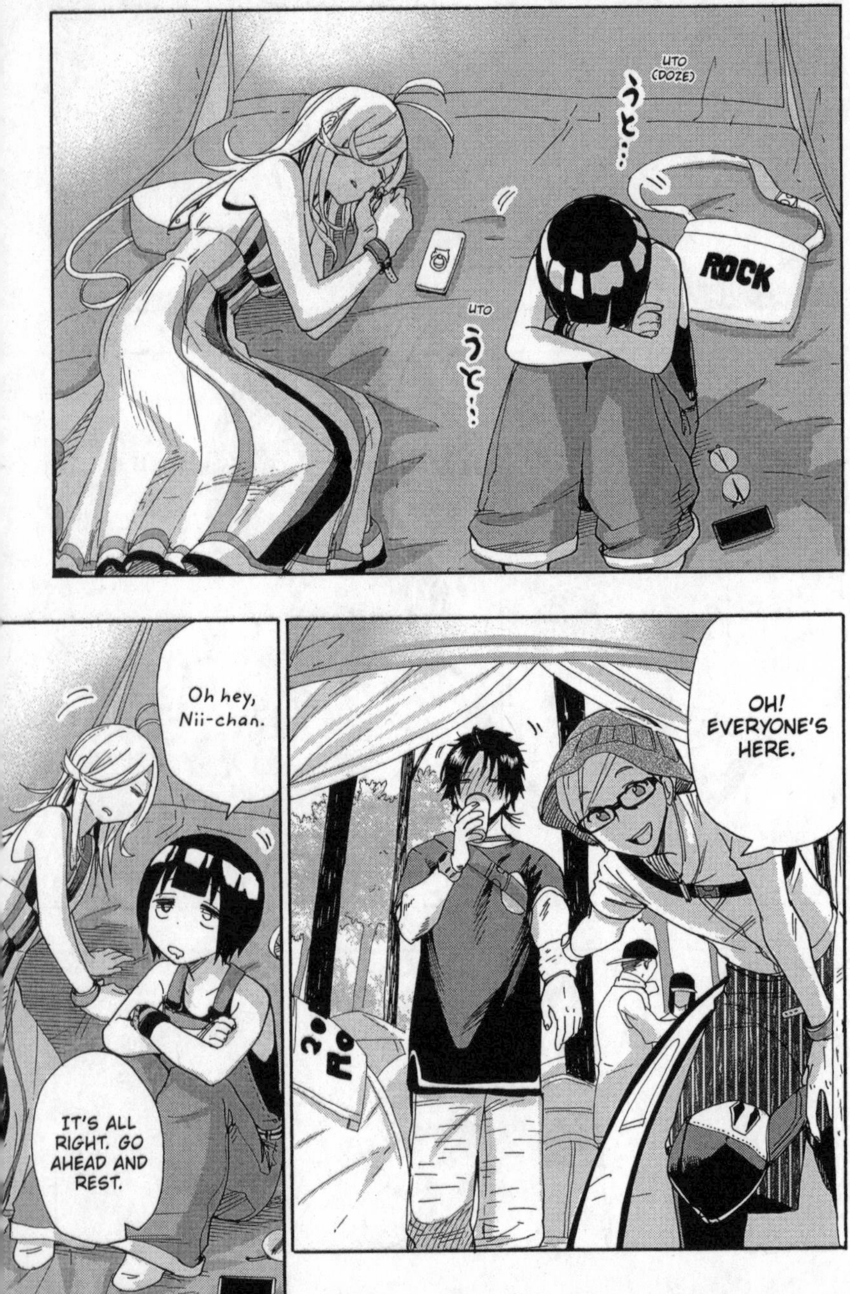
UTO (DOZE)
うと…
ROCK
UTO
うと‥
OH! EVERYONE'S HERE.
Oh hey, Nii-chan.
IT'S ALL RIGHT. GO AHEAD AND REST.

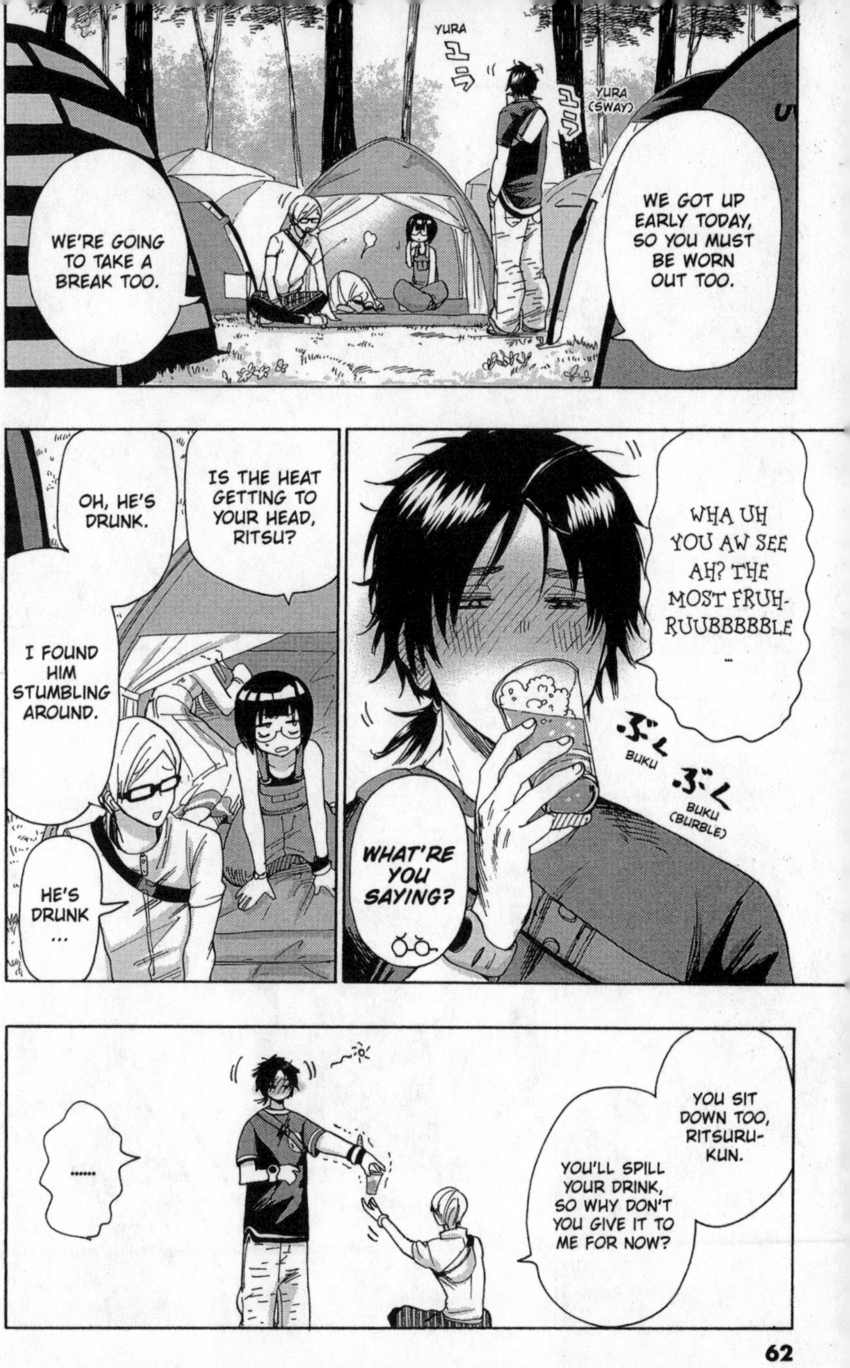
YURA
YURA (SWAY)
WE GOT UP EARLY TODAY, SO YOU MUST BE WORN OUT TOO.
WE'RE GOING TO TAKE A BREAK TOO.
WHA UH YOU AW SEE AH? THE MOST FRUH-RUUBBBBBLE ...
BUKU
BUKU (BURBLE)
WHAT'RE YOU SAYING?
IS THE HEAT GETTING TO YOUR HEAD, RITSU?
OH, HE'S DRUNK.
I FOUND HIM STUMBLING AROUND.
HE'S DRUNK ...
YOU SIT DOWN TOO, RITSURU-KUN.
YOU'LL SPILL YOUR DRINK, SO WHY DON'T YOU GIVE IT TO ME FOR NOW?
......

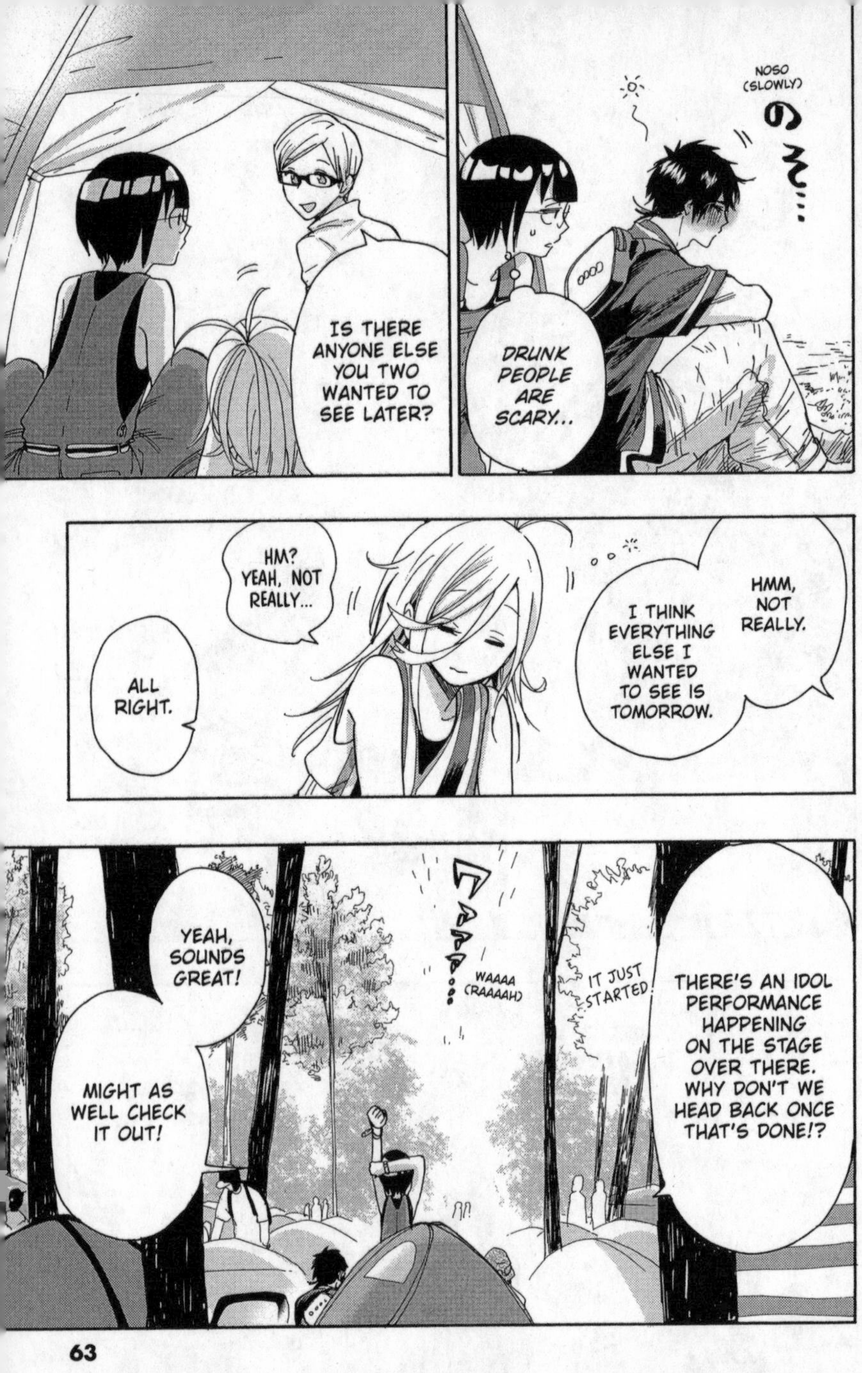
NOSO (SLOWLY)
のそ…
DRUNK PEOPLE ARE SCARY...
IS THERE ANYONE ELSE YOU TWO WANTED TO SEE LATER?
HMM, NOT REALLY.
I THINK EVERYTHING ELSE I WANTED TO SEE IS TOMORROW.
HM? YEAH, NOT REALLY...
ALL RIGHT.
THERE'S AN IDOL PERFORMANCE HAPPENING ON THE STAGE OVER THERE. WHY DON'T WE HEAD BACK ONCE THAT'S DONE!?
IT JUST STARTED!
WAAAA (RAAAAH)
YEAH, SOUNDS GREAT!
MIGHT AS WELL CHECK IT OUT!

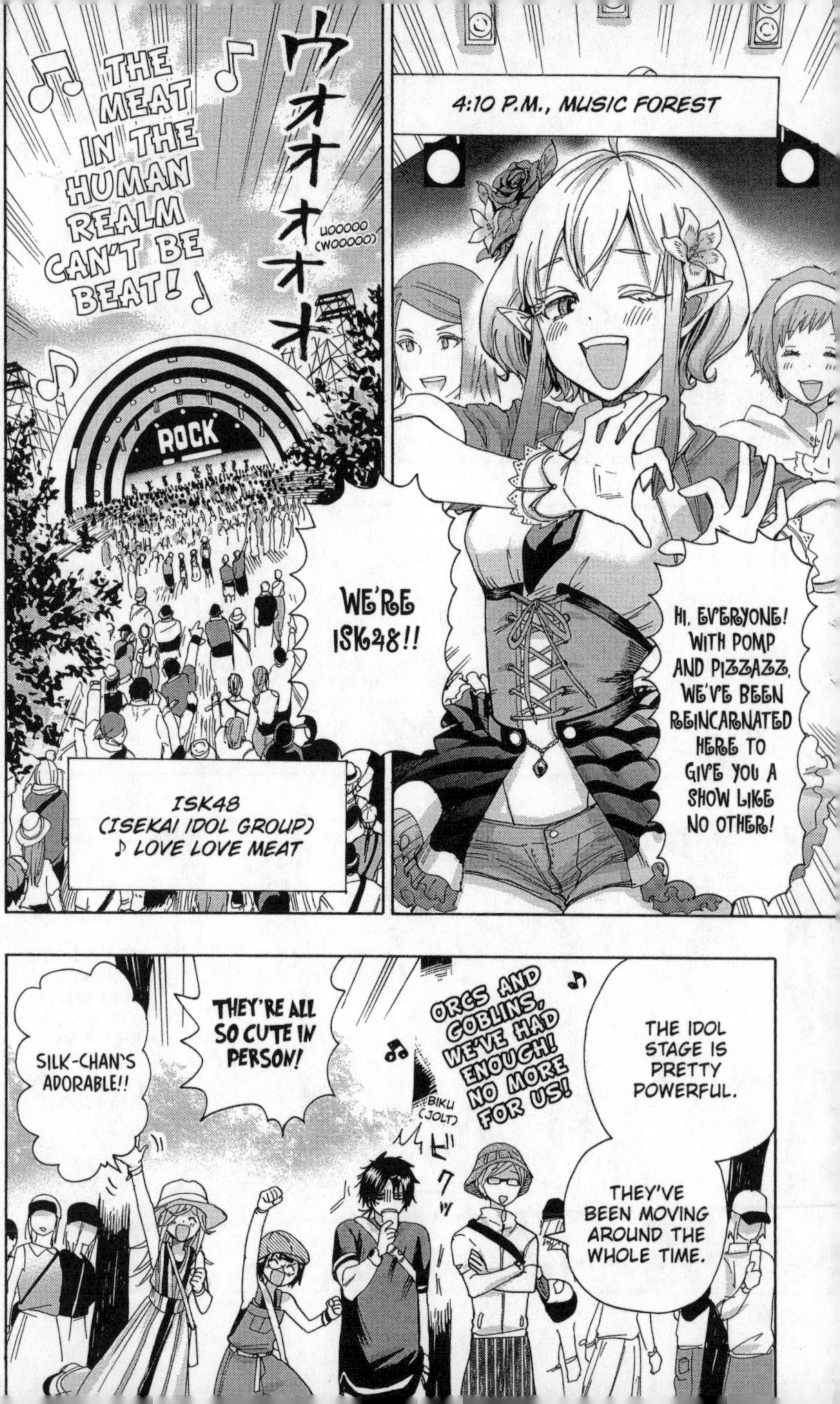

4:10 P.M., MUSIC FOREST
HI, EVERYONE! WITH POMP AND PIZZAZZ, WE'VE BEEN REINCARNATED HERE TO GIVE YOU A SHOW LIKE NO OTHER!
WE'RE ISK48!!
THE MEAT IN THE HUMAN REALM CAN'T BE BEAT! ♪
ウオオオオ
UOOOOO (WOOOOO)
ROCK
ISK48 (ISEKAI IDOL GROUP) ♪ LOVE LOVE MEAT
THE IDOL STAGE IS PRETTY POWERFUL.
THEY'VE BEEN MOVING AROUND THE WHOLE TIME.
ORCS AND GOBLINS, WE'VE HAD ENOUGH! NO MORE FOR US!
ビクッ
BIKU (JOLT)
THEY'RE ALL SO CUTE IN PERSON!
SILK-CHAN'S ADORABLE!!

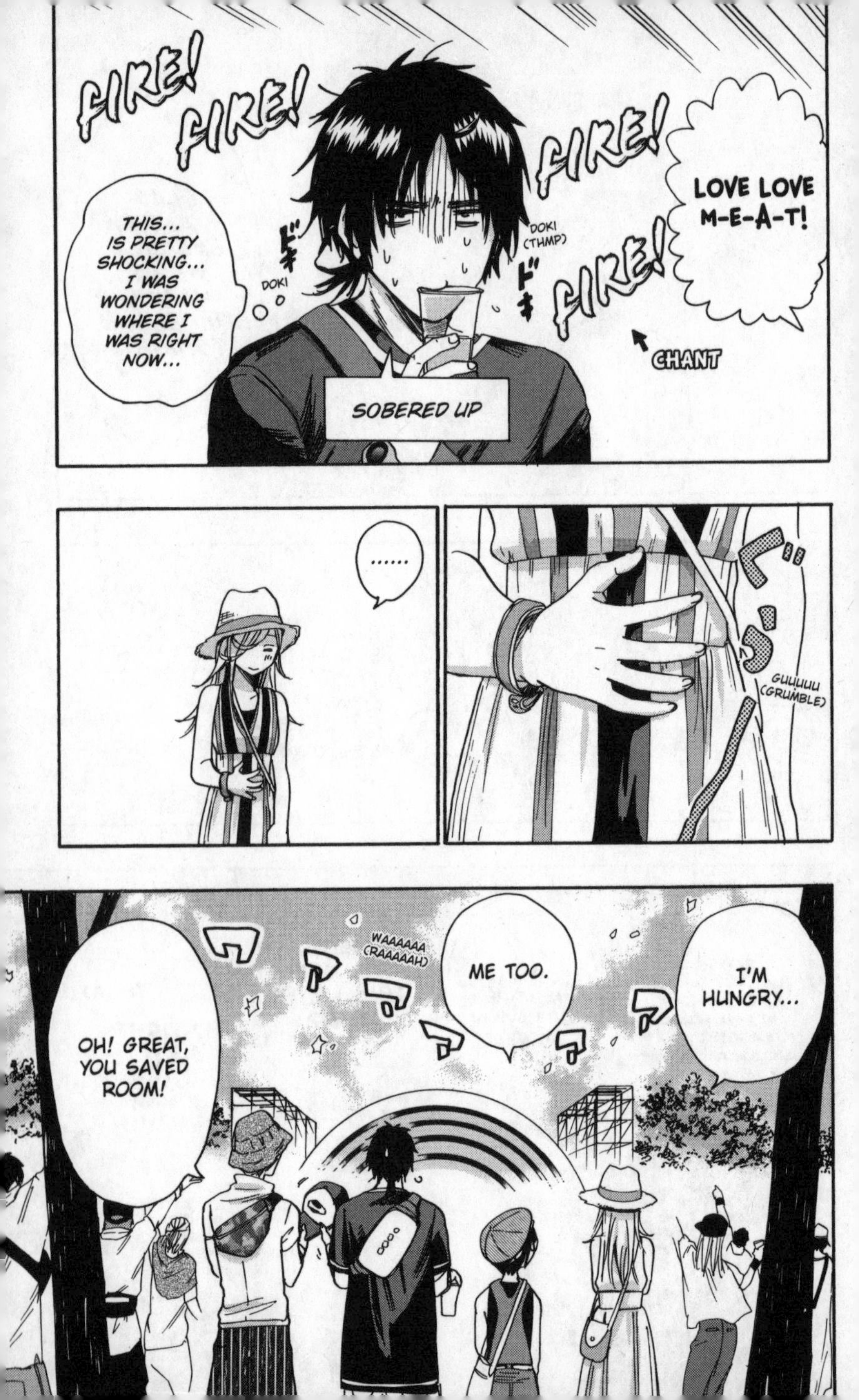
LOVE LOVE M-E-A-T!
CHANT
FIRE! FIRE! FIRE! FIRE!
DOKI (THMP)
ドキ
ドキ
SOBERED UP
THIS... IS PRETTY SHOCKING... I WAS WONDERING WHERE I WAS RIGHT NOW...
DOKI
GUUUUUU (GRUMBLE)
......
I'M HUNGRY...
ME TOO.
WAAAAAA (RAAAAAH)
OH! GREAT, YOU SAVED ROOM!

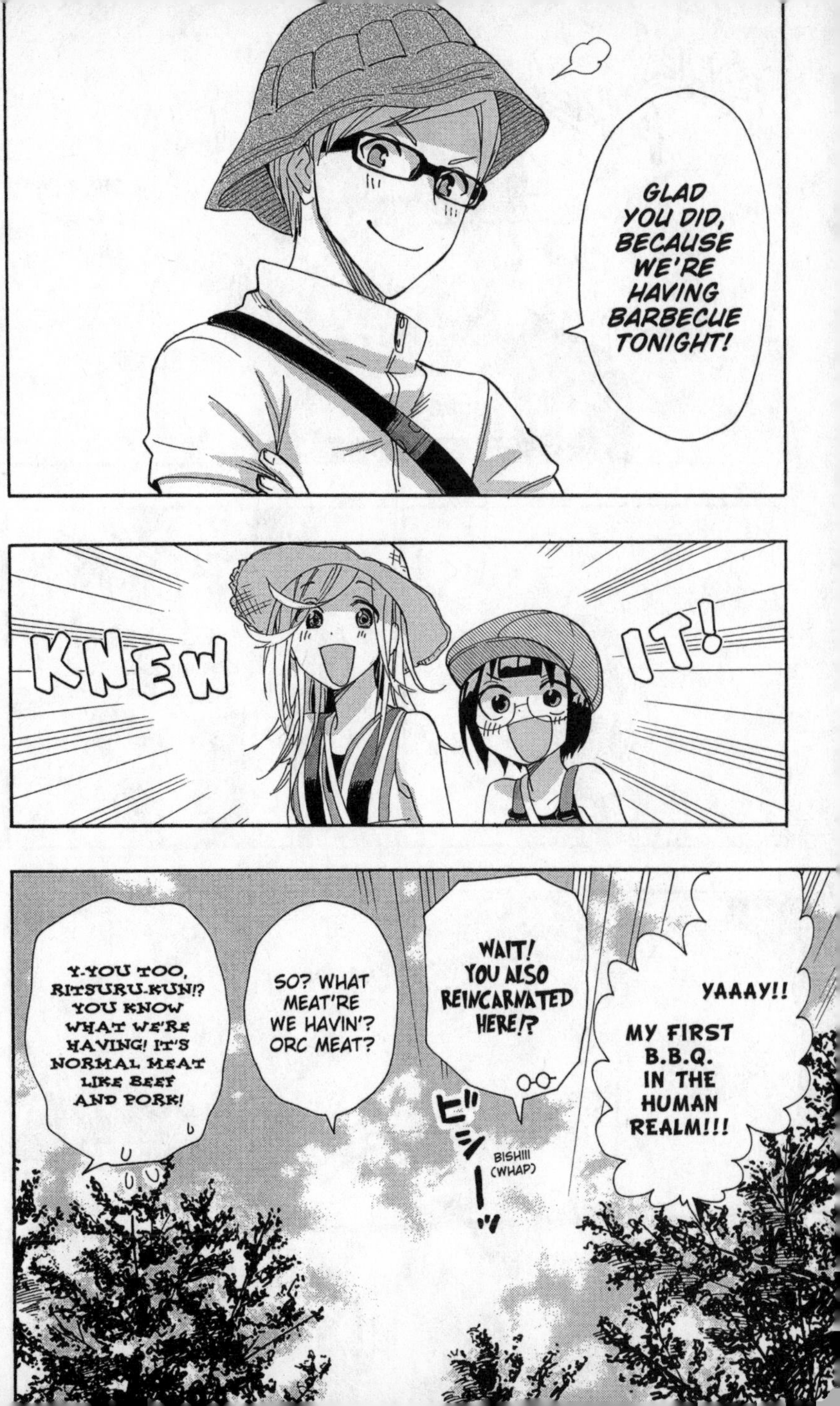
GLAD YOU DID, BECAUSE WE'RE HAVING BARBECUE TONIGHT!
KNEW IT!
YAAAY!!
MY FIRST B.B.Q. IN THE HUMAN REALM!!!
WAIT! YOU ALSO REINCARNATED HERE!?
ビシ
BISHIII (WHAP)
SO? WHAT MEAT'RE WE HAVIN'? ORC MEAT?
Y-YOU TOO, RITSURU-KUN!? YOU KNOW WHAT WE'RE HAVING! IT'S NORMAL MEAT LIKE BEEF AND PORK!

FES 7.5

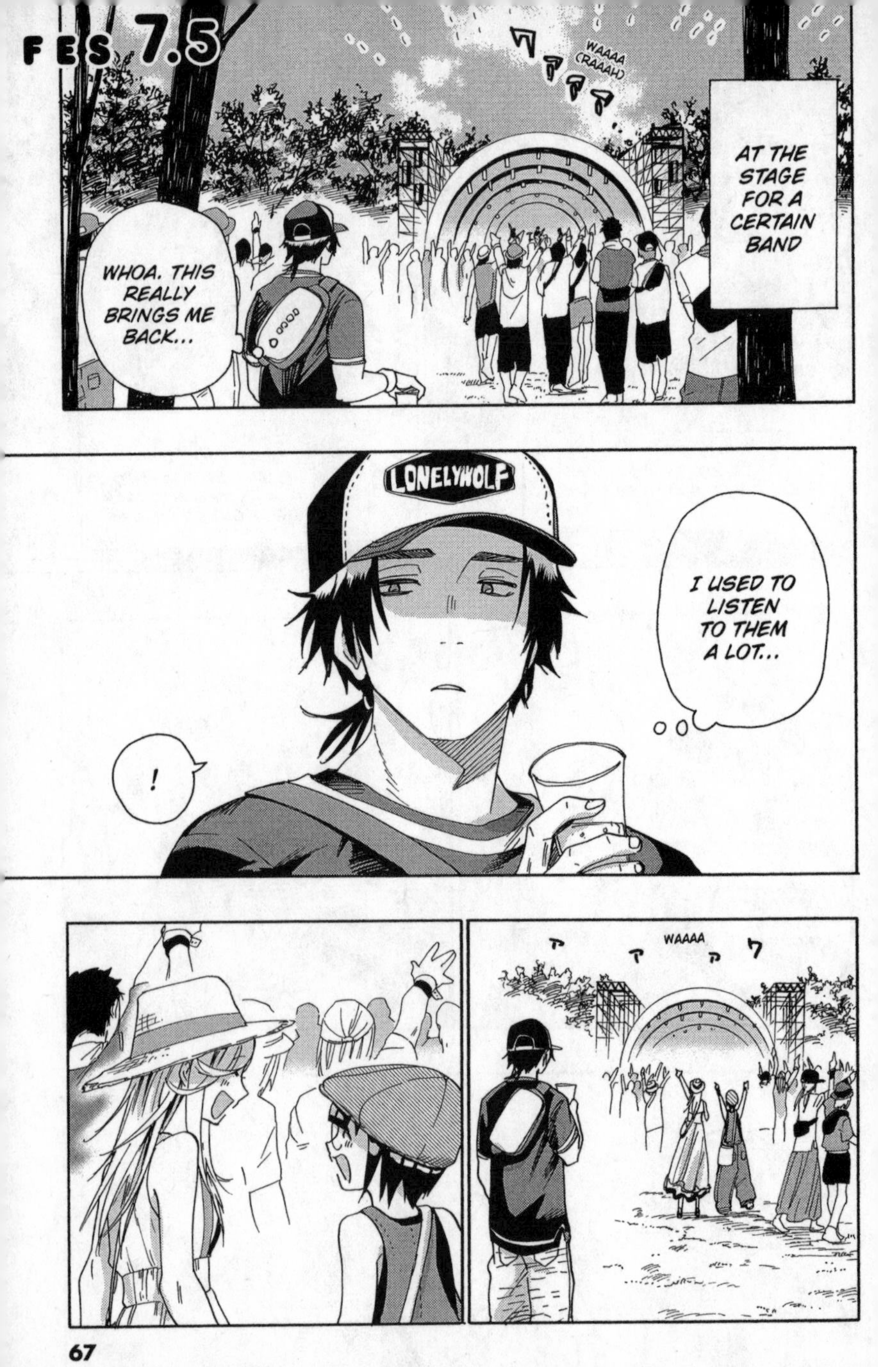

AT THE STAGE FOR A CERTAIN BAND
WAAAA (RAAAH)
WHOA. THIS REALLY BRINGS ME BACK...
LONELYWOLF
I USED TO LISTEN TO THEM A LOT...
!
WAAAA

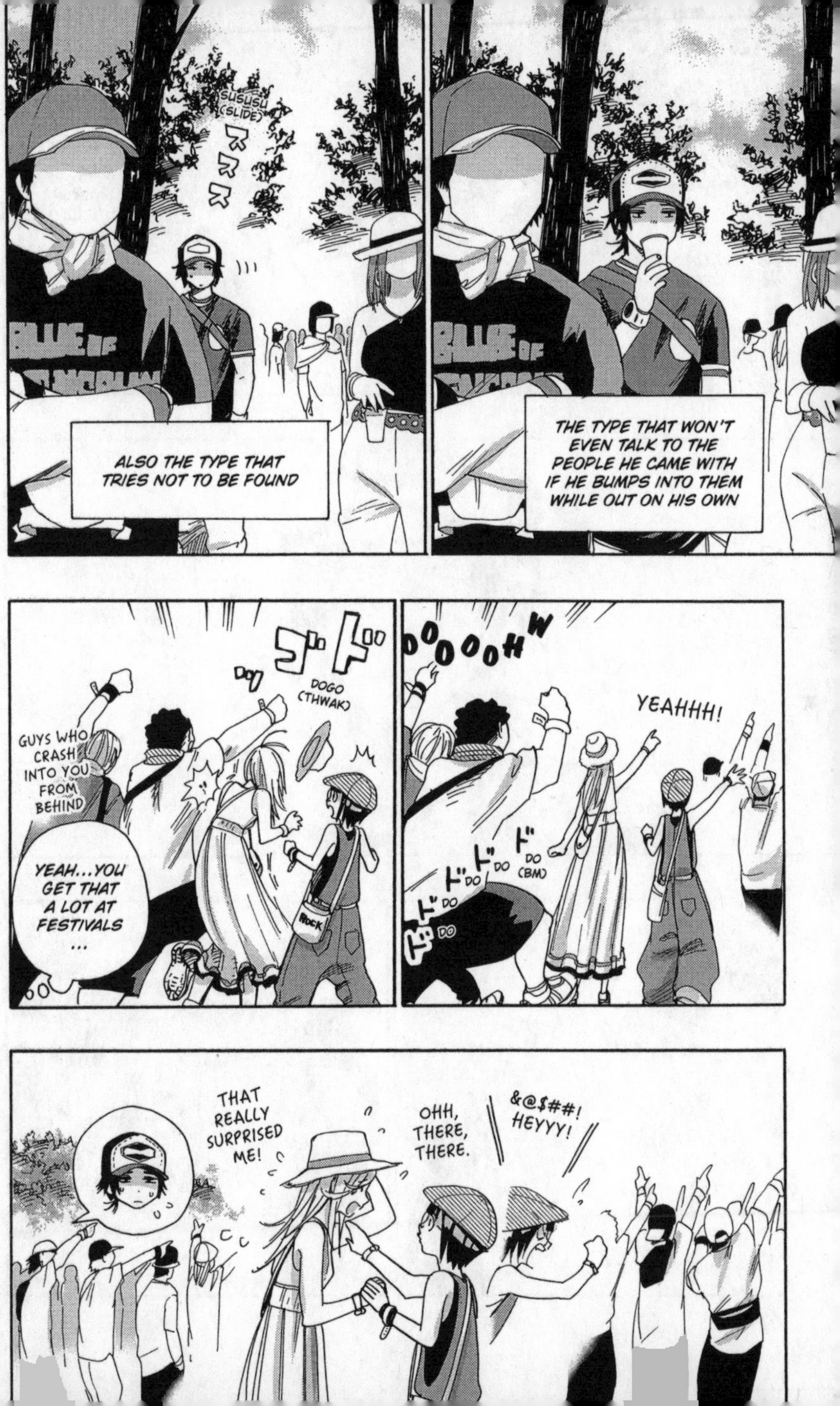
THE TYPE THAT WON'T EVEN TALK TO THE PEOPLE HE CAME WITH IF HE BUMPS INTO THEM WHILE OUT ON HIS OWN
SUSUSU (SLIDE)
ALSO THE TYPE THAT TRIES NOT TO BE FOUND
OOOOOOHW
YEAHHH!
DO DO DO DO (BM)
DOGO (THWAK)
GUYS WHO CRASH INTO YOU FROM BEHIND
YEAH...YOU GET THAT A LOT AT FESTIVALS...
&@$##! HEYYY!
OHH, THERE, THERE.
THAT REALLY SURPRISED ME!

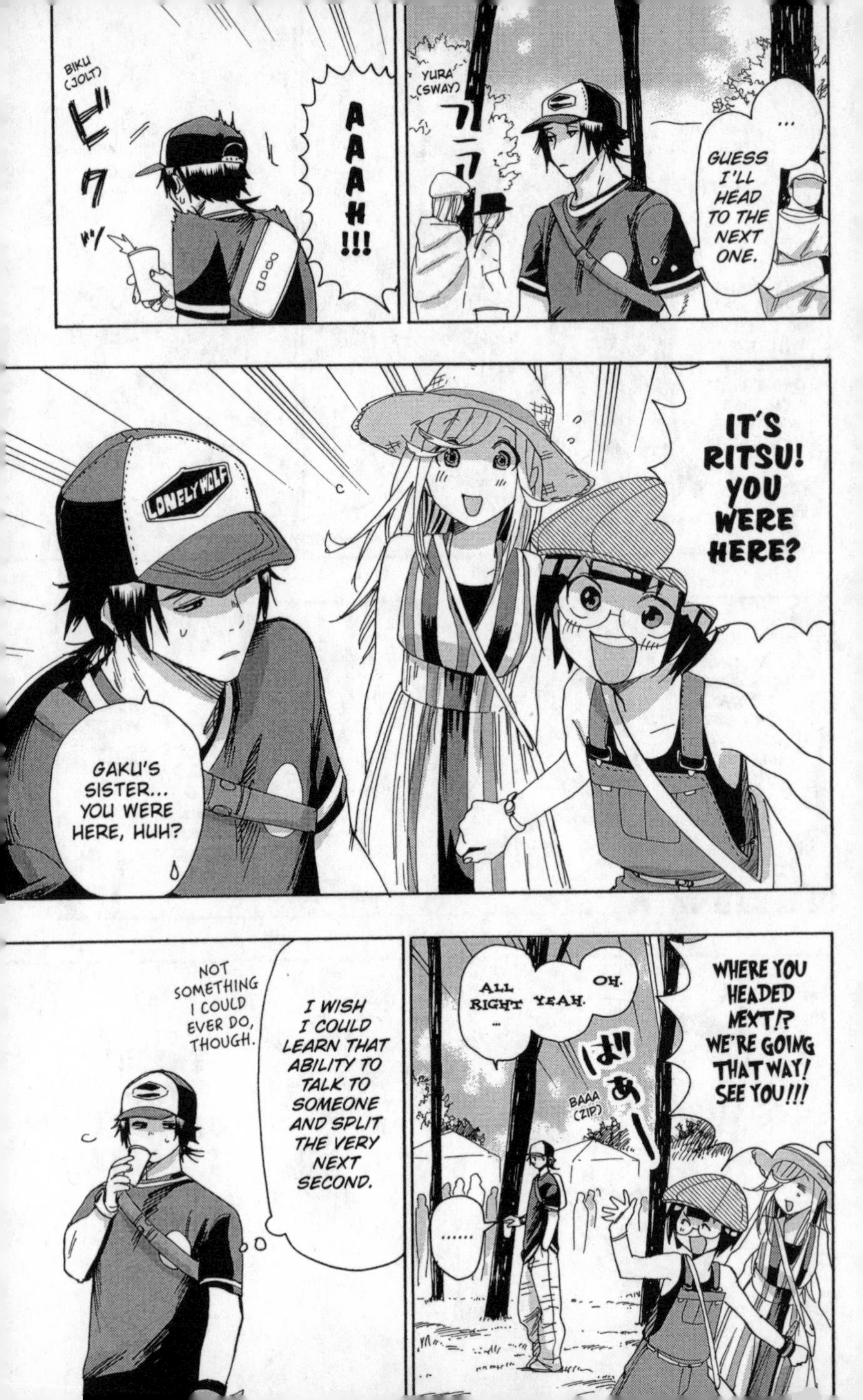
YURA (SWAY)
... GUESS I'LL HEAD TO THE NEXT ONE.
AAAAH!!!
BIKU (JOLT)
IT'S RITSU! YOU WERE HERE?
GAKU'S SISTER... YOU WERE HERE, HUH?
WHERE YOU HEADED NEXT!? WE'RE GOING THAT WAY! SEE YOU!!!
OH. YEAH. ALL RIGHT ...
BAAA (ZIP)
......
I WISH I COULD LEARN THAT ABILITY TO TALK TO SOMEONE AND SPLIT THE VERY NEXT SECOND.
NOT SOMETHING I COULD EVER DO, THOUGH.

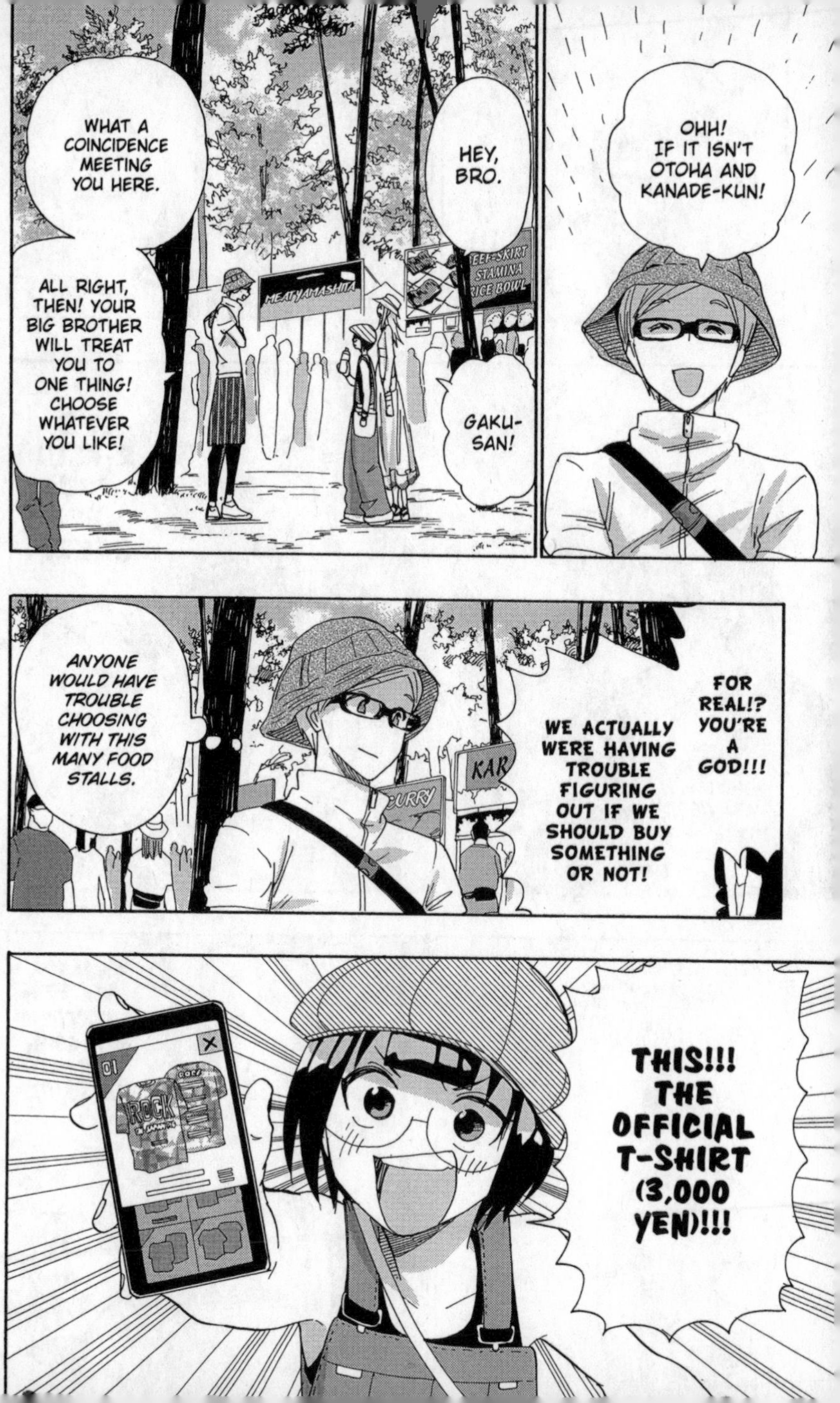
OHH! IF IT ISN'T OTOHA AND KANADE-KUN!
HEY, BRO.
GAKU-SAN!
WHAT A COINCIDENCE MEETING YOU HERE.
ALL RIGHT, THEN! YOUR BIG BROTHER WILL TREAT YOU TO ONE THING! CHOOSE WHATEVER YOU LIKE!
MEATYAMASHITA
STAMINA RICE BOWL
FOR REAL!? YOU'RE A GOD!!!
WE ACTUALLY WERE HAVING TROUBLE FIGURING OUT IF WE SHOULD BUY SOMETHING OR NOT!
ANYONE WOULD HAVE TROUBLE CHOOSING WITH THIS MANY FOOD STALLS.
KAR
CURRY
THIS!!! THE OFFICIAL T-SHIRT (3,000 YEN)!!!
ROCK

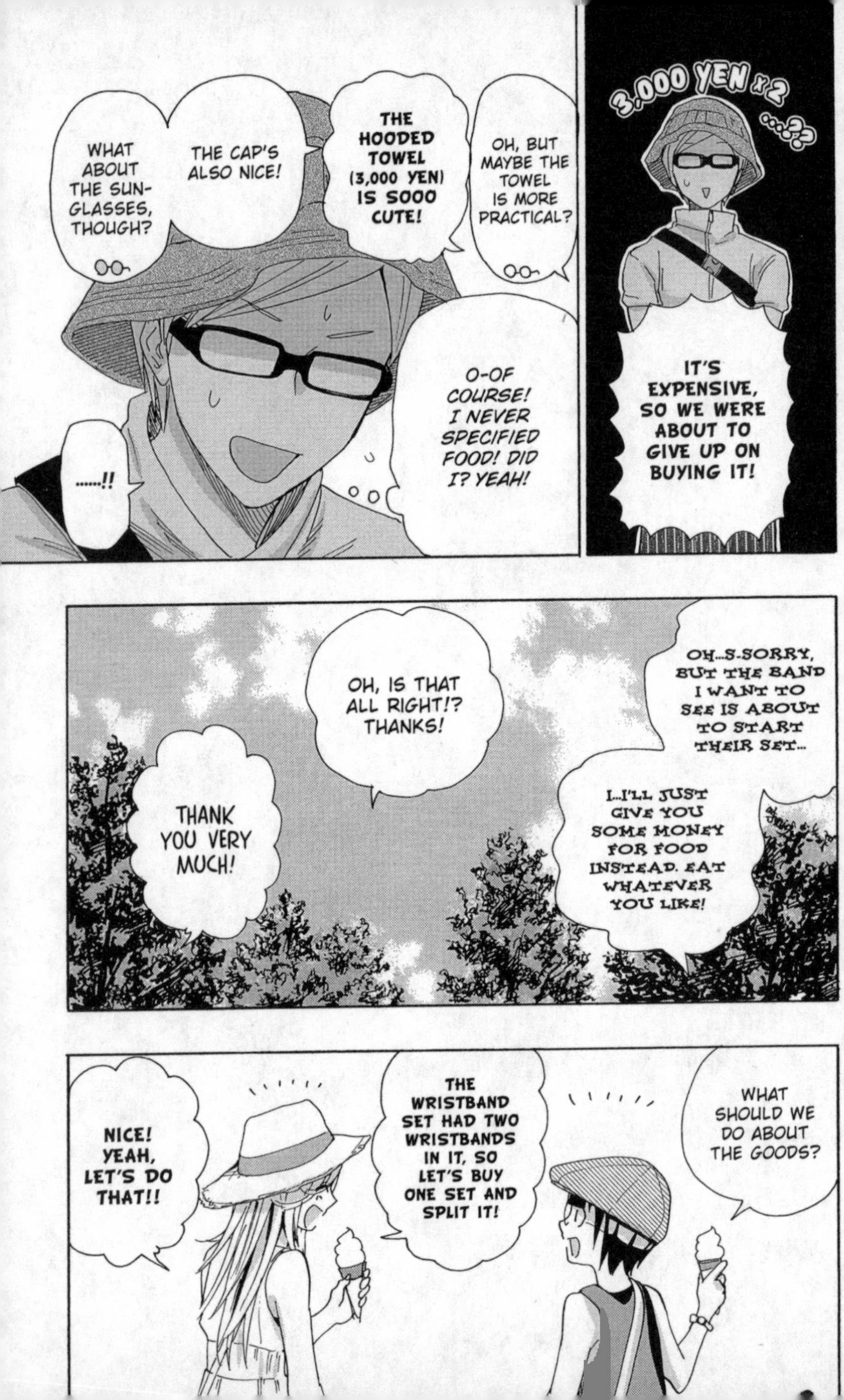
3,000 YEN x 2 ...??
IT'S EXPENSIVE, SO WE WERE ABOUT TO GIVE UP ON BUYING IT!
OH, BUT MAYBE THE TOWEL IS MORE PRACTICAL?
THE HOODED TOWEL (3,000 YEN) IS SOOO CUTE!
THE CAP'S ALSO NICE!
WHAT ABOUT THE SUN-GLASSES, THOUGH?
O-OF COURSE! I NEVER SPECIFIED FOOD! DID I? YEAH!
......!!
OH...S-SORRY, BUT THE BAND I WANT TO SEE IS ABOUT TO START THEIR SET...
I...I'LL JUST GIVE YOU SOME MONEY FOR FOOD INSTEAD. EAT WHATEVER YOU LIKE!
OH, IS THAT ALL RIGHT!? THANKS!
THANK YOU VERY MUCH!
WHAT SHOULD WE DO ABOUT THE GOODS?
THE WRISTBAND SET HAD TWO WRISTBANDS IN IT, SO LET'S BUY ONE SET AND SPLIT IT!
NICE! YEAH, LET'S DO THAT!!

Days on Fes

FES 8

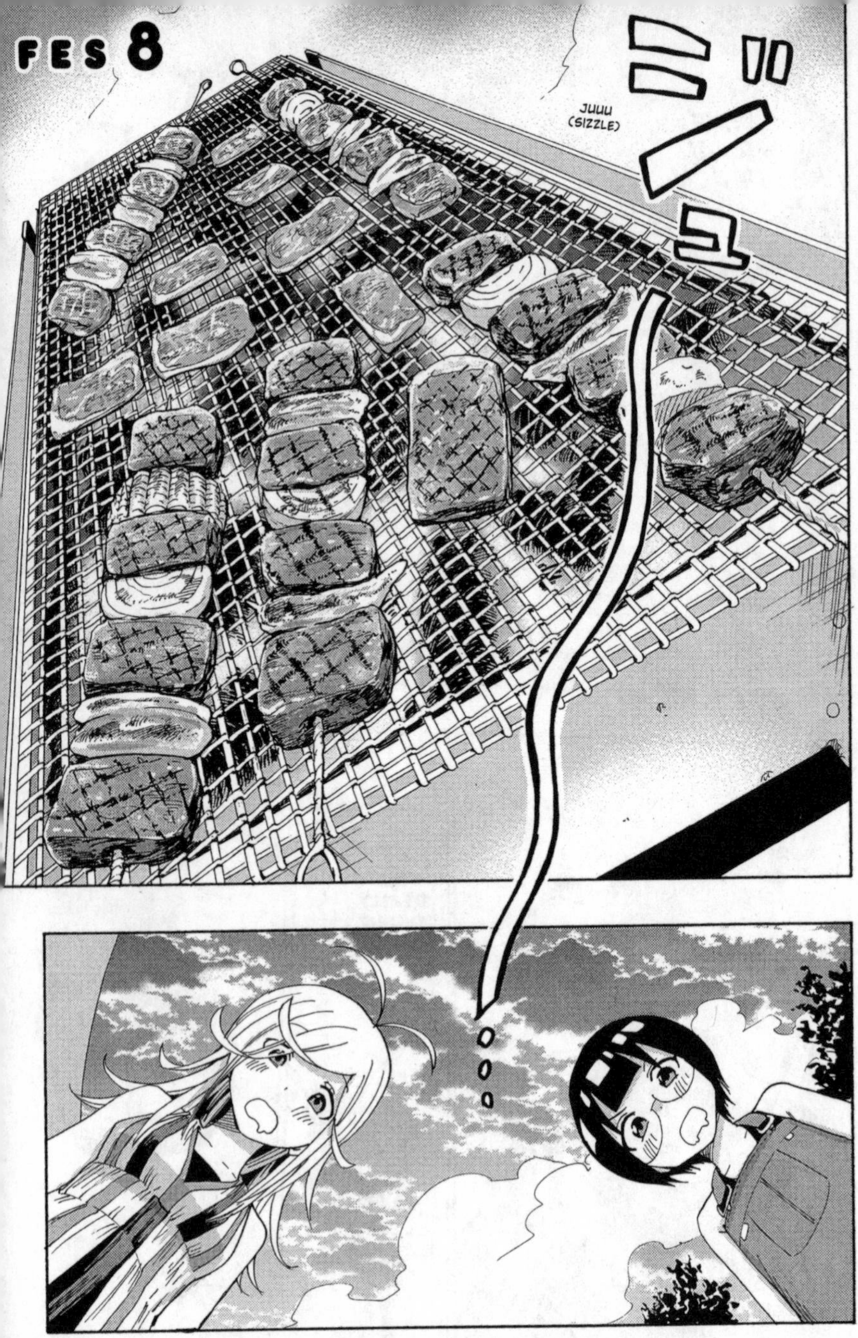
JUUU
(SIZZLE)

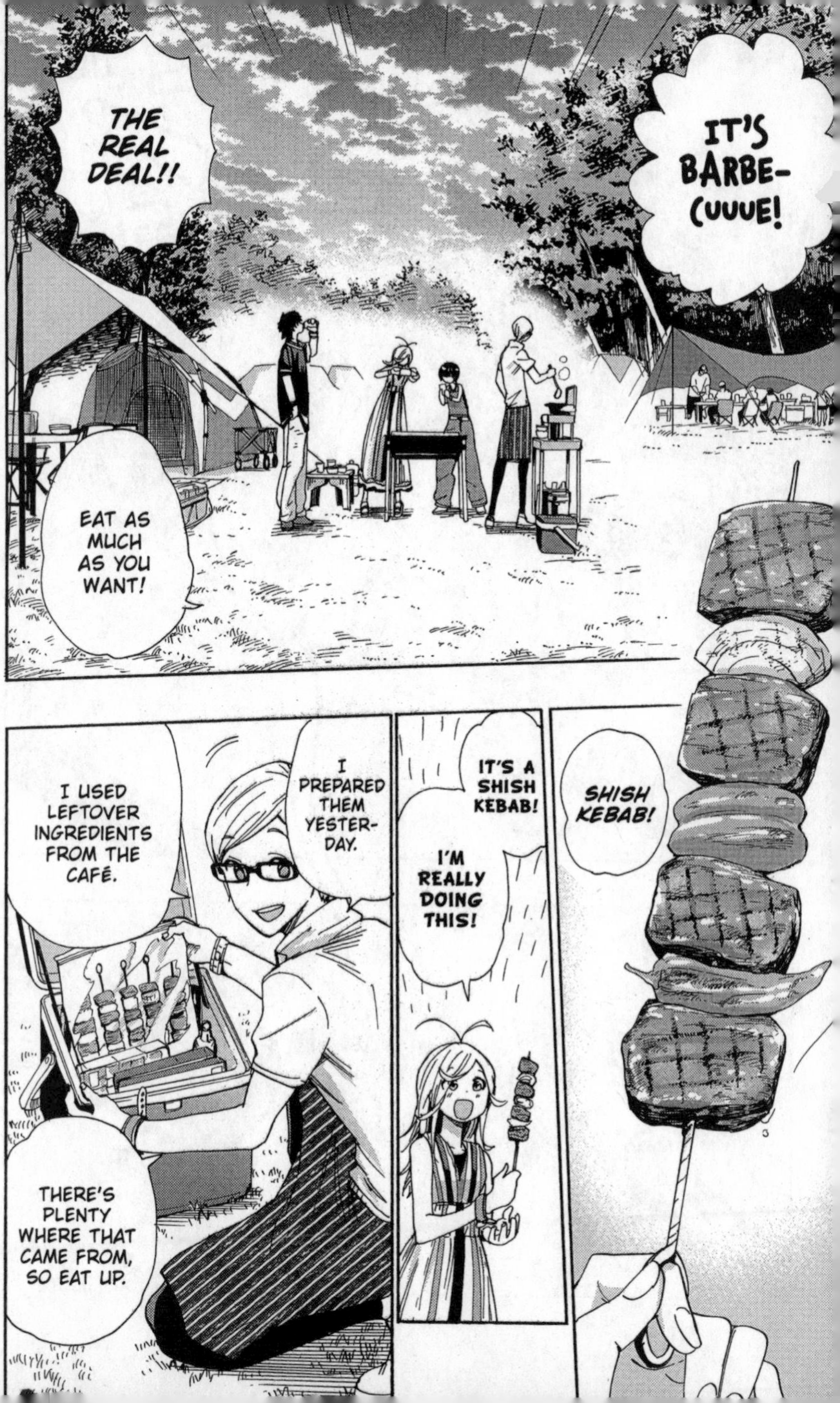
IT'S BARBE-CUUUE!
THE REAL DEAL!!
EAT AS MUCH AS YOU WANT!
SHISH KEBAB!
IT'S A SHISH KEBAB!
I'M REALLY DOING THIS!
I PREPARED THEM YESTER-DAY.
I USED LEFTOVER INGREDIENTS FROM THE CAFÉ.
THERE'S PLENTY WHERE THAT CAME FROM, SO EAT UP.

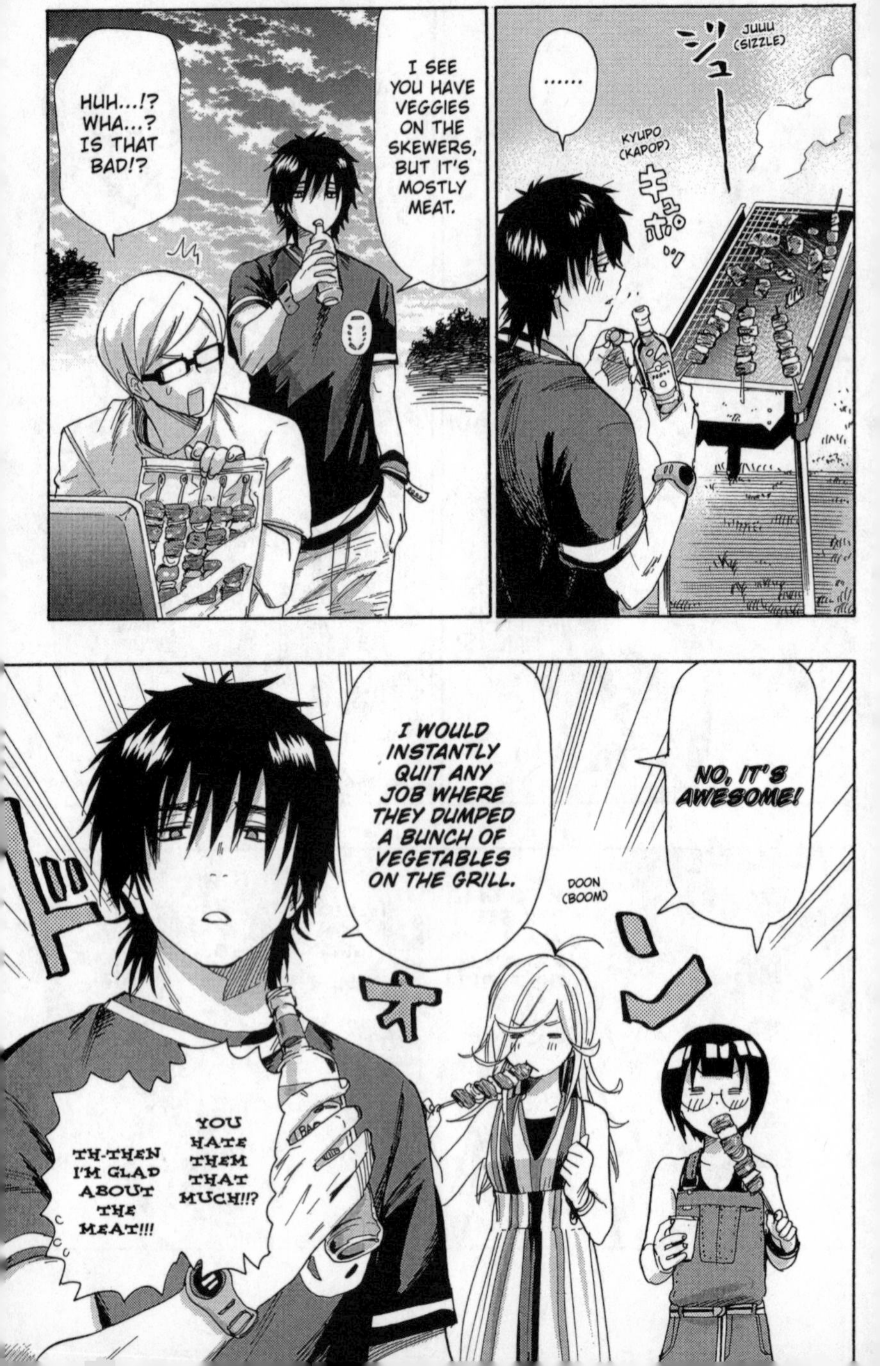
JUUU (SIZZLE)
......
KYUPO (KAPOP)
I SEE YOU HAVE VEGGIES ON THE SKEWERS, BUT IT'S MOSTLY MEAT.
HUH...!? WHA...? IS THAT BAD!?
NO, IT'S AWESOME!
I WOULD INSTANTLY QUIT ANY JOB WHERE THEY DUMPED A BUNCH OF VEGETABLES ON THE GRILL.
DOON (BOOM)
YOU HATE THEM THAT MUCH!!?
TH-THEN I'M GLAD ABOUT THE MEAT!!!

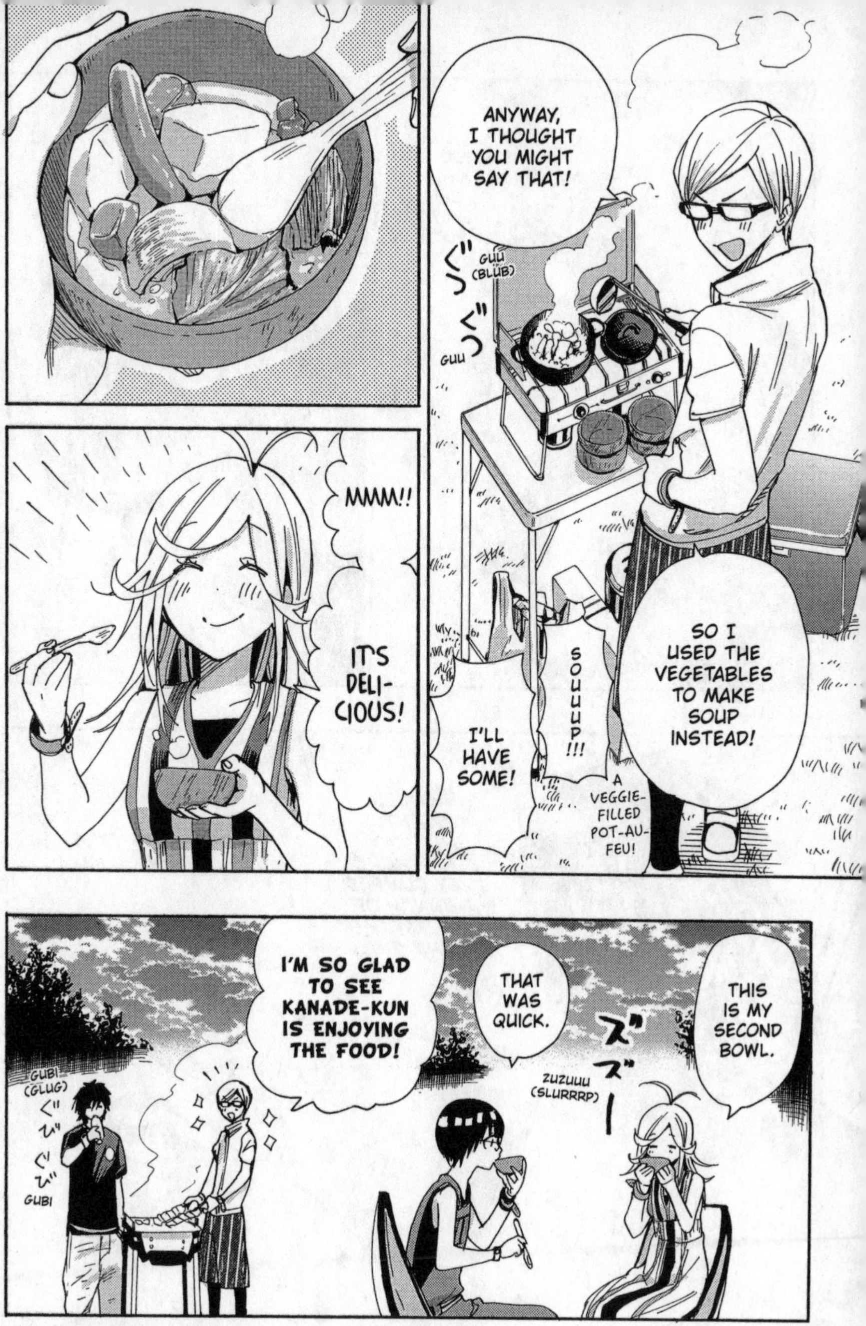
ANYWAY, I THOUGHT YOU MIGHT SAY THAT!
GUU (BLUB)
GUU
SO I USED THE VEGETABLES TO MAKE SOUP INSTEAD!
A VEGGIE-FILLED POT-AU-FEU!
SOUUUP!!!
I'LL HAVE SOME!
MMMM!!
IT'S DELI-CIOUS!
THIS IS MY SECOND BOWL.
ZUZUUU (SLURRRP)
THAT WAS QUICK.
I'M SO GLAD TO SEE KANADE-KUN IS ENJOYING THE FOOD!
GUBI (GLUG)
GUBI

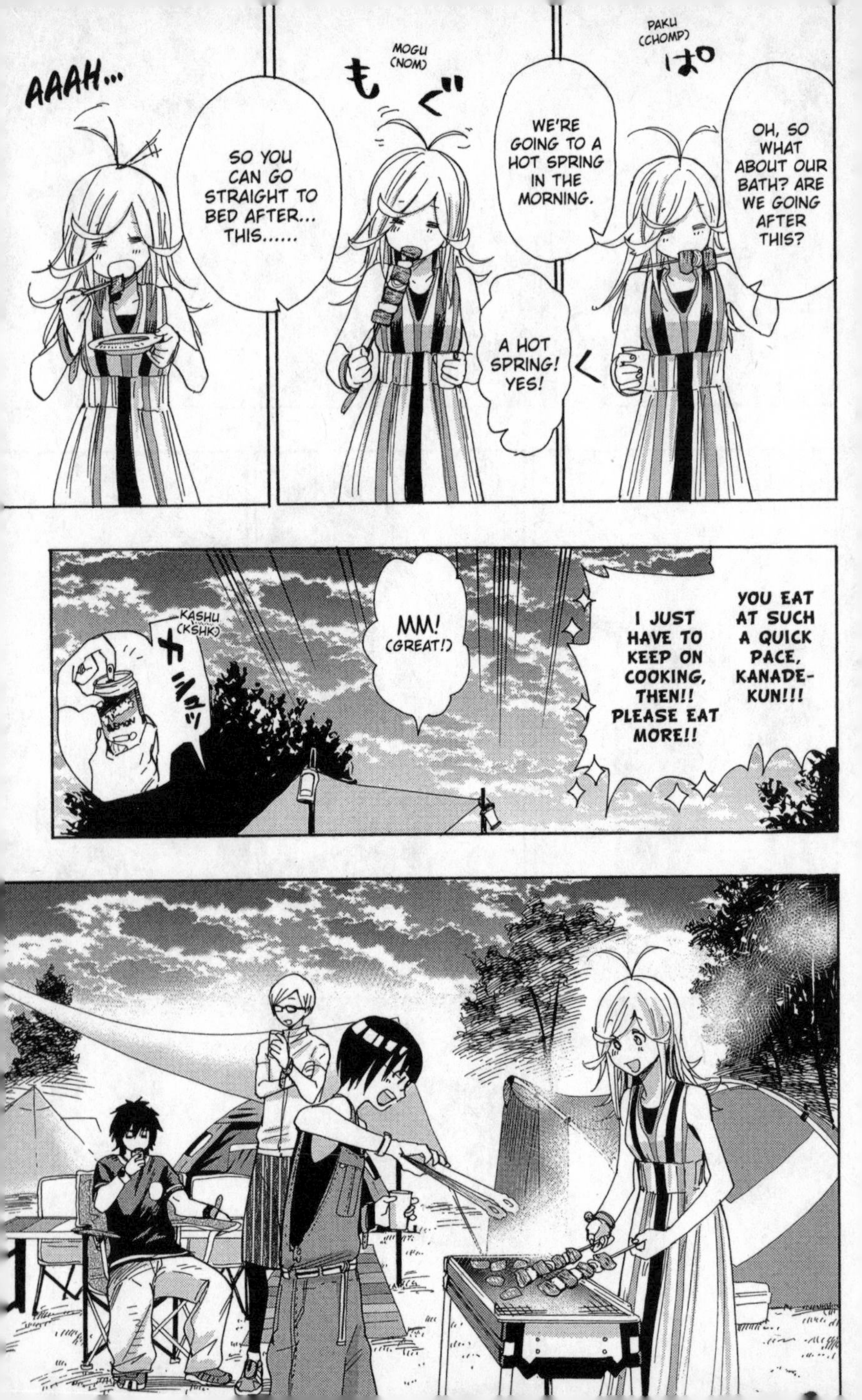
PAKU (CHOMP)
OH, SO WHAT ABOUT OUR BATH? ARE WE GOING AFTER THIS?
WE'RE GOING TO A HOT SPRING IN THE MORNING.
MOGU (NOM)
A HOT SPRING! YES!
SO YOU CAN GO STRAIGHT TO BED AFTER... THIS......
AAAH...
YOU EAT AT SUCH A QUICK PACE, KANADE-KUN!!!
I JUST HAVE TO KEEP ON COOKING, THEN!! PLEASE EAT MORE!!
MM! (GREAT!)
KASHU (KSHK)

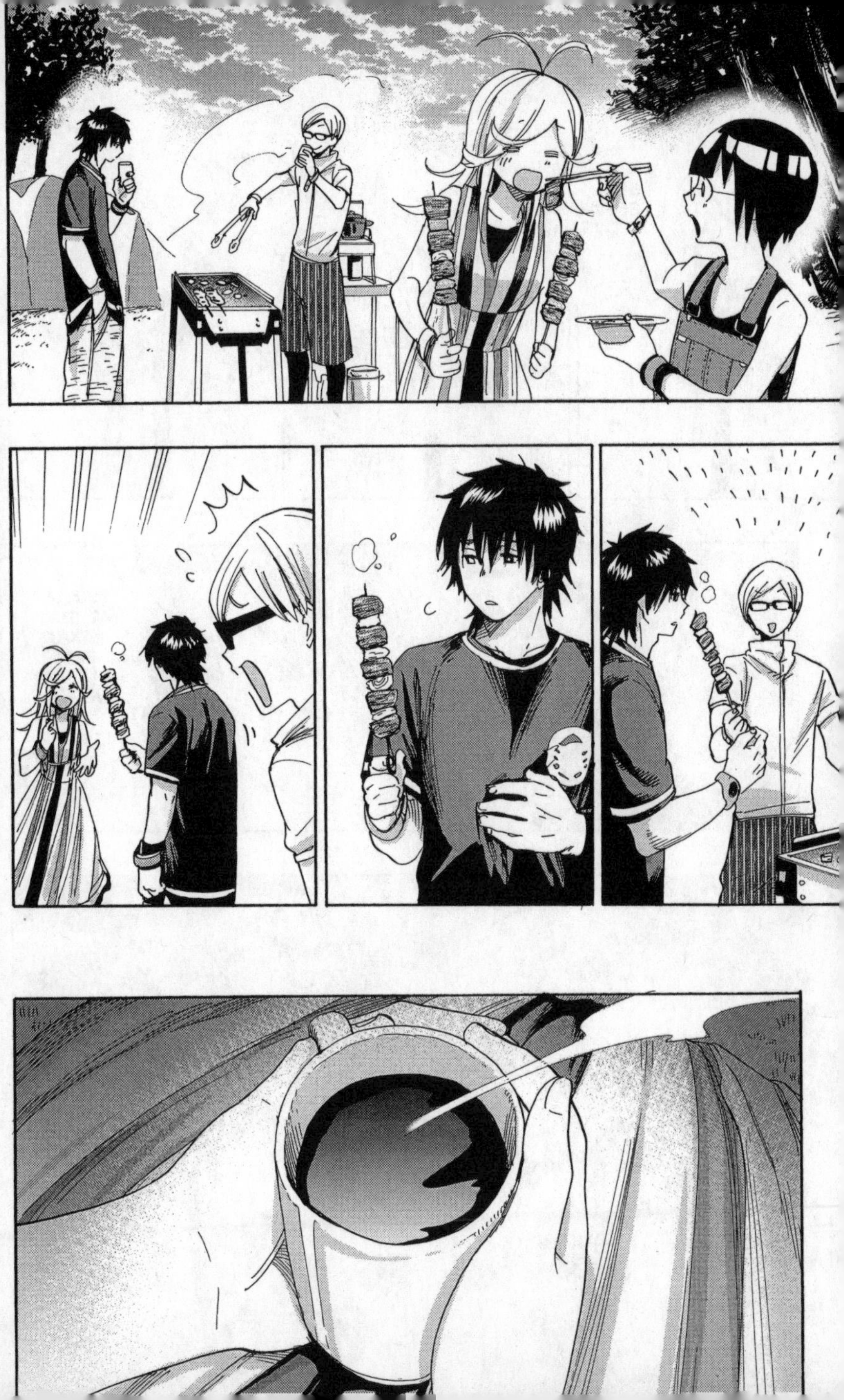

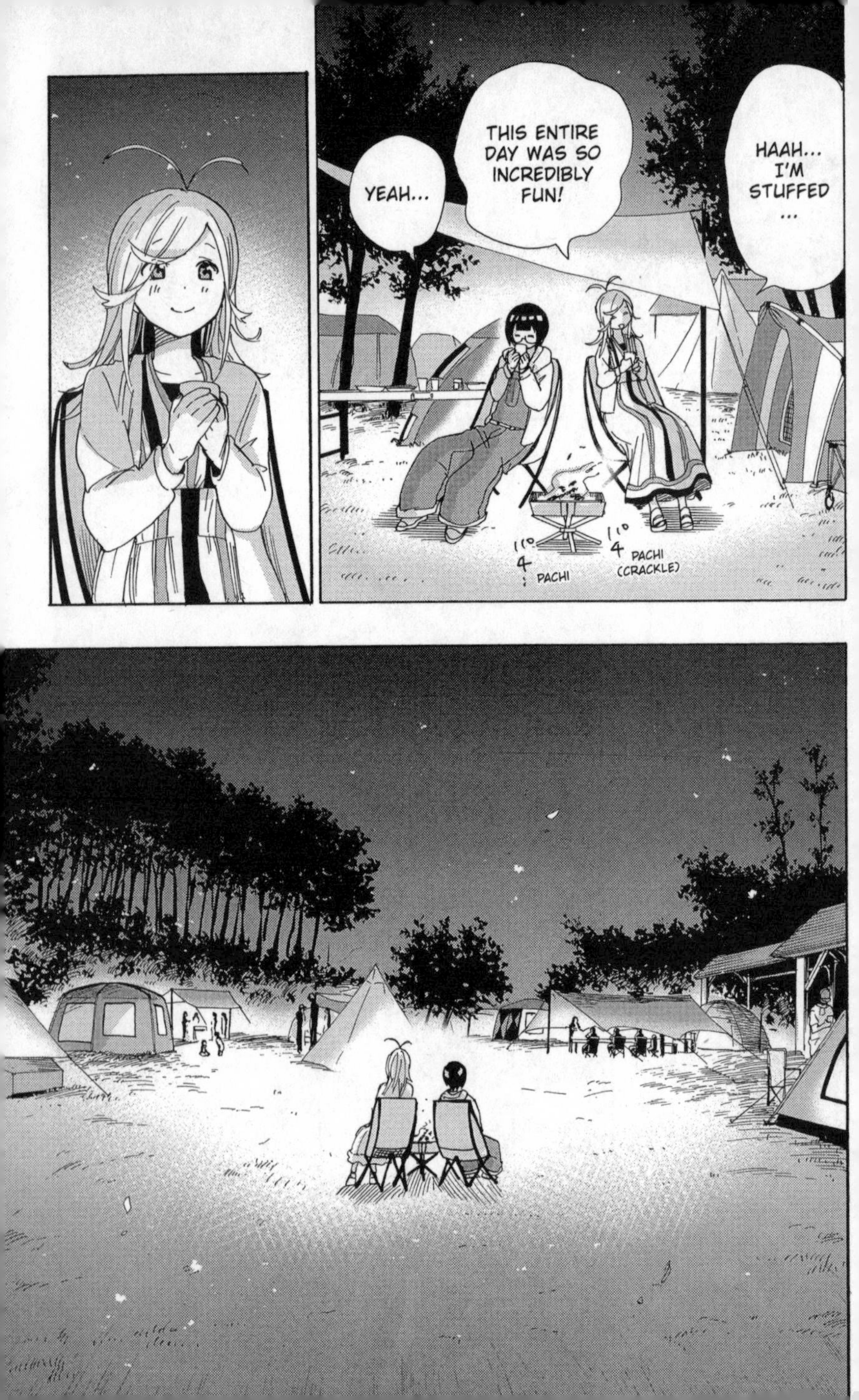
HAAH... I'M STUFFED ...
THIS ENTIRE DAY WAS SO INCREDIBLY FUN!
YEAH...
PACHI (CRACKLE)
PACHI

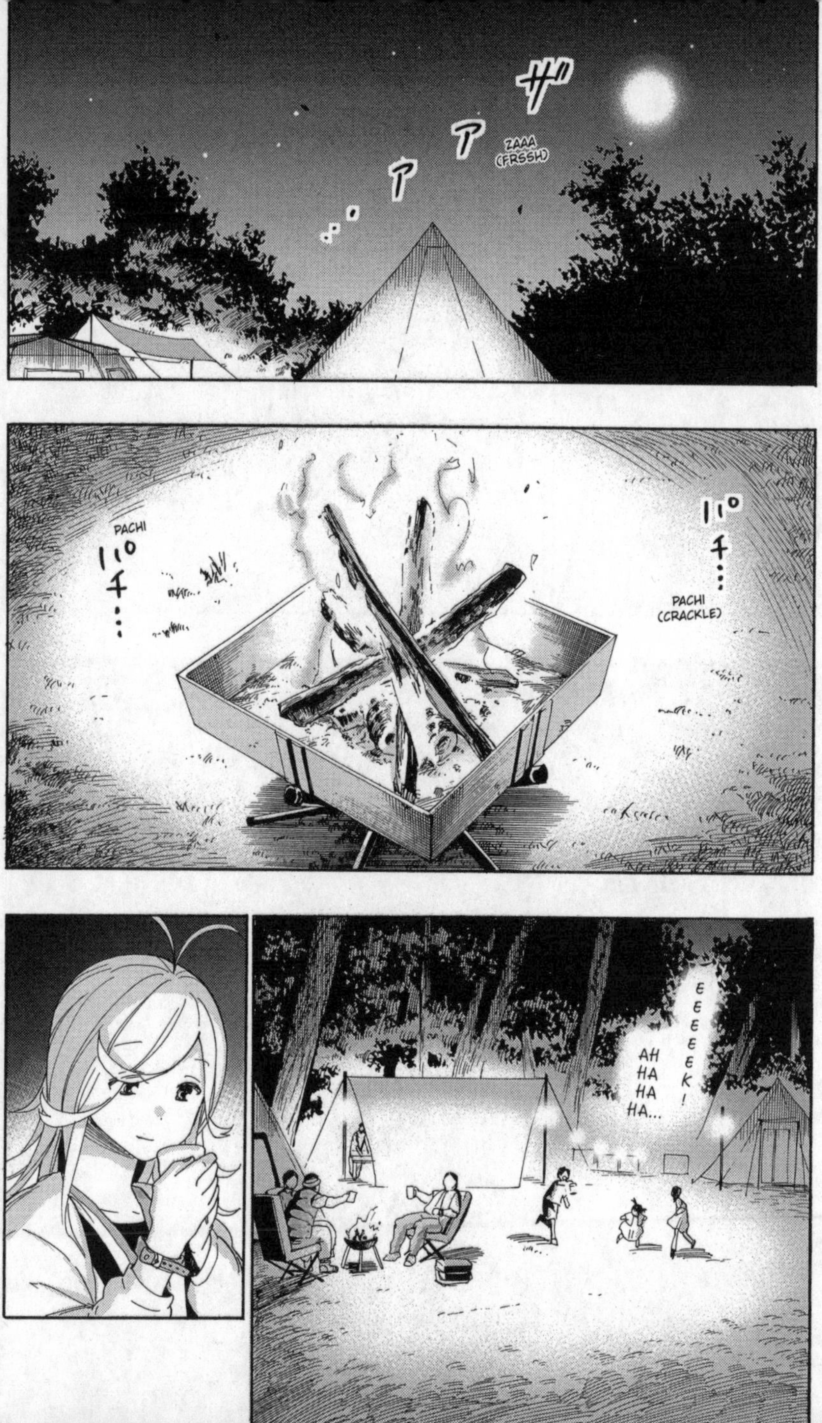
ザァァ。。
ZAAA (FRSSH)
パチ…
PACHI (CRACKLE)
PACHI
パチ…
EEEEEK!
AH HA HA HA...

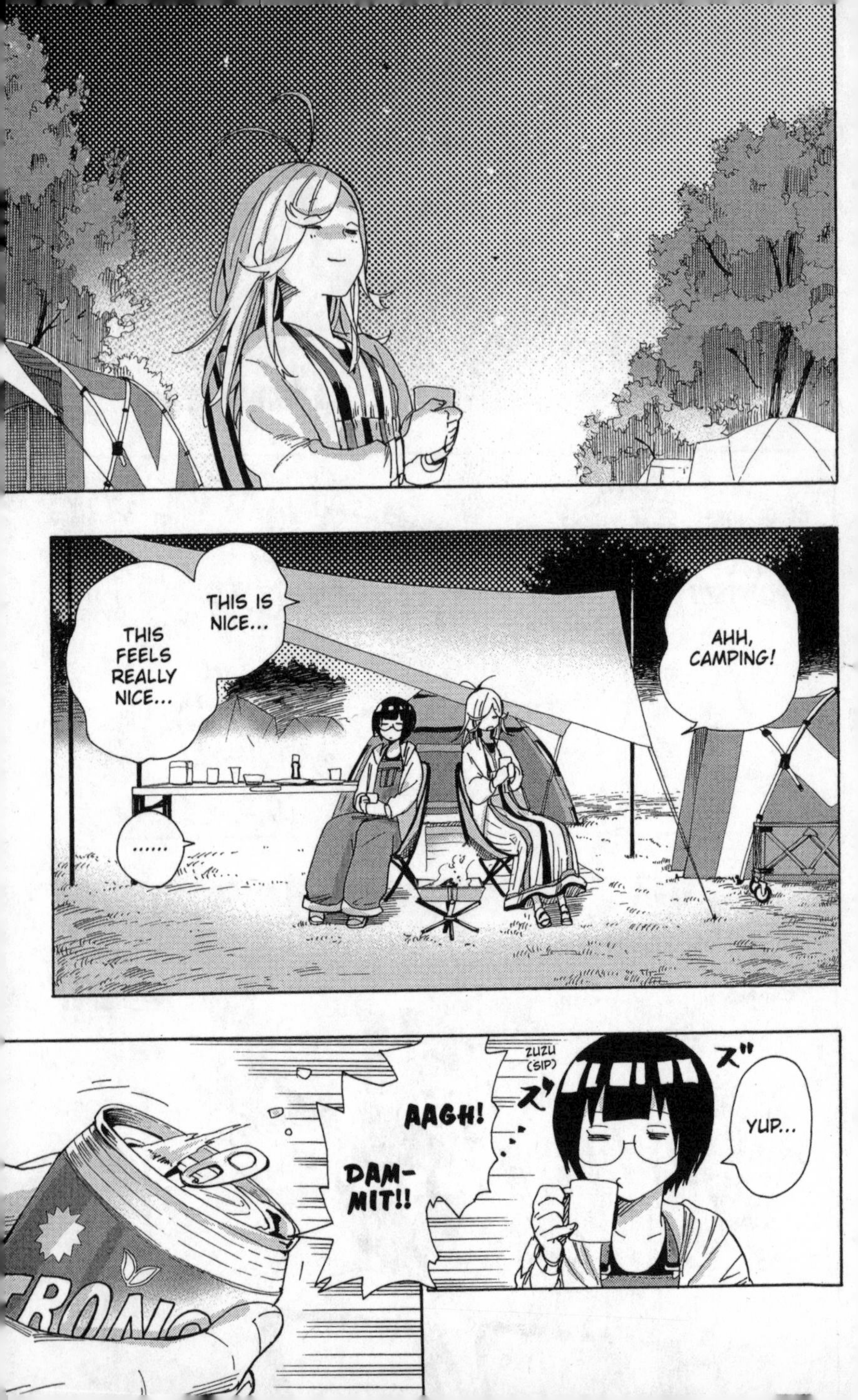
AHH, CAMPING!
THIS IS NICE...
THIS FEELS REALLY NICE...
......
YUP...
ZUZU (SIP)
AAGH!
DAM-MIT!!

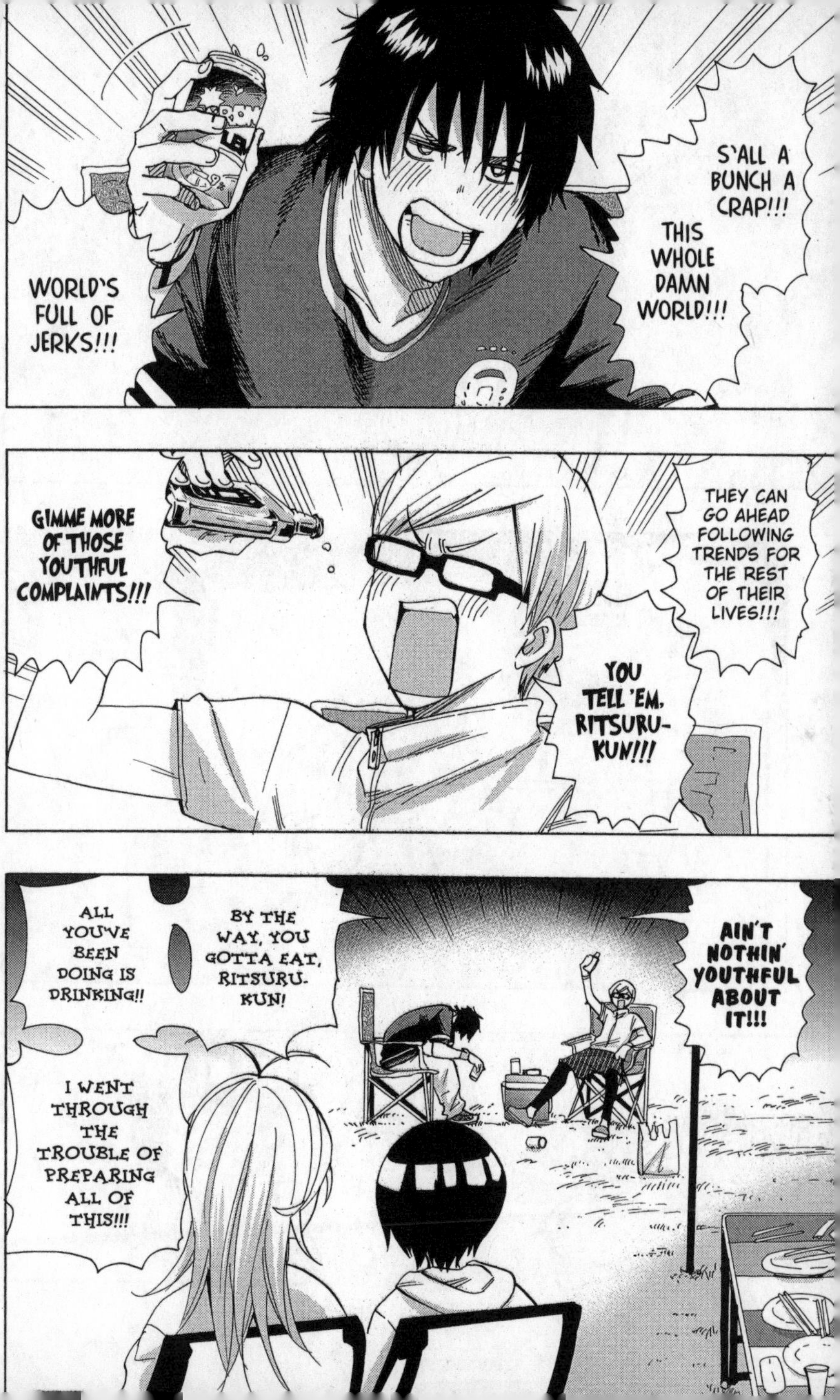
S'ALL A BUNCH A CRAP!!!
THIS WHOLE DAMN WORLD!!!
WORLD'S FULL OF JERKS!!!
THEY CAN GO AHEAD FOLLOWING TRENDS FOR THE REST OF THEIR LIVES!!!
YOU TELL 'EM, RITSURU-KUN!!!
GIMME MORE OF THOSE YOUTHFUL COMPLAINTS!!!
AIN'T NOTHIN' YOUTHFUL ABOUT IT!!!
BY THE WAY, YOU GOTTA EAT, RITSURU-KUN!
ALL YOU'VE BEEN DOING IS DRINKING!!
I WENT THROUGH THE TROUBLE OF PREPARING ALL OF THIS!!!

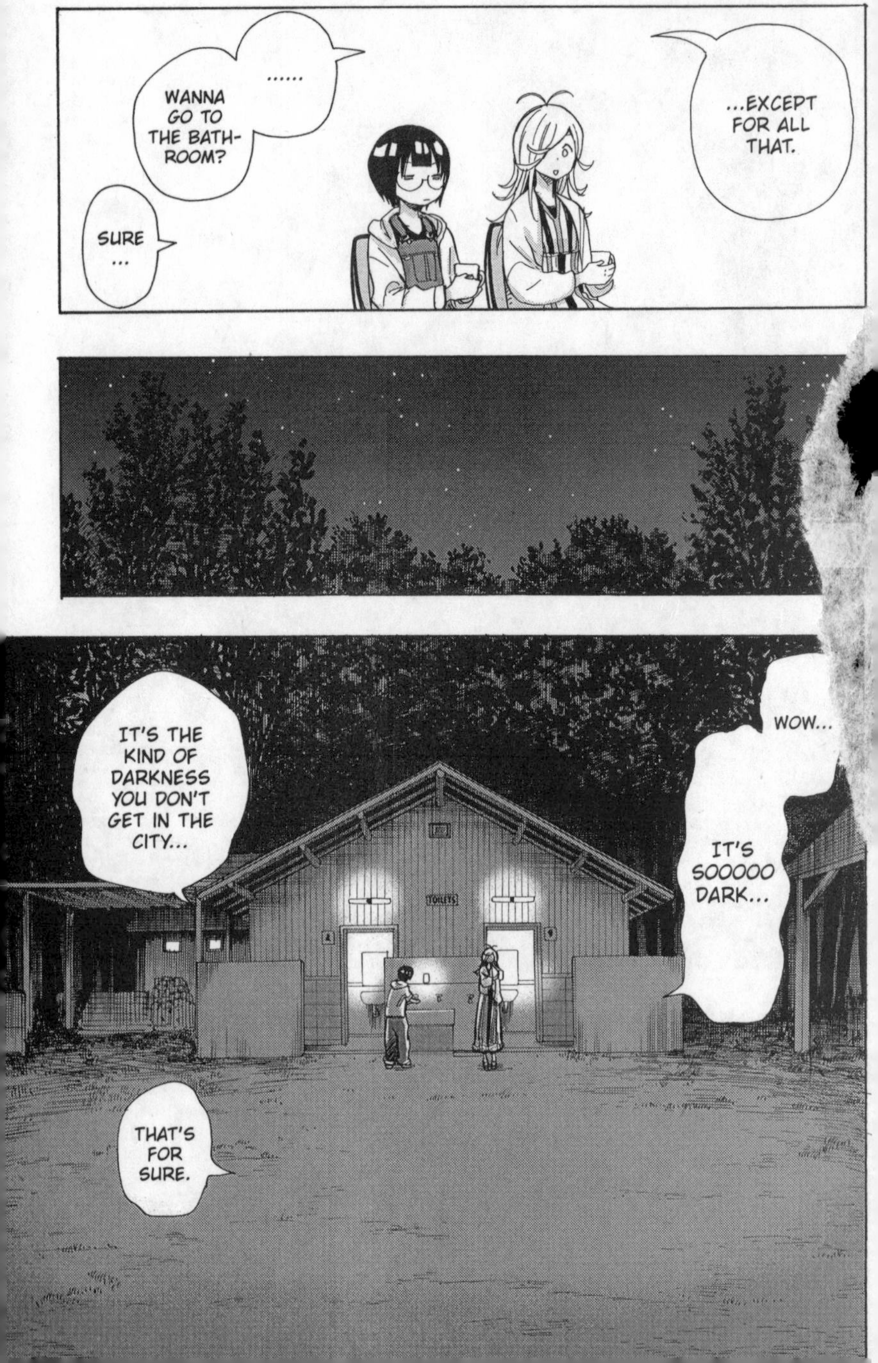
...EXCEPT FOR ALL THAT.
......
WANNA GO TO THE BATH-ROOM?
SURE ...
WOW...
IT'S SOOOOO DARK...
IT'S THE KIND OF DARKNESS YOU DON'T GET IN THE CITY...
THAT'S FOR SURE.

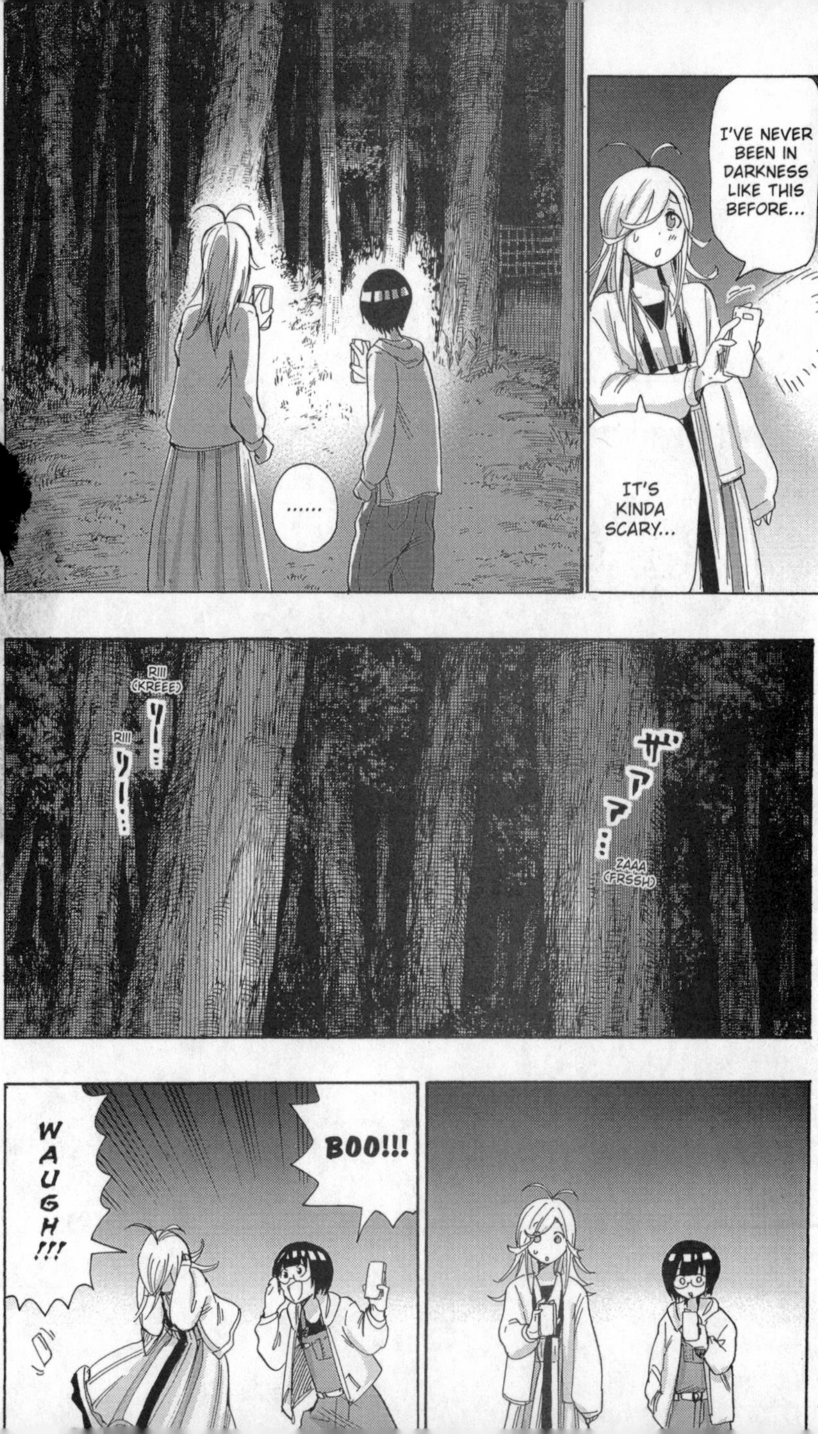
I'VE NEVER BEEN IN DARKNESS LIKE THIS BEFORE...
IT'S KINDA SCARY...
......
ZAAA (FRSSH)
RIII (KREEE)
RIII
BOO!!!
WAUGH!!!

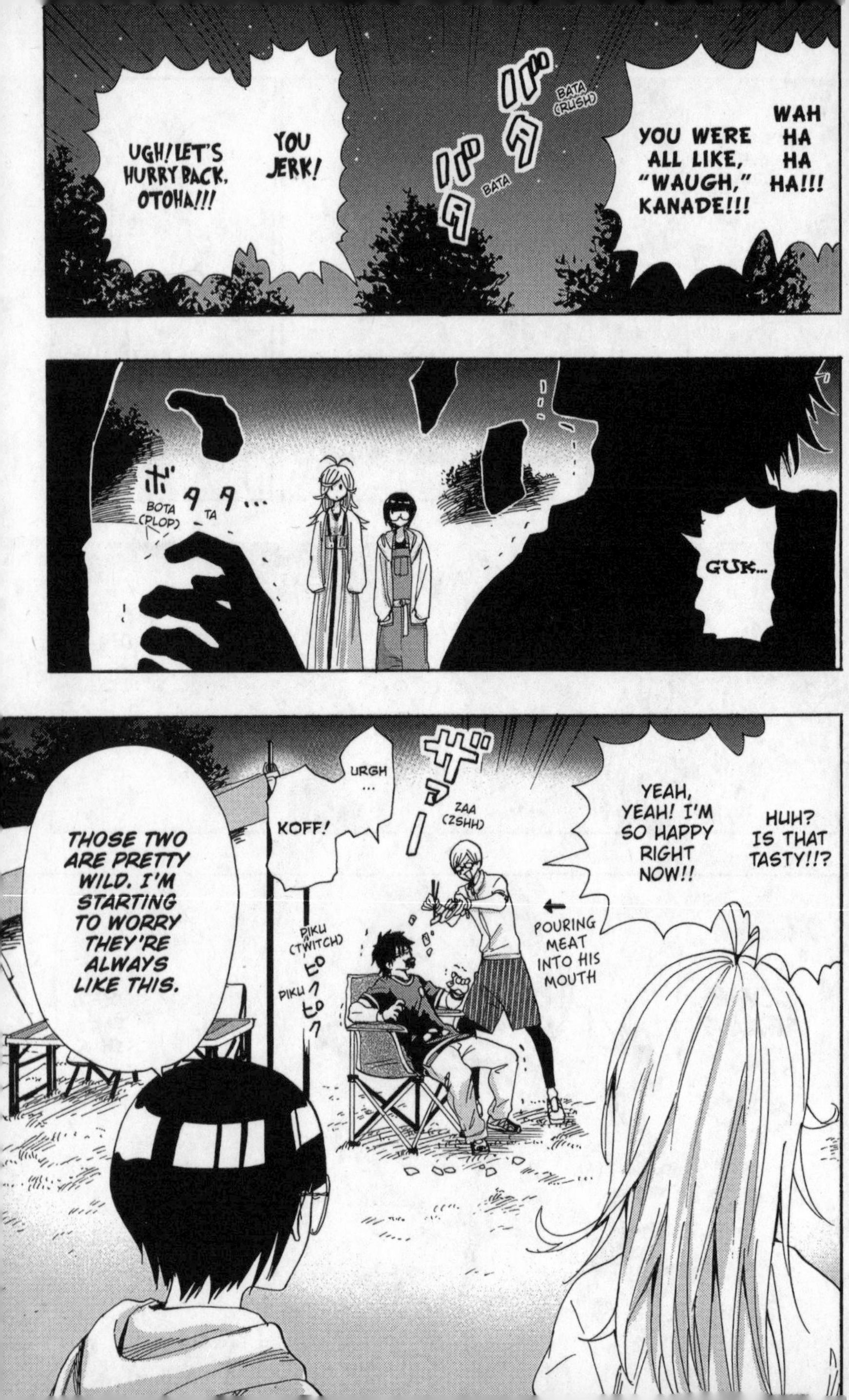
WAH HA HA HA!!!
YOU WERE ALL LIKE, "WAUGH," KANADE!!!
バタ
BATA (RUSH)
バタ
BATA
YOU JERK!
UGH! LET'S HURRY BACK, OTOHA!!!
GUK...
ボタタ...
BOTA (PLOP)
TA
HUH? IS THAT TASTY!!?
YEAH, YEAH! I'M SO HAPPY RIGHT NOW!!
← POURING MEAT INTO HIS MOUTH
ザァー
ZAA (ZSHH)
URGH ...
KOFF!
PIKU (TWITCH)
ピク
PIKU
ピクピク
THOSE TWO ARE PRETTY WILD. I'M STARTING TO WORRY THEY'RE ALWAYS LIKE THIS.

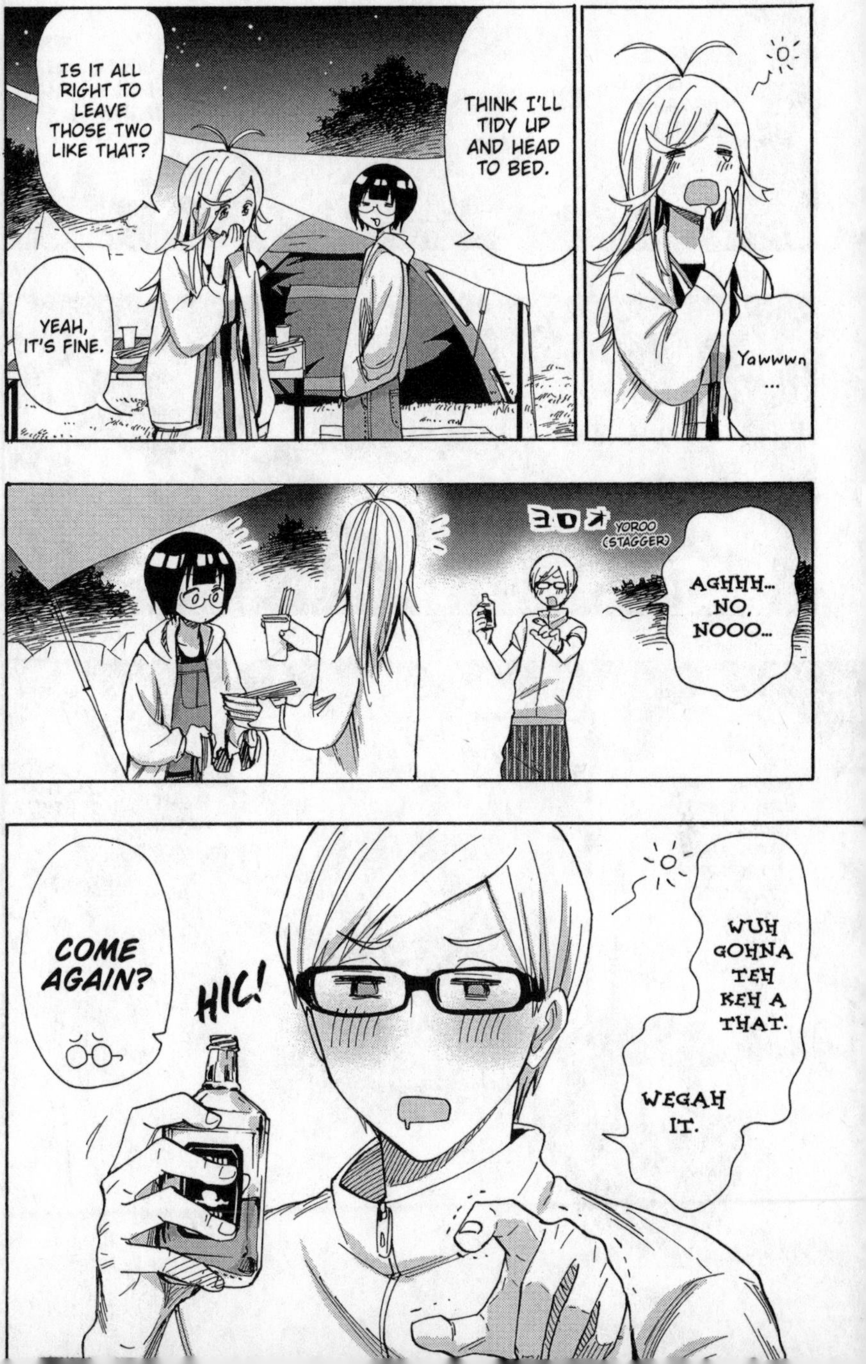
Yawwwn ...
THINK I'LL TIDY UP AND HEAD TO BED.
IS IT ALL RIGHT TO LEAVE THOSE TWO LIKE THAT?
YEAH, IT'S FINE.
ヨロォ YOROO (STAGGER)
AGHHH... NO, NOOO...
WUH GOHNA TEH KEH A THAT.
WEGAH IT.
HIC!
COME AGAIN?

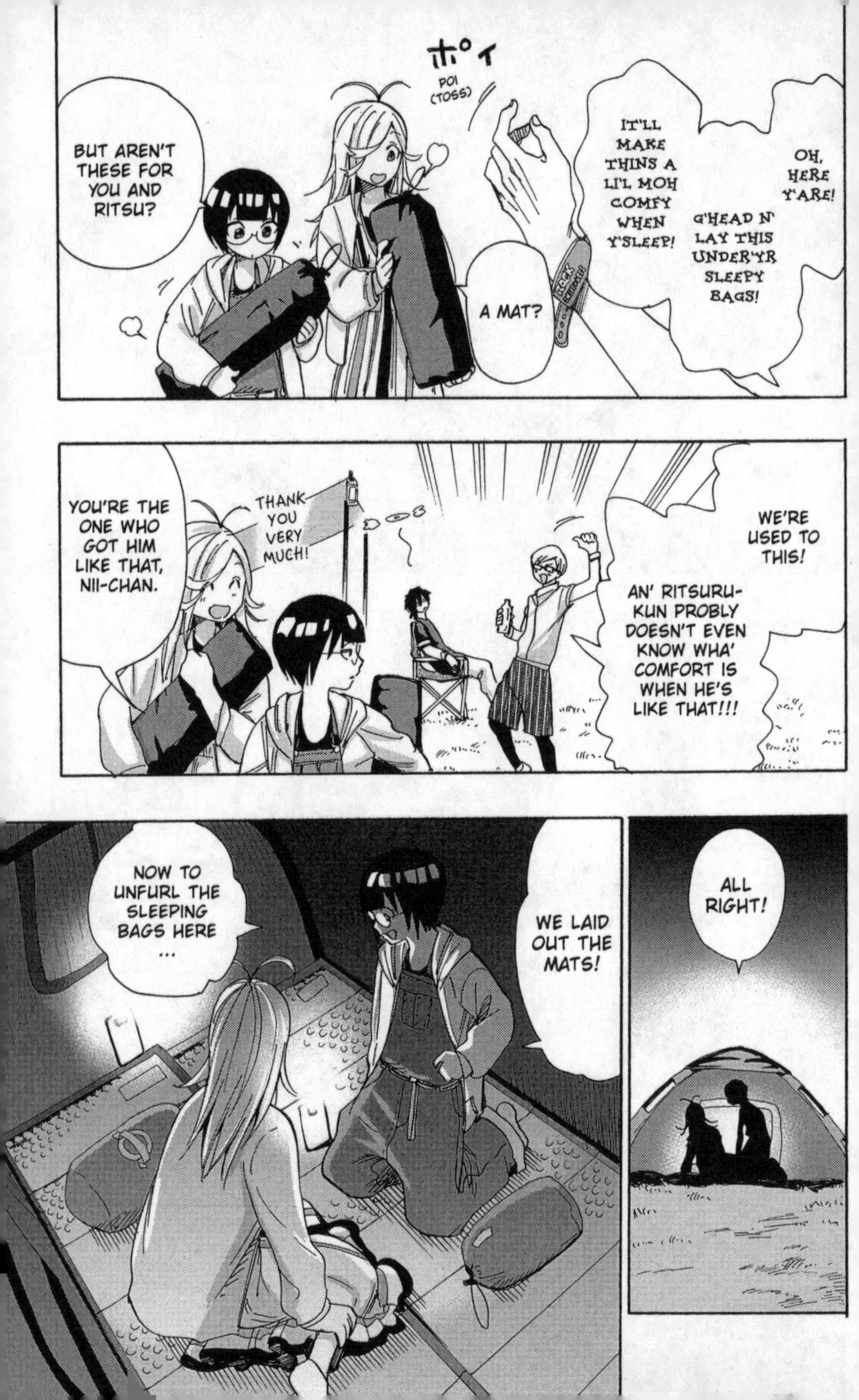
ポイ
POI (TOSS)
OH, HERE Y'ARE!
G'HEAD N' LAY THIS UNDER'YR SLEEPY BAGS!
IT'LL MAKE THINS A LI'L MOH COMFY WHEN Y'SLEEP!
A MAT?
BUT AREN'T THESE FOR YOU AND RITSU?
WE'RE USED TO THIS!
AN' RITSURU-KUN PROBLY DOESN'T EVEN KNOW WHA' COMFORT IS WHEN HE'S LIKE THAT!!!
THANK YOU VERY MUCH!
YOU'RE THE ONE WHO GOT HIM LIKE THAT, NII-CHAN.
ALL RIGHT!
WE LAID OUT THE MATS!
NOW TO UNFURL THE SLEEPING BAGS HERE ...

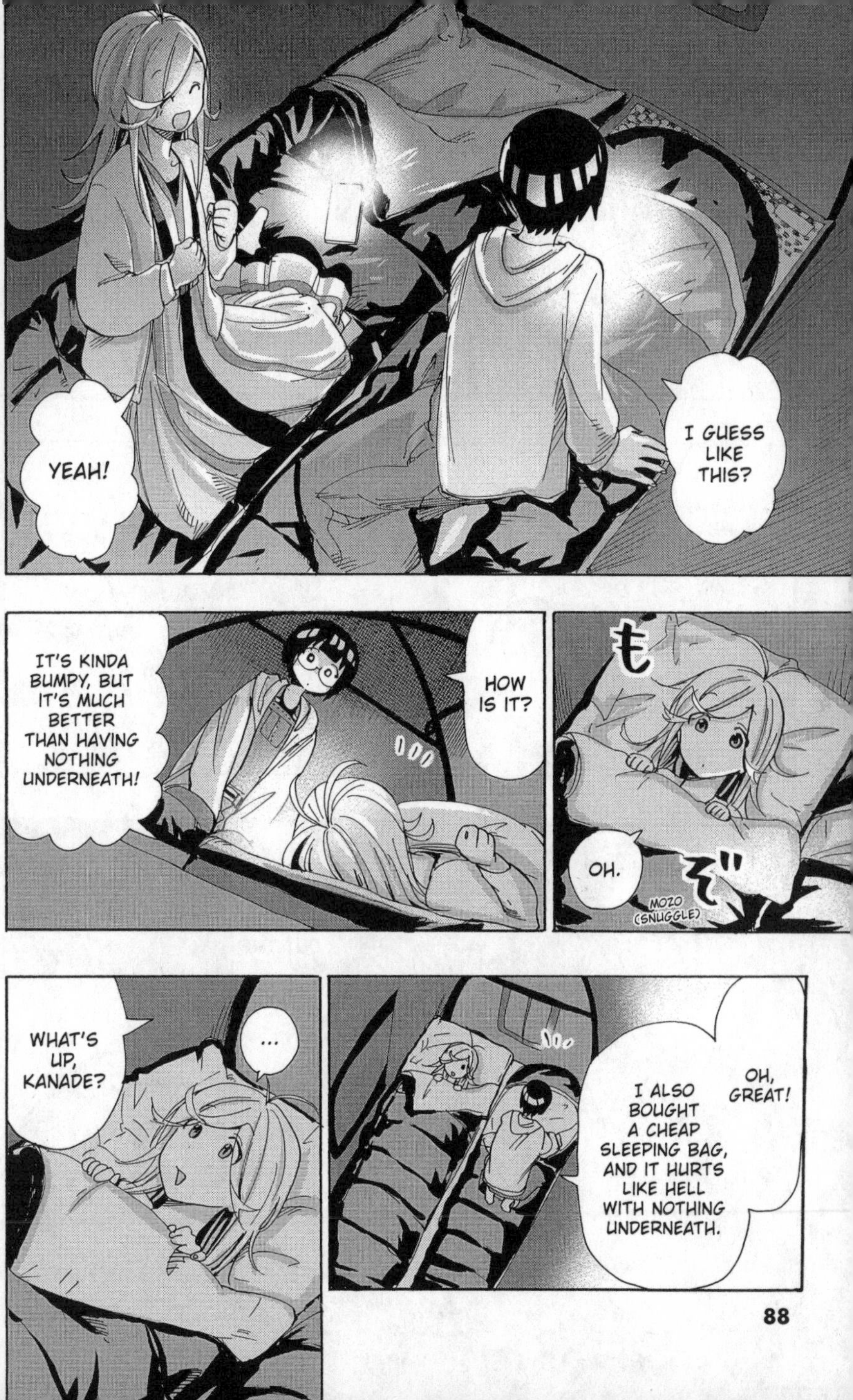
I GUESS LIKE THIS?
YEAH!
もぞ
OH.
MOZO (SNUGGLE)
HOW IS IT?
IT'S KINDA BUMPY, BUT IT'S MUCH BETTER THAN HAVING NOTHING UNDERNEATH!
OH, GREAT!
I ALSO BOUGHT A CHEAP SLEEPING BAG, AND IT HURTS LIKE HELL WITH NOTHING UNDERNEATH.
...
WHAT'S UP, KANADE?

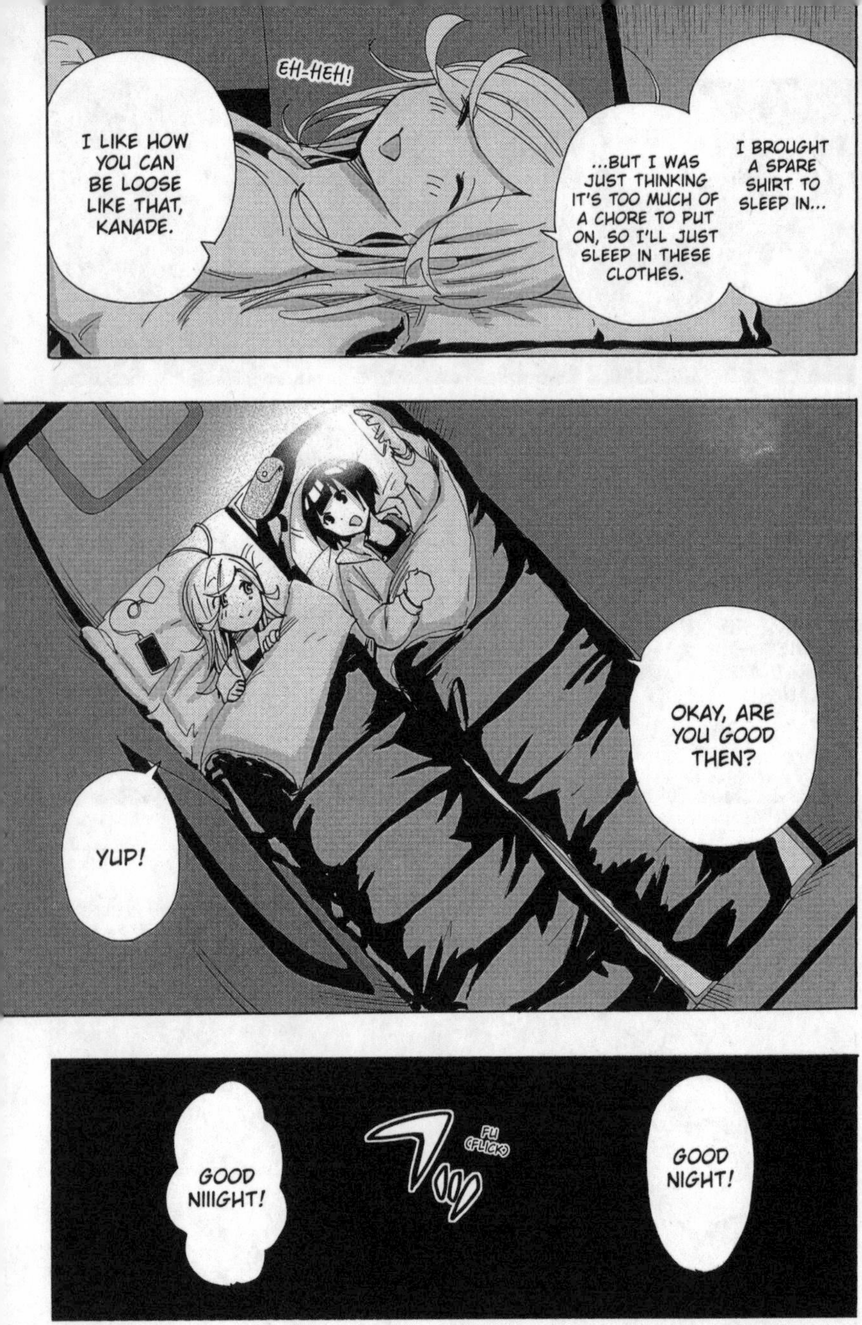
I BROUGHT A SPARE SHIRT TO SLEEP IN...
...BUT I WAS JUST THINKING IT'S TOO MUCH OF A CHORE TO PUT ON, SO I'LL JUST SLEEP IN THESE CLOTHES.
EH-HEH!
I LIKE HOW YOU CAN BE LOOSE LIKE THAT, KANADE.
OKAY, ARE YOU GOOD THEN?
YUP!
GOOD NIGHT!
FU (FLICK)
GOOD NIIIGHT!

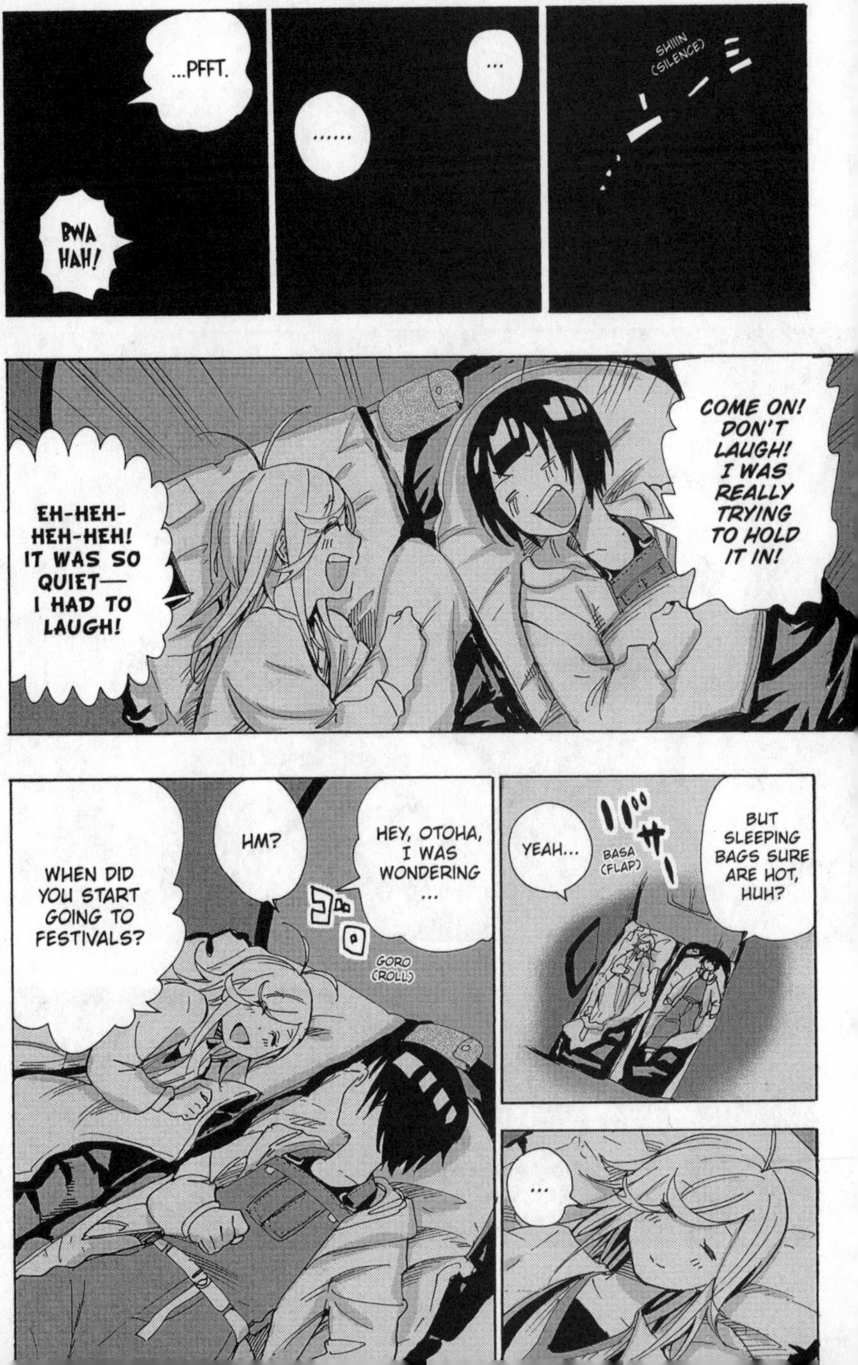
SHIIIN (SILENCE)
...
....
...PFFT.
BWA HAH!
COME ON! DON'T LAUGH! I WAS REALLY TRYING TO HOLD IT IN!
EH-HEH-HEH-HEH! IT WAS SO QUIET— I HAD TO LAUGH!
BUT SLEEPING BAGS SURE ARE HOT, HUH?
BASA (FLAP)
YEAH...
...
HEY, OTOHA, I WAS WONDERING ...
GORO (ROLL)
HM?
WHEN DID YOU START GOING TO FESTIVALS?

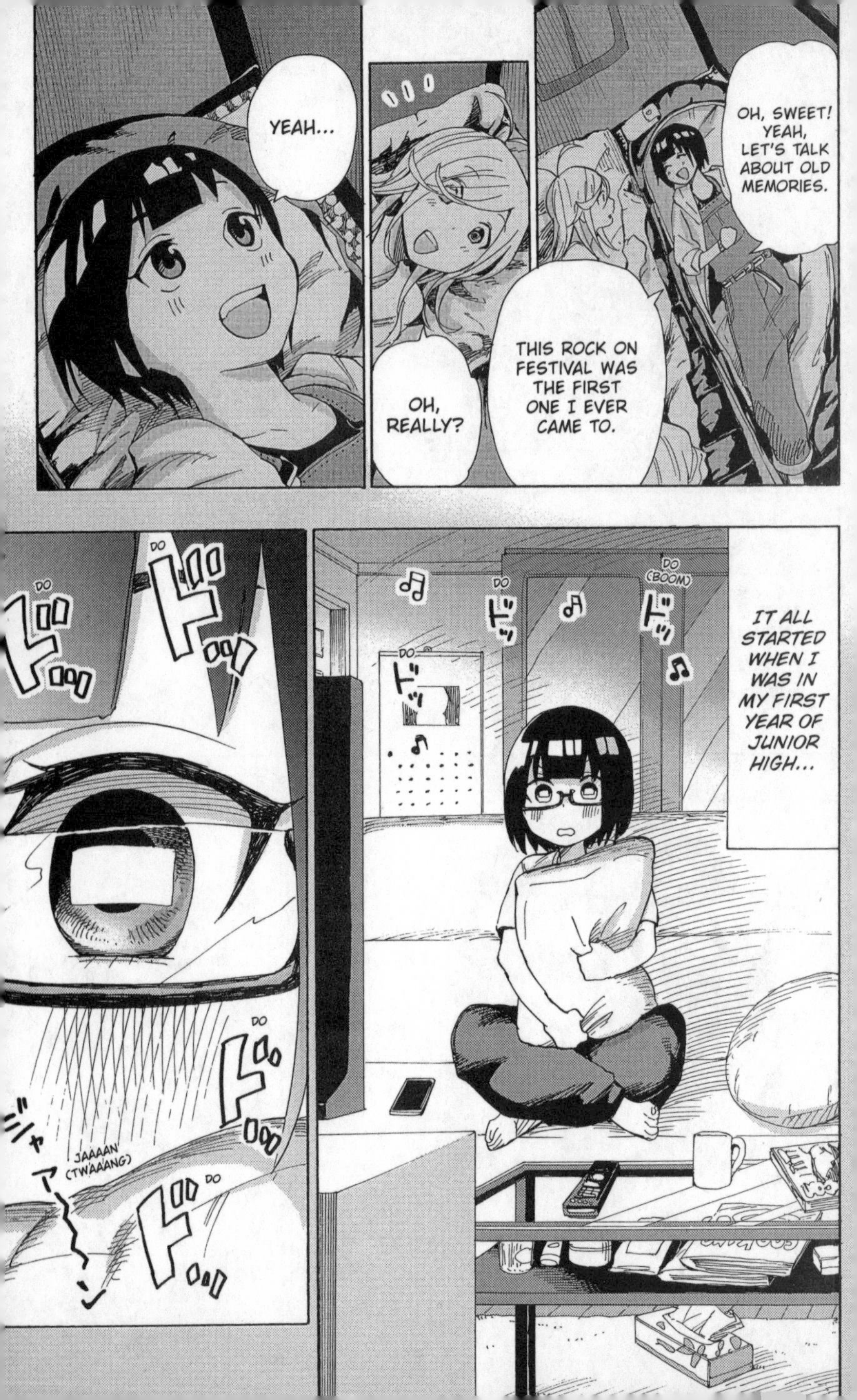
OH, SWEET! YEAH, LET'S TALK ABOUT OLD MEMORIES.
THIS ROCK ON FESTIVAL WAS THE FIRST ONE I EVER CAME TO.
OH, REALLY?
YEAH...
IT ALL STARTED WHEN I WAS IN MY FIRST YEAR OF JUNIOR HIGH...
DO (BOOM)
DO
DO
DO
DO
DO
JAAAAN (TWAAANG)
DO

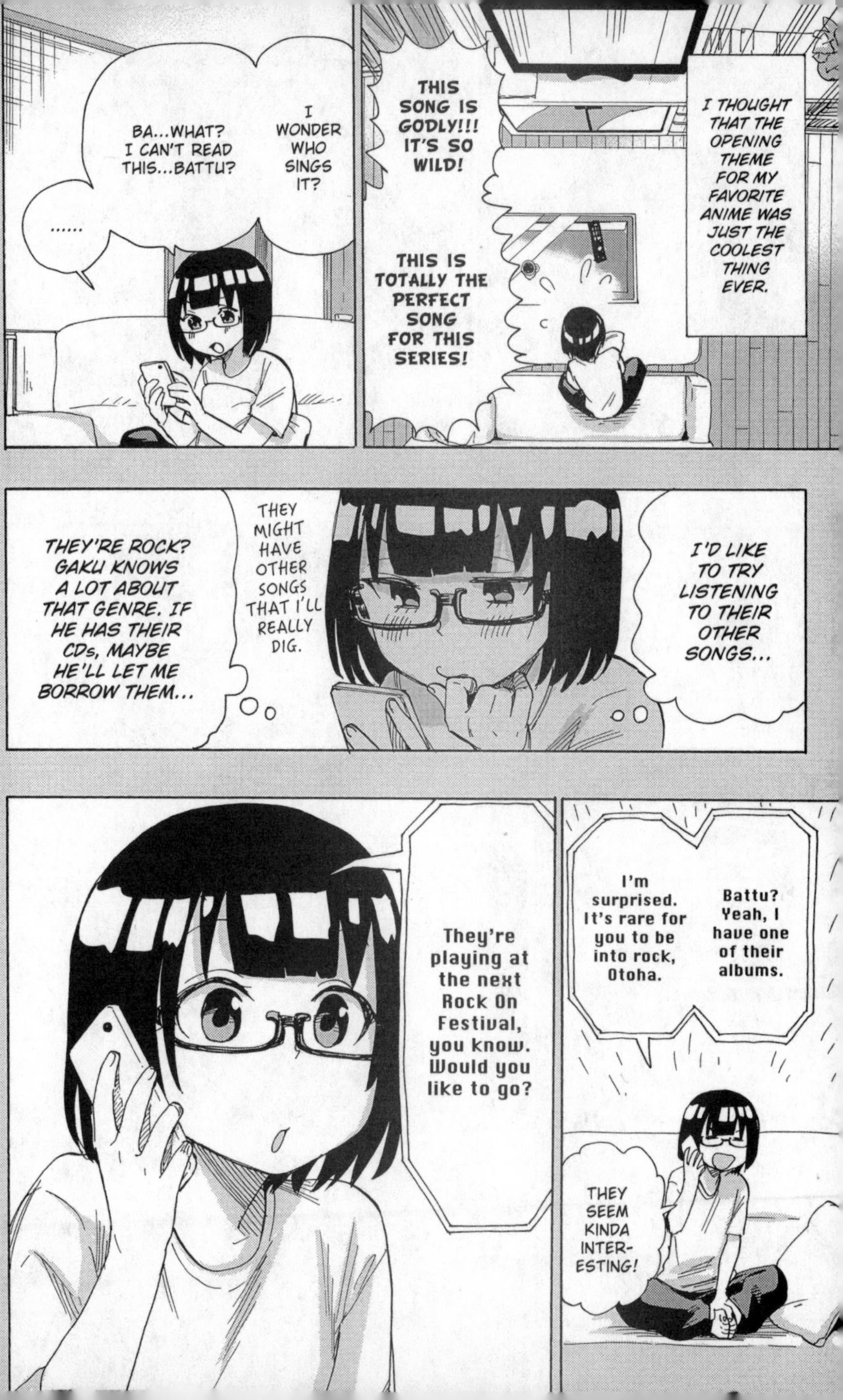
I THOUGHT THAT THE OPENING THEME FOR MY FAVORITE ANIME WAS JUST THE COOLEST THING EVER.
THIS SONG IS GODLY!!! IT'S SO WILD!
THIS IS TOTALLY THE PERFECT SONG FOR THIS SERIES!
I WONDER WHO SINGS IT?
BA...WHAT? I CAN'T READ THIS...BATTU?
......
I'D LIKE TO TRY LISTENING TO THEIR OTHER SONGS...
THEY MIGHT HAVE OTHER SONGS THAT I'LL REALLY DIG.
THEY'RE ROCK? GAKU KNOWS A LOT ABOUT THAT GENRE. IF HE HAS THEIR CDs, MAYBE HE'LL LET ME BORROW THEM...
Battu? Yeah, I have one of their albums.
I'm surprised. It's rare for you to be into rock, Otoha.
THEY SEEM KINDA INTER-ESTING!
They're playing at the next Rock On Festival, you know. Would you like to go?

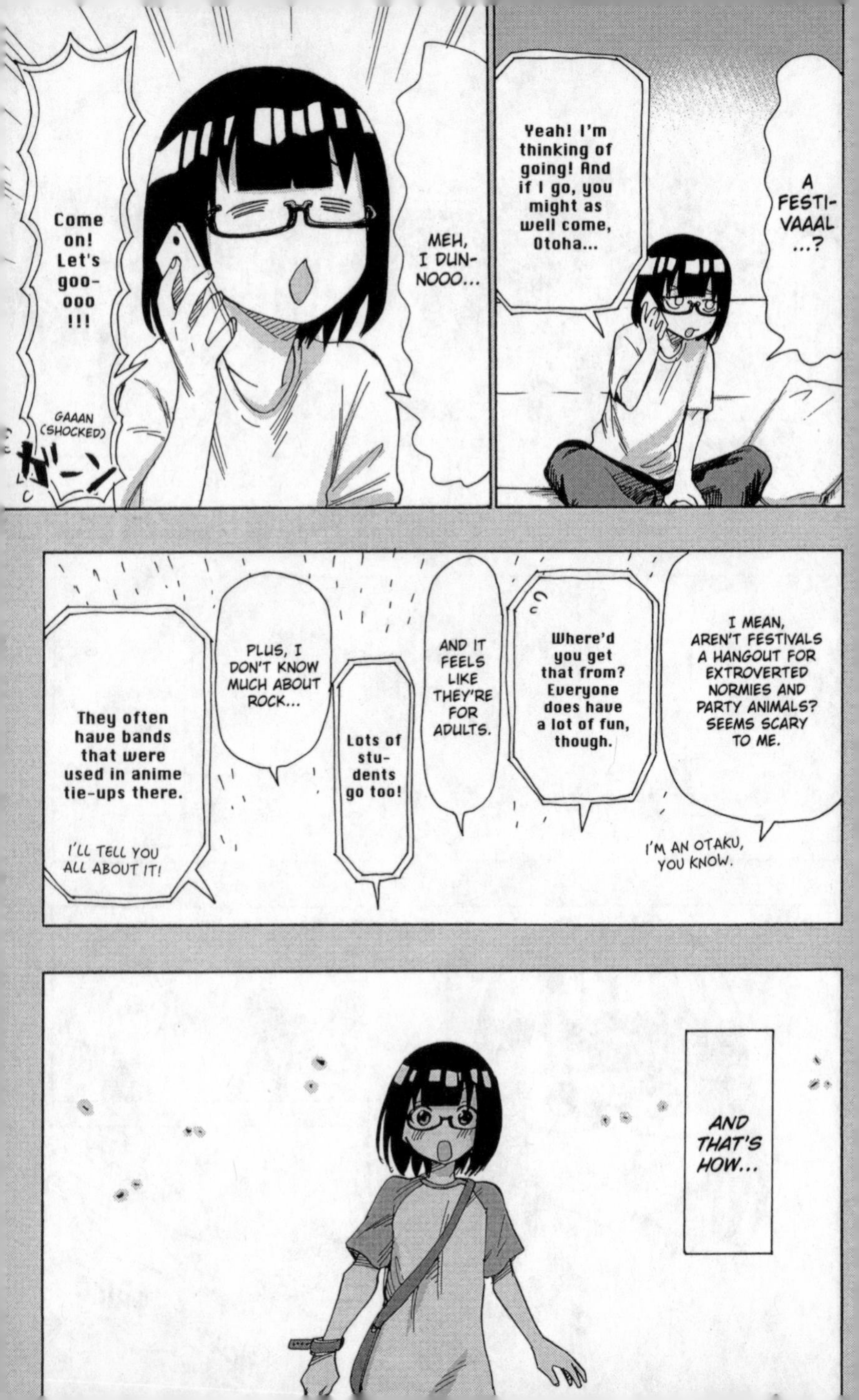
A FESTI-VAAAL ...?
Yeah! I'm thinking of going! And if I go, you might as well come, Otoha...
MEH, I DUN-NOOO...
Come on! Let's goo-ooo !!!
GAAAN (SHOCKED)
ガーン
I MEAN, AREN'T FESTIVALS A HANGOUT FOR EXTROVERTED NORMIES AND PARTY ANIMALS? SEEMS SCARY TO ME.
I'M AN OTAKU, YOU KNOW.
Where'd you get that from? Everyone does have a lot of fun, though.
AND IT FEELS LIKE THEY'RE FOR ADULTS.
Lots of stu-dents go too!
PLUS, I DON'T KNOW MUCH ABOUT ROCK...
They often have bands that were used in anime tie-ups there.
I'LL TELL YOU ALL ABOUT IT!
AND THAT'S HOW...

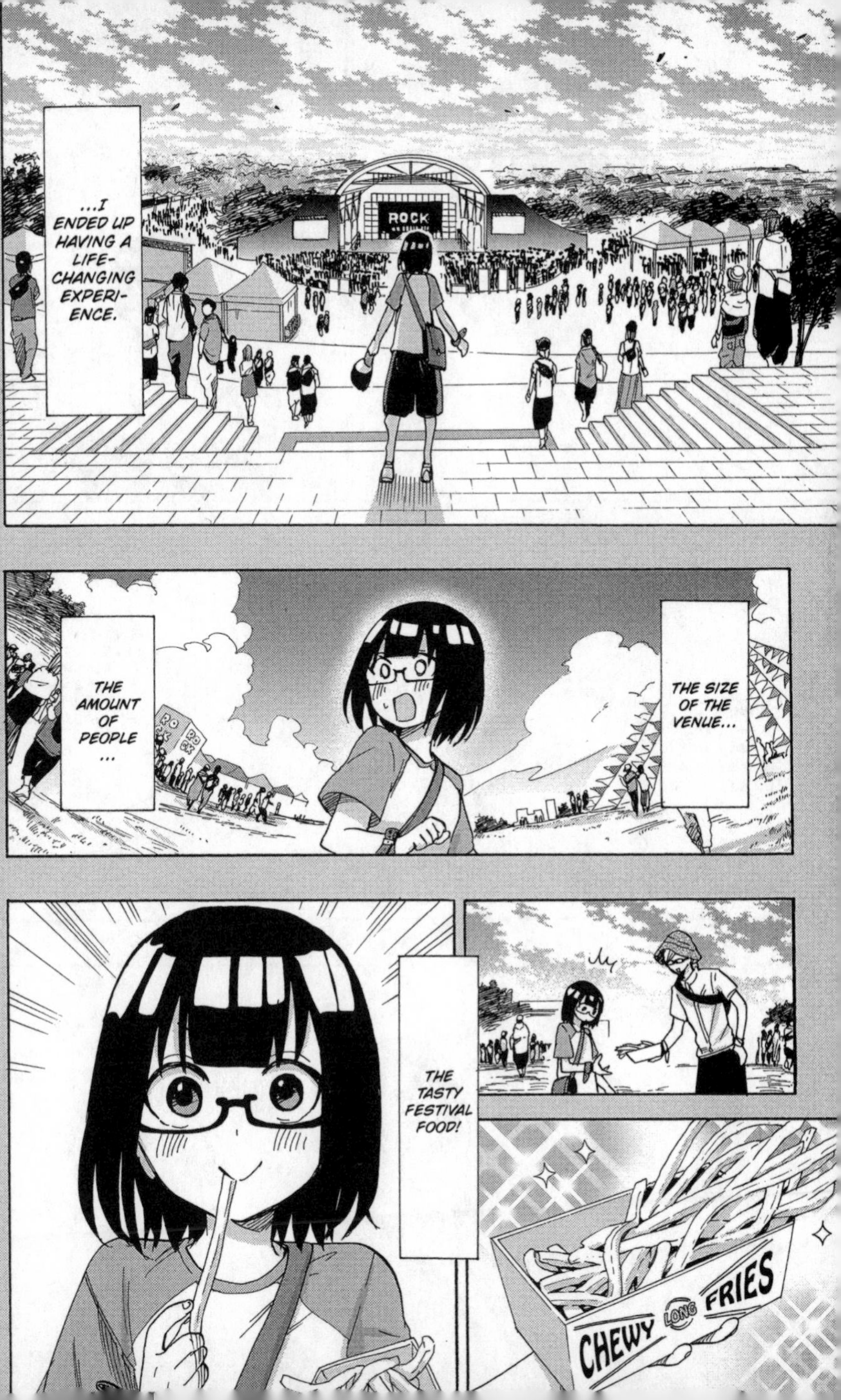
...I ENDED UP HAVING A LIFE-CHANGING EXPERI-ENCE.
ROCK
THE SIZE OF THE VENUE...
THE AMOUNT OF PEOPLE ...
ROCK
THE TASTY FESTIVAL FOOD!
CHEWY LONG FRIES

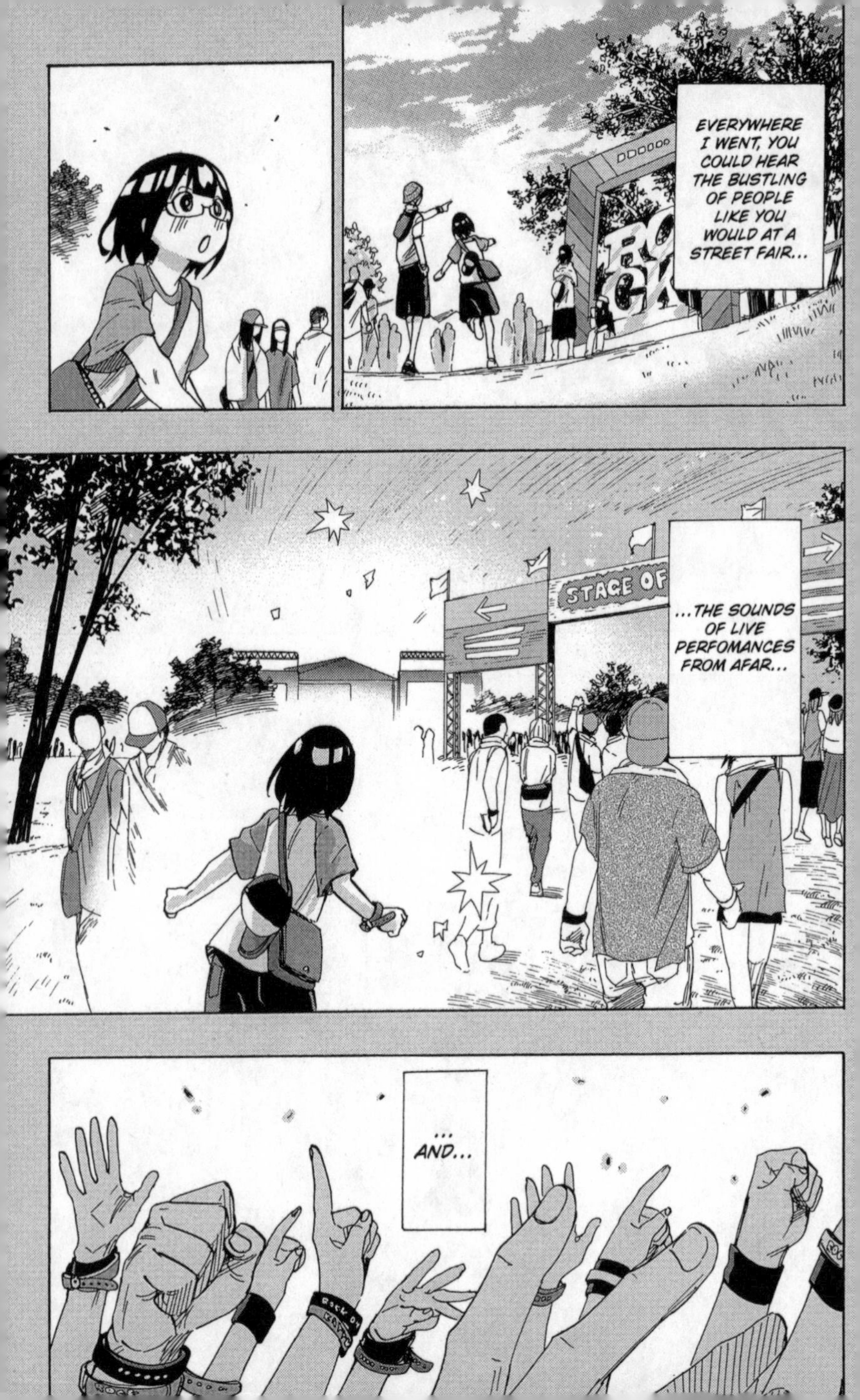
EVERYWHERE I WENT, YOU COULD HEAR THE BUSTLING OF PEOPLE LIKE YOU WOULD AT A STREET FAIR...
...THE SOUNDS OF LIVE PERFOMANCES FROM AFAR...
STAGE OF
...AND...

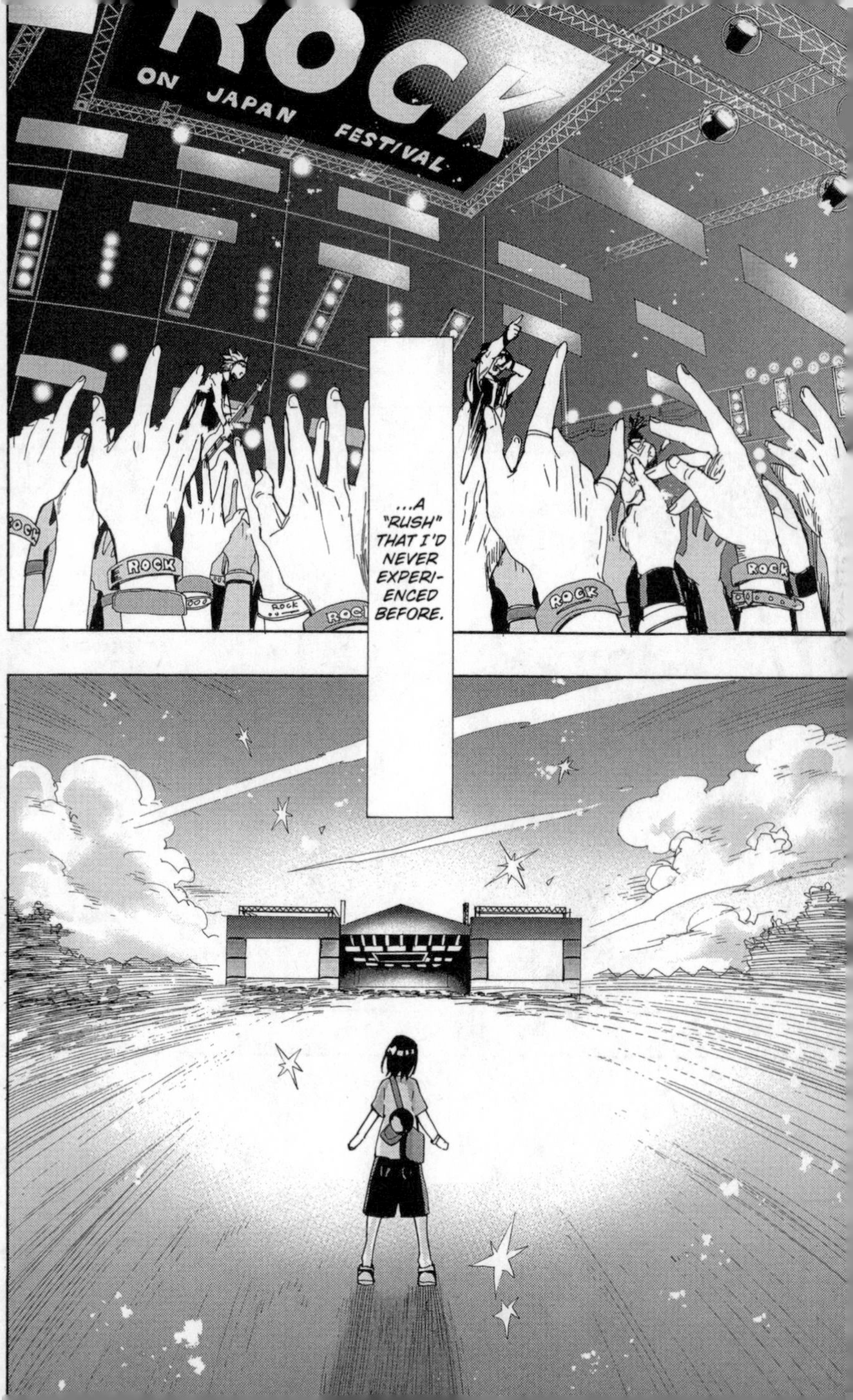
ROCK
ON JAPAN FESTIVAL
...A "RUSH" THAT I'D NEVER EXPERI-ENCED BEFORE.
ROCK
ROCK
ROCK
ROCK
ROCK
ROCK

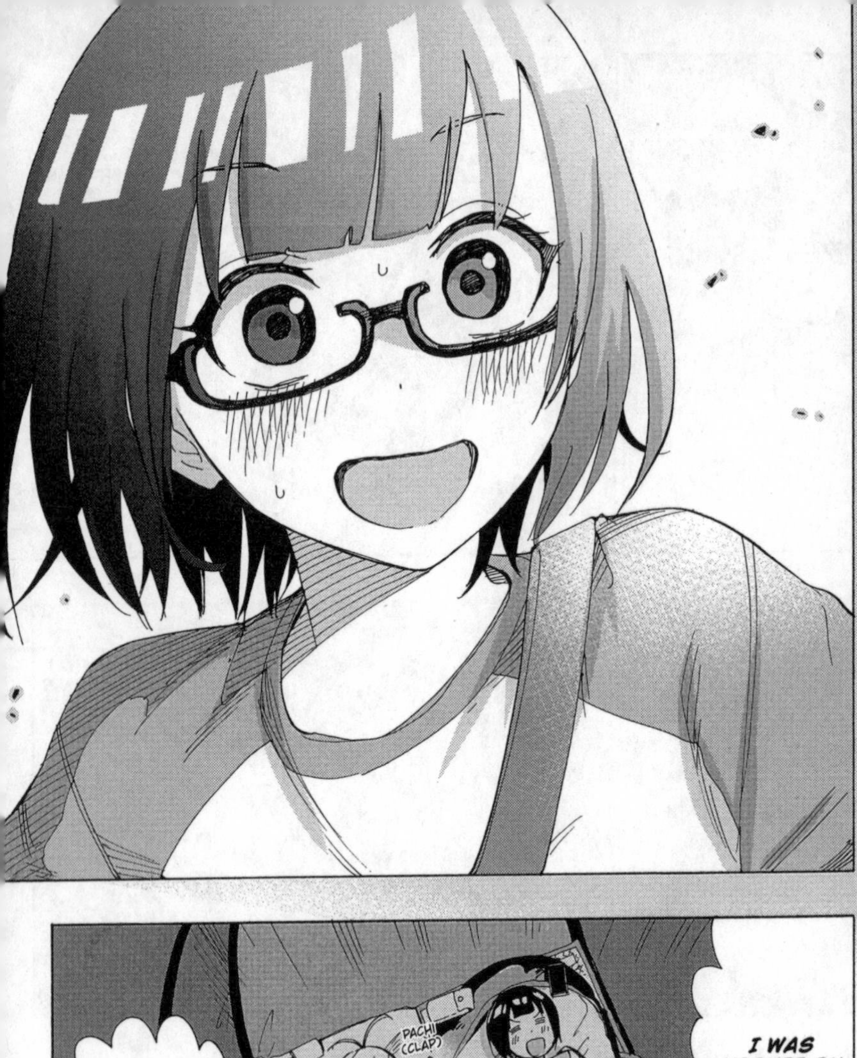

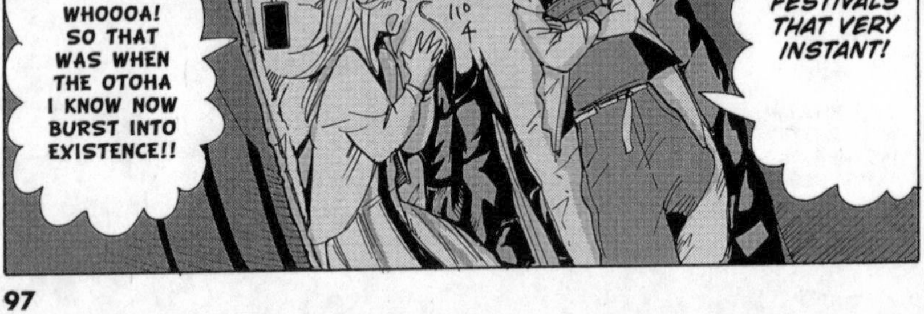
I WAS HOOKED ON FESTIVALS THAT VERY INSTANT!
PACHI
PACHI (CLAP)
WHOOOA! SO THAT WAS WHEN THE OTOHA I KNOW NOW BURST INTO EXISTENCE!!

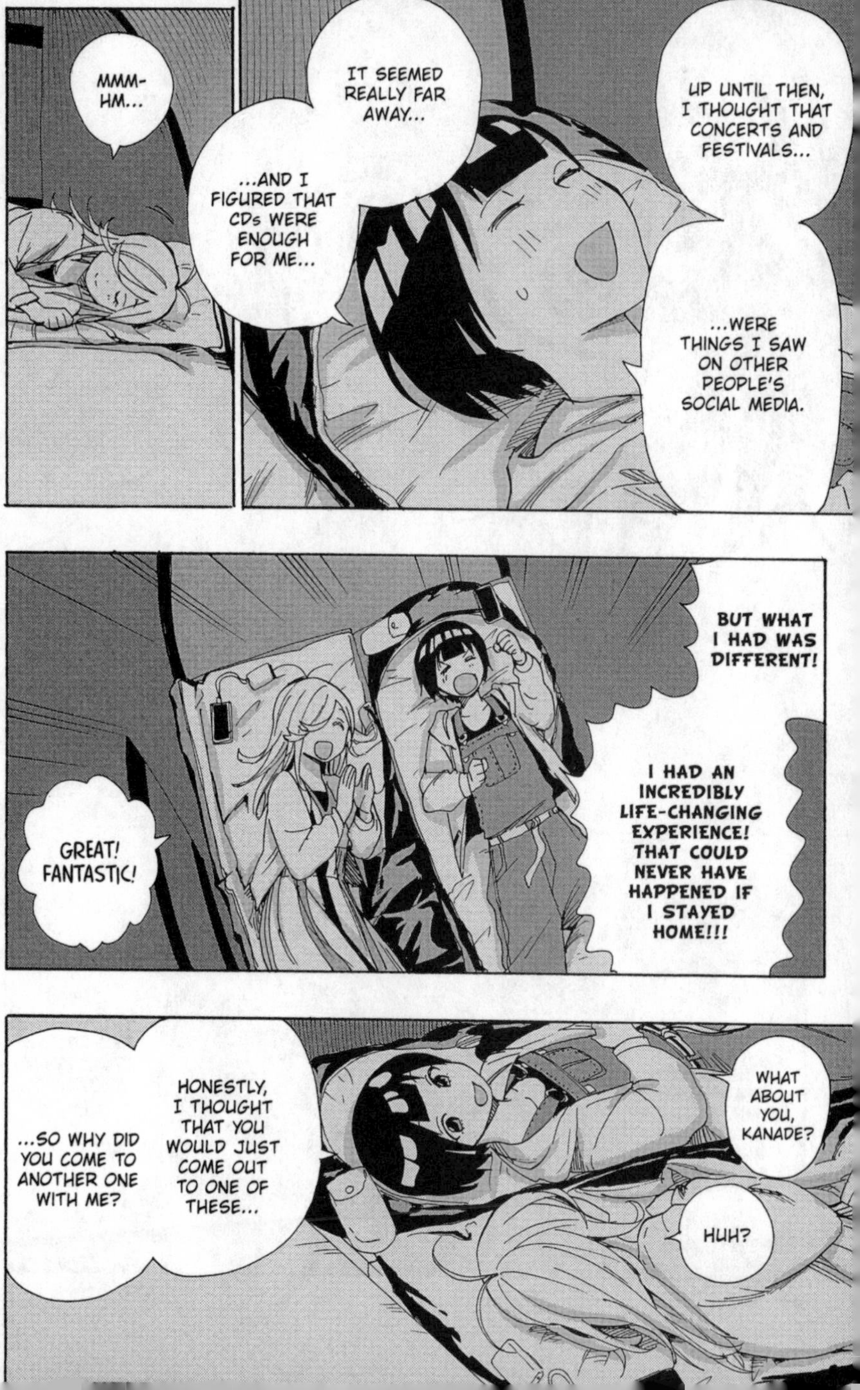
UP UNTIL THEN, I THOUGHT THAT CONCERTS AND FESTIVALS...
...WERE THINGS I SAW ON OTHER PEOPLE'S SOCIAL MEDIA.
IT SEEMED REALLY FAR AWAY...
...AND I FIGURED THAT CDs WERE ENOUGH FOR ME...
MMM-HM...
BUT WHAT I HAD WAS DIFFERENT!
I HAD AN INCREDIBLY LIFE-CHANGING EXPERIENCE! THAT COULD NEVER HAVE HAPPENED IF I STAYED HOME!!!
GREAT! FANTASTIC!
WHAT ABOUT YOU, KANADE?
HUH?
HONESTLY, I THOUGHT THAT YOU WOULD JUST COME OUT TO ONE OF THESE...
...SO WHY DID YOU COME TO ANOTHER ONE WITH ME?

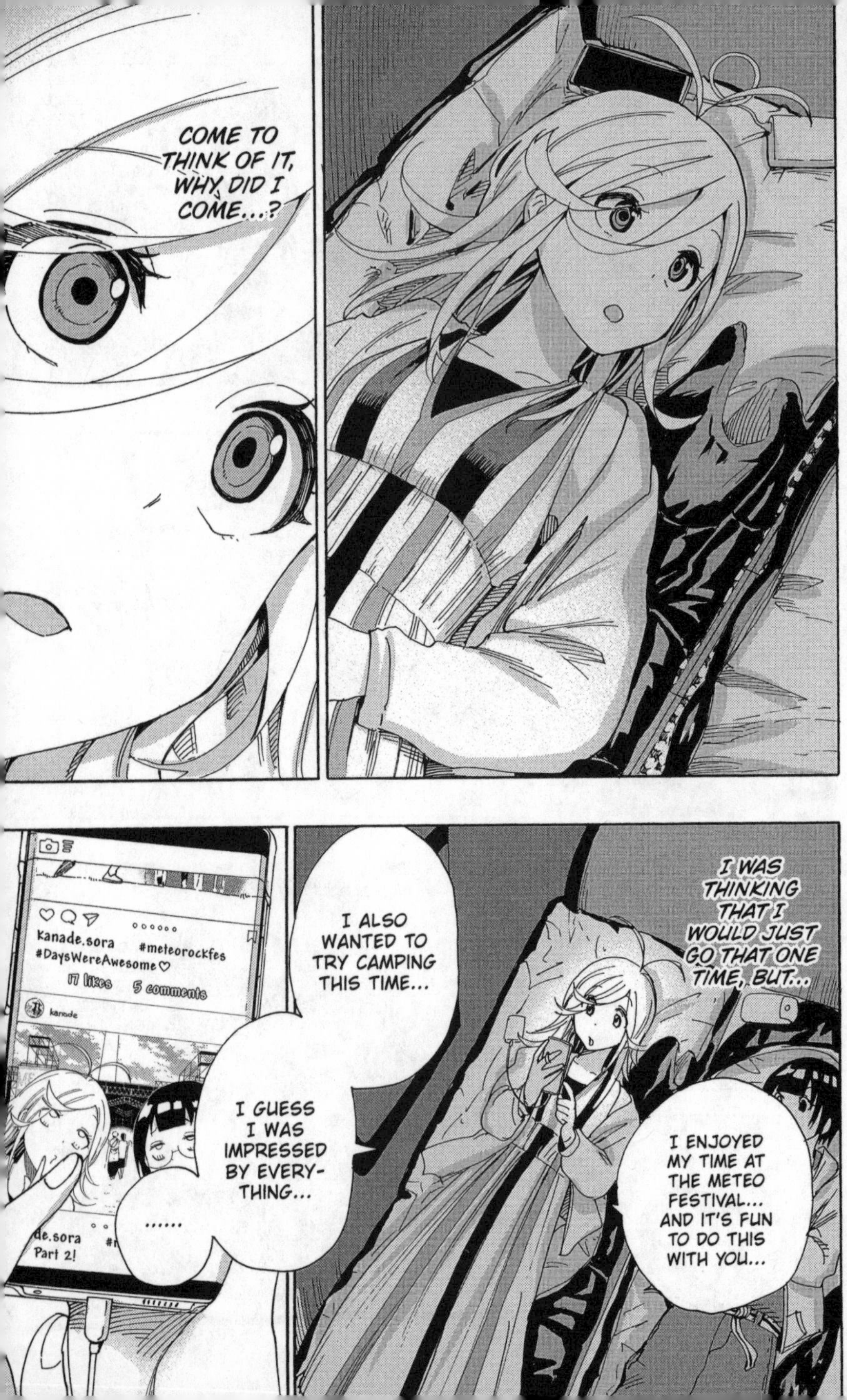
COME TO THINK OF IT, WHY DID I COME...?
I WAS THINKING THAT I WOULD JUST GO THAT ONE TIME, BUT...
I ENJOYED MY TIME AT THE METEO FESTIVAL... AND IT'S FUN TO DO THIS WITH YOU...
I ALSO WANTED TO TRY CAMPING THIS TIME...
I GUESS I WAS IMPRESSED BY EVERYTHING...
......
kanade.sora #meteorockfes
#DaysWereAwesome♡
17 likes 5 comments
kanade
de.sora
Part 2!

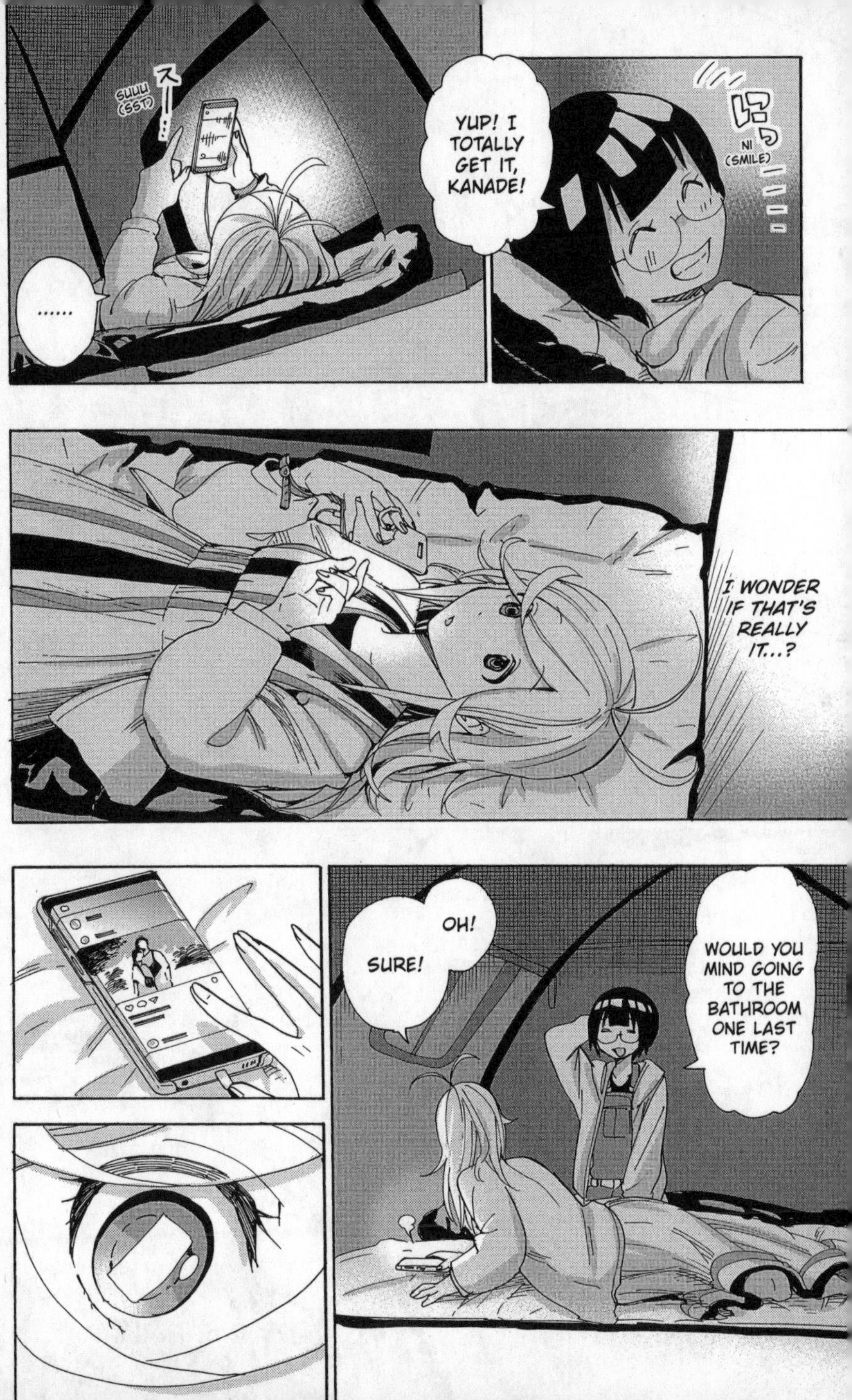
ニコッ
NI (SMILE)
YUP! I TOTALLY GET IT, KANADE!
スー…
SUUU (SSST)
......
I WONDER IF THAT'S REALLY IT...?
WOULD YOU MIND GOING TO THE BATHROOM ONE LAST TIME?
OH!
SURE!

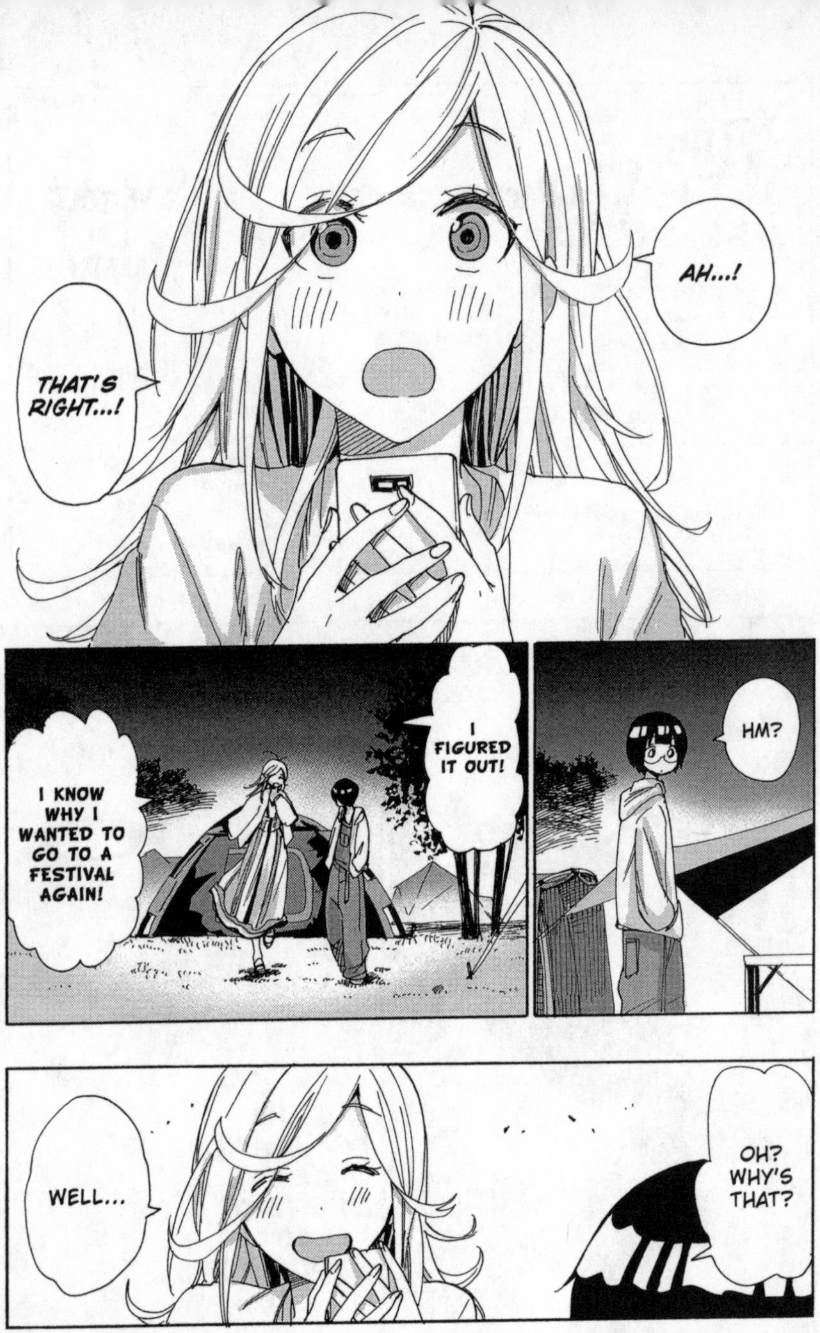
AH...!
THAT'S RIGHT...!
HM?
I FIGURED IT OUT!
I KNOW WHY I WANTED TO GO TO A FESTIVAL AGAIN!
OH? WHY'S THAT?
WELL...

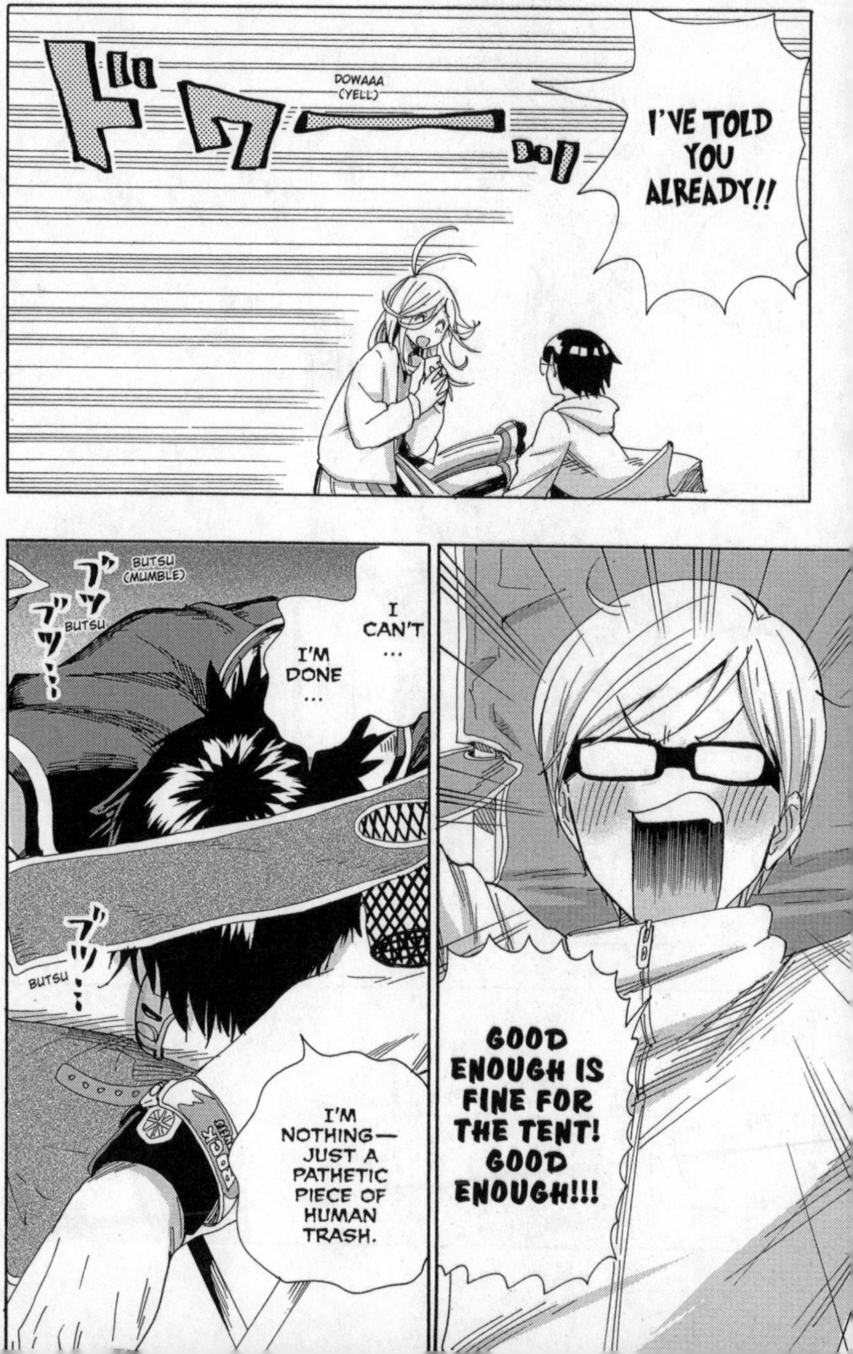
I'VE TOLD YOU ALREADY!!
DOWAAA (YELL)
GOOD ENOUGH IS FINE FOR THE TENT! GOOD ENOUGH!!!
I CAN'T ...
I'M DONE ...
BUTSU (MUMBLE)
BUTSU
BUTSU
I'M NOTHING— JUST A PATHETIC PIECE OF HUMAN TRASH.

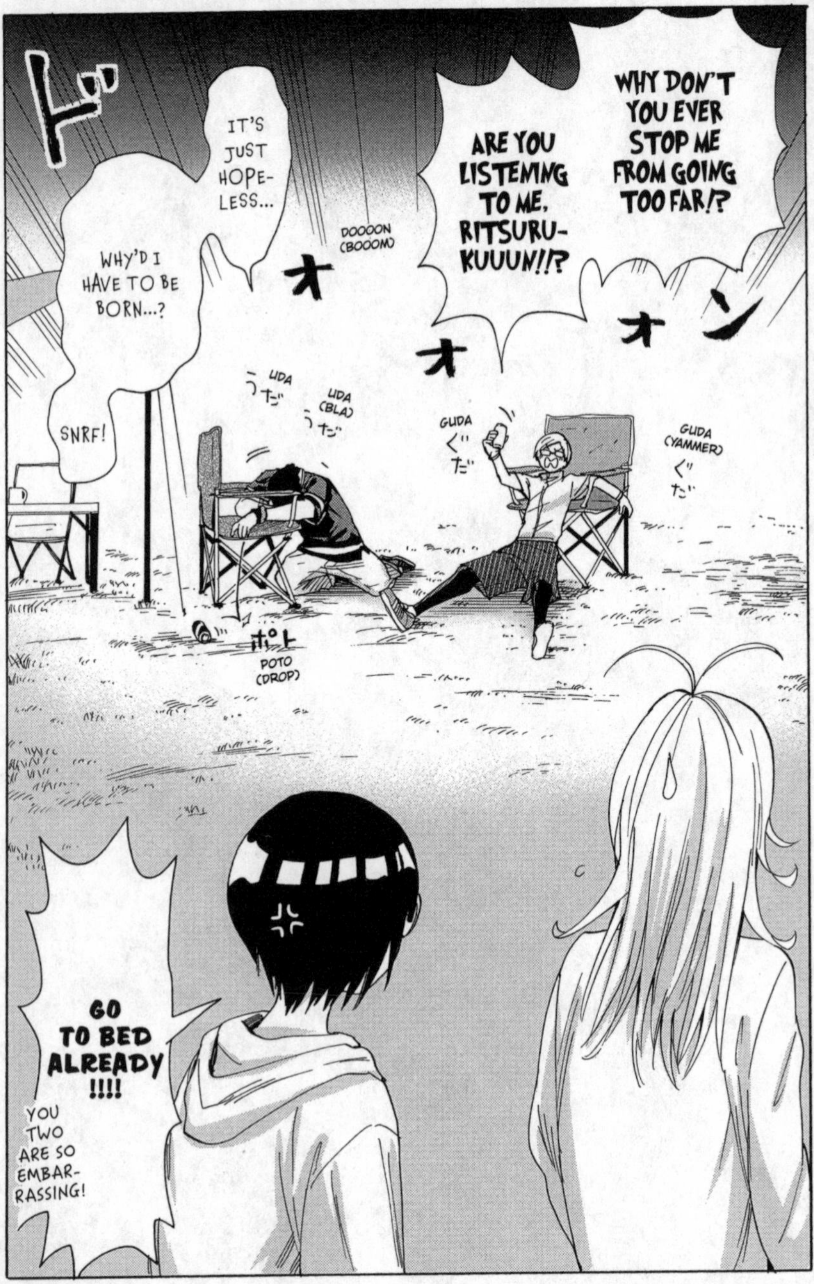
WHY DON'T YOU EVER STOP ME FROM GOING TOO FAR!?
ARE YOU LISTEMING TO ME, RITSURU-KUUUN!!?
ドォオオン
DOOOON (BOOOM)
IT'S JUST HOPELESS...
WHY'D I HAVE TO BE BORN...?
SNRF!
ぐだ
GUDA (YAMMER)
ぐだ
GUDA
うだ
UDA (BLA)
うだ
UDA
ポト
POTO (DROP)
GO TO BED ALREADY!!!!
YOU TWO ARE SO EMBARRASSING!

Days on Fes

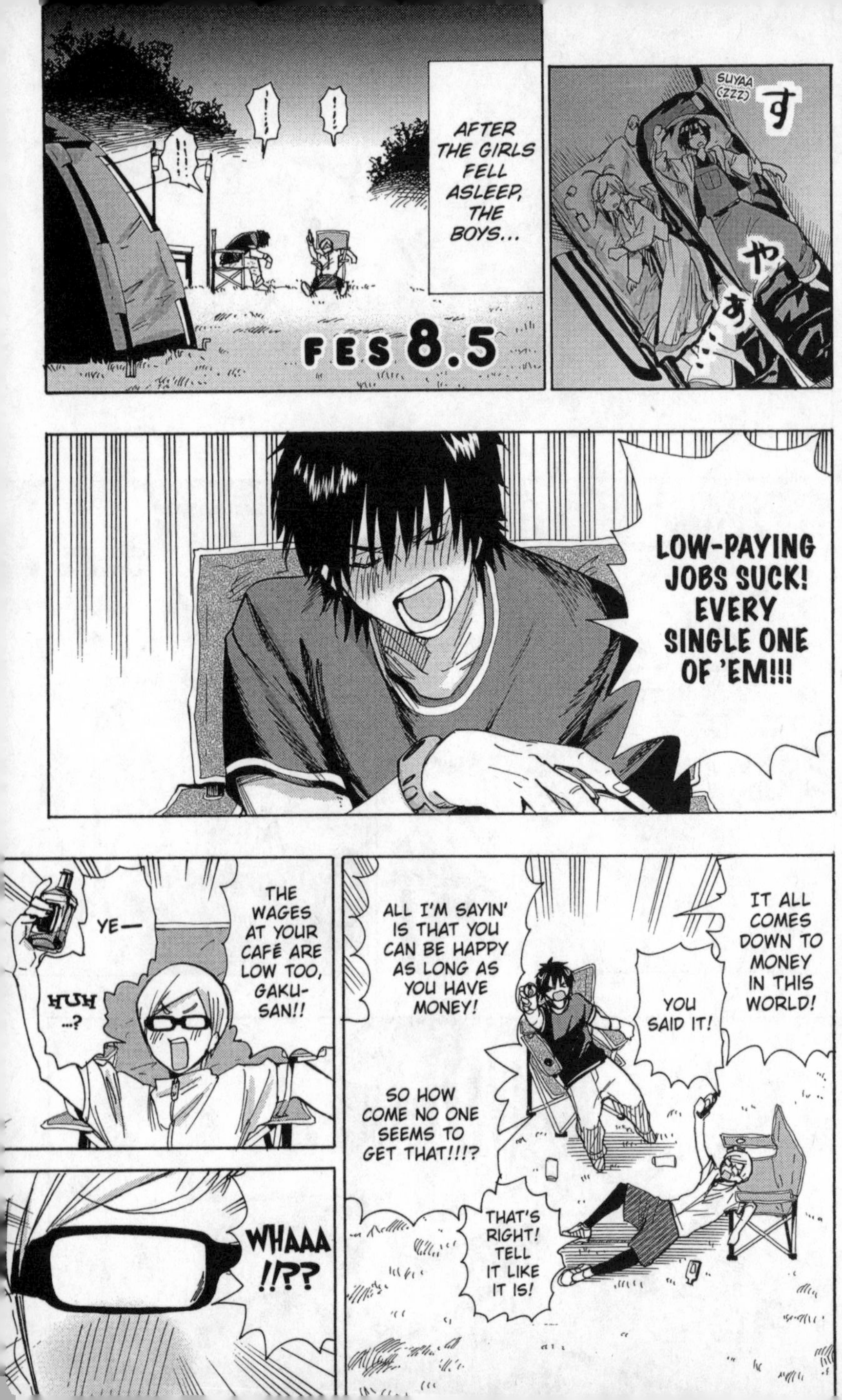
SUYAA (ZZZ)
す
や
す
AFTER THE GIRLS FELL ASLEEP, THE BOYS...
FES 8.5
LOW-PAYING JOBS SUCK! EVERY SINGLE ONE OF 'EM!!!
IT ALL COMES DOWN TO MONEY IN THIS WORLD!
YOU SAID IT!
ALL I'M SAYIN' IS THAT YOU CAN BE HAPPY AS LONG AS YOU HAVE MONEY!
SO HOW COME NO ONE SEEMS TO GET THAT!!!?
THAT'S RIGHT! TELL IT LIKE IT IS!
THE WAGES AT YOUR CAFÉ ARE LOW TOO, GAKU-SAN!!
YE—
HUH ...?
WHAAA !!??

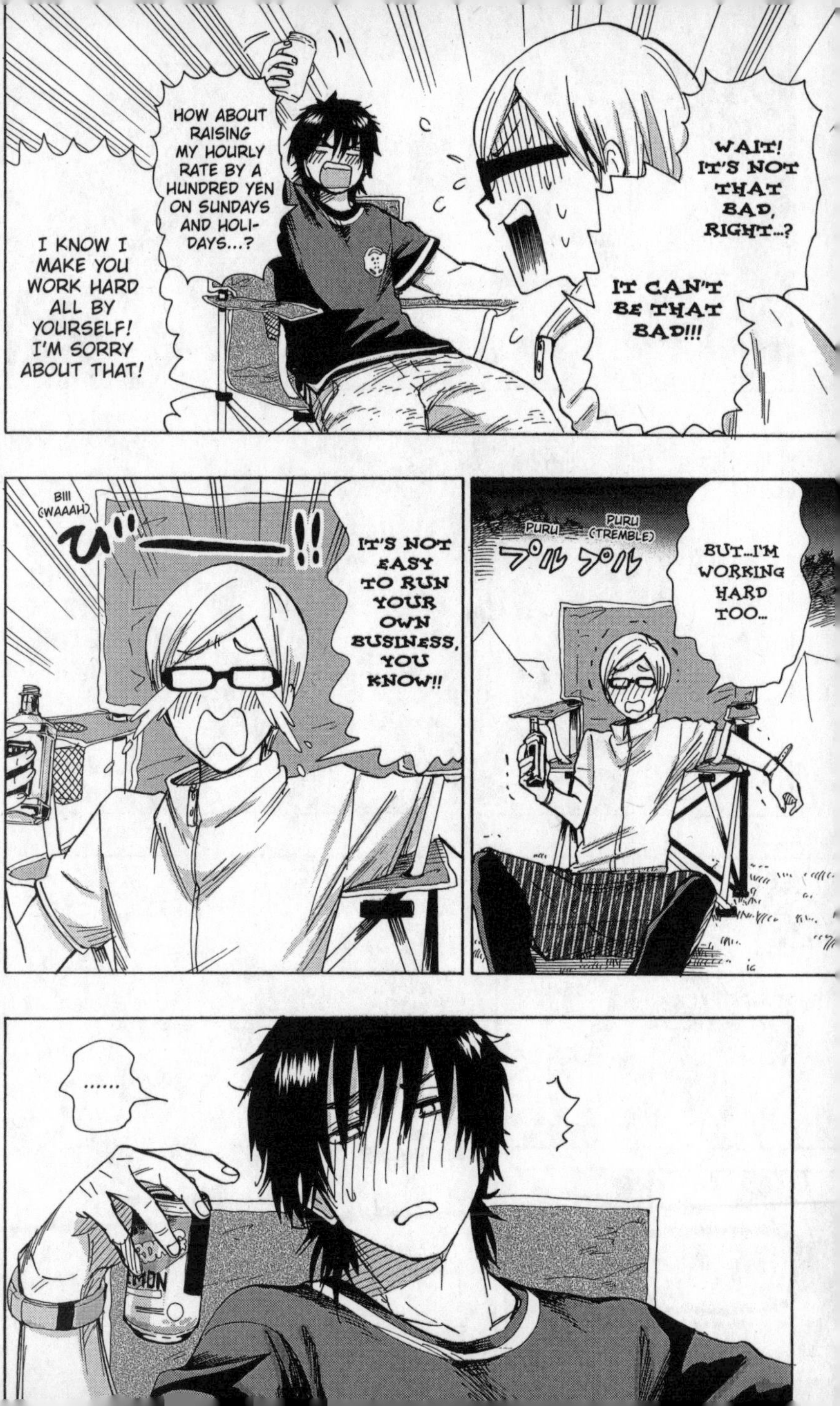
WAIT! IT'S NOT THAT BAD, RIGHT...?
IT CAN'T BE THAT BAD!!!
HOW ABOUT RAISING MY HOURLY RATE BY A HUNDRED YEN ON SUNDAYS AND HOLI-DAYS...?
I KNOW I MAKE YOU WORK HARD ALL BY YOURSELF! I'M SORRY ABOUT THAT!
PURU PURU (TREMBLE)
プル プル
BUT...I'M WORKING HARD TOO...
BIII (WAAAH)
IT'S NOT EASY TO RUN YOUR OWN BUSINESS, YOU KNOW!!
......

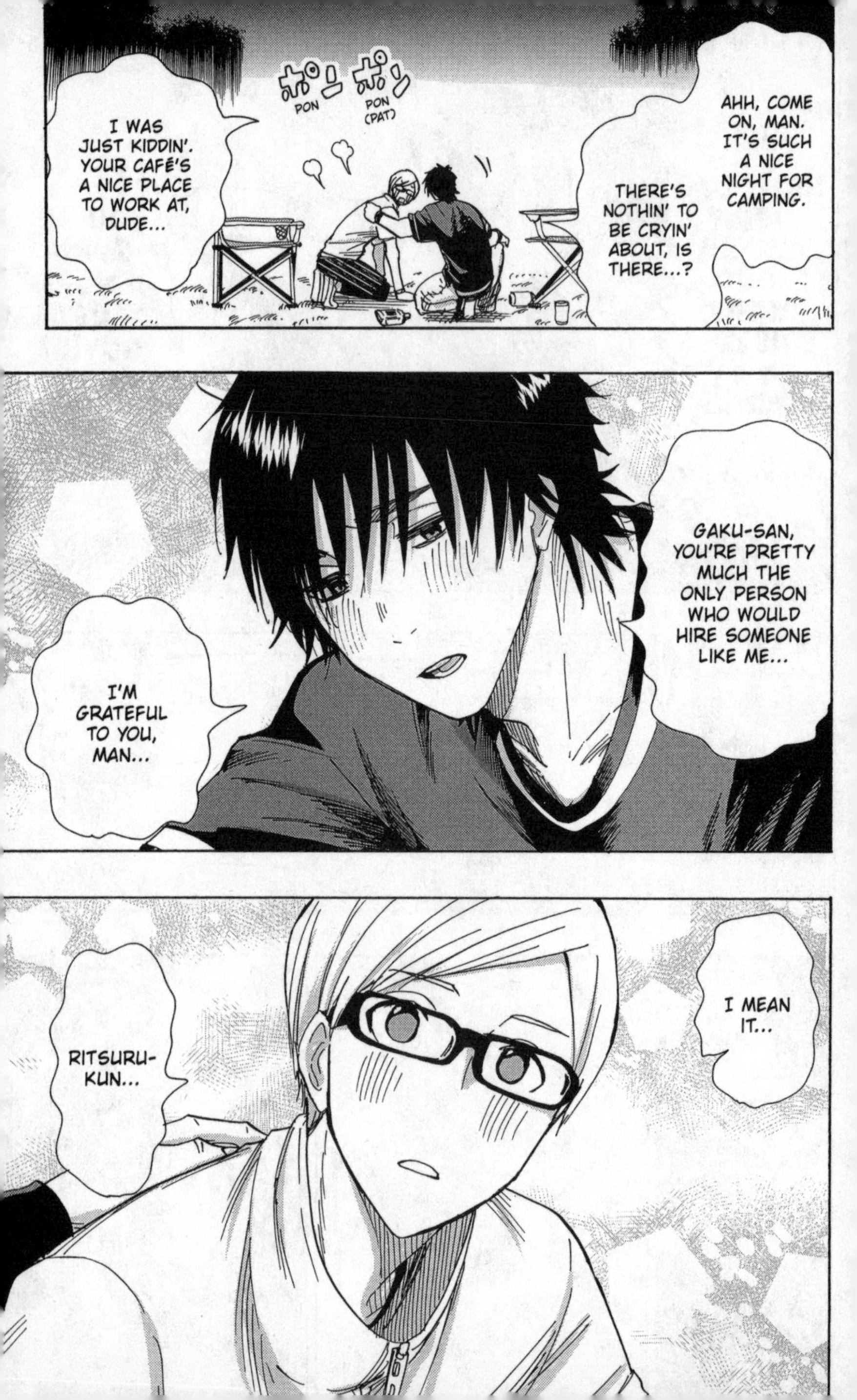
AHH, COME ON, MAN. IT'S SUCH A NICE NIGHT FOR CAMPING.
THERE'S NOTHIN' TO BE CRYIN' ABOUT, IS THERE...?
PON (PAT)
PON
I WAS JUST KIDDIN'. YOUR CAFÉ'S A NICE PLACE TO WORK AT, DUDE...
GAKU-SAN, YOU'RE PRETTY MUCH THE ONLY PERSON WHO WOULD HIRE SOMEONE LIKE ME...
I'M GRATEFUL TO YOU, MAN...
I MEAN IT...
RITSURU-KUN...

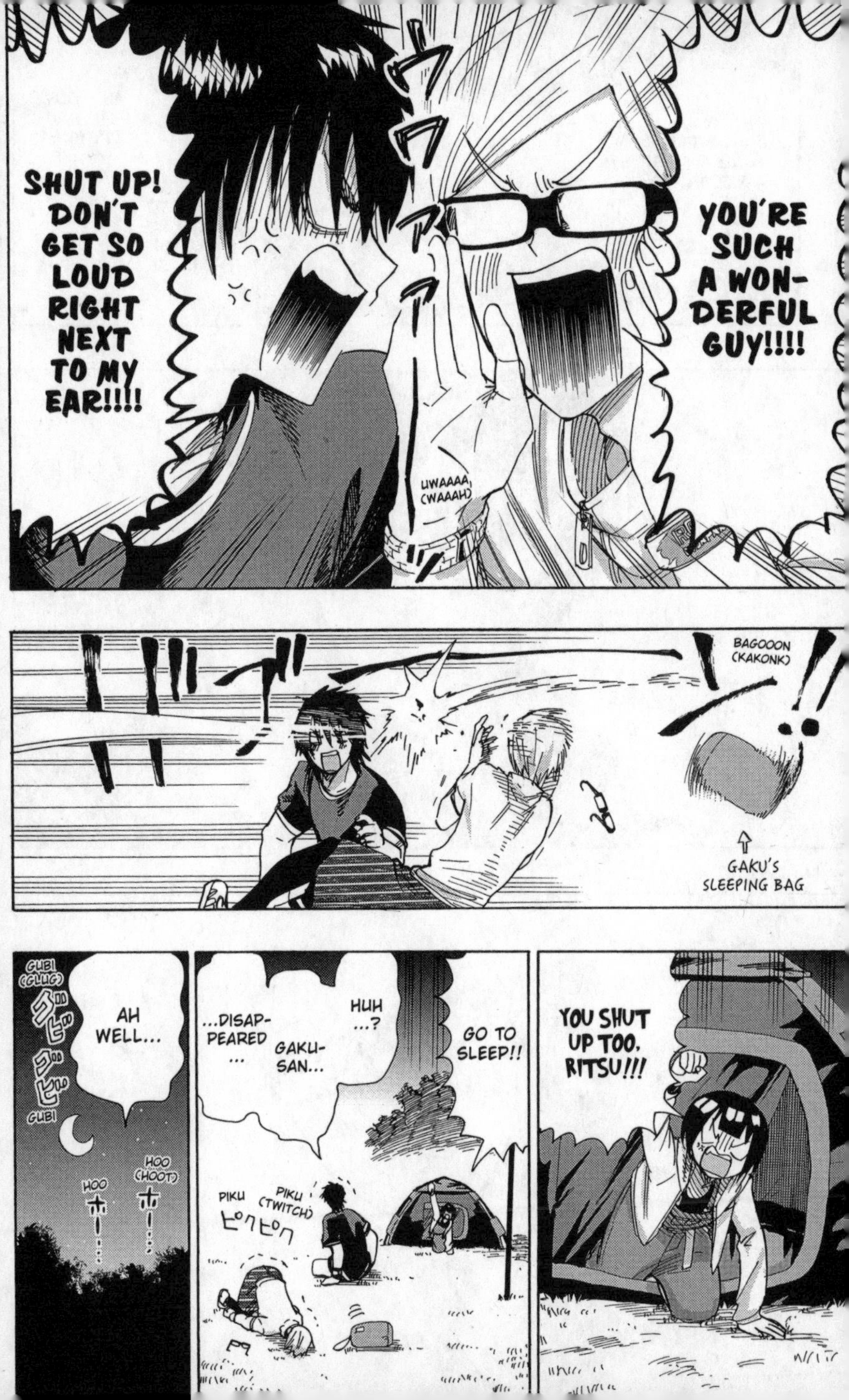
YOU'RE SUCH A WON-DERFUL GUY!!!!
SHUT UP! DON'T GET SO LOUD RIGHT NEXT TO MY EAR!!!!
UWAAAA (WAAAH)
BAGOOON (KAKONK)
GAKU'S SLEEPING BAG
YOU SHUT UP TOO, RITSU!!!
GO TO SLEEP!!
HUH ...?
GAKU-SAN...
...DISAP-PEARED ...
PIKU PIKU (TWITCH)
GUBI (GLUG) GUBI
AH WELL...
HOO (HOOT) HOO

Days on Fes

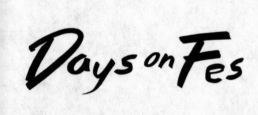

Days on Fes

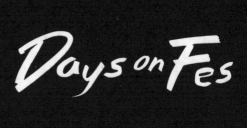

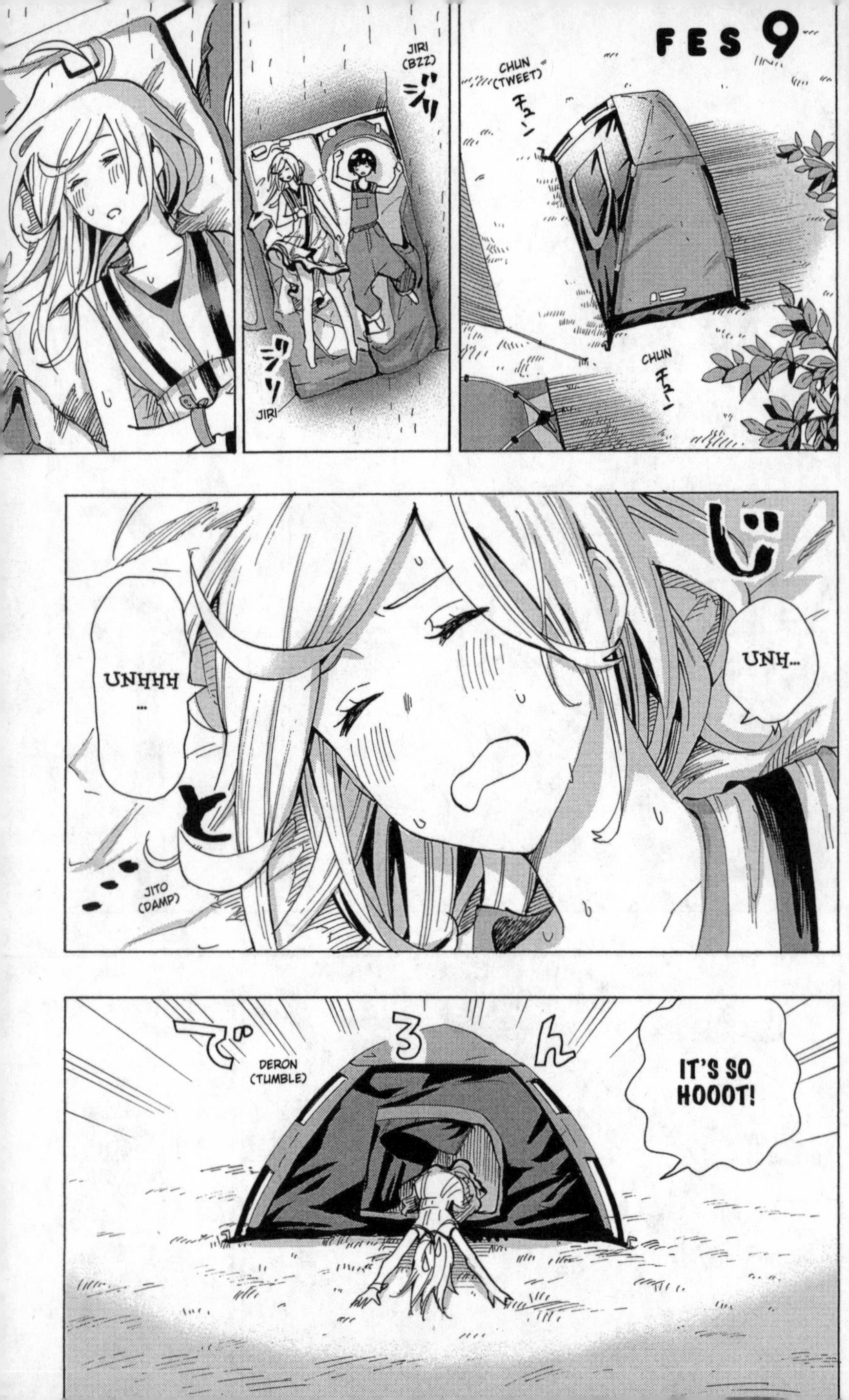
FES 9
CHUN (TWEET)
チュン
CHUN
チュン
JIRI (BZZ)
ジリ
ジリ
JIRI
じ
UNH...
UNHHH...
と
JITO (DAMP)
IT'S SO HOOOT!
でろん
DERON (TUMBLE)

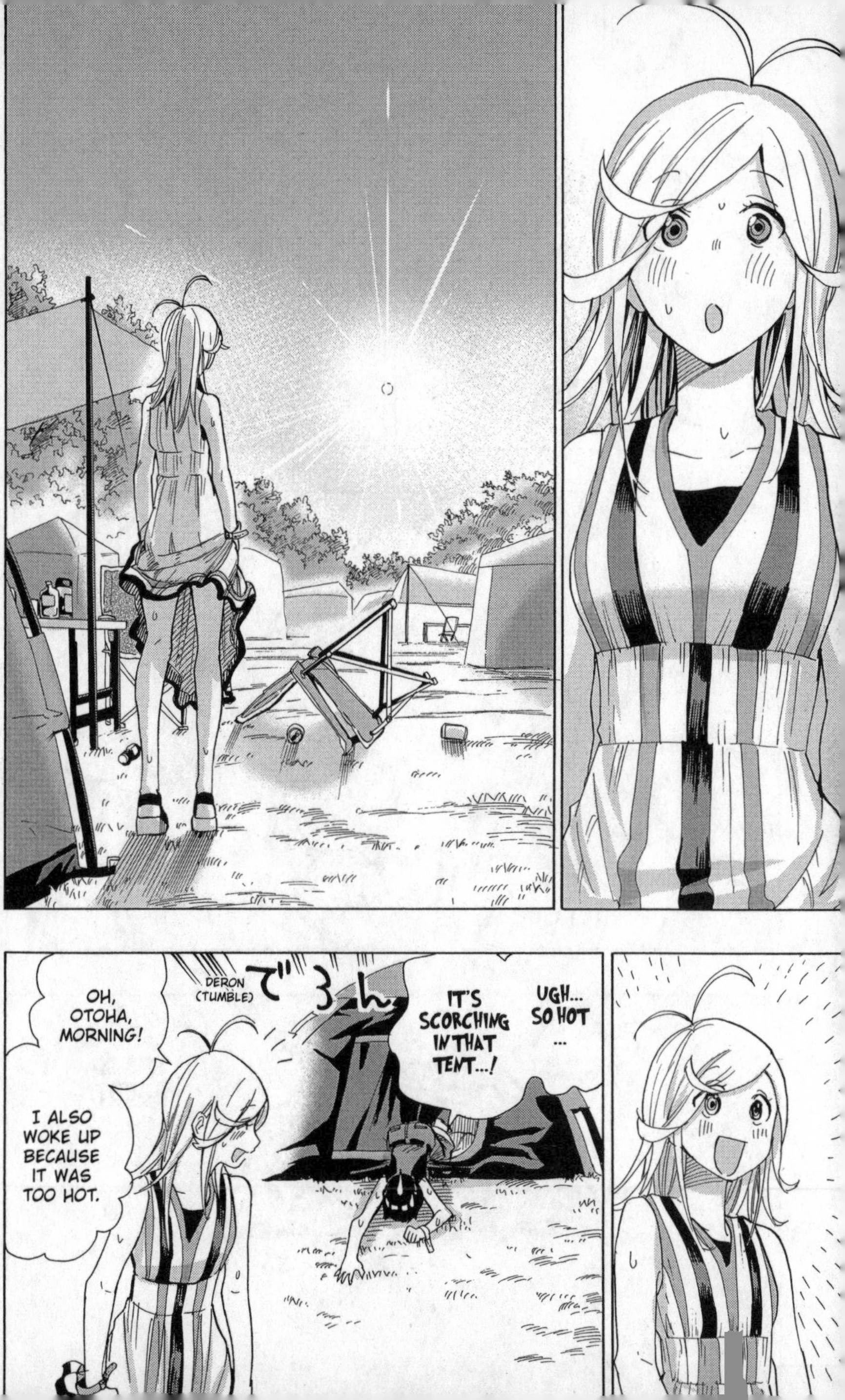
UGH... SO HOT ...
IT'S SCORCHING IN THAT TENT...!
DERON (TUMBLE)
でろん
OH, OTOHA, MORNING!
I ALSO WOKE UP BECAUSE IT WAS TOO HOT.

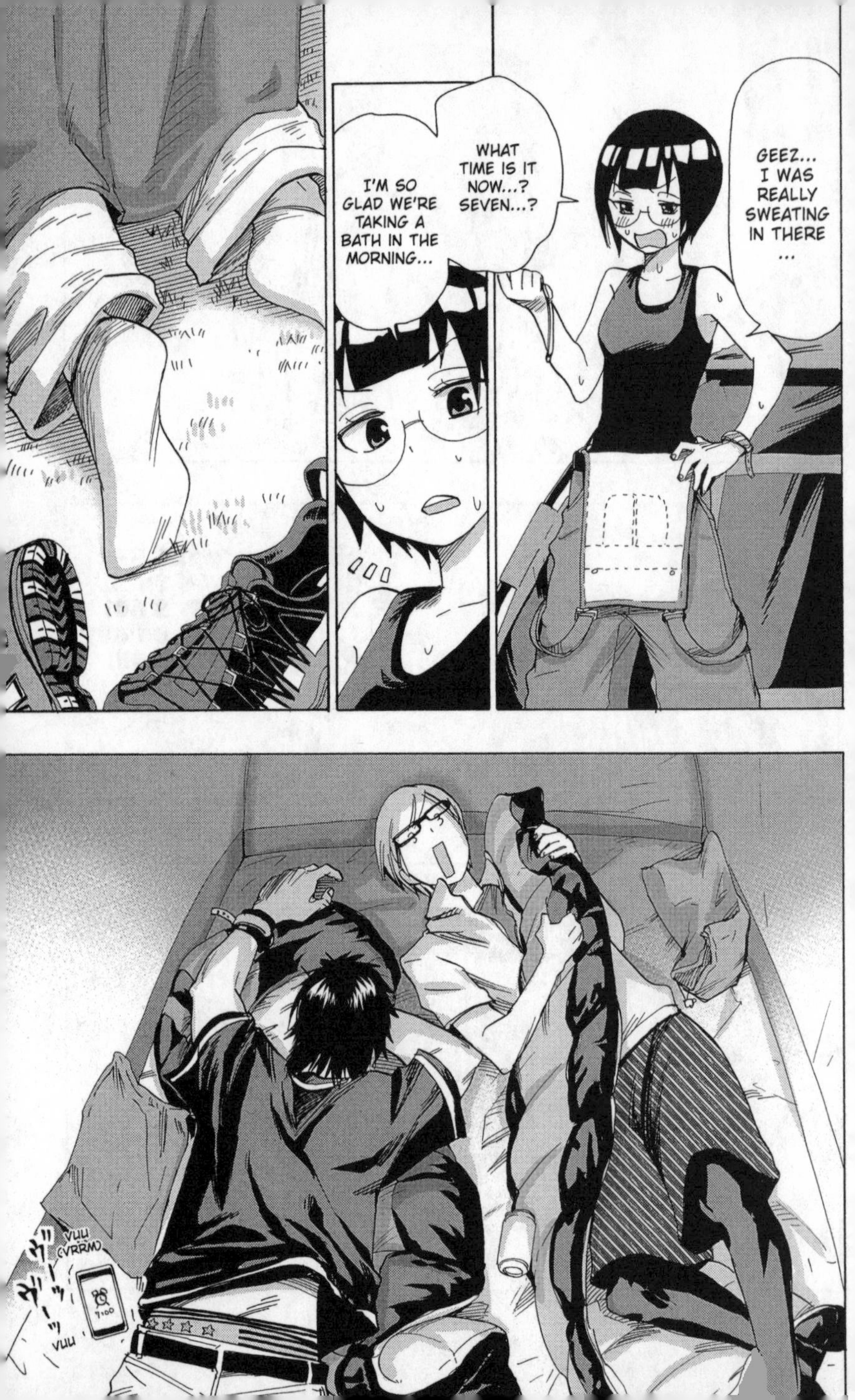
GEEZ... I WAS REALLY SWEATING IN THERE ...
WHAT TIME IS IT NOW...? SEVEN...?
I'M SO GLAD WE'RE TAKING A BATH IN THE MORNING...
VUU (VRRM)
VUU

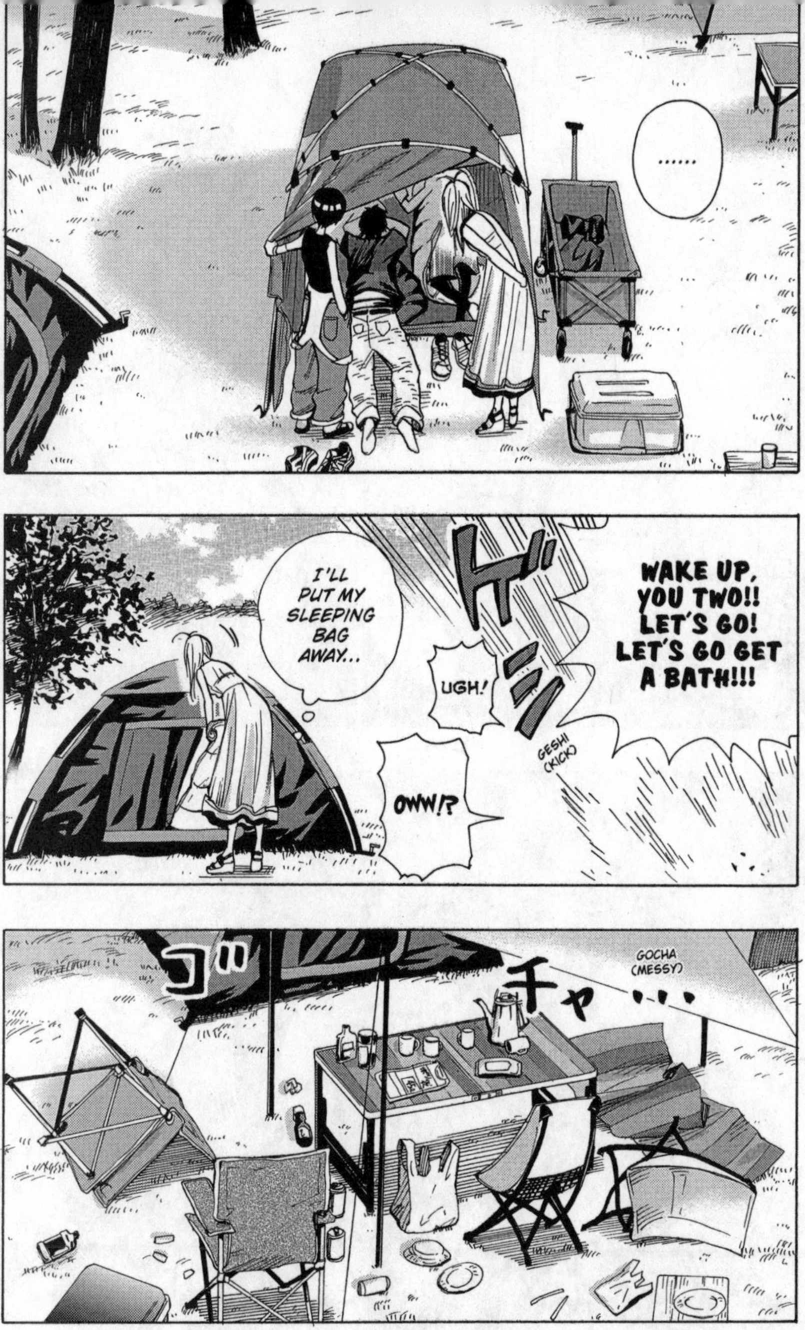
......
WAKE UP, YOU TWO!! LET'S GO! LET'S GO GET A BATH!!!
GESHI (KICK)
UGH!
OWW!?
I'LL PUT MY SLEEPING BAG AWAY...
GOCHA (MESSY)

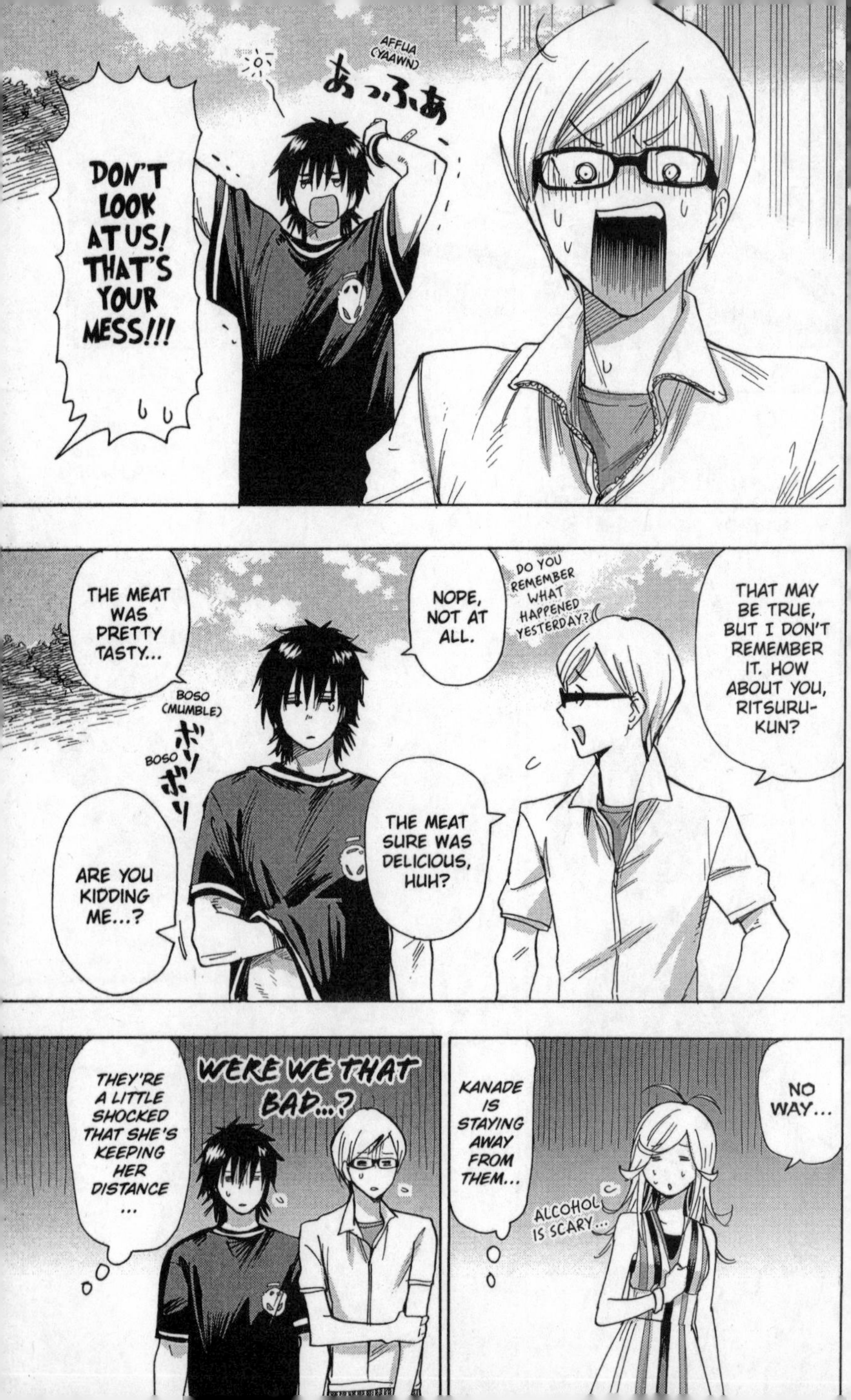
AFFUA (YAAWN)
あっふあ
DON'T LOOK AT US! THAT'S YOUR MESS!!!
THAT MAY BE TRUE, BUT I DON'T REMEMBER IT. HOW ABOUT YOU, RITSURU-KUN?
DO YOU REMEMBER WHAT HAPPENED YESTERDAY?
NOPE, NOT AT ALL.
THE MEAT WAS PRETTY TASTY...
BOSO (MUMBLE)
BOSO
ボソボソ
THE MEAT SURE WAS DELICIOUS, HUH?
ARE YOU KIDDING ME...?
NO WAY...
KANADE IS STAYING AWAY FROM THEM...
ALCOHOL IS SCARY...
WERE WE THAT BAD...?
THEY'RE A LITTLE SHOCKED THAT SHE'S KEEPING HER DISTANCE ...

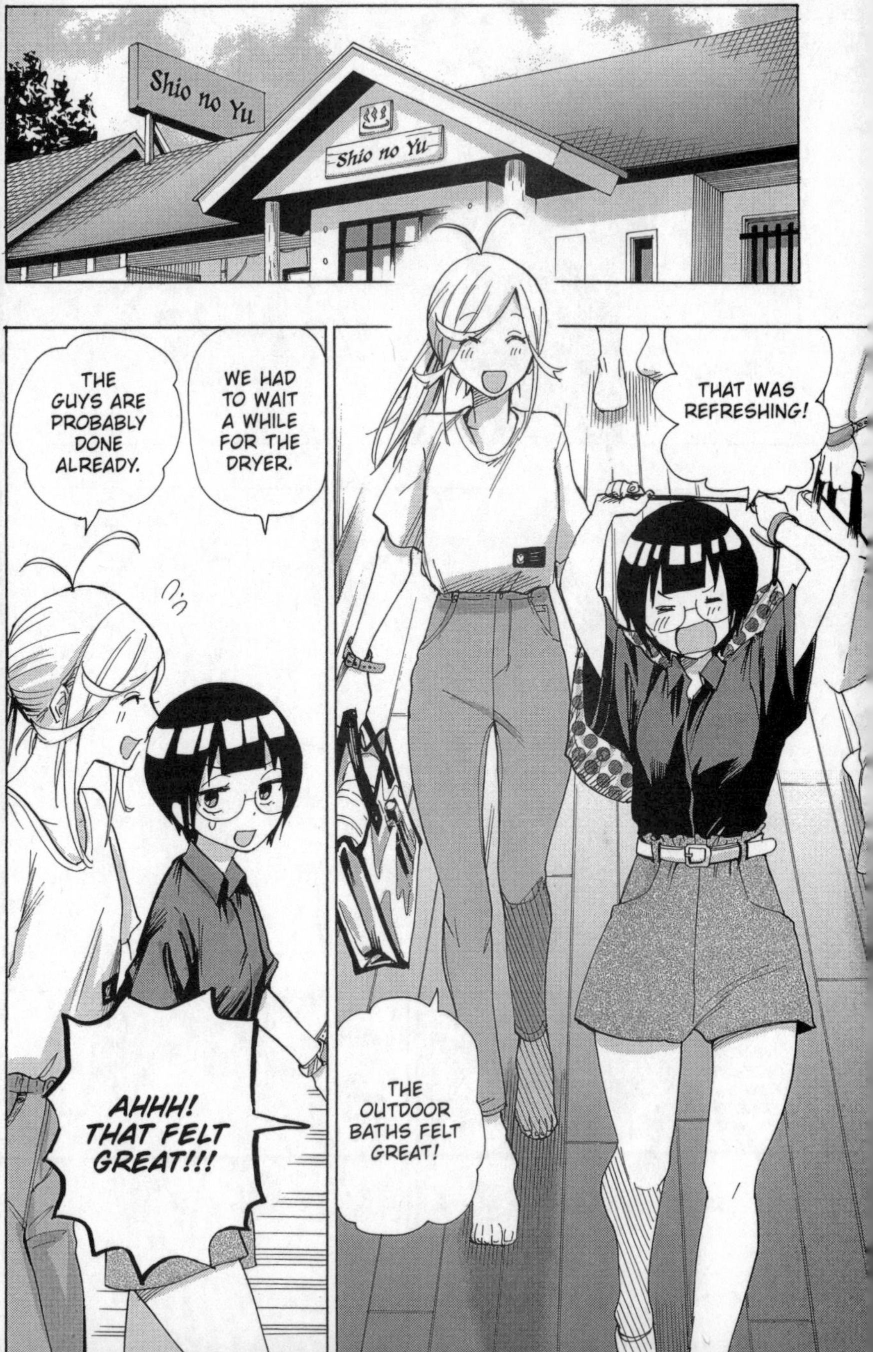
Shio no Yu
Shio no Yu
THAT WAS REFRESHING!
THE OUTDOOR BATHS FELT GREAT!
WE HAD TO WAIT A WHILE FOR THE DRYER.
THE GUYS ARE PROBABLY DONE ALREADY.
AHHH! THAT FELT GREAT!!!

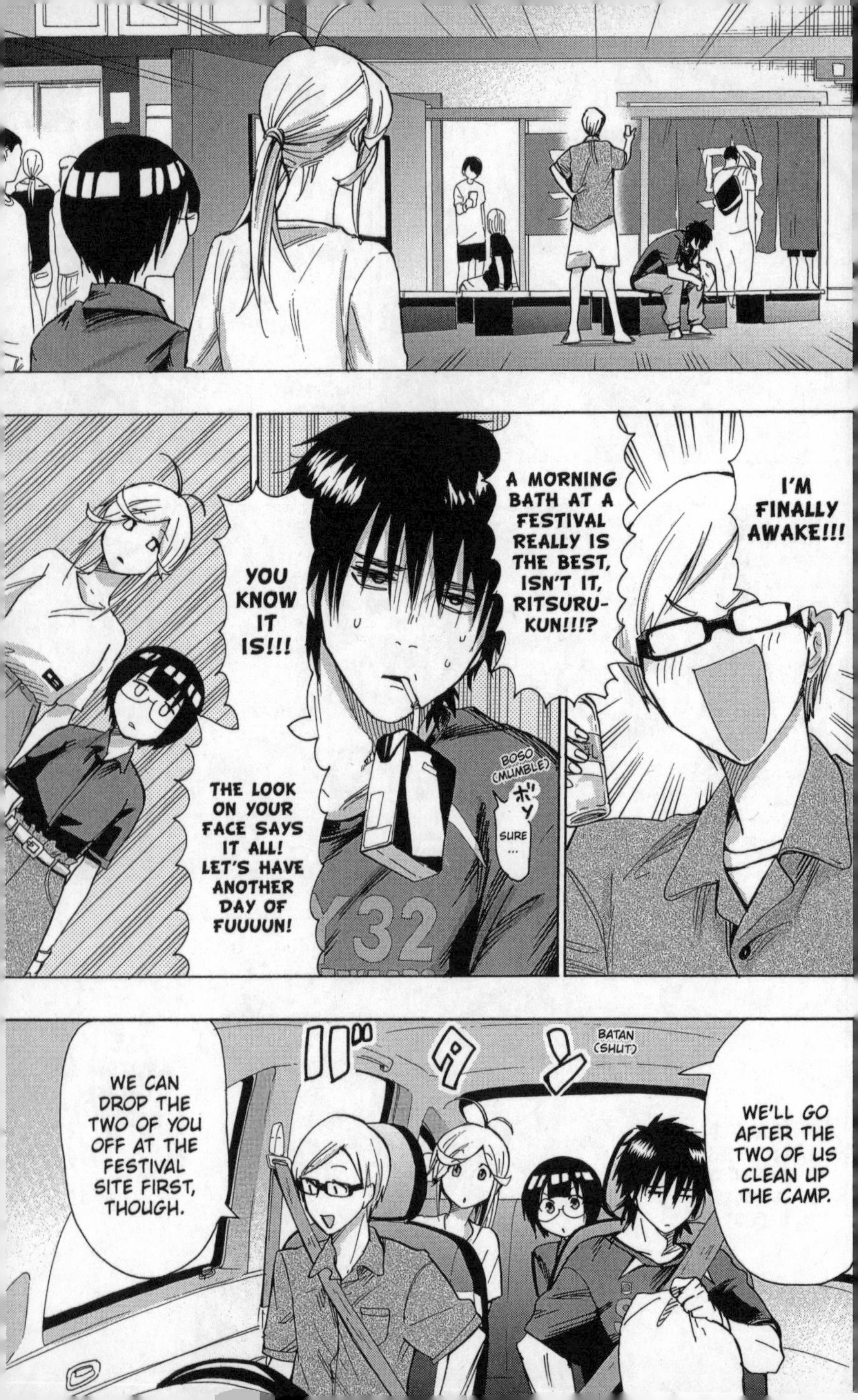
I'M FINALLY AWAKE!!!
A MORNING BATH AT A FESTIVAL REALLY IS THE BEST, ISN'T IT, RITSURU-KUN!!!?
BOSO (MUMBLE)
ボソ
SURE...
YOU KNOW IT IS!!!
THE LOOK ON YOUR FACE SAYS IT ALL! LET'S HAVE ANOTHER DAY OF FUUUUN!
バタン
BATAN (SHUT)
WE'LL GO AFTER THE TWO OF US CLEAN UP THE CAMP.
WE CAN DROP THE TWO OF YOU OFF AT THE FESTIVAL SITE FIRST, THOUGH.

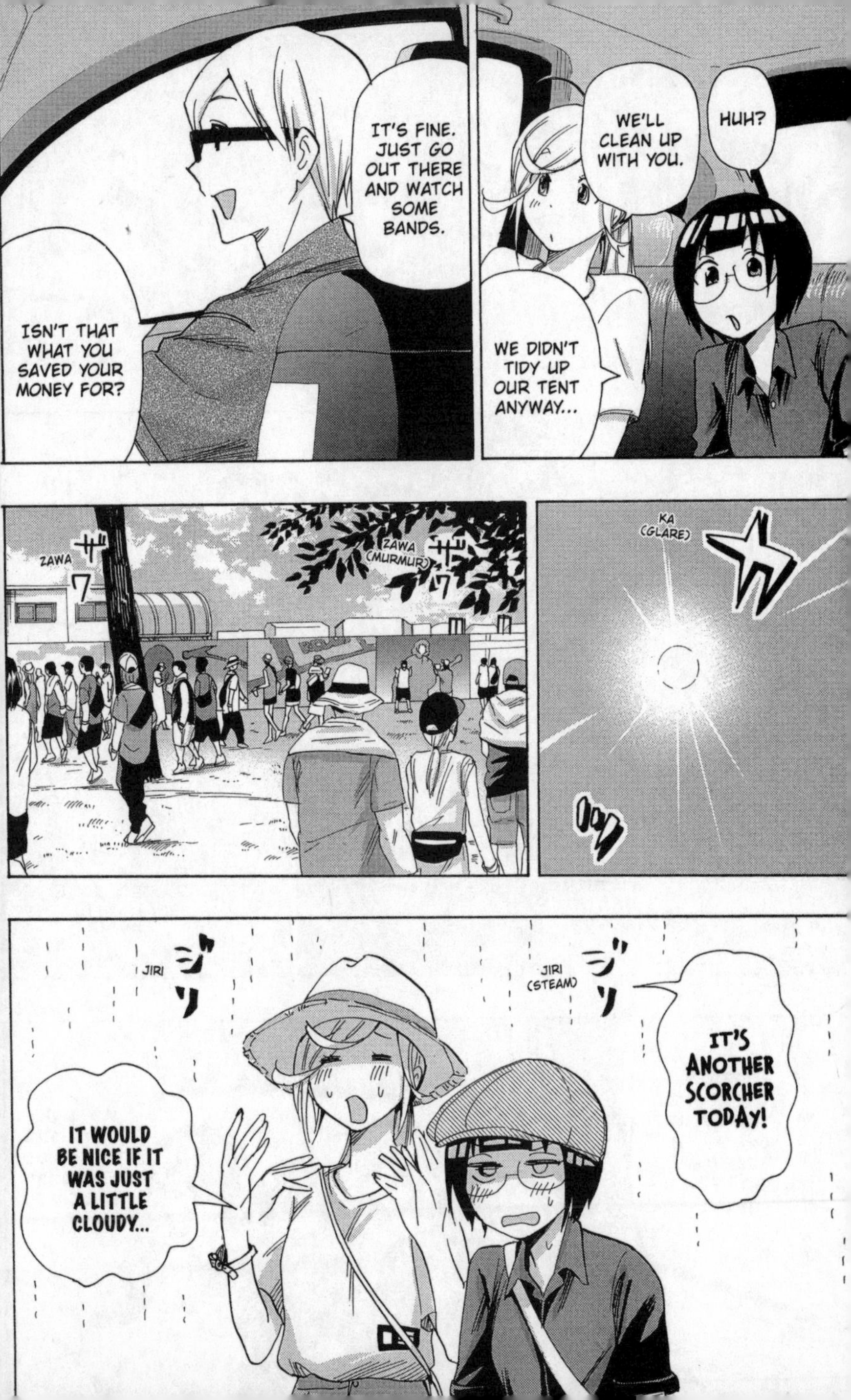
HUH?
WE'LL CLEAN UP WITH YOU.
WE DIDN'T TIDY UP OUR TENT ANYWAY...
IT'S FINE. JUST GO OUT THERE AND WATCH SOME BANDS.
ISN'T THAT WHAT YOU SAVED YOUR MONEY FOR?
KA (GLARE)
ZAWA (MURMUR)
ZAWA
JIRI (STEAM)
IT'S ANOTHER SCORCHER TODAY!
JIRI
IT WOULD BE NICE IF IT WAS JUST A LITTLE CLOUDY...

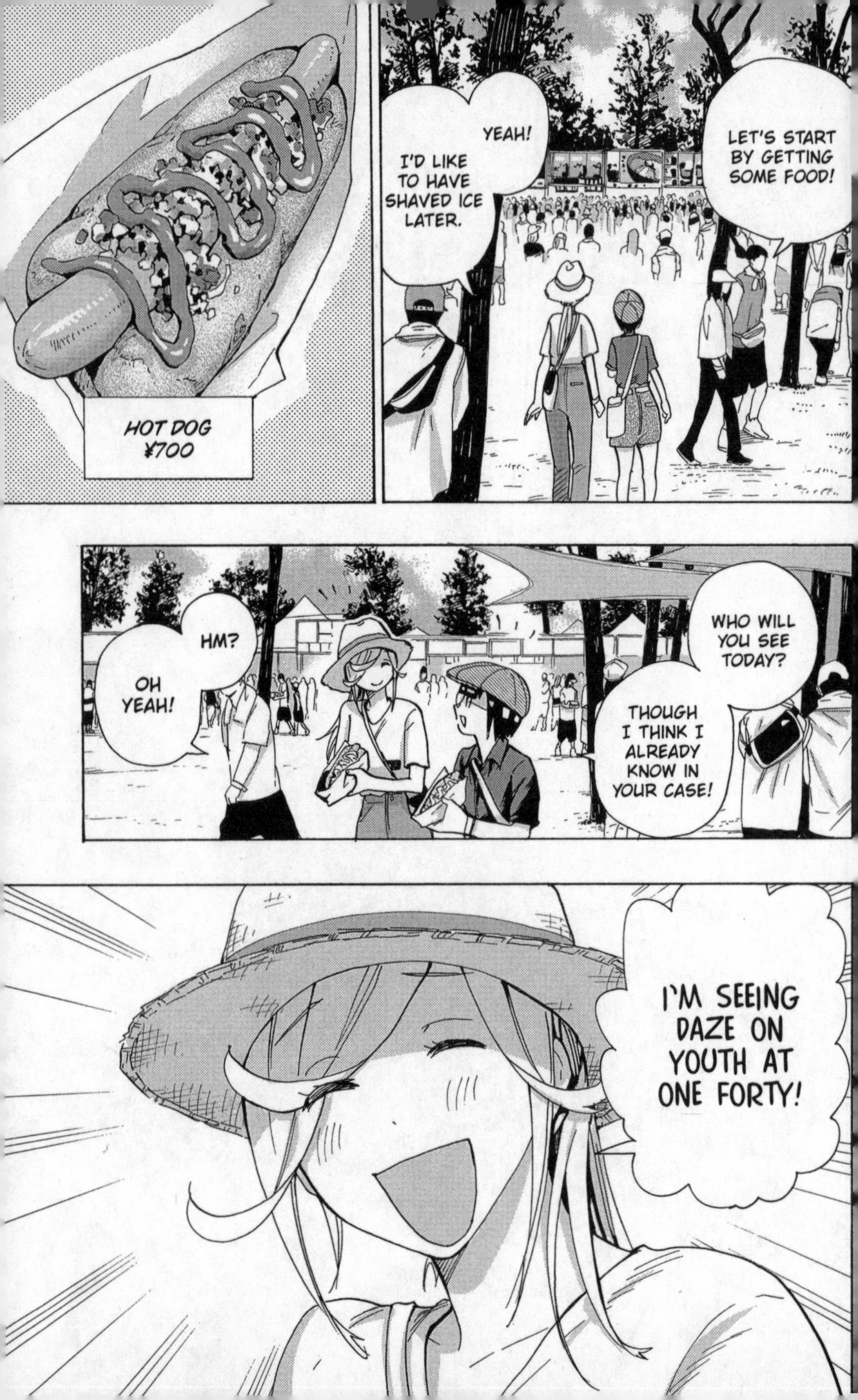
LET'S START BY GETTING SOME FOOD!
YEAH!
I'D LIKE TO HAVE SHAVED ICE LATER.
HOT DOG ¥700
WHO WILL YOU SEE TODAY?
THOUGH I THINK I ALREADY KNOW IN YOUR CASE!
HM?
OH YEAH!
I'M SEEING DAZE ON YOUTH AT ONE FORTY!

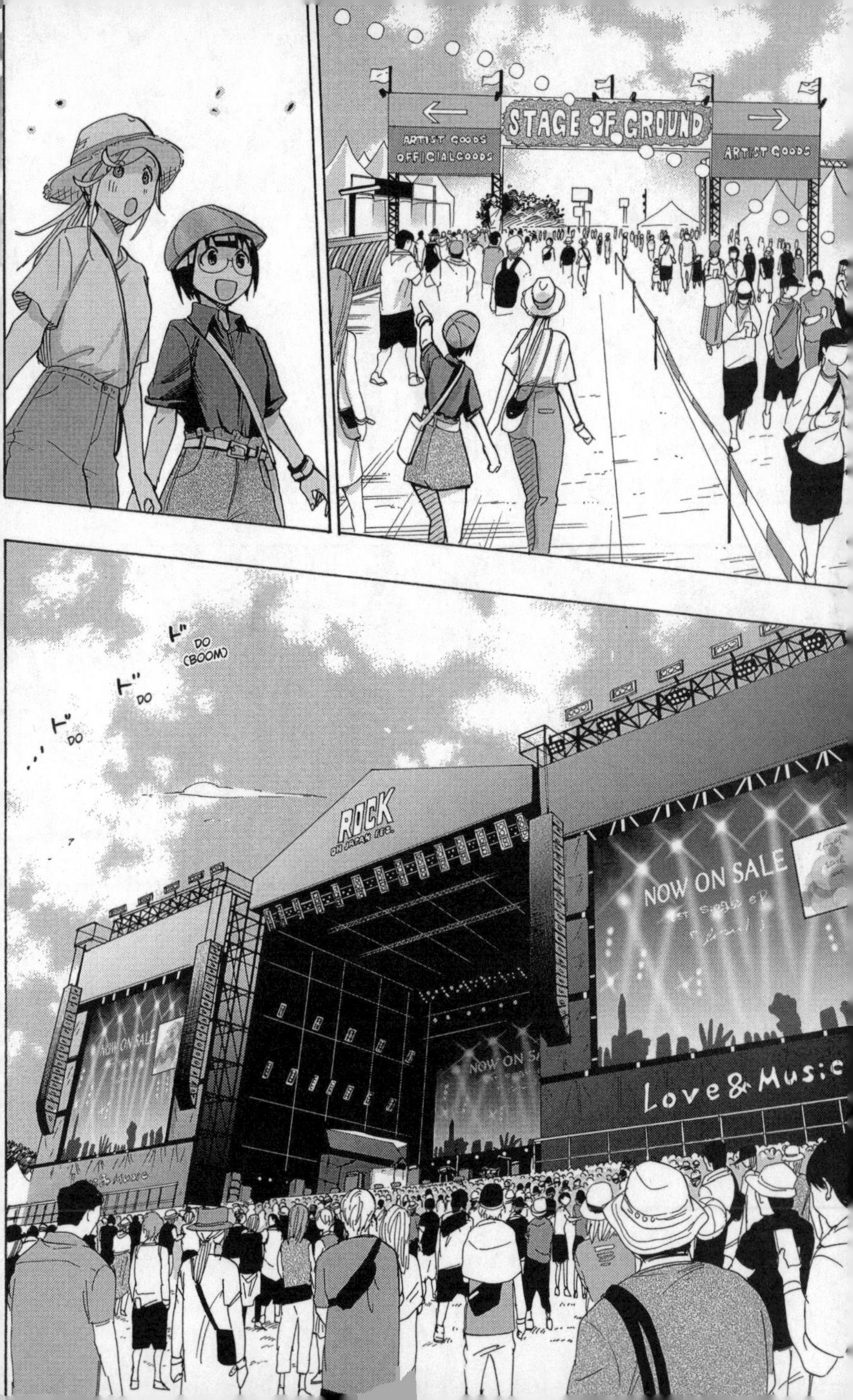
STAGE OF GROUND
ARTIST GOODS
ARTIST GOODS
OFFICIAL GOODS
ド DO (BOOM)
ド DO
ド DO
ROCK ON JAPAN FES.
NOW ON SALE
NOW ON SALE
NOW ON SA
Love & Music

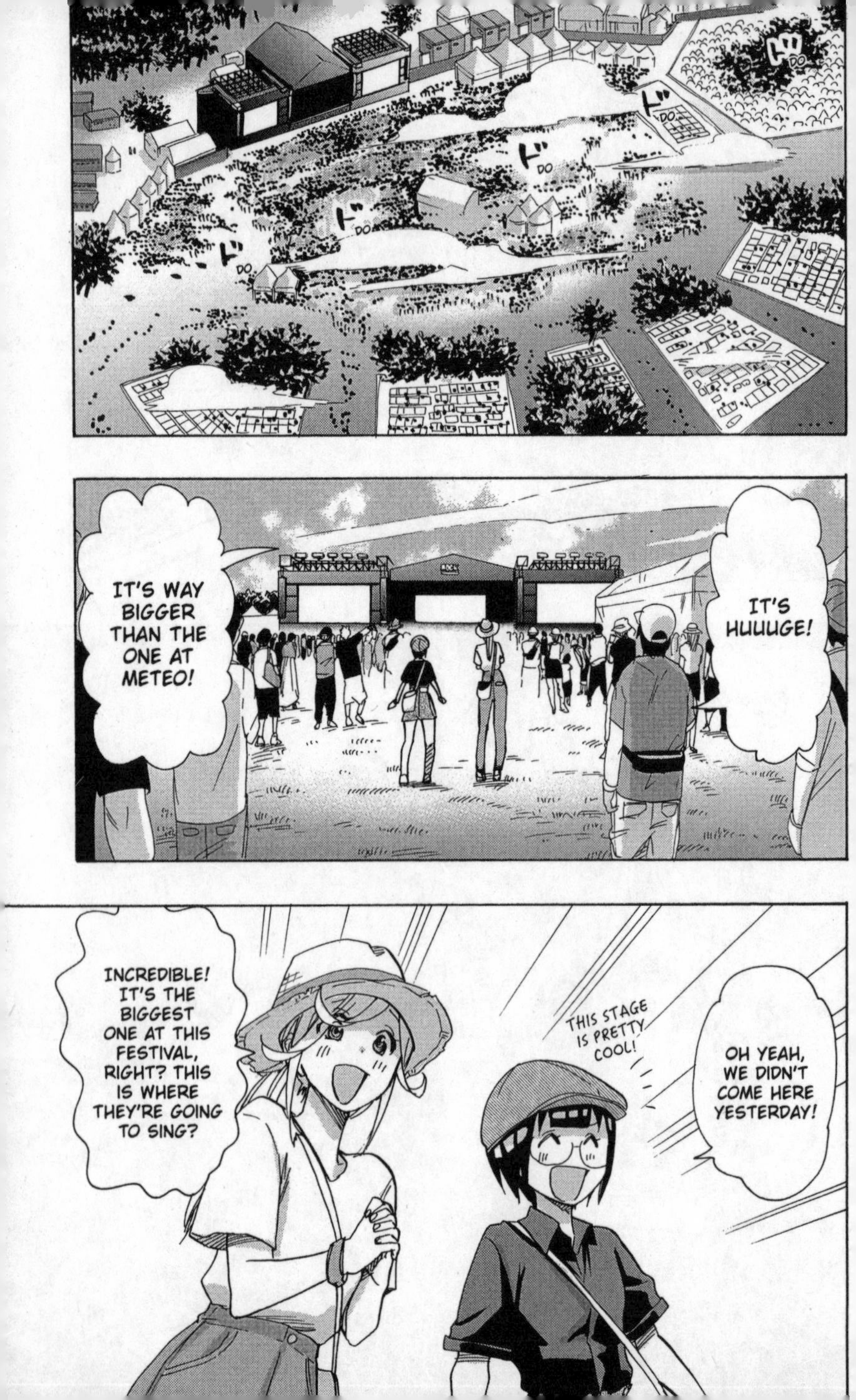
ドド DO
ド DO
ド DO
ド DO
ド DO
IT'S HUUUGE!
IT'S WAY BIGGER THAN THE ONE AT METEO!
OH YEAH, WE DIDN'T COME HERE YESTERDAY!
THIS STAGE IS PRETTY COOL!
INCREDIBLE! IT'S THE BIGGEST ONE AT THIS FESTIVAL, RIGHT? THIS IS WHERE THEY'RE GOING TO SING?

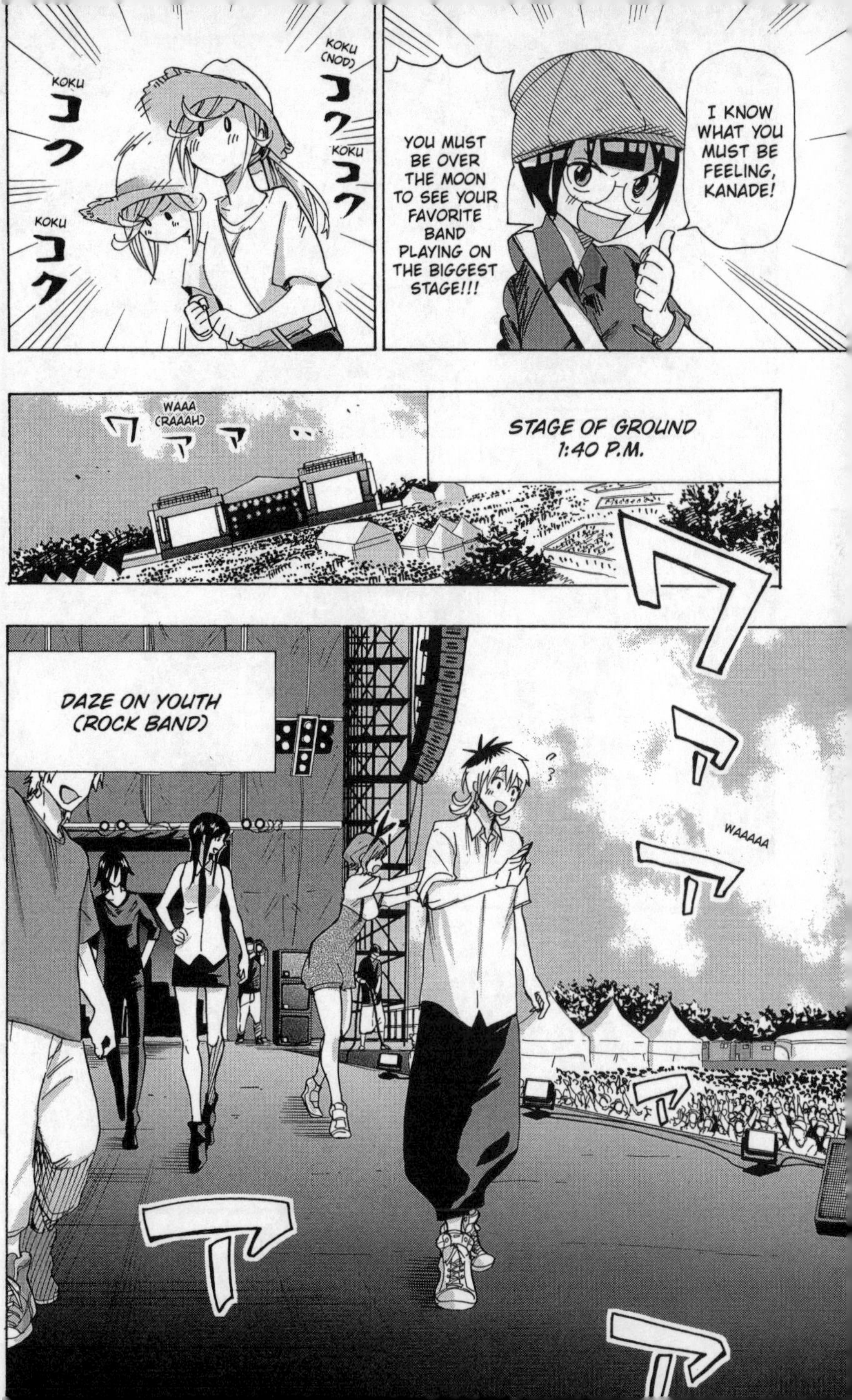
I KNOW WHAT YOU MUST BE FEELING, KANADE!
YOU MUST BE OVER THE MOON TO SEE YOUR FAVORITE BAND PLAYING ON THE BIGGEST STAGE!!!
KOKU (NOD)
コク
KOKU
コク
KOKU
コク
KOKU
コク
STAGE OF GROUND 1:40 P.M.
WAAA (RAAAH)
ワァァ..
DAZE ON YOUTH (ROCK BAND)
WAAAAA
ワァァァァ

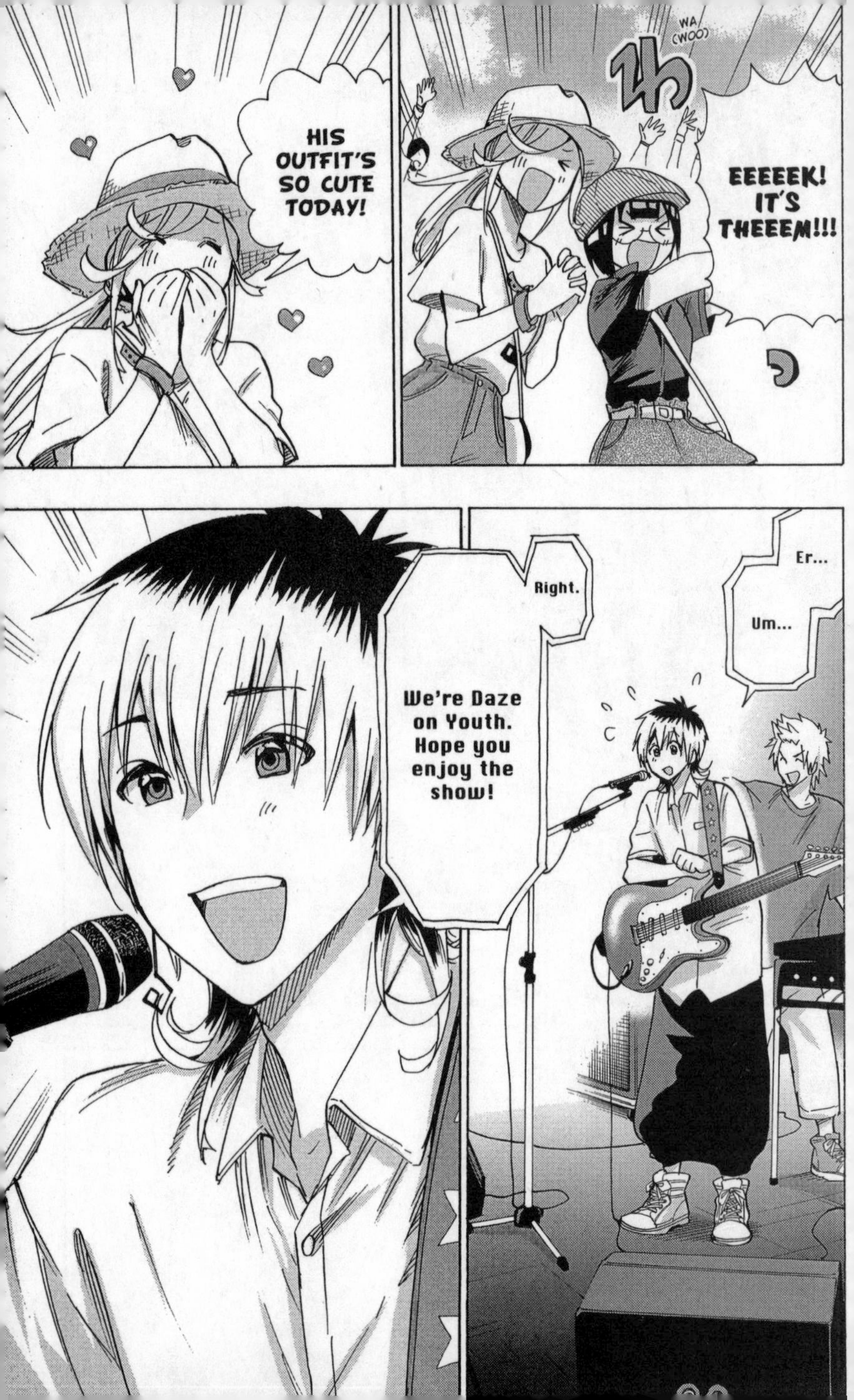
WA (WOO)
EEEEEK! IT'S THEEEM!!!
HIS OUTFIT'S SO CUTE TODAY!
Er...
Um...
Right.
We're Daze on Youth. Hope you enjoy the show!

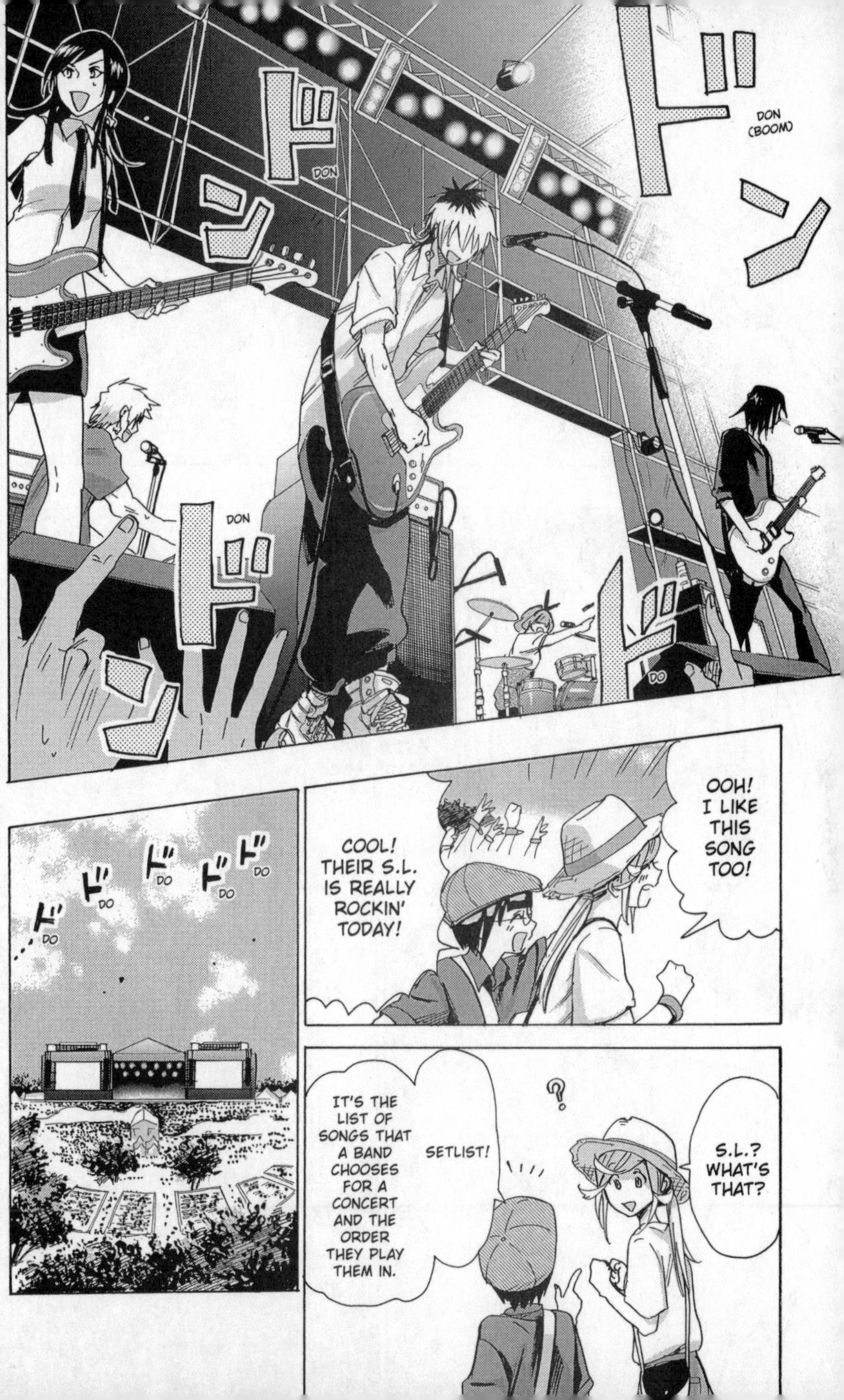
ドン
DON (BOOM)
ドン
DON
ド
DO
ドン
DON
OOH! I LIKE THIS SONG TOO!
COOL! THEIR S.L. IS REALLY ROCKIN' TODAY!
ド DO ド DO ド DO ド DO
S.L.? WHAT'S THAT?
?
SETLIST!
IT'S THE LIST OF SONGS THAT A BAND CHOOSES FOR A CONCERT AND THE ORDER THEY PLAY THEM IN.

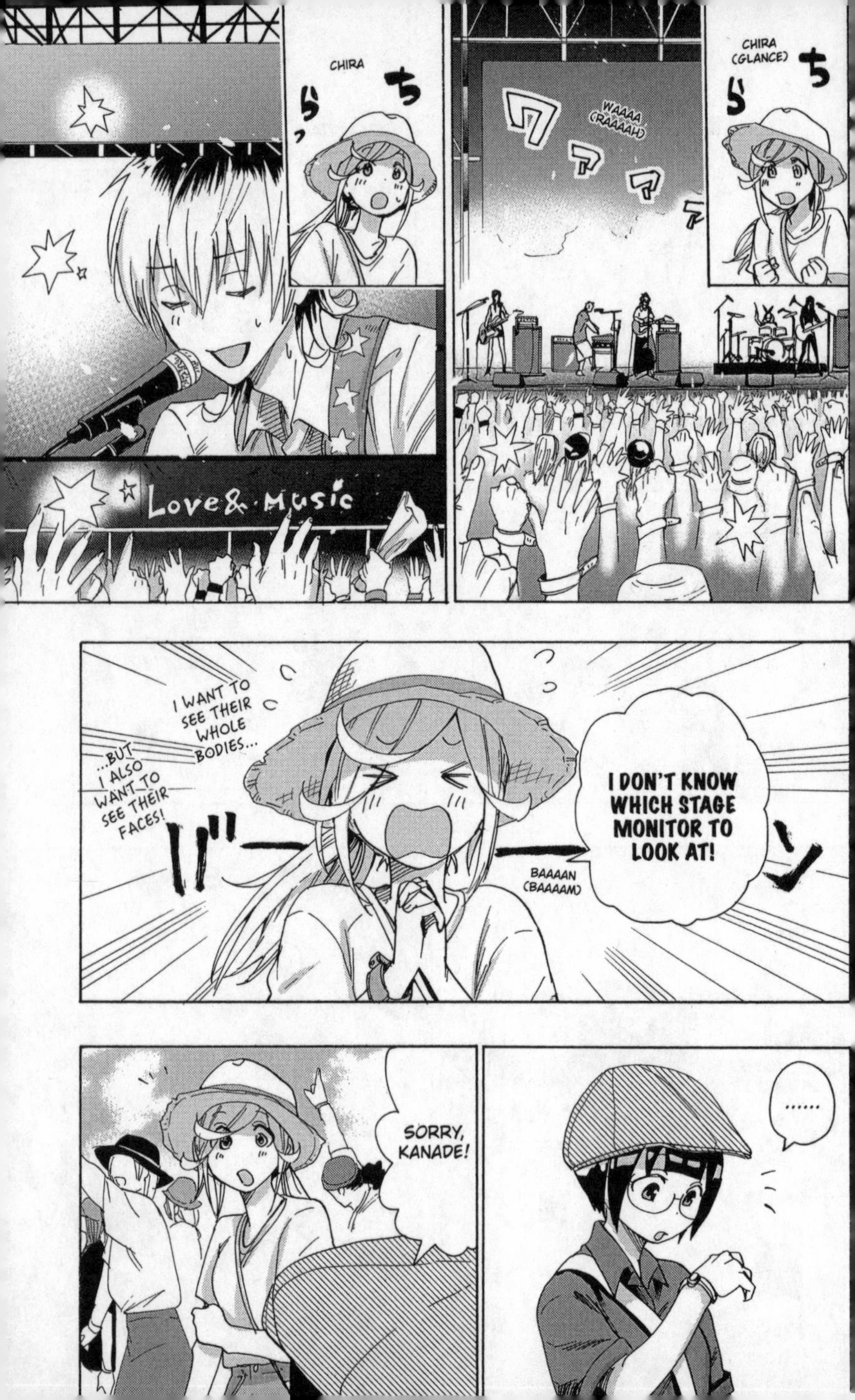

CHIRA (GLANCE)
WAAAA (RAAAAH)
CHIRA
Love & Music
I DON'T KNOW WHICH STAGE MONITOR TO LOOK AT!
I WANT TO SEE THEIR WHOLE BODIES...
...BUT I ALSO WANT TO SEE THEIR FACES!
BAAAAN (BAAAAM)
......
SORRY, KANADE!

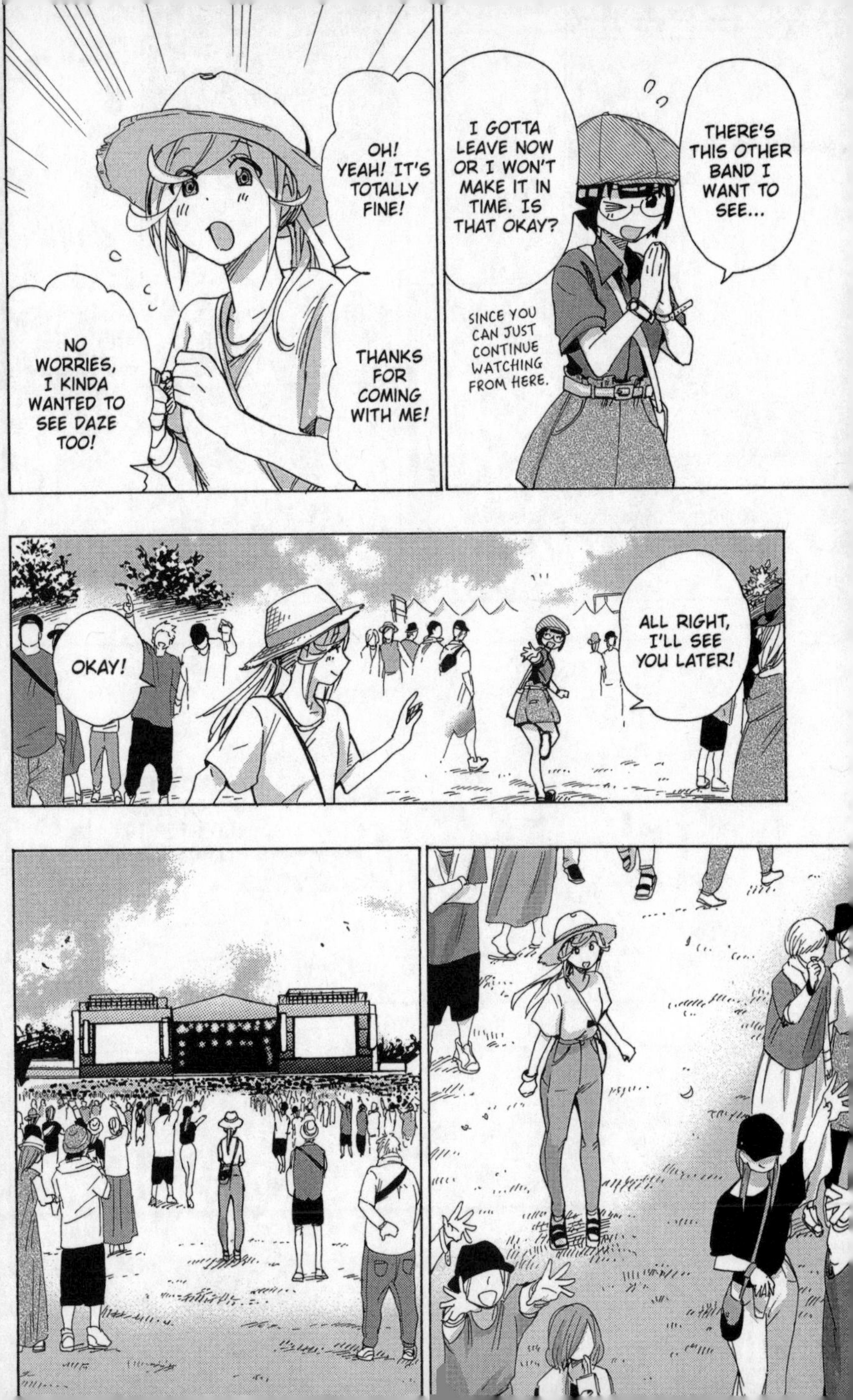
THERE'S THIS OTHER BAND I WANT TO SEE...
I GOTTA LEAVE NOW OR I WON'T MAKE IT IN TIME. IS THAT OKAY?
SINCE YOU CAN JUST CONTINUE WATCHING FROM HERE.
OH! YEAH! IT'S TOTALLY FINE!
THANKS FOR COMING WITH ME!
NO WORRIES, I KINDA WANTED TO SEE DAZE TOO!
ALL RIGHT, I'LL SEE YOU LATER!
OKAY!

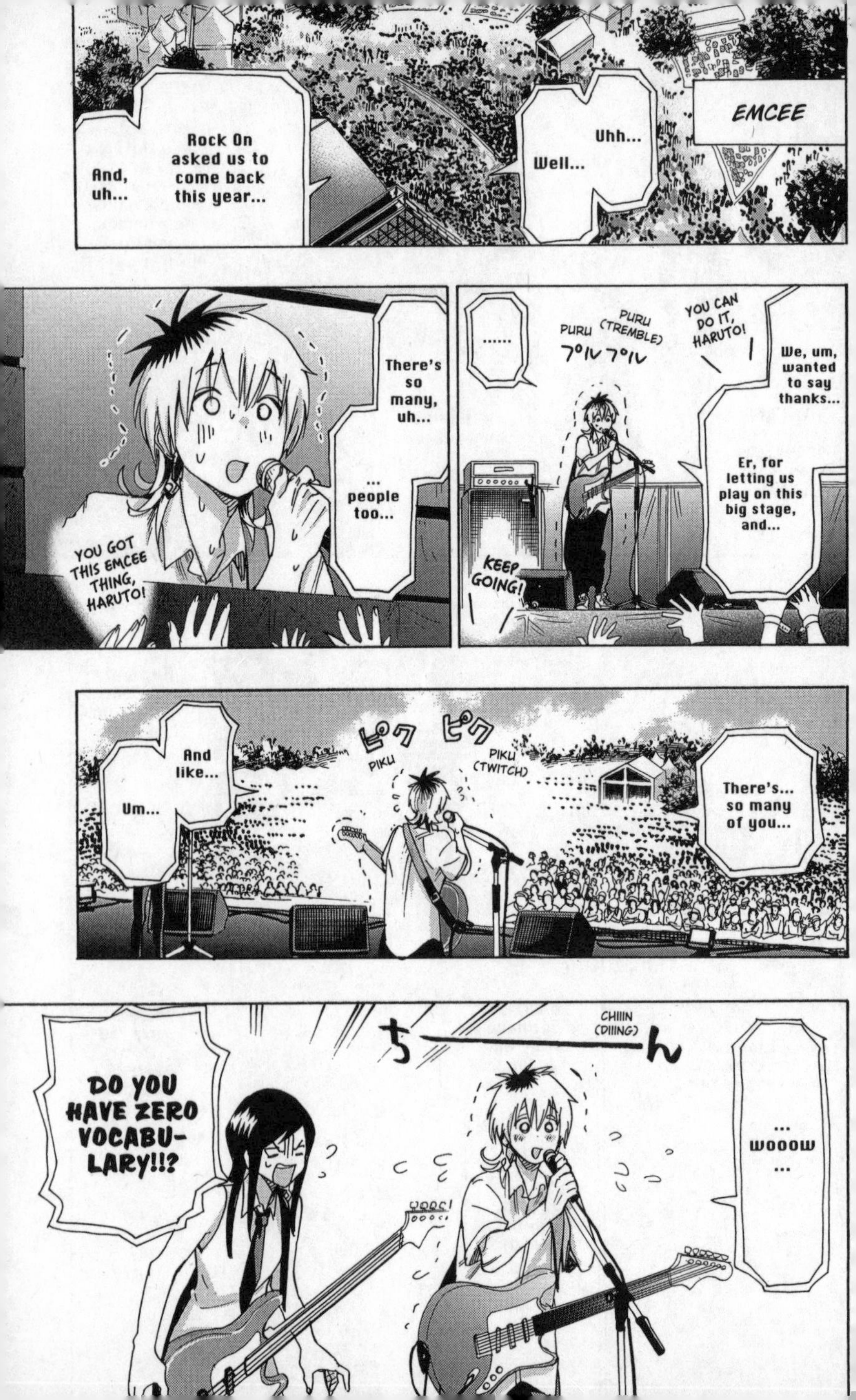
EMCEE
Uhh... Well...
And, uh... Rock On asked us to come back this year...
We, um, wanted to say thanks... Er, for letting us play on this big stage, and...
YOU CAN DO IT, HARUTO!
プルプル
PURU PURU (TREMBLE)
......
KEEP GOING!
There's so many, uh... ... people too...
YOU GOT THIS EMCEE THING, HARUTO!
There's... so many of you...
ピクピク
PIKU PIKU (TWITCH)
And like... Um...
... wooow ...
ち――ん
CHIIIN (DIIING)
DO YOU HAVE ZERO VOCABULARY!!!?

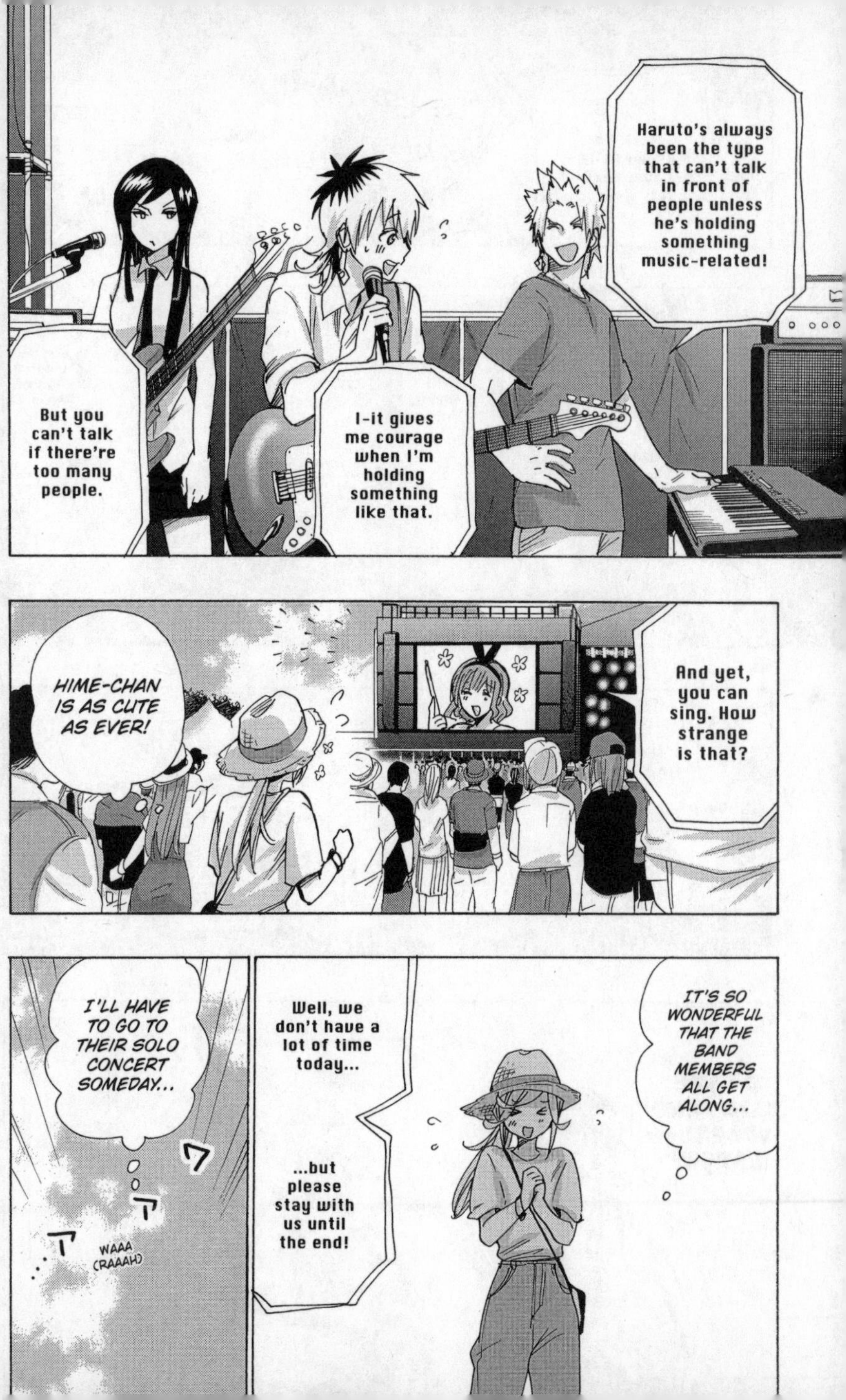
Haruto's always been the type that can't talk in front of people unless he's holding something music-related!
I-it gives me courage when I'm holding something like that.
But you can't talk if there're too many people.
And yet, you can sing. How strange is that?
HIME-CHAN IS AS CUTE AS EVER!
IT'S SO WONDERFUL THAT THE BAND MEMBERS ALL GET ALONG...
Well, we don't have a lot of time today...
...but please stay with us until the end!
I'LL HAVE TO GO TO THEIR SOLO CONCERT SOMEDAY...
WAAA (RAAAH)

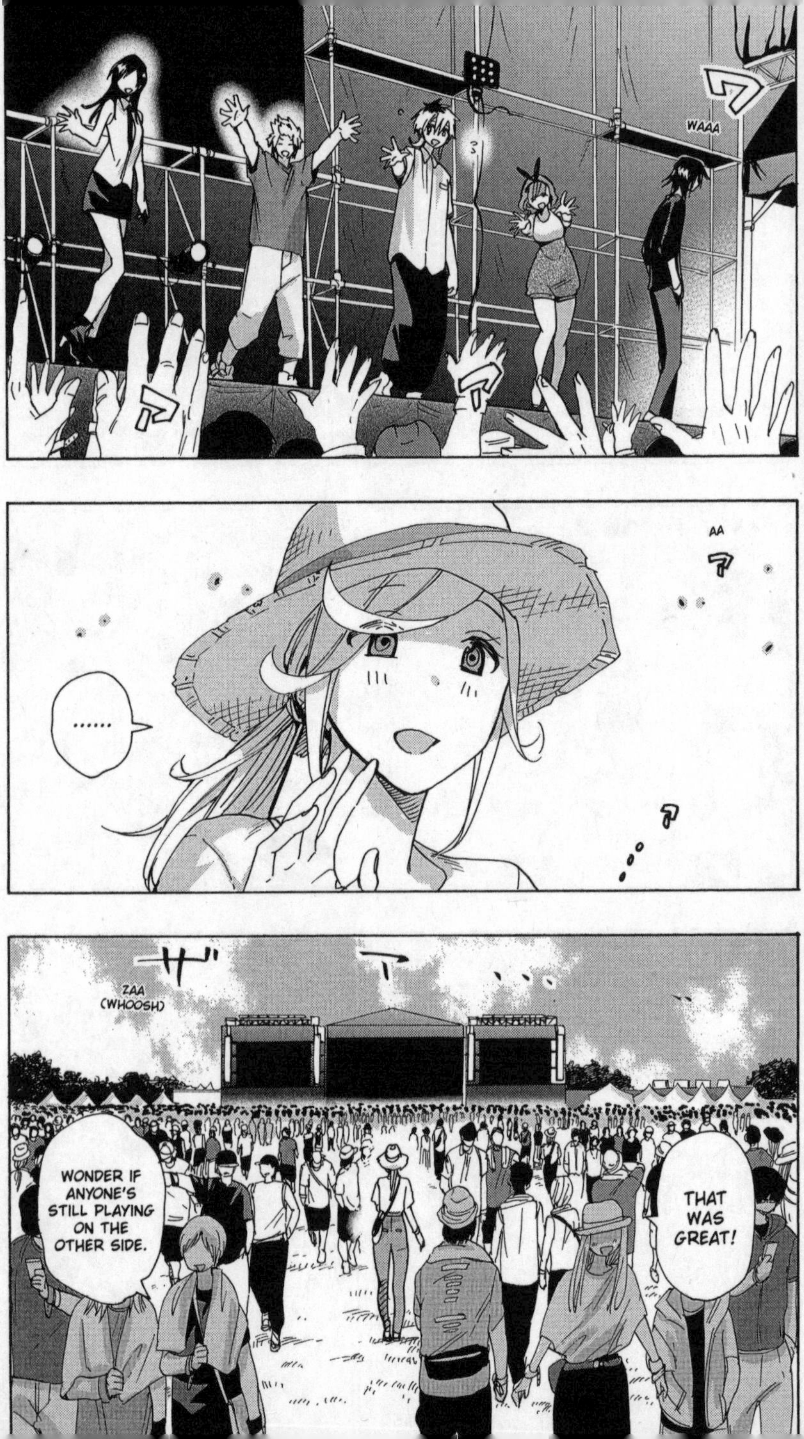
WAAA
AA
......
ZAA (WHOOSH)
THAT WAS GREAT!
WONDER IF ANYONE'S STILL PLAYING ON THE OTHER SIDE.

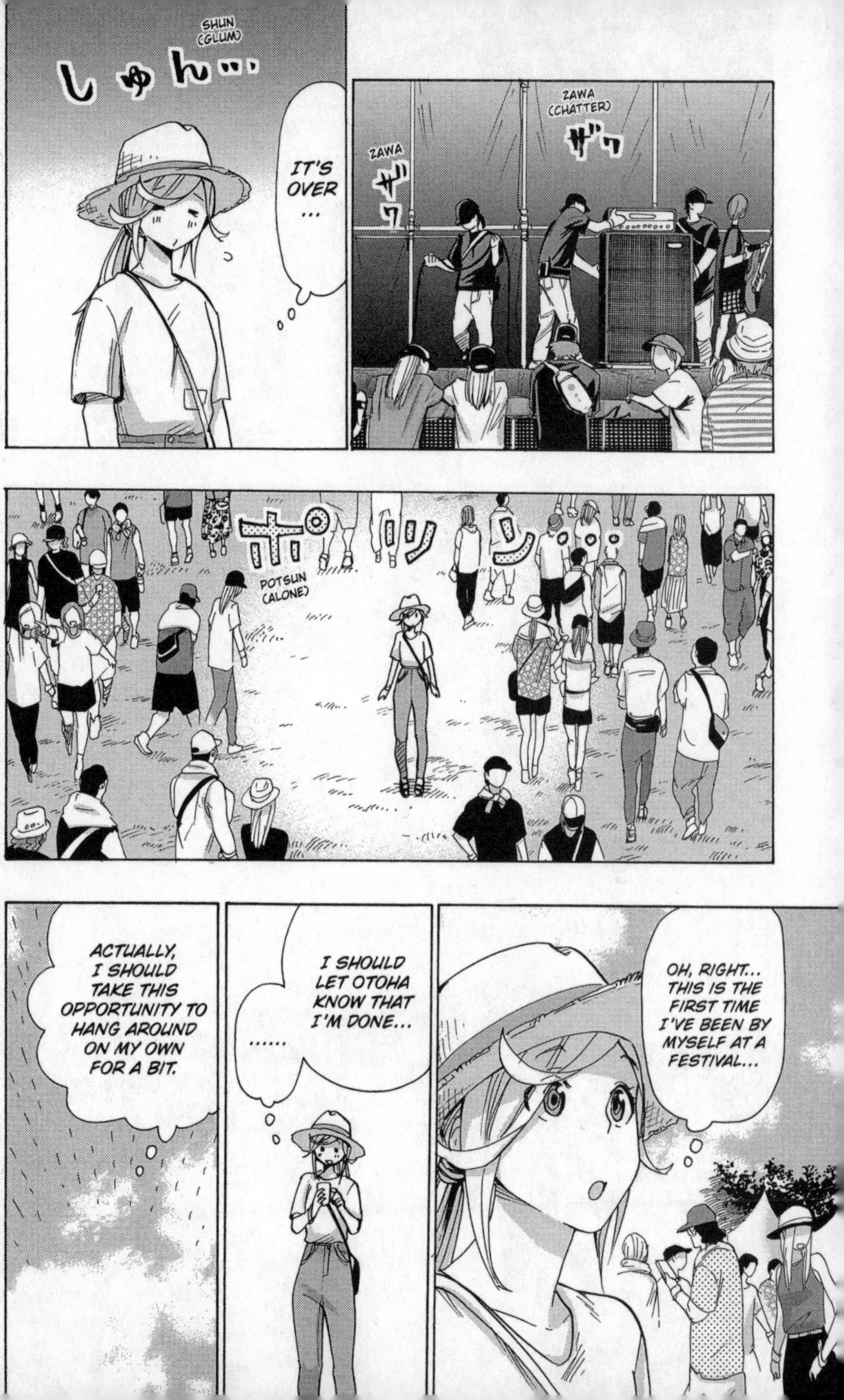
ZAWA (CHATTER)
ザワ
ZAWA
ザワ
SHUN (GLUM)
しゅん…
IT'S OVER...
ポツン
POTSUN (ALONE)
OH, RIGHT... THIS IS THE FIRST TIME I'VE BEEN BY MYSELF AT A FESTIVAL...
I SHOULD LET OTOHA KNOW THAT I'M DONE...
......
ACTUALLY, I SHOULD TAKE THIS OPPORTUNITY TO HANG AROUND ON MY OWN FOR A BIT.

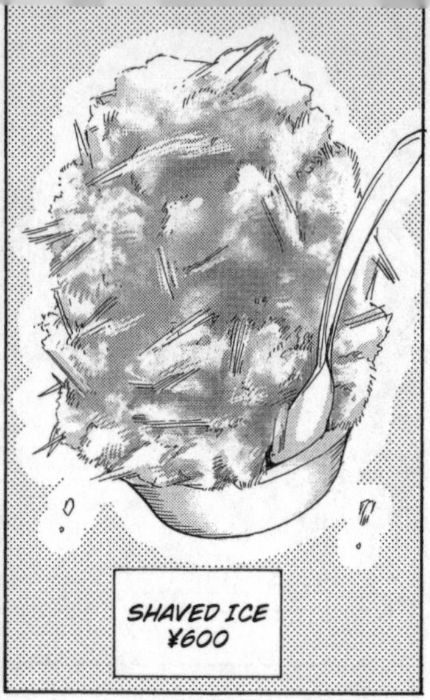
SHAVED ICE
¥600

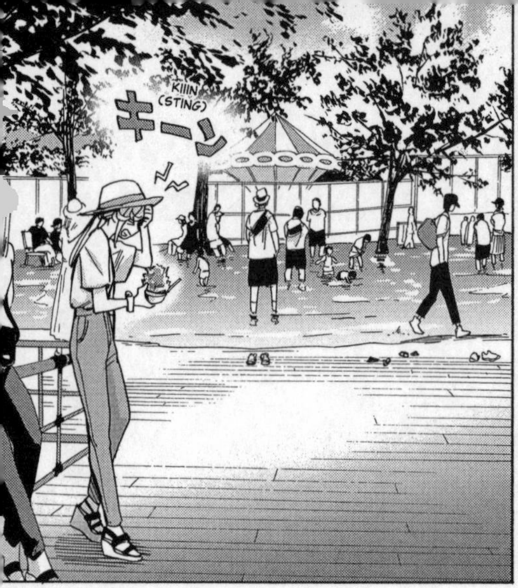
KIIIN
(STING)
キーン

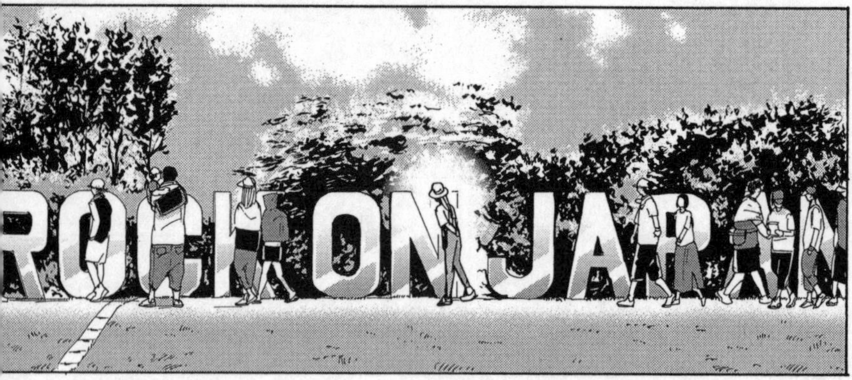

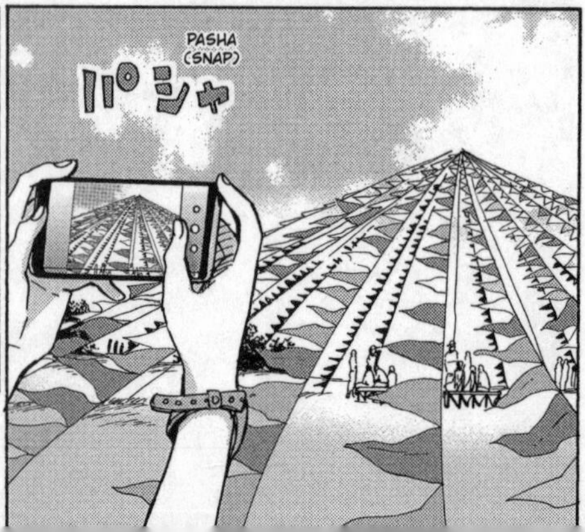
PASHA
(SNAP)
パシャ

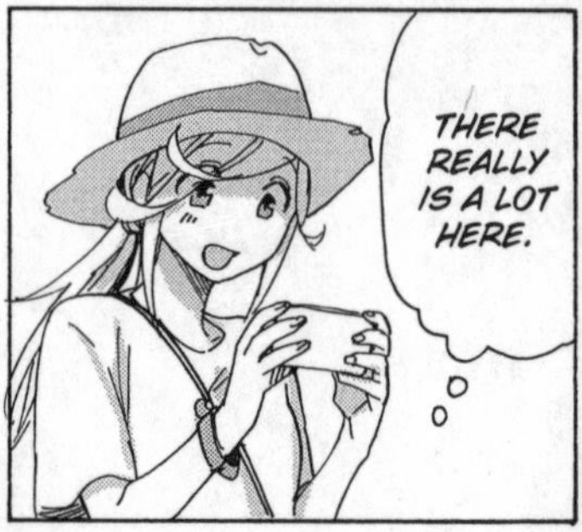
THERE REALLY IS A LOT HERE.

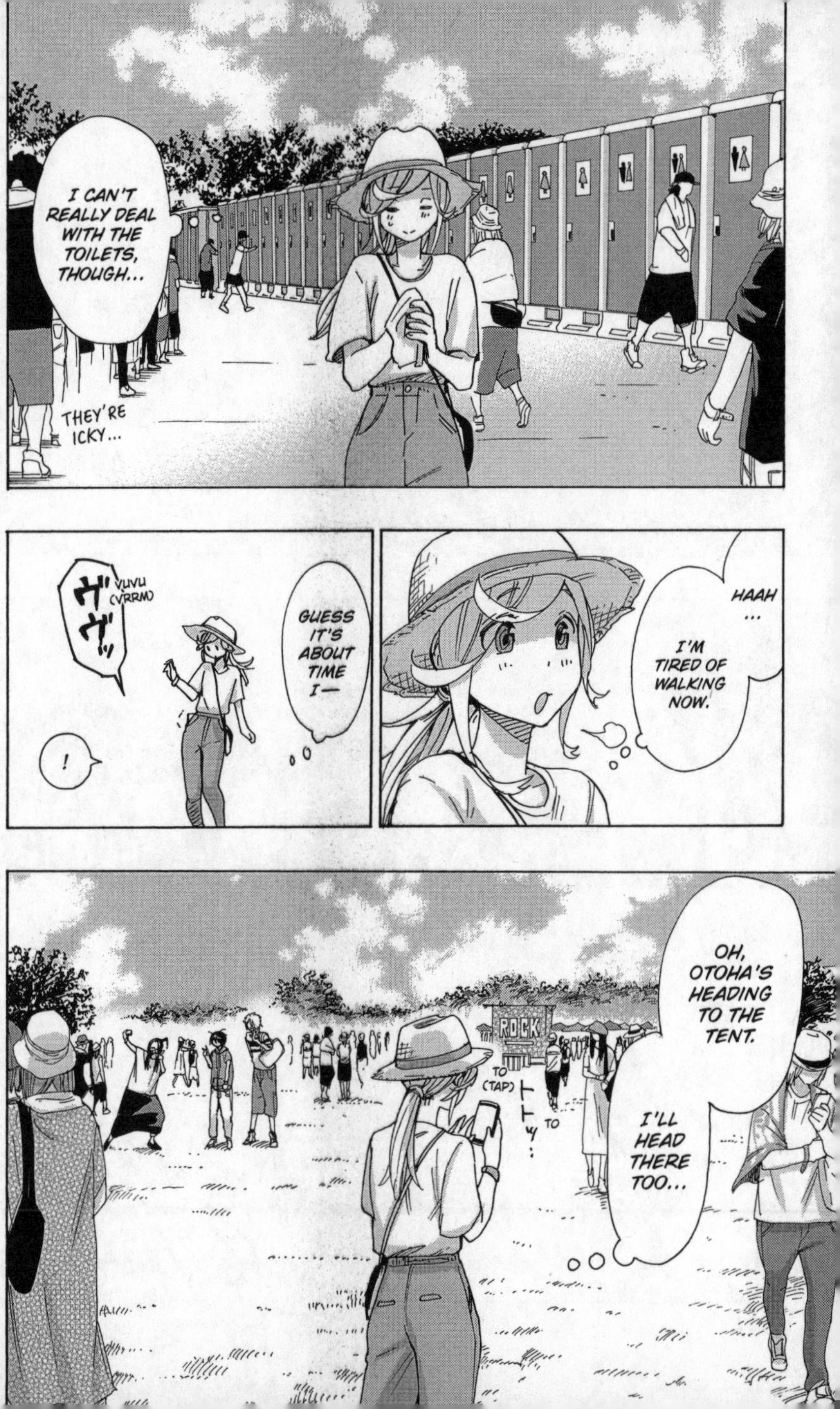
I CAN'T REALLY DEAL WITH THE TOILETS, THOUGH...
THEY'RE ICKY...
HAAH...
I'M TIRED OF WALKING NOW.
GUESS IT'S ABOUT TIME I—
ヴヴッ
VUVU (VRRM)
!
OH, OTOHA'S HEADING TO THE TENT.
I'LL HEAD THERE TOO...
ROCK
TO (TAP)
TO

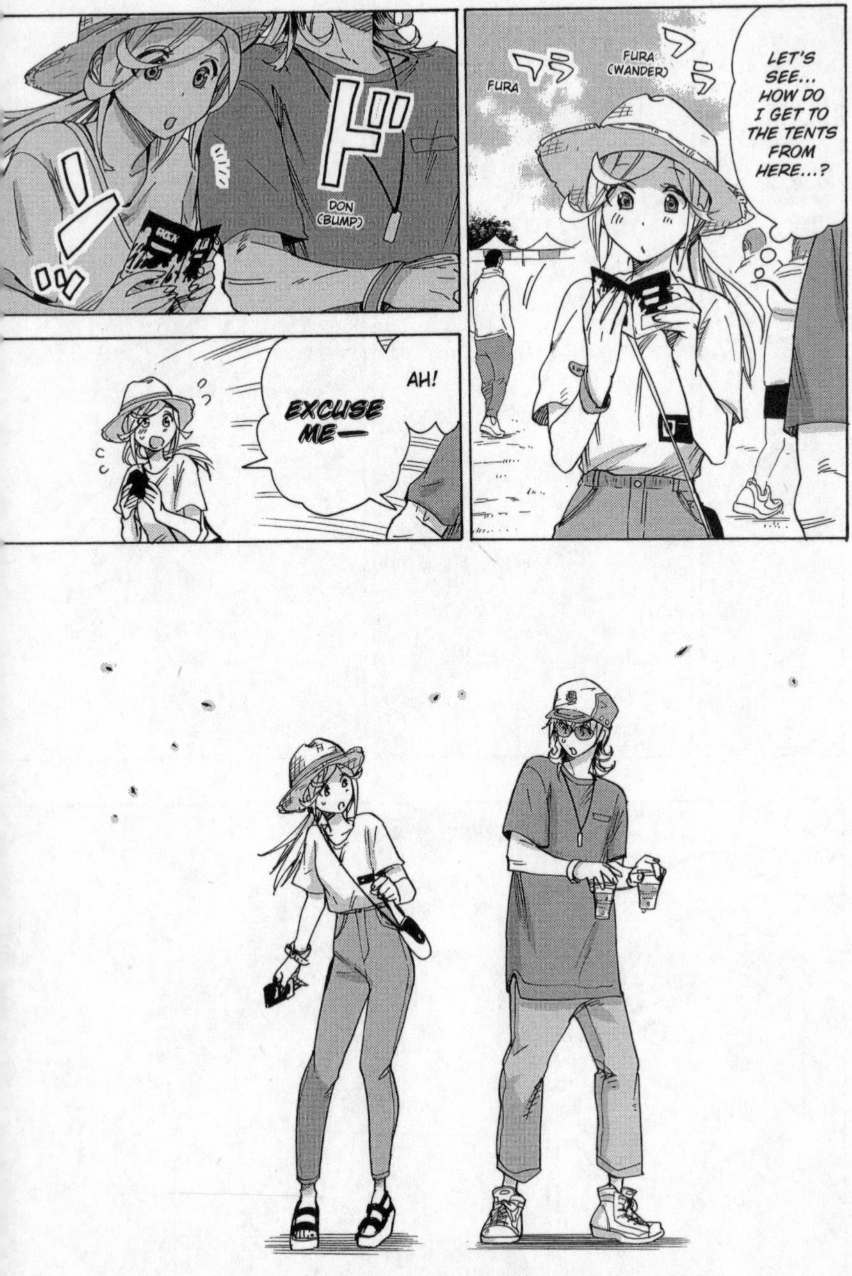
LET'S SEE... HOW DO I GET TO THE TENTS FROM HERE...?
FURA (WANDER)
FURA
DON (BUMP)
AH!
EXCUSE ME—

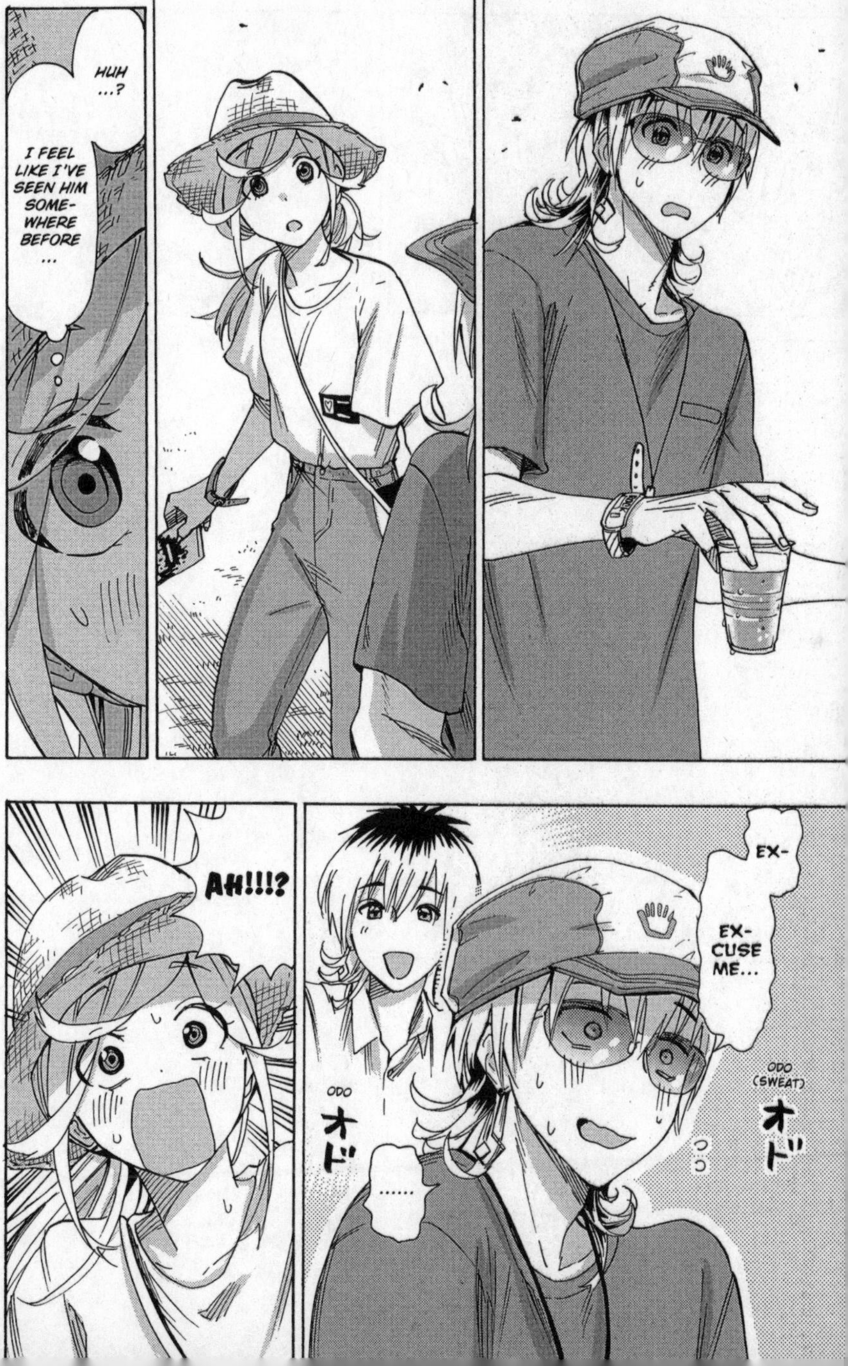
HUH ...?
I FEEL LIKE I'VE SEEN HIM SOME-WHERE BEFORE ...
EX-
EX-CUSE ME...
ODO (SWEAT)
オド
......
ODO
オド
AH!!!?

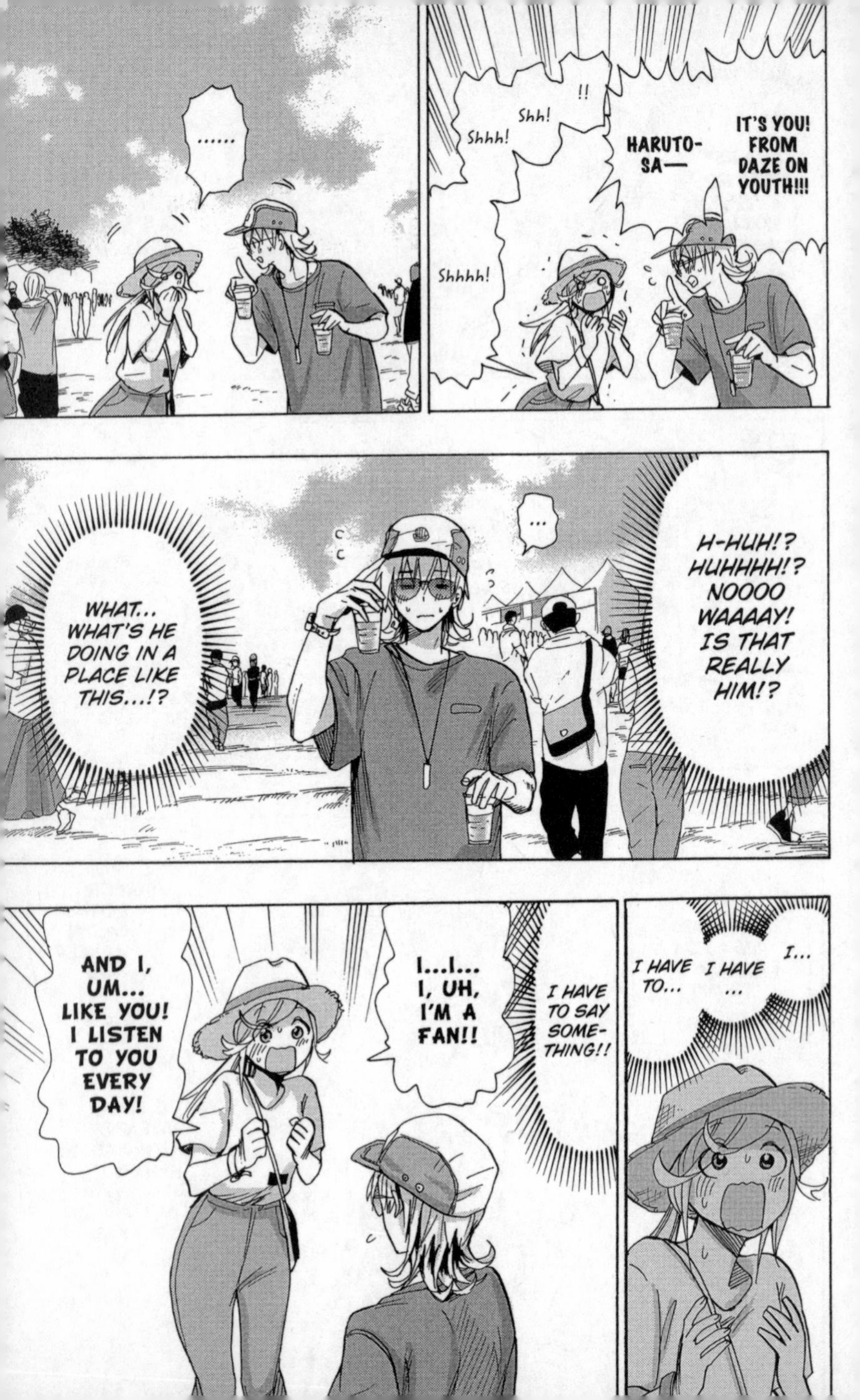
IT'S YOU! FROM DAZE ON YOUTH!!!
HARUTO-SA—
!!
Shh!
Shhh!
Shhhh!
......
H-HUH!? HUHHHH!? NOOOO WAAAAY! IS THAT REALLY HIM!?
...
WHAT... WHAT'S HE DOING IN A PLACE LIKE THIS...!?
I...
I HAVE ...
I HAVE TO...
I HAVE TO SAY SOME-THING!!
I...I... I, UH, I'M A FAN!!
AND I, UM... LIKE YOU! I LISTEN TO YOU EVERY DAY!

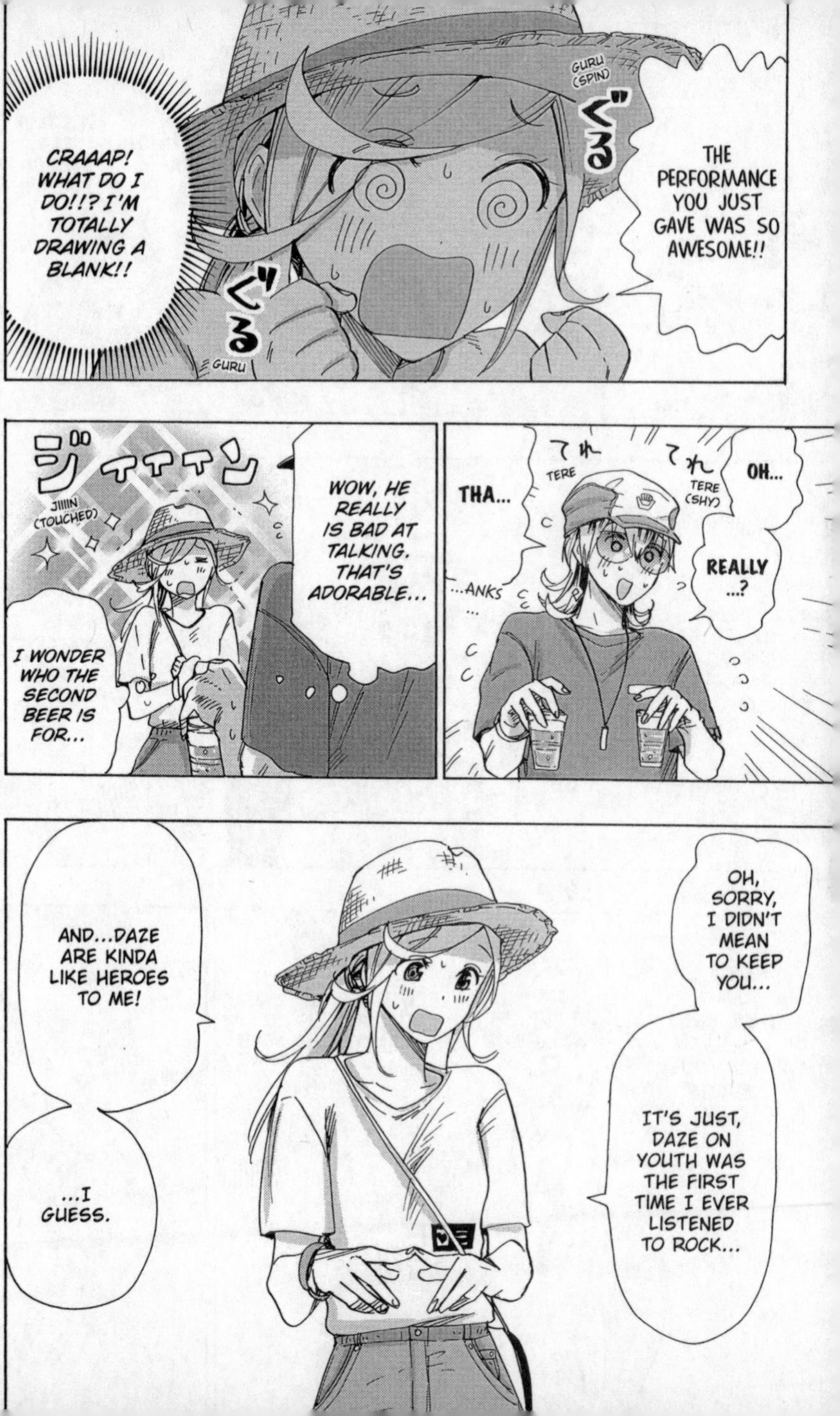
ぐる
GURU (SPIN)
THE PERFORMANCE YOU JUST GAVE WAS SO AWESOME!!
CRAAAP! WHAT DO I DO!!? I'M TOTALLY DRAWING A BLANK!!
ぐる
GURU
OH... REALLY ...?
てれ
TERE (SHY)
てれ
TERE
THA... ...ANKS ...
WOW, HE REALLY IS BAD AT TALKING. THAT'S ADORABLE...
ジイイイン
JIIIIN (TOUCHED)
I WONDER WHO THE SECOND BEER IS FOR...
OH, SORRY, I DIDN'T MEAN TO KEEP YOU...
IT'S JUST, DAZE ON YOUTH WAS THE FIRST TIME I EVER LISTENED TO ROCK...
AND...DAZE ARE KINDA LIKE HEROES TO ME!
...I GUESS.

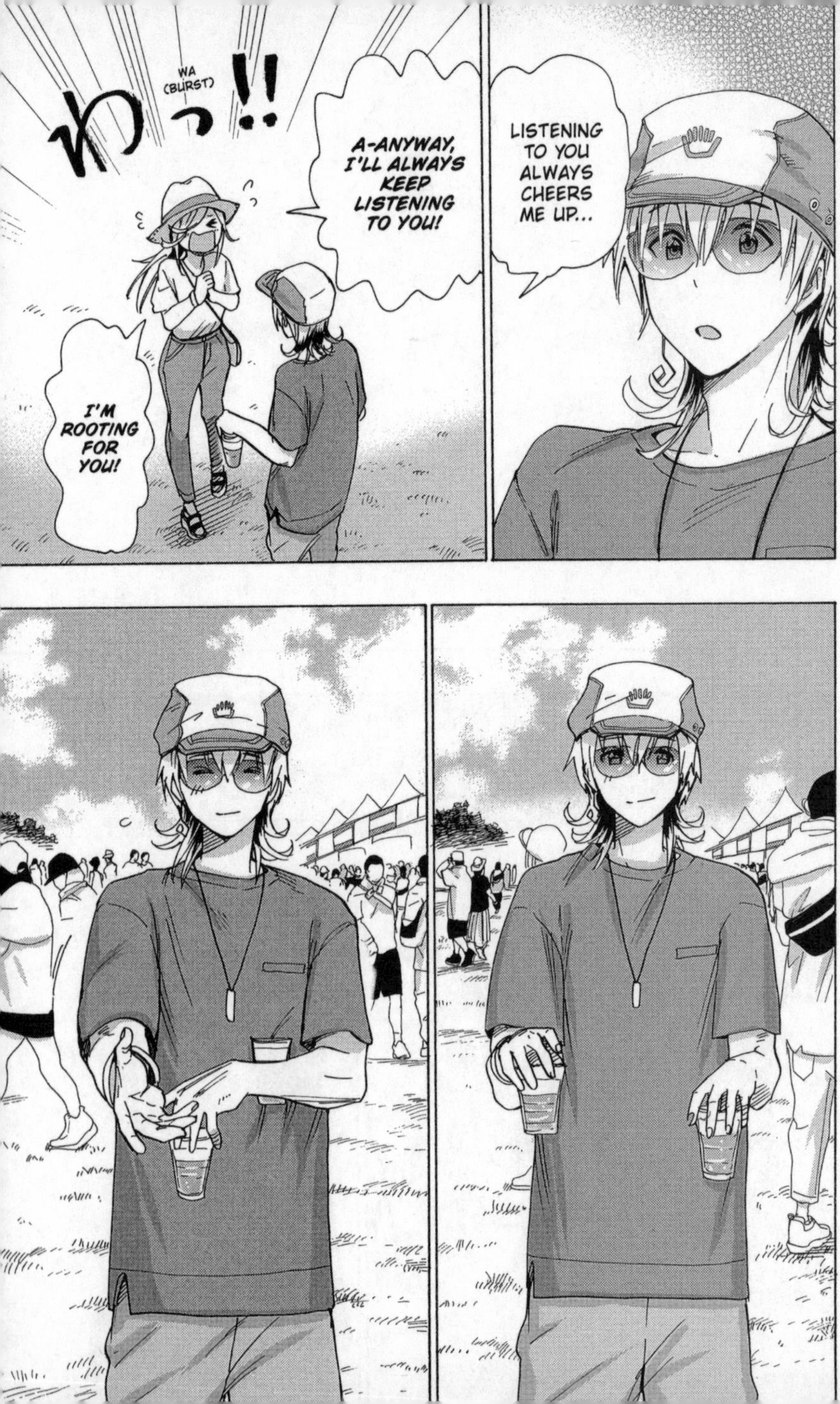
LISTENING TO YOU ALWAYS CHEERS ME UP...
A-ANYWAY, I'LL ALWAYS KEEP LISTENING TO YOU!
わっ!!
WA (BURST)
I'M ROOTING FOR YOU!

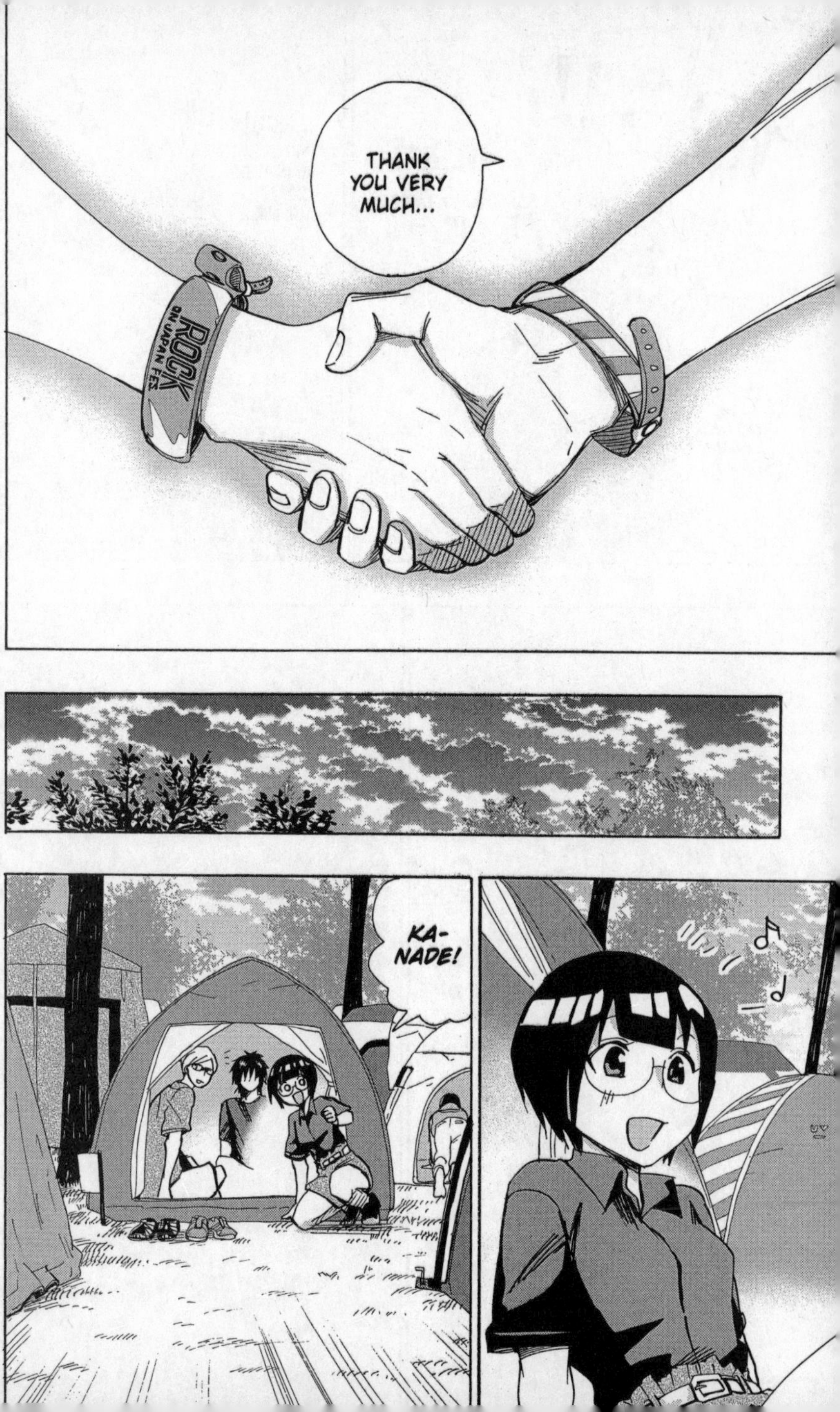
THANK YOU VERY MUCH...
ROCK
KA-NADE!

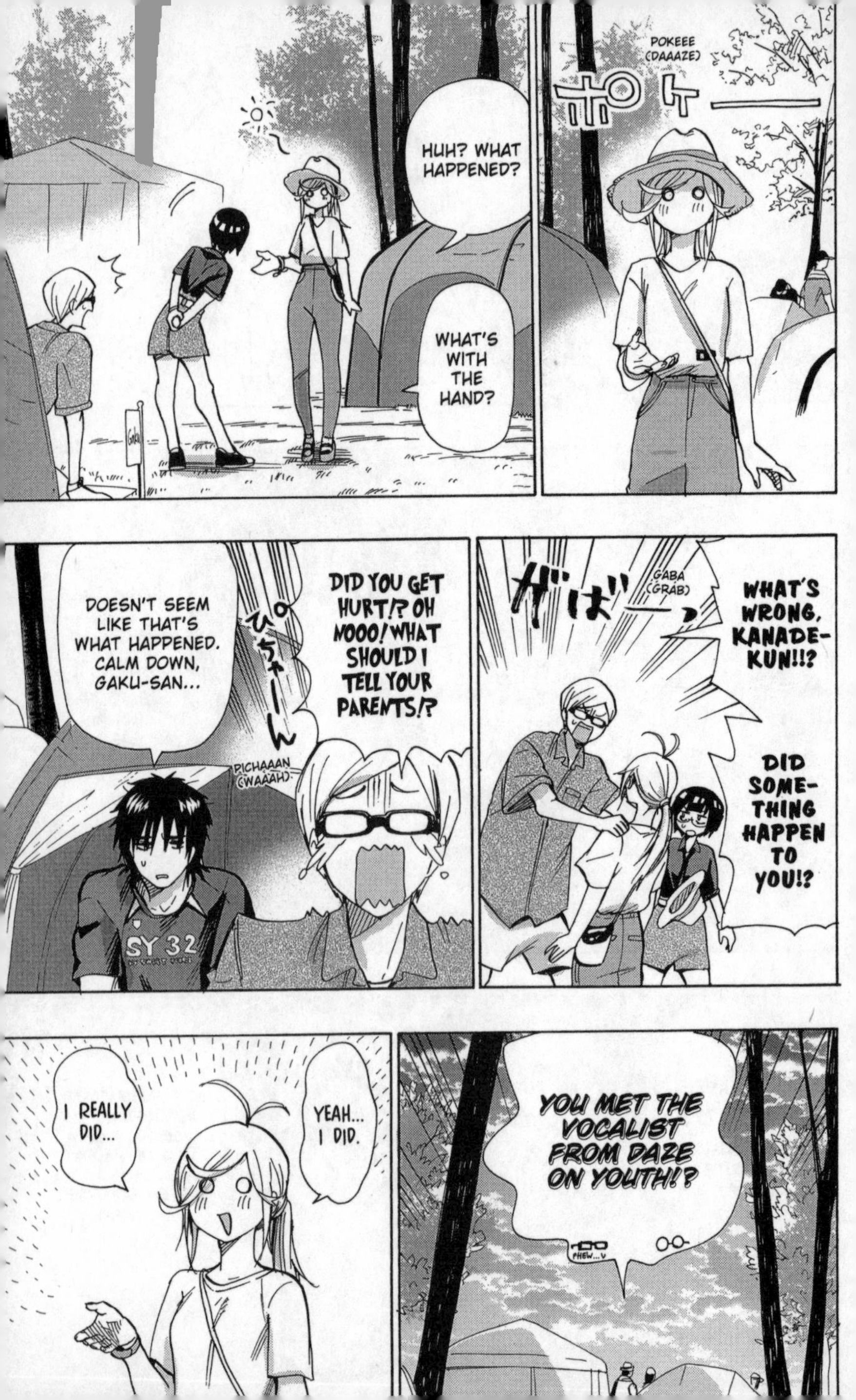
POKEEE (DAAAZE)
ポケー
HUH? WHAT HAPPENED?
WHAT'S WITH THE HAND?
ガばっ
GABA (GRAB)
WHAT'S WRONG, KANADE-KUN!!?
DID SOMETHING HAPPEN TO YOU!?
DID YOU GET HURT!? OH NOOO! WHAT SHOULD I TELL YOUR PARENTS!?
ぴちゃーん
PICHAAAN (WAAAH)
DOESN'T SEEM LIKE THAT'S WHAT HAPPENED. CALM DOWN, GAKU-SAN...
YOU MET THE VOCALIST FROM DAZE ON YOUTH!?
PHEW...♥
YEAH... I DID.
I REALLY DID...

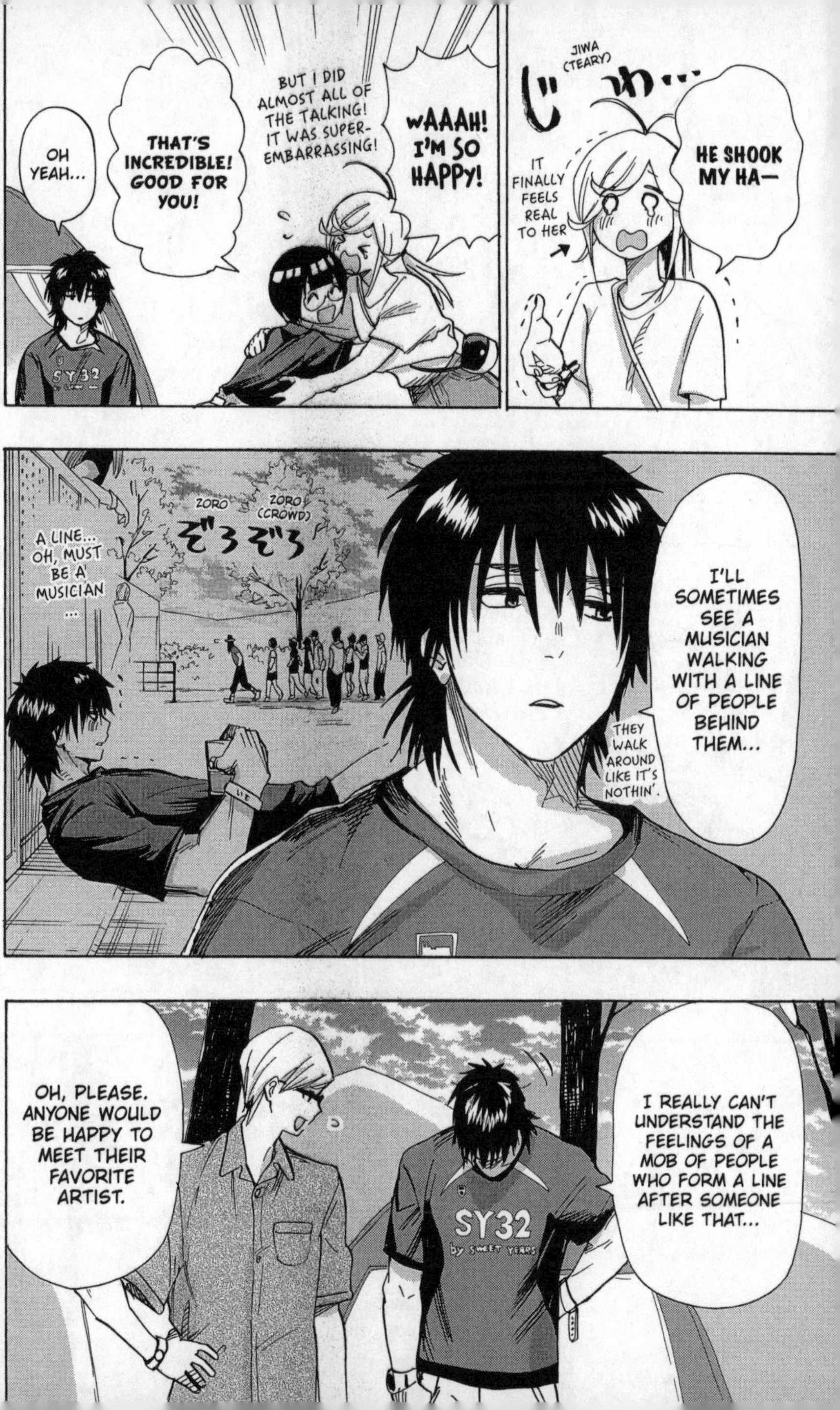
JIWA (TEARY)
じわ…
HE SHOOK MY HA—
IT FINALLY FEELS REAL TO HER
WAAAH! I'M SO HAPPY!
BUT I DID ALMOST ALL OF THE TALKING! IT WAS SUPER-EMBARRASSING!
THAT'S INCREDIBLE! GOOD FOR YOU!
OH YEAH...
SY32
I'LL SOMETIMES SEE A MUSICIAN WALKING WITH A LINE OF PEOPLE BEHIND THEM...
THEY WALK AROUND LIKE IT'S NOTHIN'.
ZORO ZORO (CROWD)
ぞろぞろ
A LINE... OH, MUST BE A MUSICIAN...
I REALLY CAN'T UNDERSTAND THE FEELINGS OF A MOB OF PEOPLE WHO FORM A LINE AFTER SOMEONE LIKE THAT...
SY32 by SWEET YEARS
OH, PLEASE. ANYONE WOULD BE HAPPY TO MEET THEIR FAVORITE ARTIST.

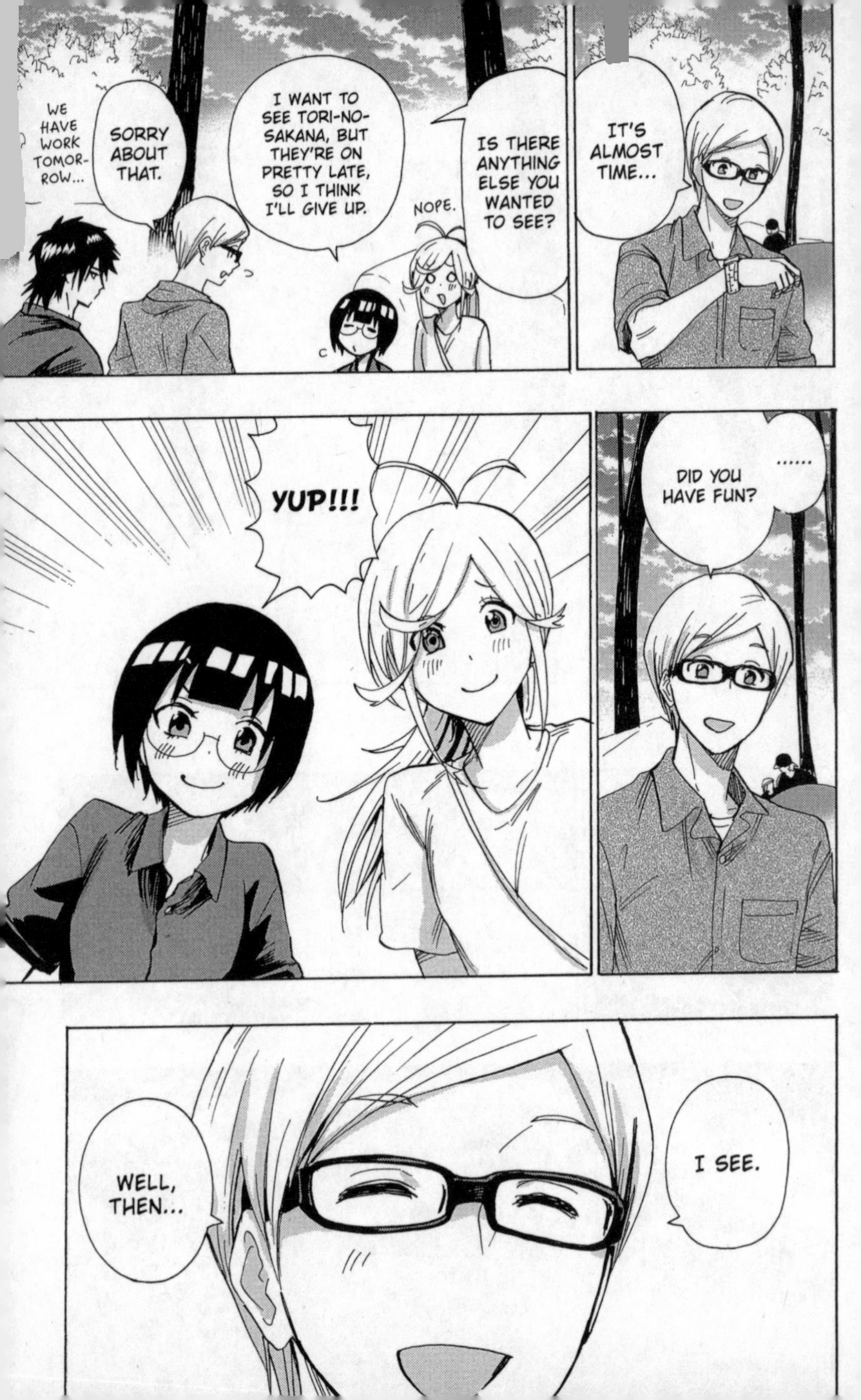
IT'S ALMOST TIME...
IS THERE ANYTHING ELSE YOU WANTED TO SEE?
NOPE.
I WANT TO SEE TORI-NO-SAKANA, BUT THEY'RE ON PRETTY LATE, SO I THINK I'LL GIVE UP.
SORRY ABOUT THAT.
WE HAVE WORK TOMORROW...
......
DID YOU HAVE FUN?
YUP!!!
I SEE.
WELL, THEN...

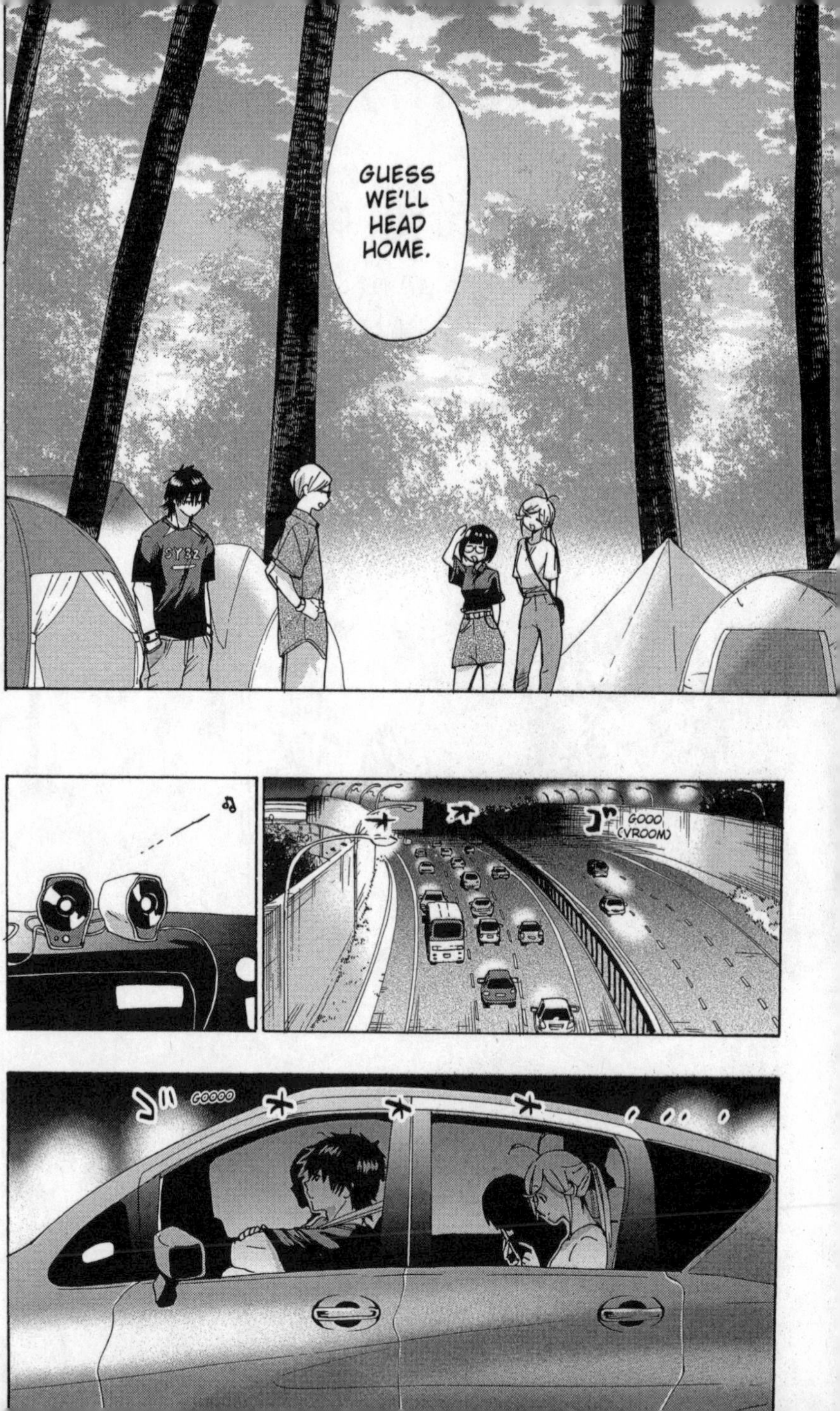
GUESS WE'LL HEAD HOME.
GOOO (VROOM)
GOOOO

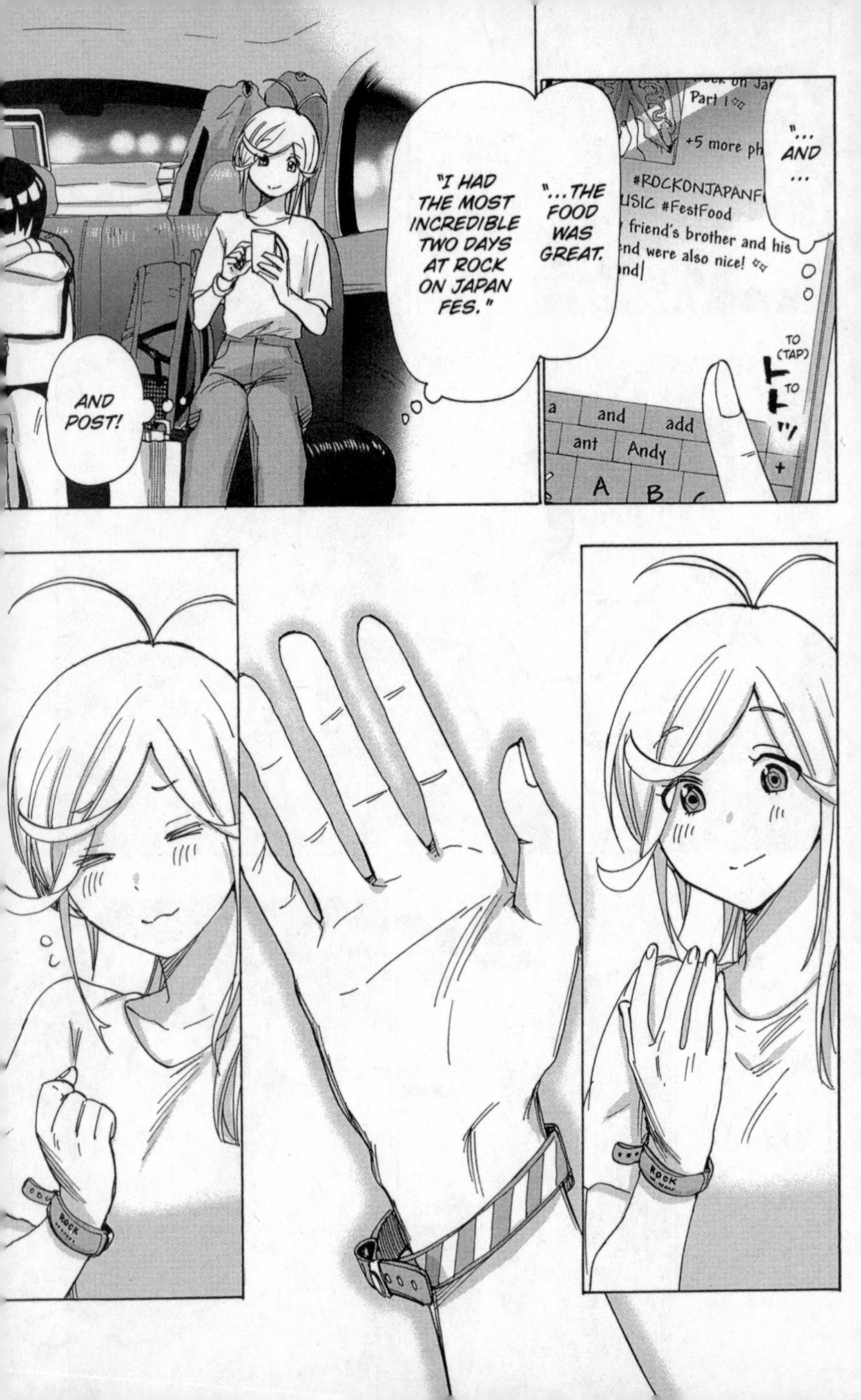
"I HAD THE MOST INCREDIBLE TWO DAYS AT ROCK ON JAPAN FES."
"...THE FOOD WAS GREAT.
Part 1
+5 more ph
#ROCKONJAPANF
USIC #FestFood
friend's brother and his
end were also nice!
nd|
"... AND ...
TO (TAP) TO
a and add
ant Andy
A B
AND POST!

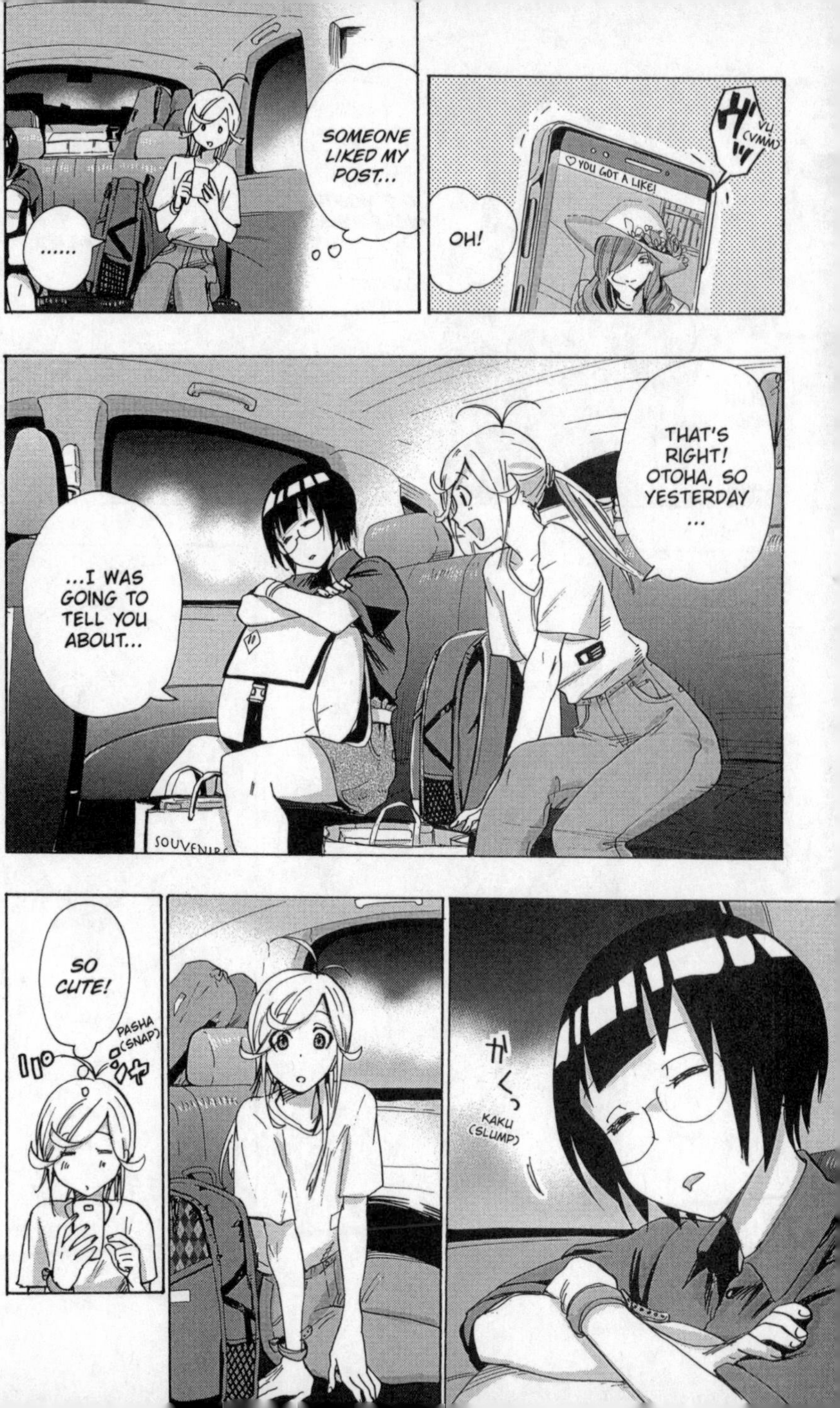
VU (VMM)
YOU GOT A LIKE!
OH!
SOMEONE LIKED MY POST...
....
THAT'S RIGHT! OTOHA, SO YESTERDAY ...
...I WAS GOING TO TELL YOU ABOUT...
KAKU (SLUMP)
SO CUTE!
PASHA (SNAP)

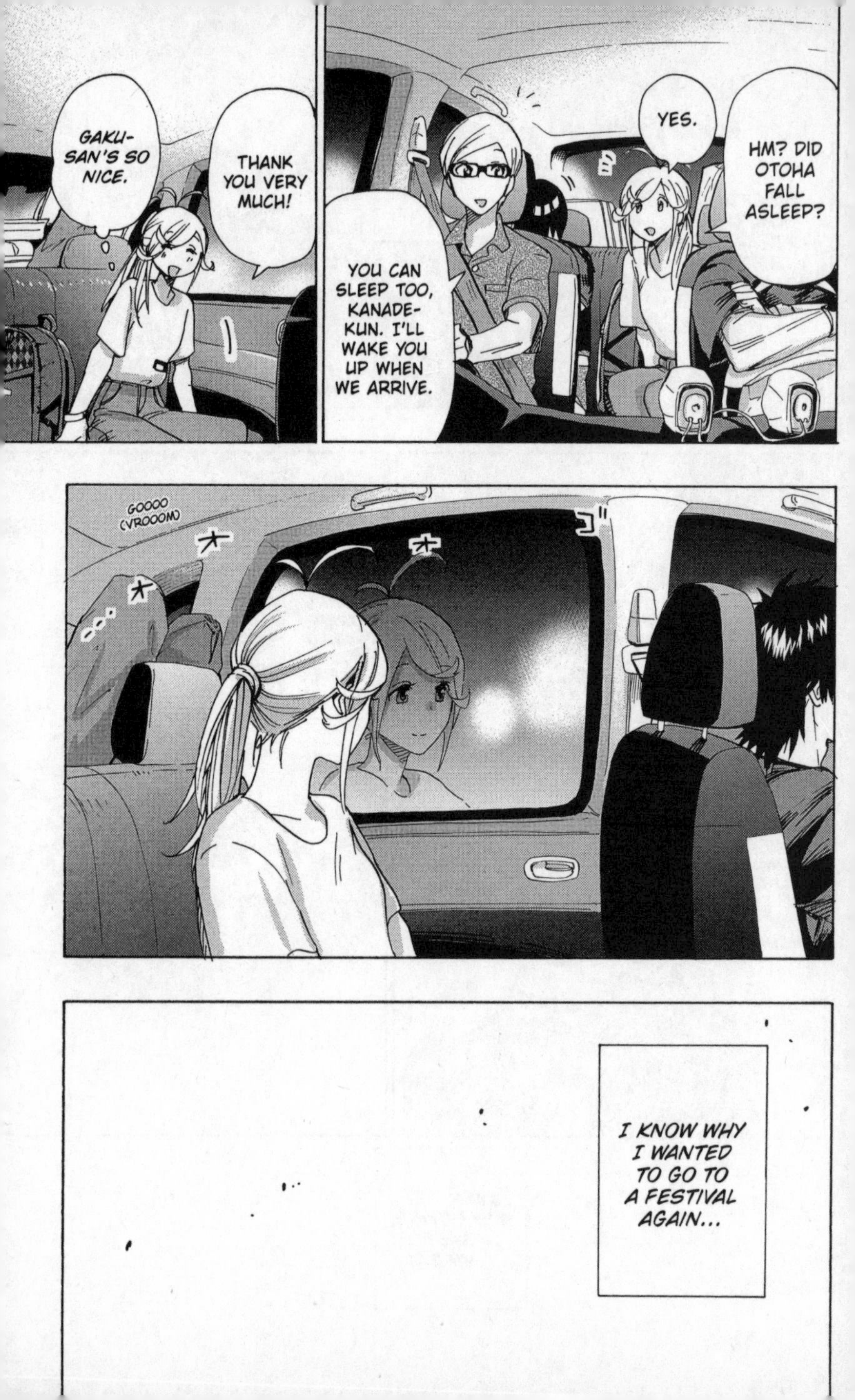
HM? DID OTOHA FALL ASLEEP?
YES.
YOU CAN SLEEP TOO, KANADE-KUN. I'LL WAKE YOU UP WHEN WE ARRIVE.
THANK YOU VERY MUCH!
GAKU-SAN'S SO NICE.
GOOOO (VROOOM)
I KNOW WHY I WANTED TO GO TO A FESTIVAL AGAIN...

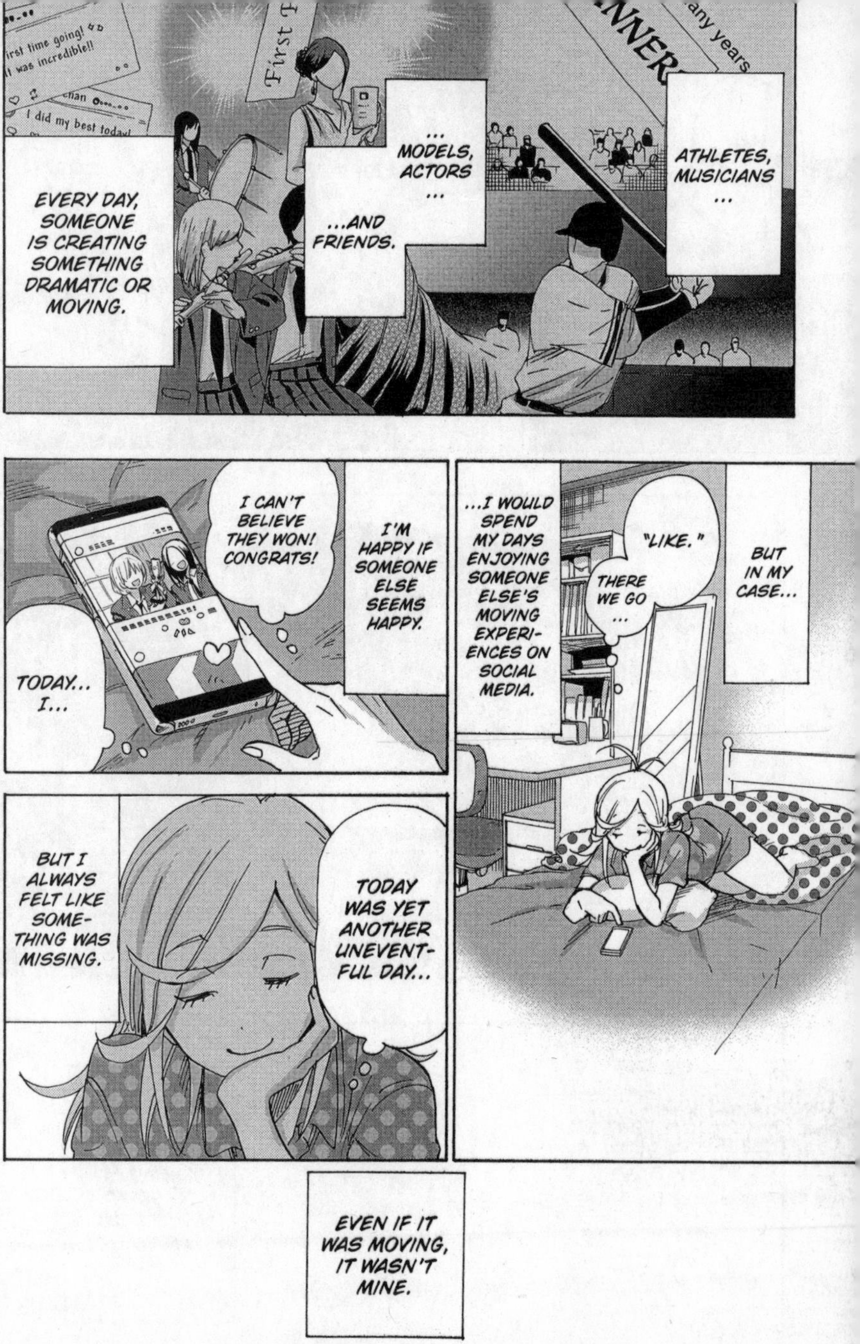
First time going!
I did my best today!
ATHLETES, MUSICIANS ...
... MODELS, ACTORS ...
...AND FRIENDS.
EVERY DAY, SOMEONE IS CREATING SOMETHING DRAMATIC OR MOVING.
BUT IN MY CASE...
...I WOULD SPEND MY DAYS ENJOYING SOMEONE ELSE'S MOVING EXPERI-ENCES ON SOCIAL MEDIA.
"LIKE."
THERE WE GO ...
I'M HAPPY IF SOMEONE ELSE SEEMS HAPPY.
I CAN'T BELIEVE THEY WON! CONGRATS!
TODAY... I...
TODAY WAS YET ANOTHER UNEVENT-FUL DAY...
BUT I ALWAYS FELT LIKE SOME-THING WAS MISSING.
EVEN IF IT WAS MOVING, IT WASN'T MINE.

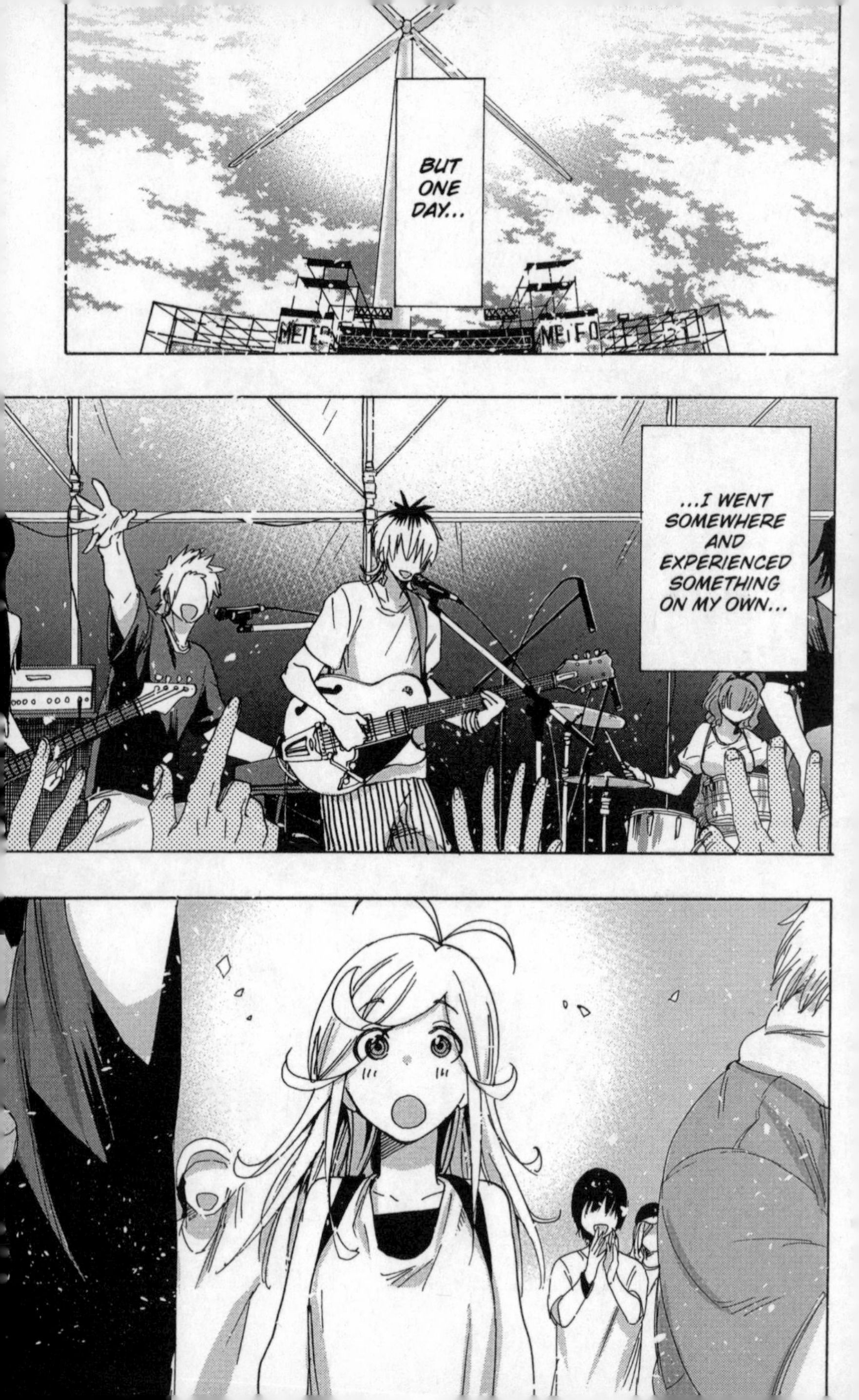
BUT ONE DAY...
...I WENT SOMEWHERE AND EXPERIENCED SOMETHING ON MY OWN...

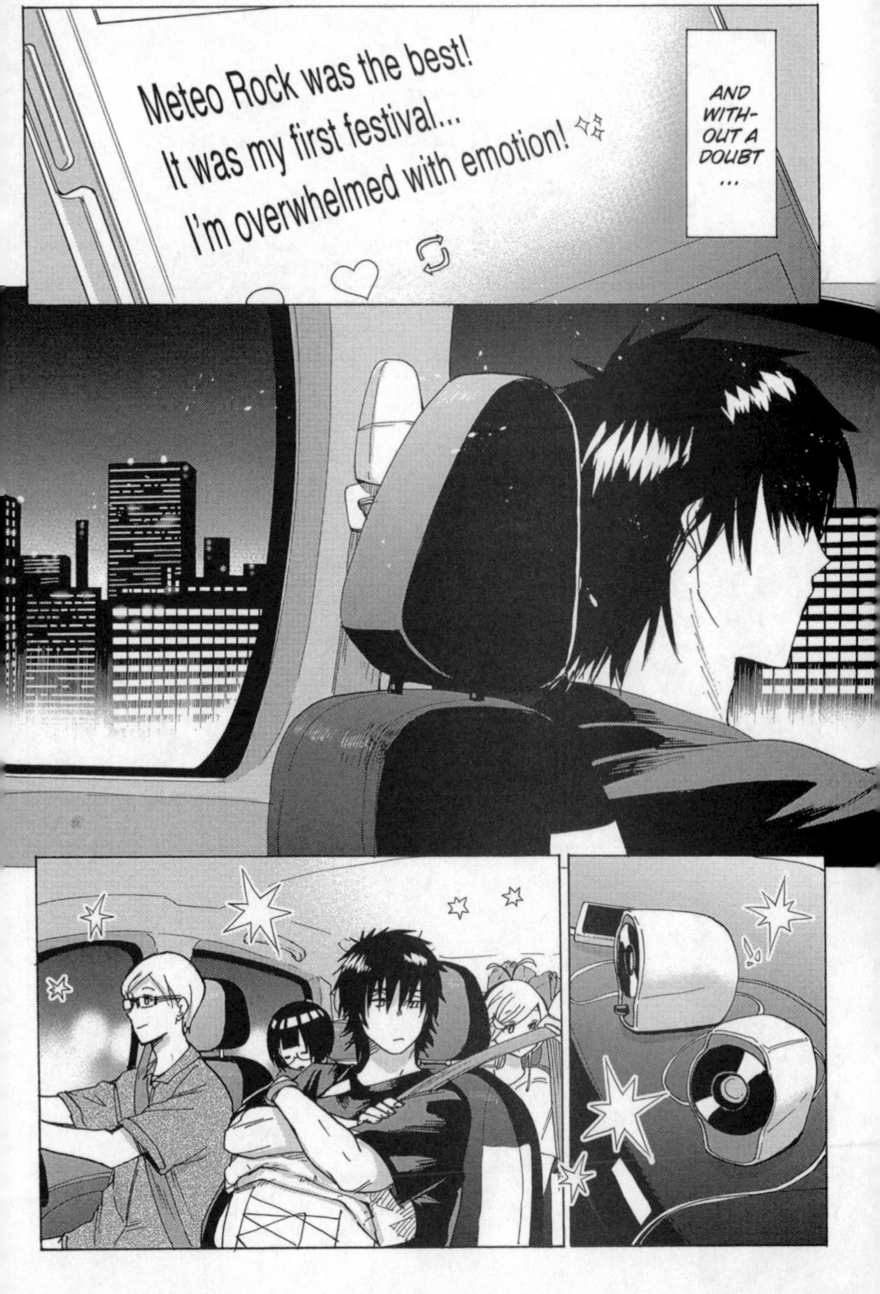
AND WITHOUT A DOUBT...
Meteo Rock was the best!
It was my first festival...
I'm overwhelmed with emotion!

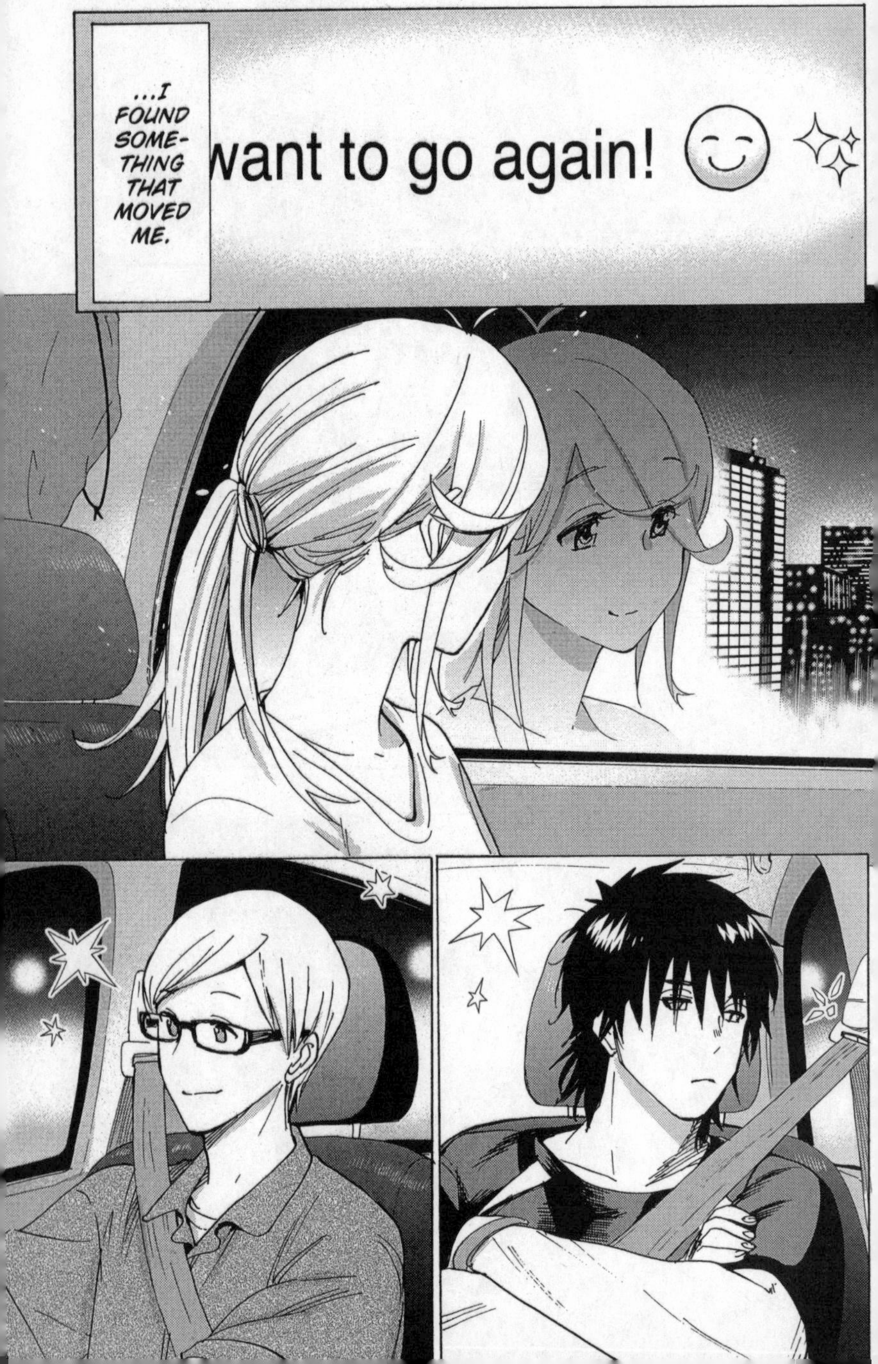
...I FOUND SOMETHING THAT MOVED ME.
want to go again!

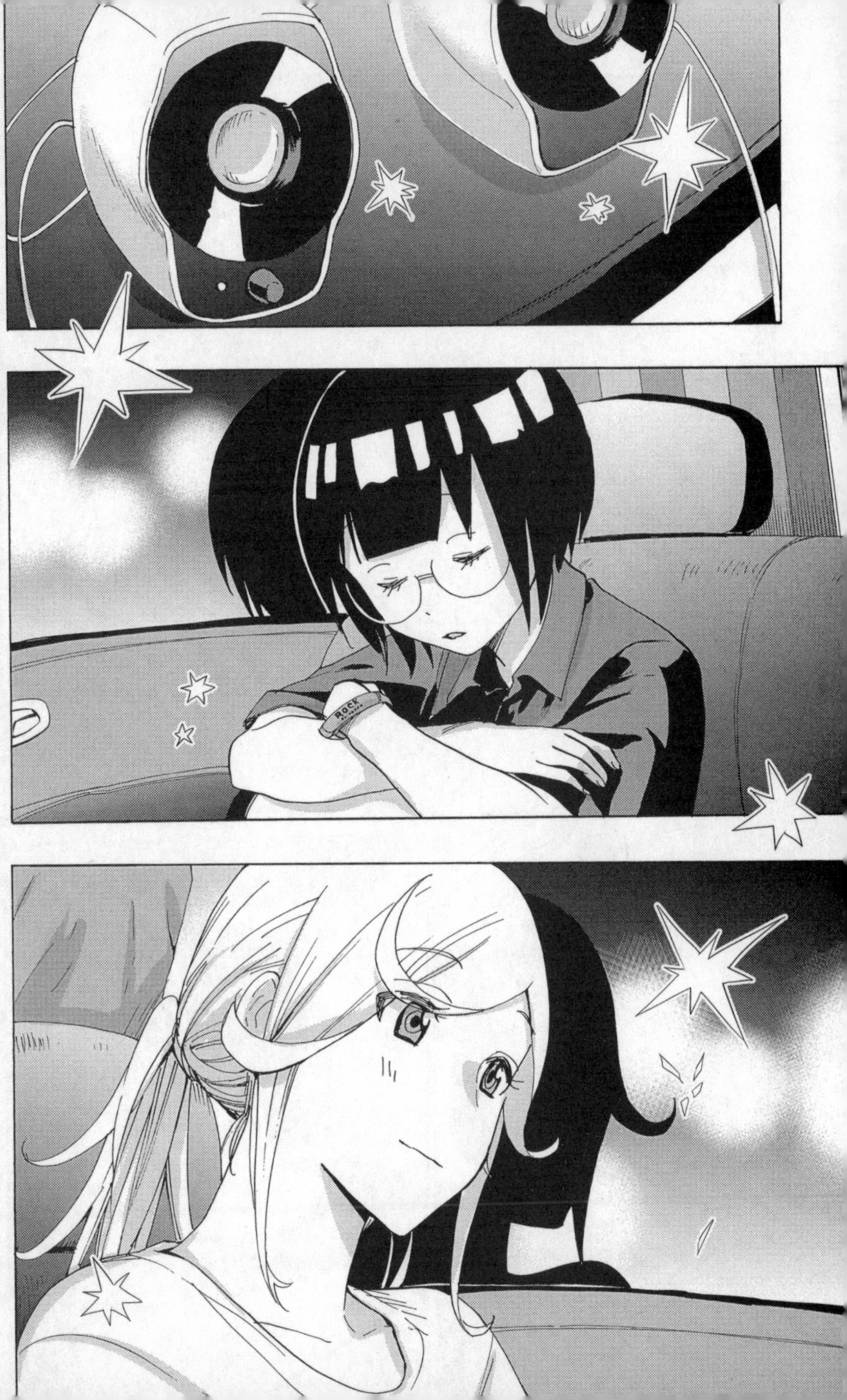
ROCK

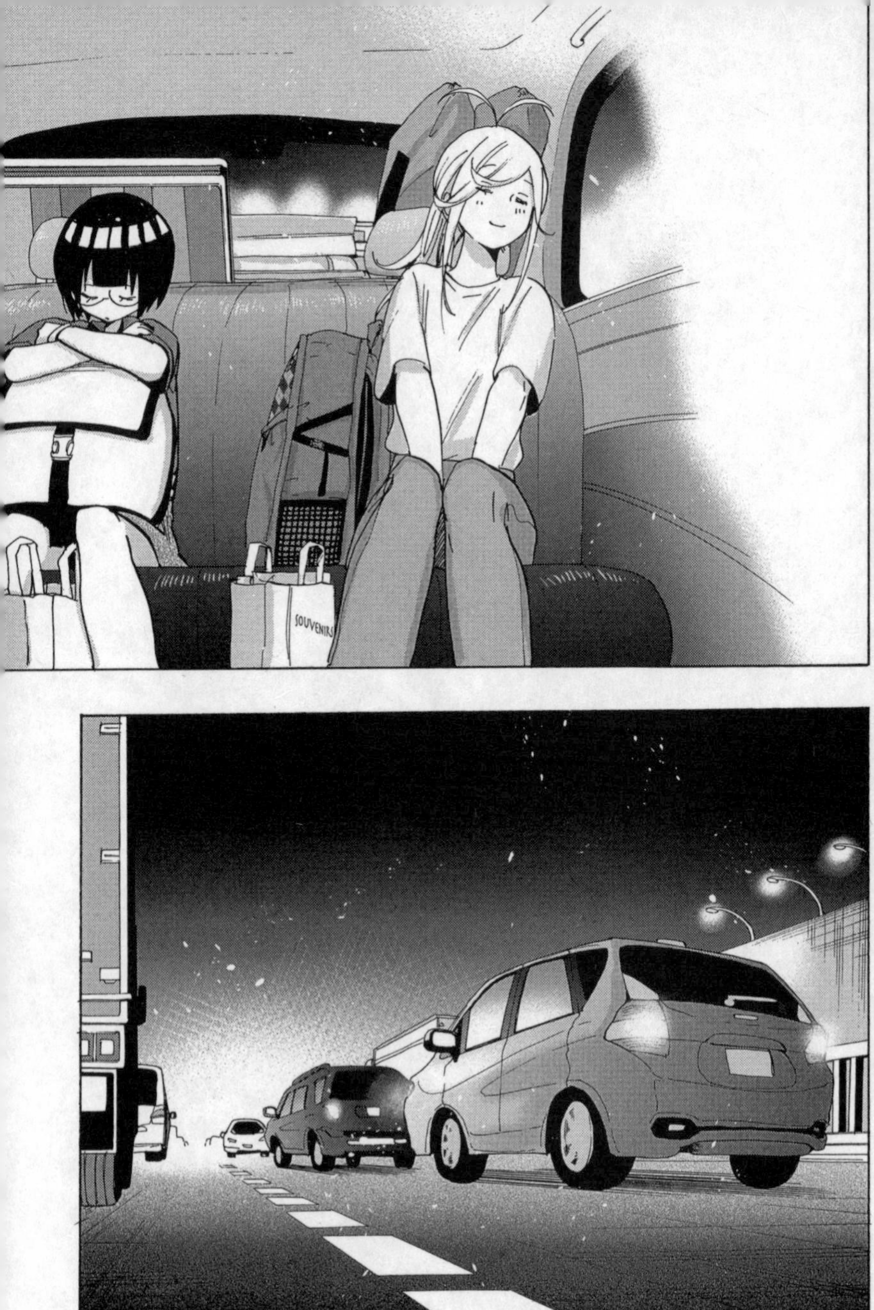
SOUVENIRS

Days on Fes

FES 9.5

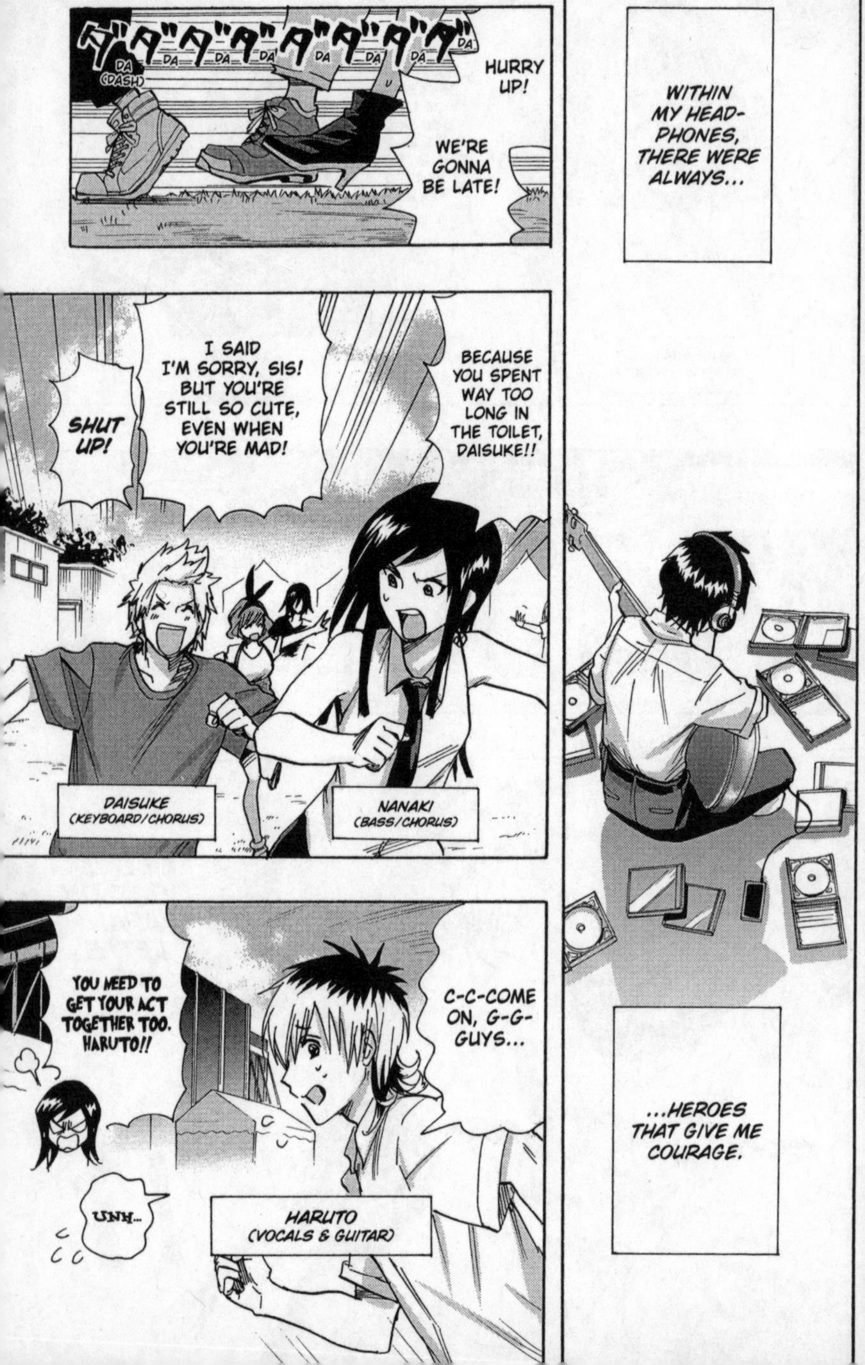
WITHIN MY HEAD-PHONES, THERE WERE ALWAYS...
...HEROES THAT GIVE ME COURAGE.
HURRY UP!
WE'RE GONNA BE LATE!
DA DA DA DA DA DA DA DA DA DA (DASH)
BECAUSE YOU SPENT WAY TOO LONG IN THE TOILET, DAISUKE!!
I SAID I'M SORRY, SIS! BUT YOU'RE STILL SO CUTE, EVEN WHEN YOU'RE MAD!
SHUT UP!
NANAKI (BASS/CHORUS)
DAISUKE (KEYBOARD/CHORUS)
C-C-COME ON, G-G-GUYS...
YOU NEED TO GET YOUR ACT TOGETHER TOO. HARUTO!!
HARUTO (VOCALS & GUITAR)
UNH...

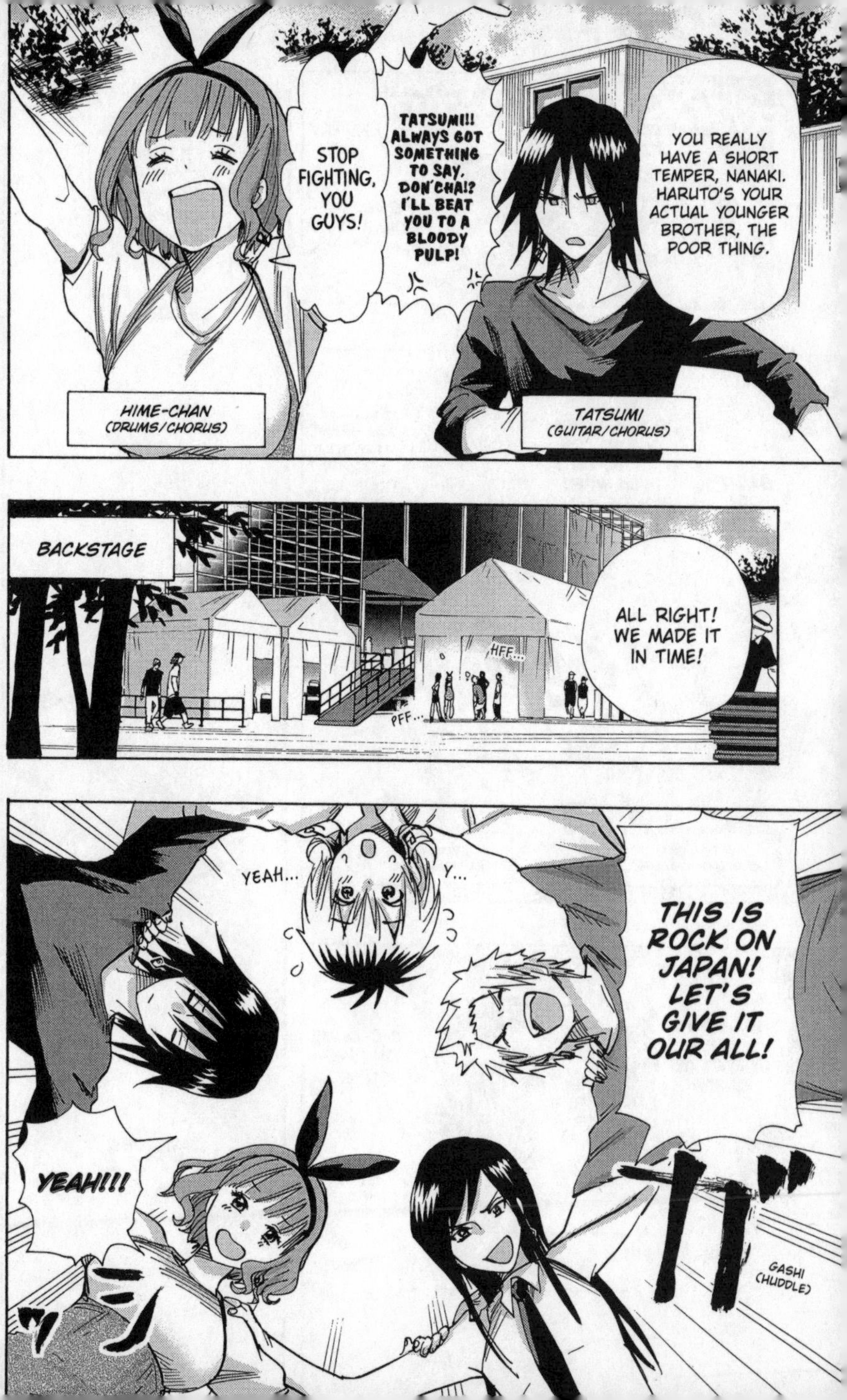
YOU REALLY HAVE A SHORT TEMPER, NANAKI. HARUTO'S YOUR ACTUAL YOUNGER BROTHER, THE POOR THING.
TATSUMI!! ALWAYS GOT SOMETHING TO SAY, DON'CHA!? I'LL BEAT YOU TO A BLOODY PULP!
STOP FIGHTING, YOU GUYS!
TATSUMI (GUITAR/CHORUS)
HIME-CHAN (DRUMS/CHORUS)
BACKSTAGE
ALL RIGHT! WE MADE IT IN TIME!
HFF...
PFF...
THIS IS ROCK ON JAPAN! LET'S GIVE IT OUR ALL!
Y...
YEAH...
GASHI (HUDDLE)
YEAH!!!

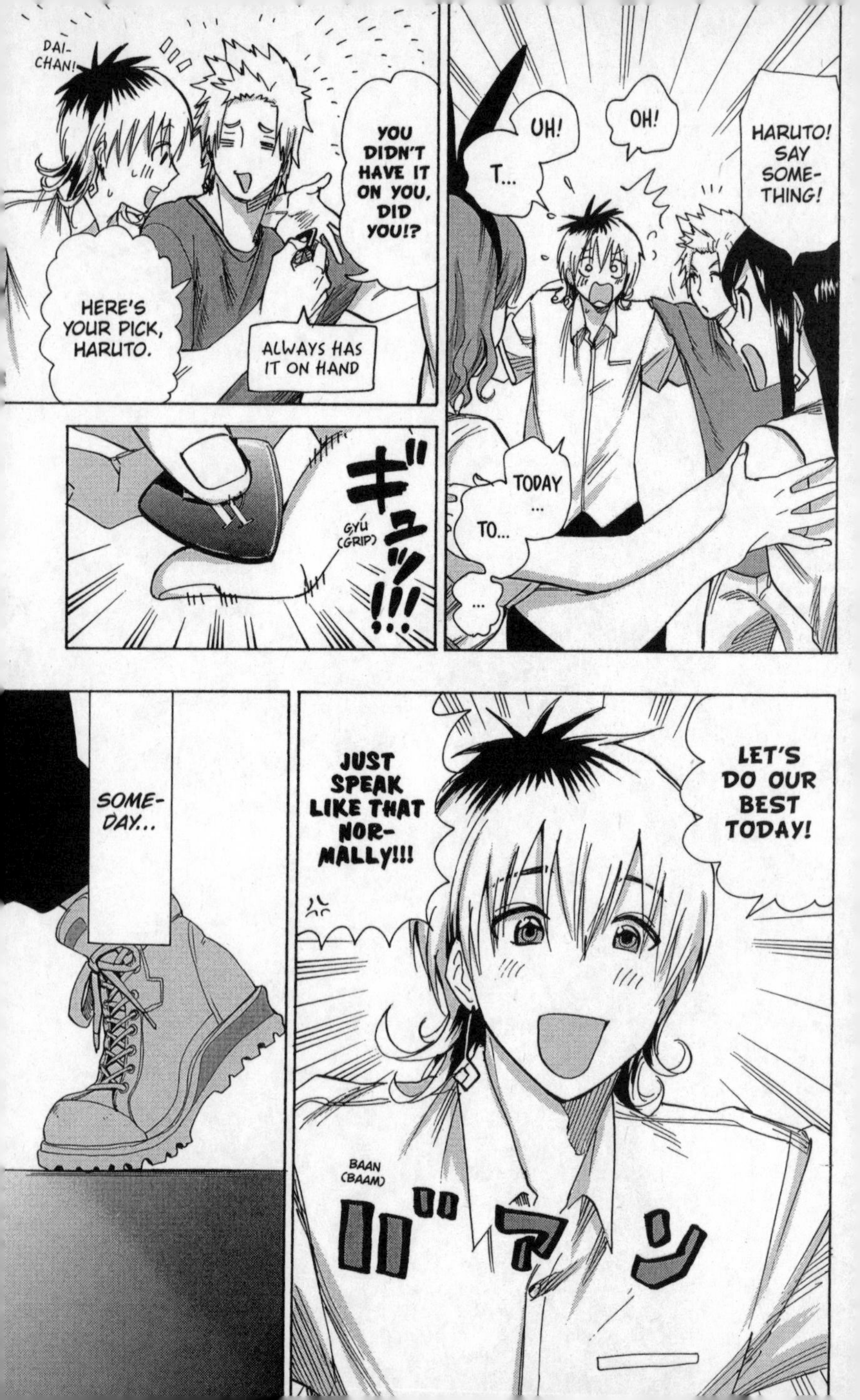

HARUTO! SAY SOMETHING!
OH!
UH!
T...
TODAY ...
TO...
...
YOU DIDN'T HAVE IT ON YOU, DID YOU!?
DAI-CHAN!
ALWAYS HAS IT ON HAND
HERE'S YOUR PICK, HARUTO.
ギュッ!!!
GYU (GRIP)
LET'S DO OUR BEST TODAY!
JUST SPEAK LIKE THAT NORMALLY!!!
BAAN (BAAM)
バアン
SOME-DAY...

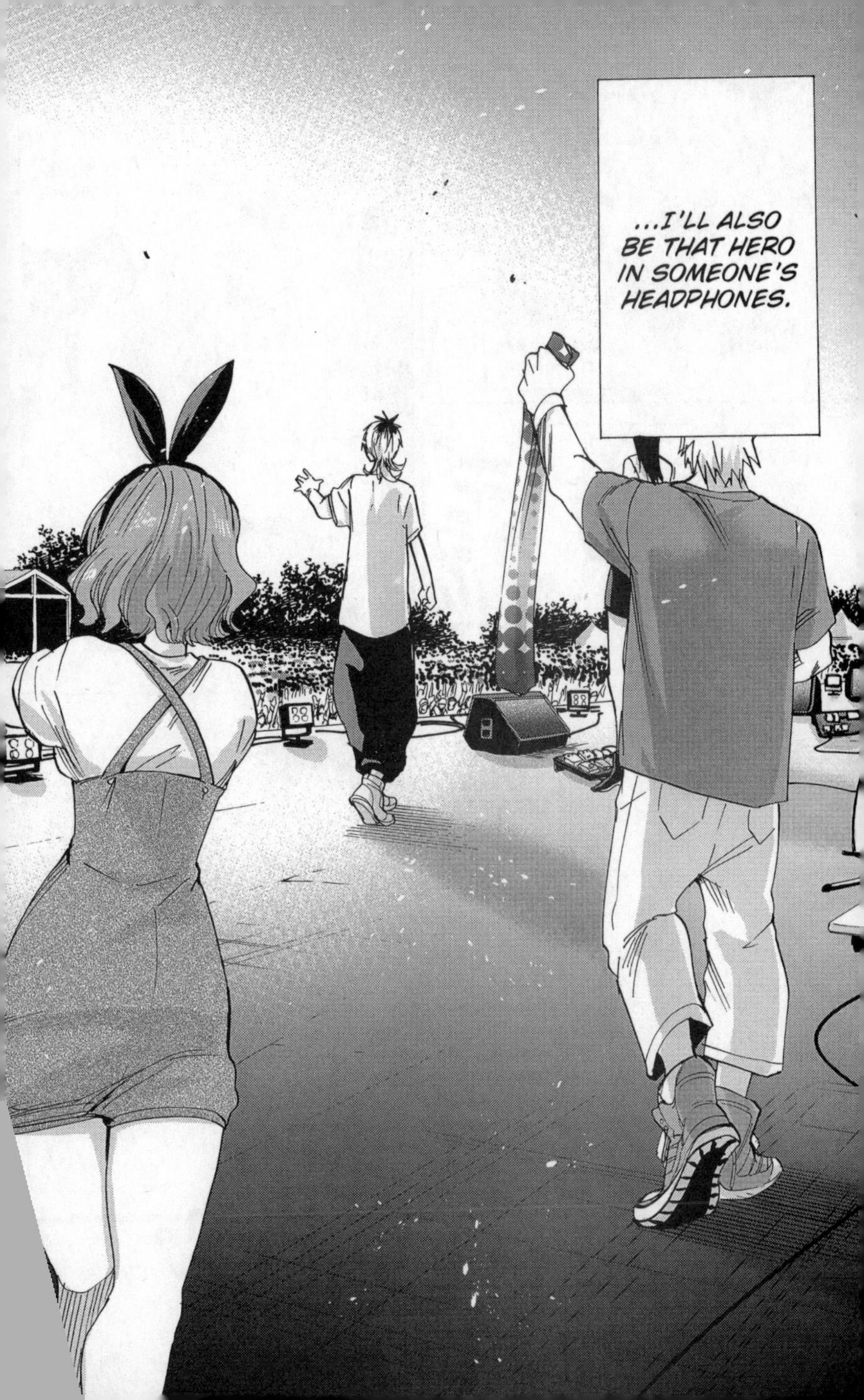
...I'LL ALSO BE THAT HERO IN SOMEONE'S HEADPHONES.

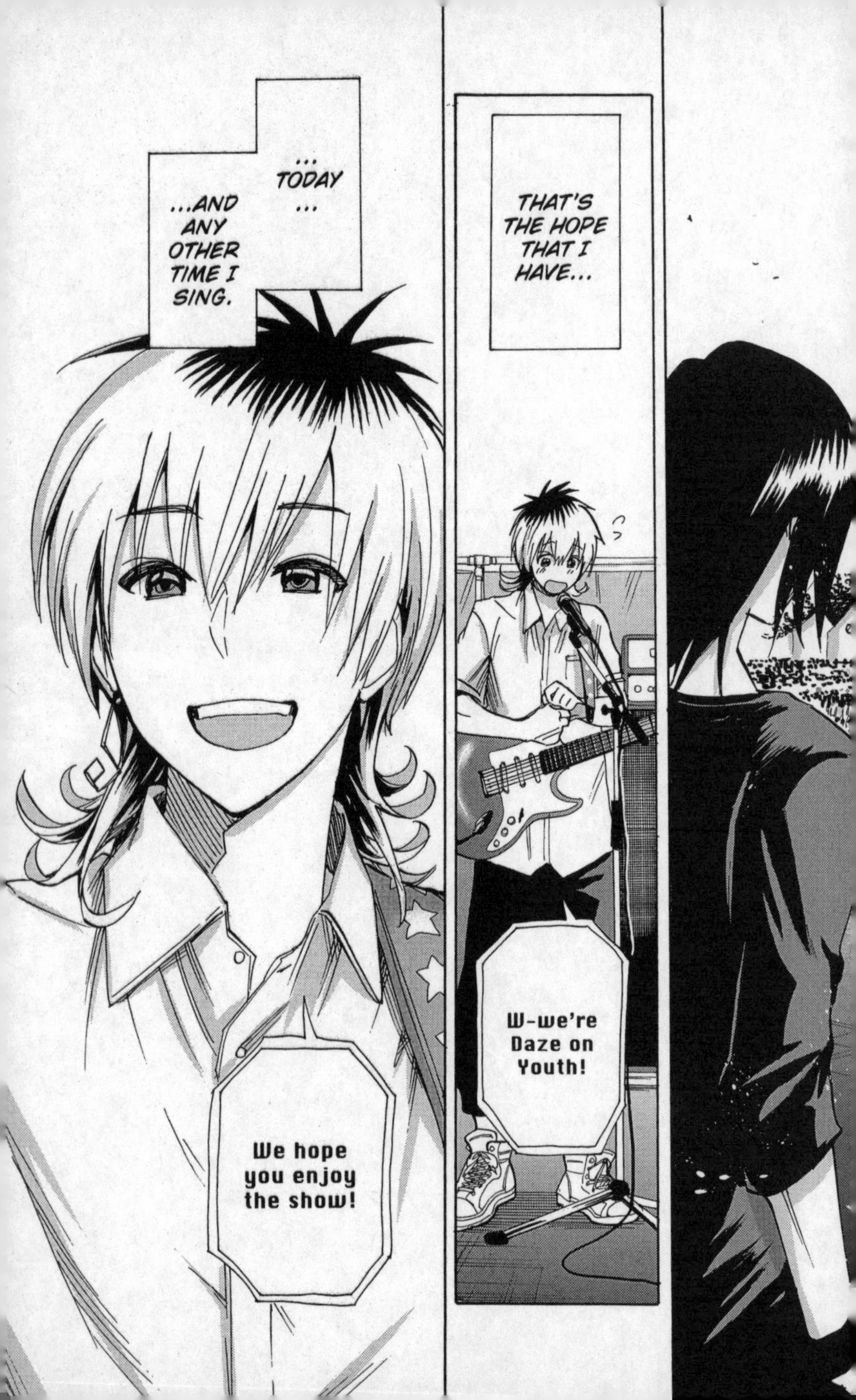
THAT'S THE HOPE THAT I HAVE...
W-we're Daze on Youth!
... TODAY ...
...AND ANY OTHER TIME I SING.
We hope you enjoy the show!

Days on Fes

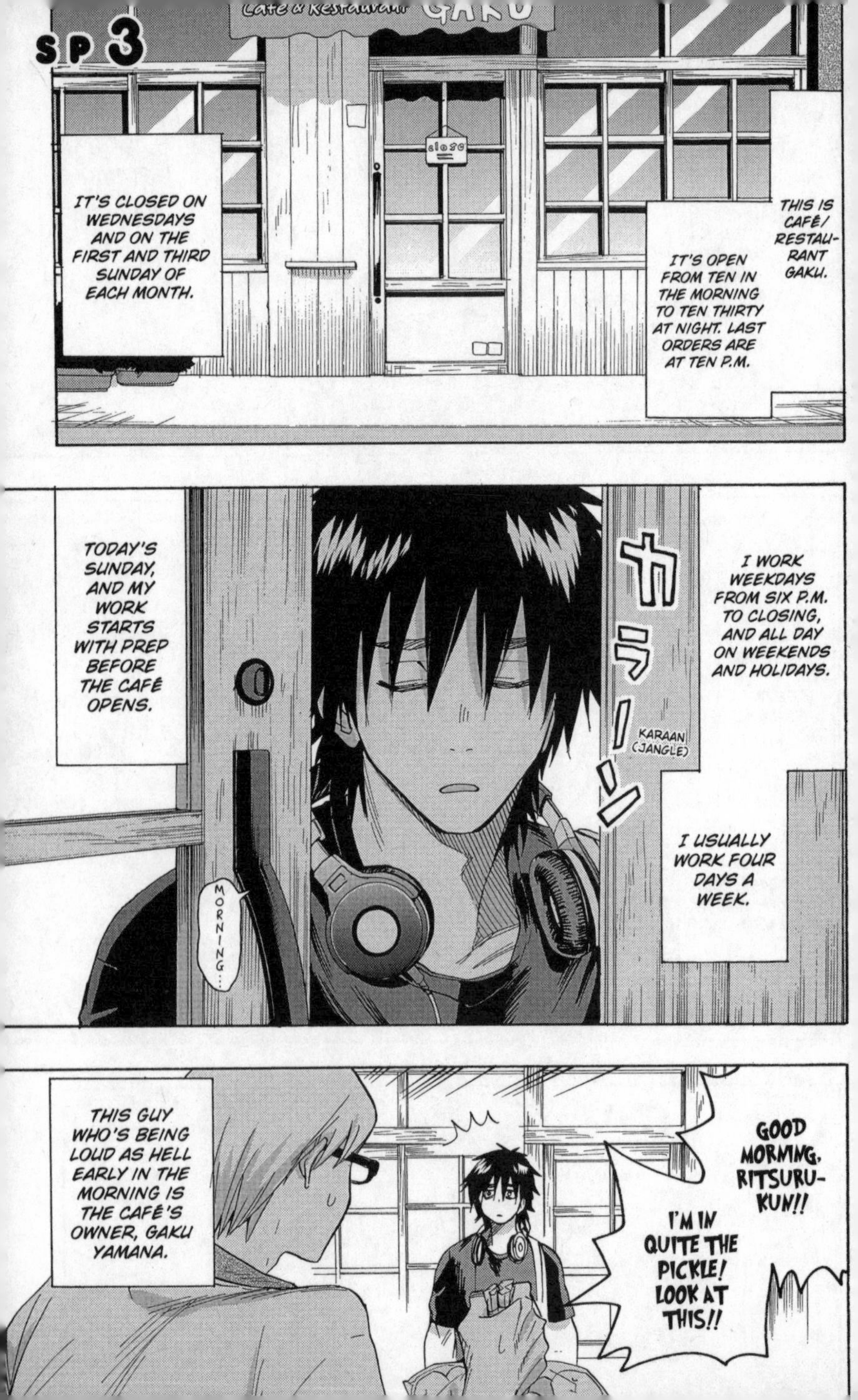
SP 3
Cafe & Restaurant GAKU
close
THIS IS CAFÉ/ RESTAURANT GAKU.
IT'S OPEN FROM TEN IN THE MORNING TO TEN THIRTY AT NIGHT. LAST ORDERS ARE AT TEN P.M.
IT'S CLOSED ON WEDNESDAYS AND ON THE FIRST AND THIRD SUNDAY OF EACH MONTH.
I WORK WEEKDAYS FROM SIX P.M. TO CLOSING, AND ALL DAY ON WEEKENDS AND HOLIDAYS.
I USUALLY WORK FOUR DAYS A WEEK.
KARAAN (JANGLE)
MORNING...
TODAY'S SUNDAY, AND MY WORK STARTS WITH PREP BEFORE THE CAFÉ OPENS.
GOOD MORNING, RITSURU-KUN!!
I'M IN QUITE THE PICKLE! LOOK AT THIS!!
THIS GUY WHO'S BEING LOUD AS HELL EARLY IN THE MORNING IS THE CAFÉ'S OWNER, GAKU YAMANA.

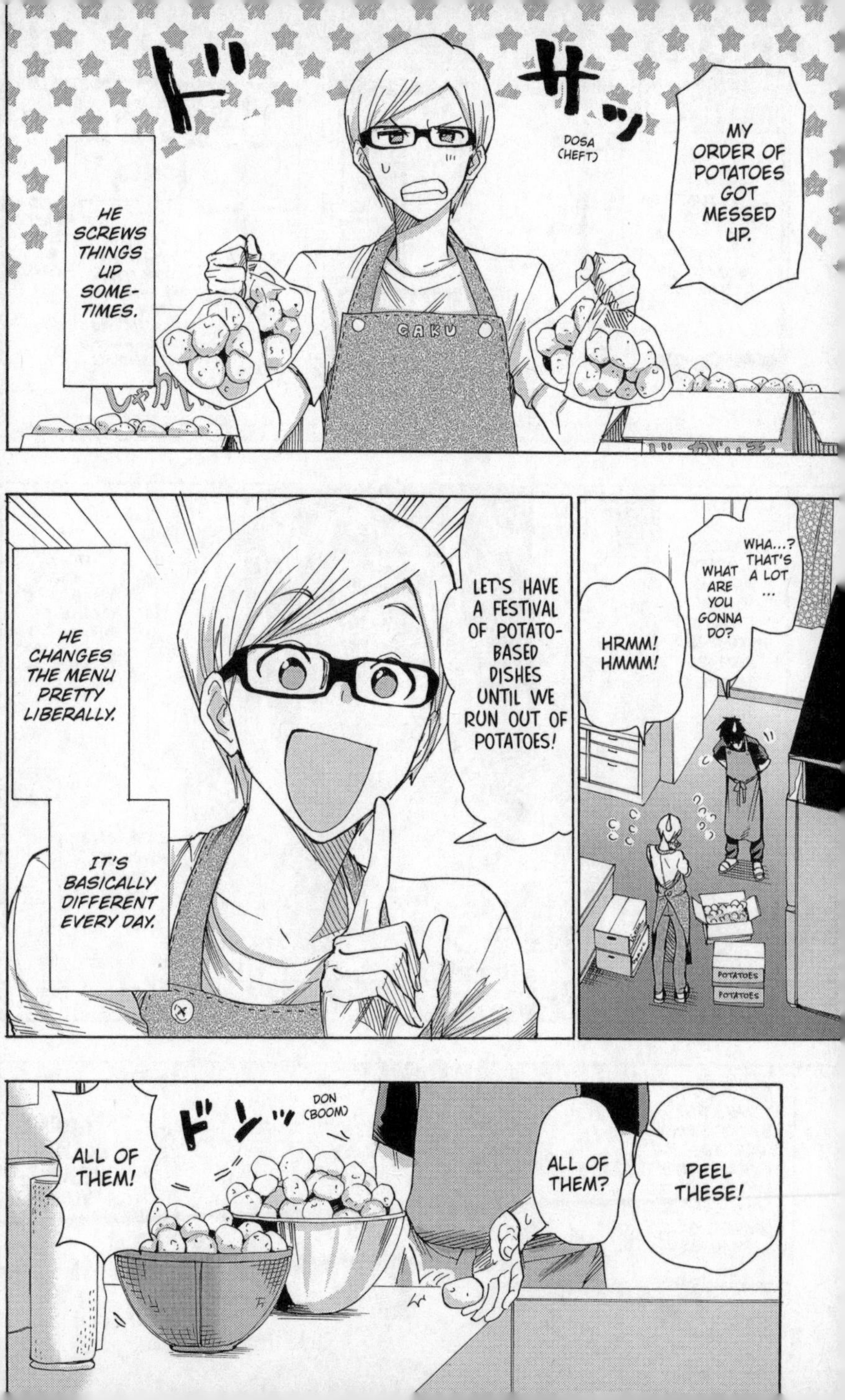 ドサッ
DOSA (HEFT)
MY ORDER OF POTATOES GOT MESSED UP.
HE SCREWS THINGS UP SOMETIMES.
WHA...? THAT'S A LOT...
WHAT ARE YOU GONNA DO?
HRMM! HMMM!
LET'S HAVE A FESTIVAL OF POTATO-BASED DISHES UNTIL WE RUN OUT OF POTATOES!
HE CHANGES THE MENU PRETTY LIBERALLY.
IT'S BASICALLY DIFFERENT EVERY DAY.
POTATOES
POTATOES
PEEL THESE!
ALL OF THEM?
ドンッ
DON (BOOM)
ALL OF THEM!

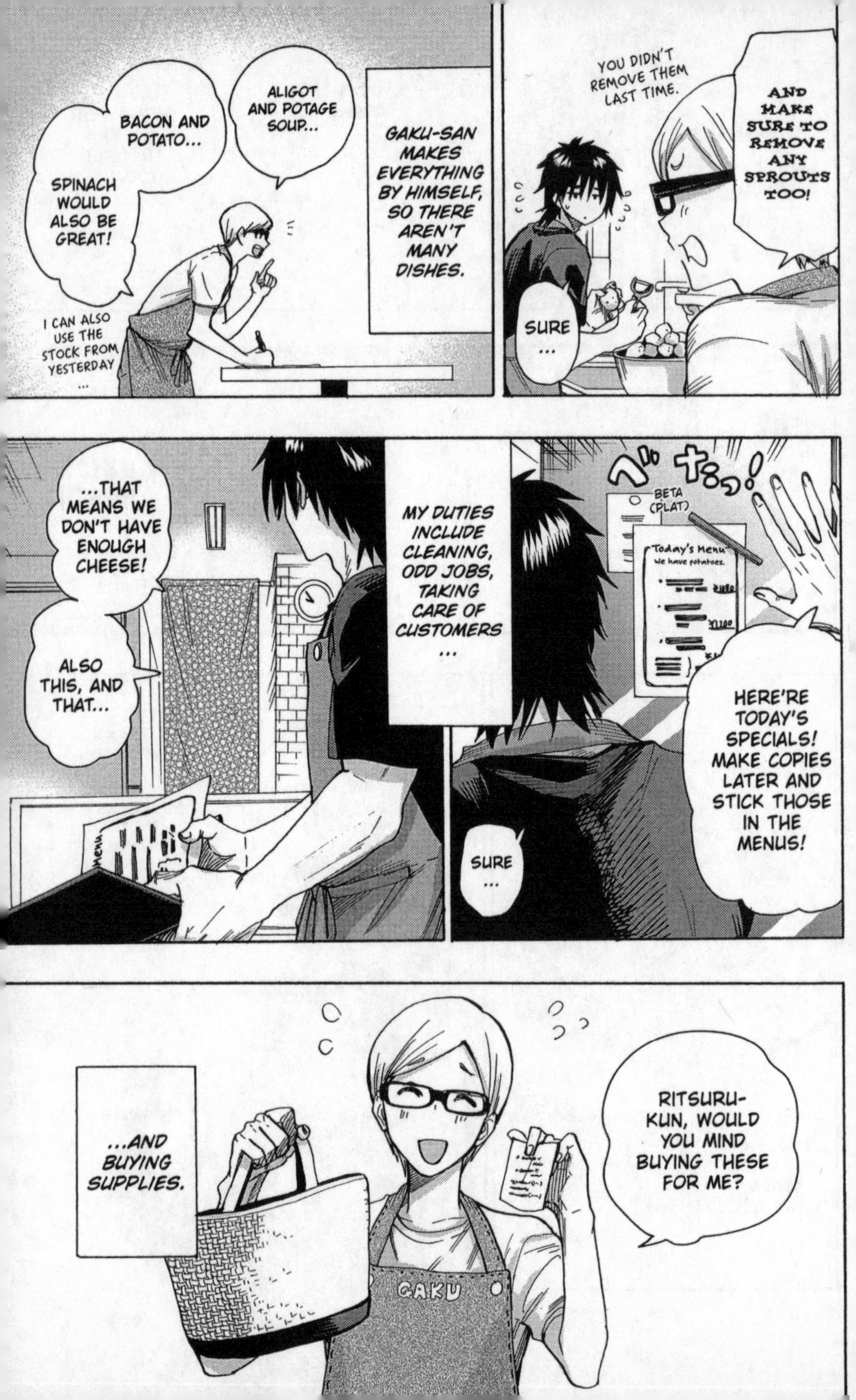
AND MAKE SURE TO REMOVE ANY SPROUTS TOO!
YOU DIDN'T REMOVE THEM LAST TIME.
SURE ...
GAKU-SAN MAKES EVERYTHING BY HIMSELF, SO THERE AREN'T MANY DISHES.
ALIGOT AND POTAGE SOUP...
BACON AND POTATO...
SPINACH WOULD ALSO BE GREAT!
I CAN ALSO USE THE STOCK FROM YESTERDAY ...
BETA (PLAT)
Today's Menu
We have potatoes.
HERE'RE TODAY'S SPECIALS! MAKE COPIES LATER AND STICK THOSE IN THE MENUS!
SURE ...
MY DUTIES INCLUDE CLEANING, ODD JOBS, TAKING CARE OF CUSTOMERS ...
...THAT MEANS WE DON'T HAVE ENOUGH CHEESE!
ALSO THIS, AND THAT...
Menu
RITSURU-KUN, WOULD YOU MIND BUYING THESE FOR ME?
...AND BUYING SUPPLIES.
GAKU

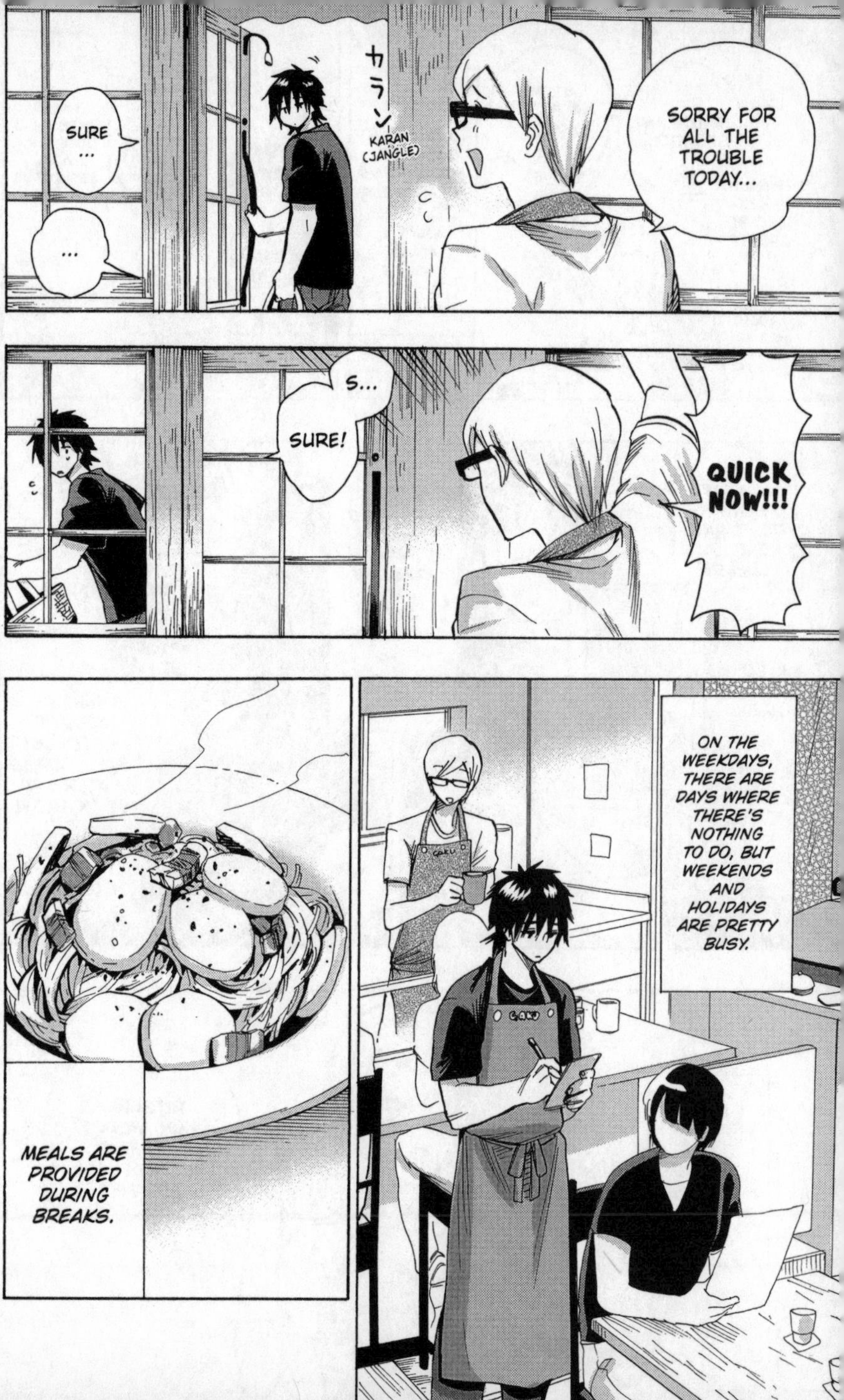

SORRY FOR ALL THE TROUBLE TODAY...
カラン
KARAN (JANGLE)
SURE ...
...
QUICK NOW!!!
S... SURE!
ON THE WEEKDAYS, THERE ARE DAYS WHERE THERE'S NOTHING TO DO, BUT WEEKENDS AND HOLIDAYS ARE PRETTY BUSY.
MEALS ARE PROVIDED DURING BREAKS.

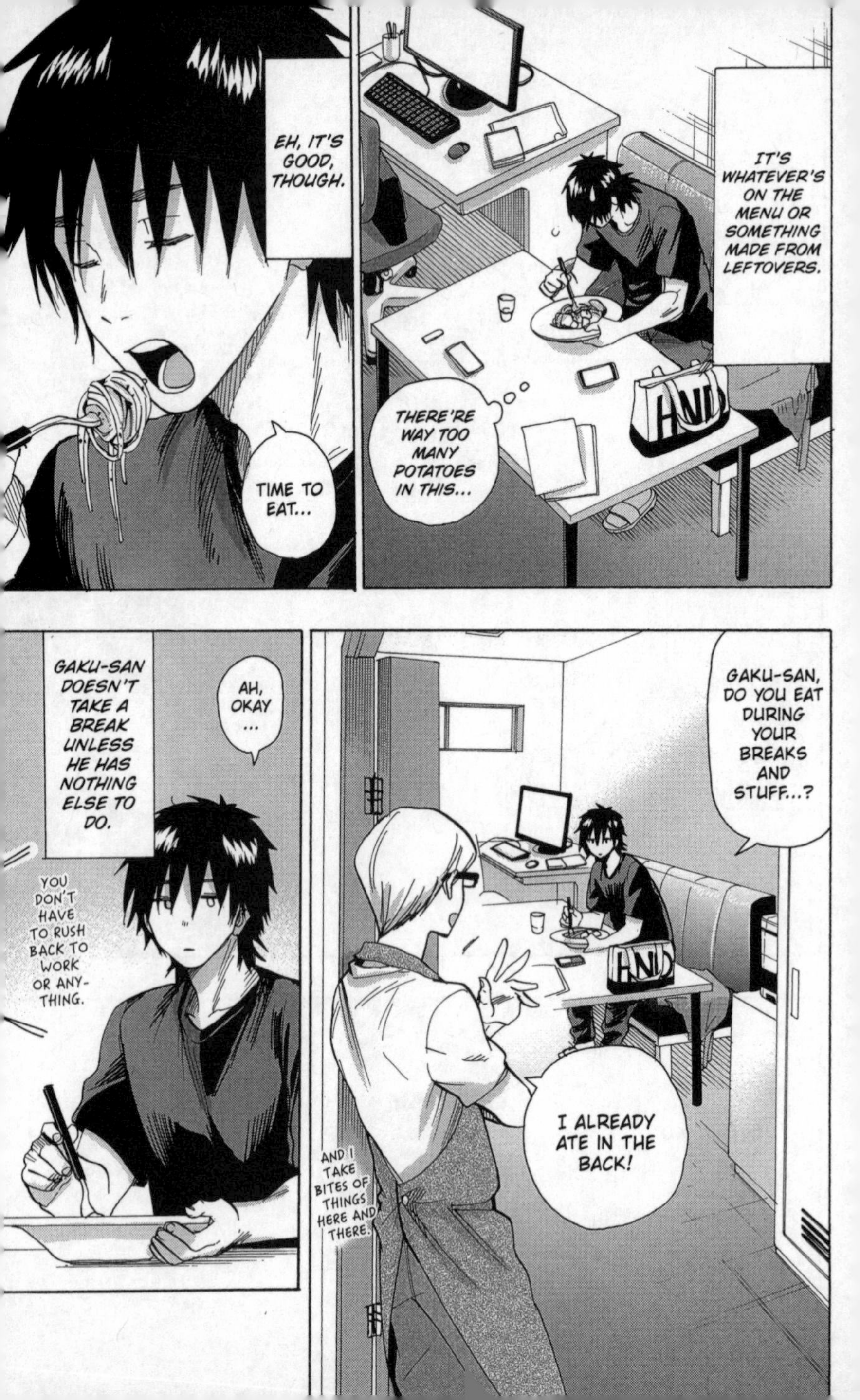
IT'S WHATEVER'S ON THE MENU OR SOMETHING MADE FROM LEFTOVERS.
THERE'RE WAY TOO MANY POTATOES IN THIS...
EH, IT'S GOOD, THOUGH.
TIME TO EAT...
GAKU-SAN, DO YOU EAT DURING YOUR BREAKS AND STUFF...?
I ALREADY ATE IN THE BACK!
AND I TAKE BITES OF THINGS HERE AND THERE.
AH, OKAY...
GAKU-SAN DOESN'T TAKE A BREAK UNLESS HE HAS NOTHING ELSE TO DO.
YOU DON'T HAVE TO RUSH BACK TO WORK OR ANY-THING.

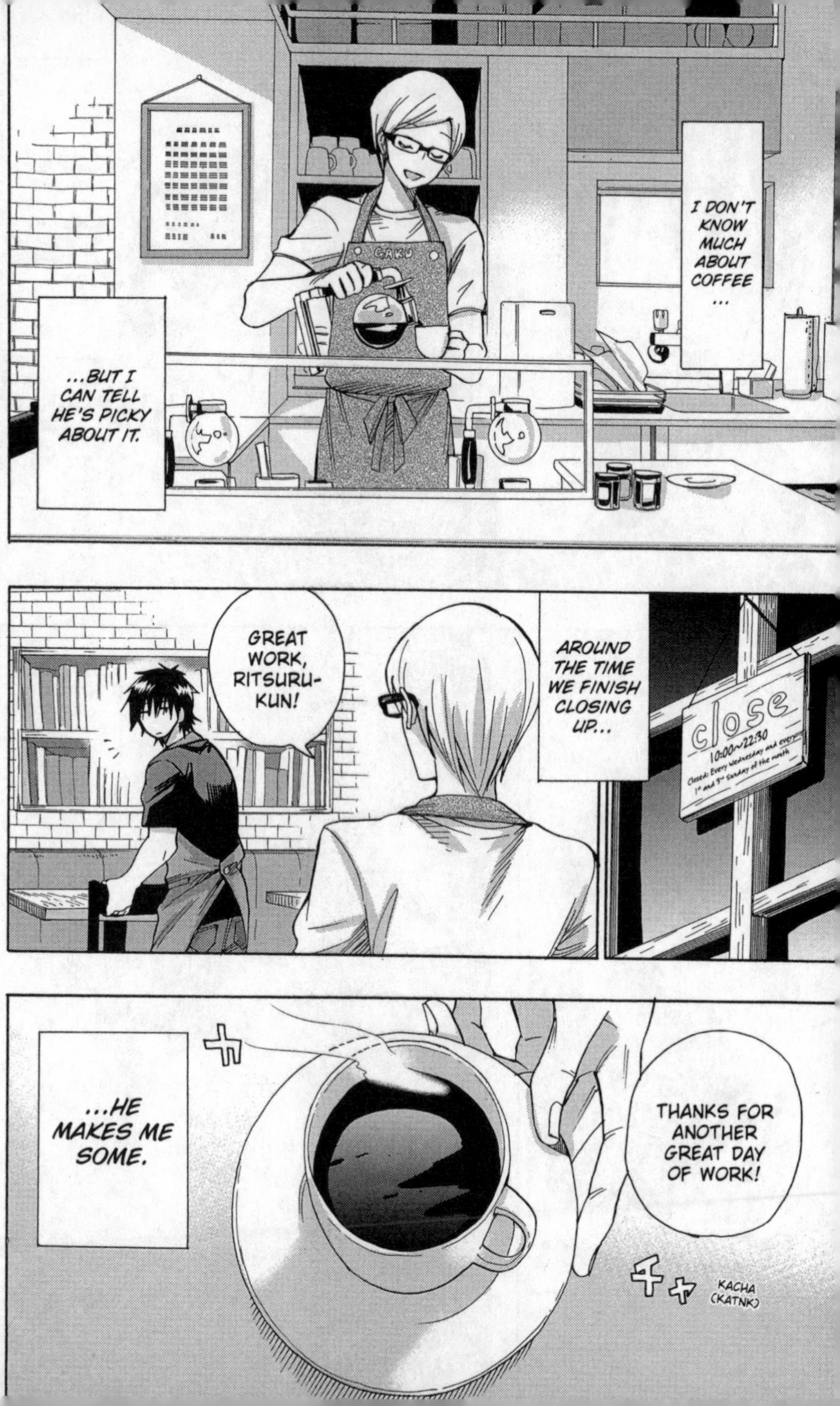
I DON'T KNOW MUCH ABOUT COFFEE...
...BUT I CAN TELL HE'S PICKY ABOUT IT.
close
10:00~22:30
Closed: Every Wednesday and every 1st and 3rd Sunday of the month
AROUND THE TIME WE FINISH CLOSING UP...
GREAT WORK, RITSURU-KUN!
THANKS FOR ANOTHER GREAT DAY OF WORK!
KACHA (KATNK)
...HE MAKES ME SOME.

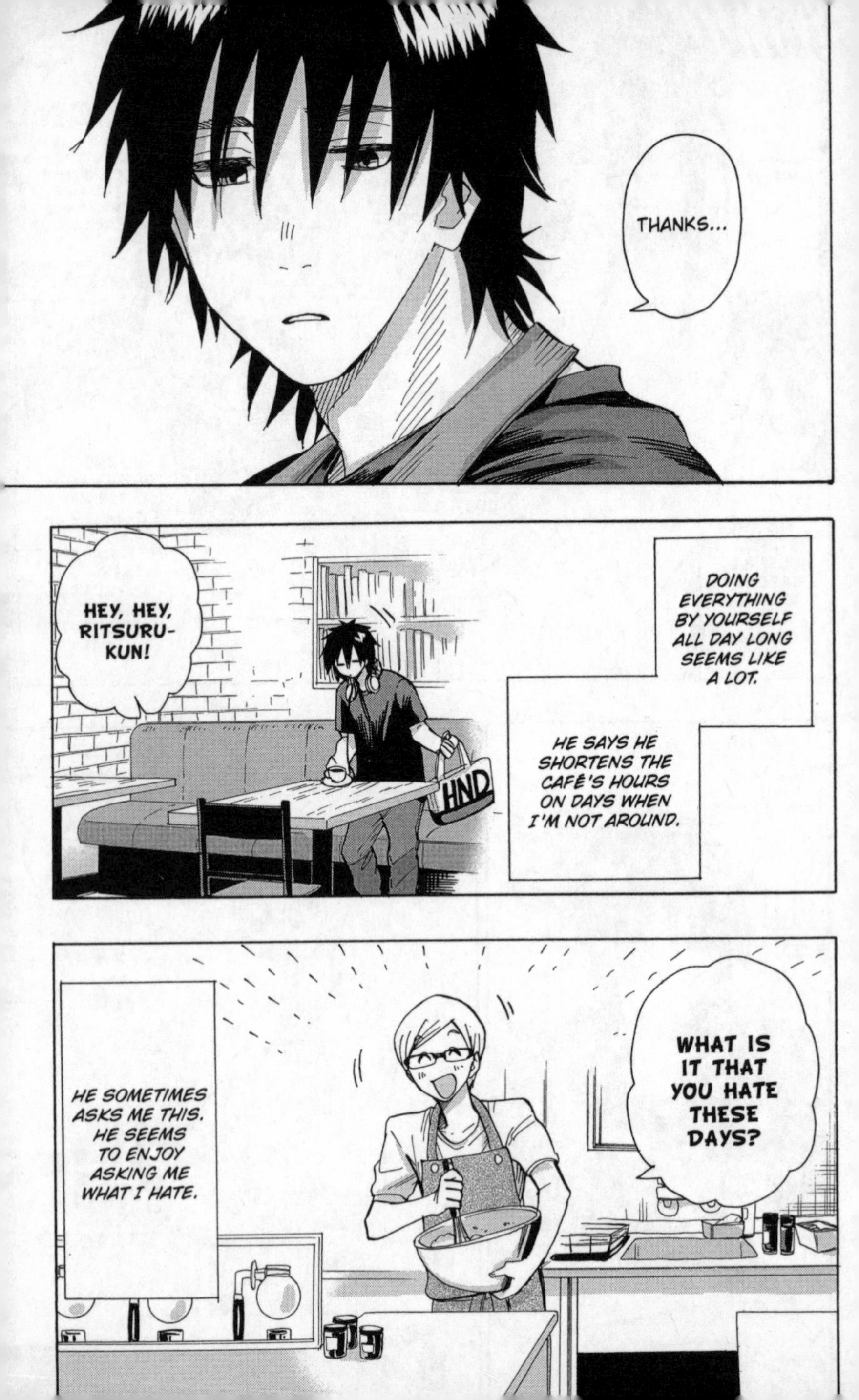
THANKS...
DOING EVERYTHING BY YOURSELF ALL DAY LONG SEEMS LIKE A LOT.
HE SAYS HE SHORTENS THE CAFÉ'S HOURS ON DAYS WHEN I'M NOT AROUND.
HEY, HEY, RITSURU-KUN!
WHAT IS IT THAT YOU HATE THESE DAYS?
HE SOMETIMES ASKS ME THIS. HE SEEMS TO ENJOY ASKING ME WHAT I HATE.
HND

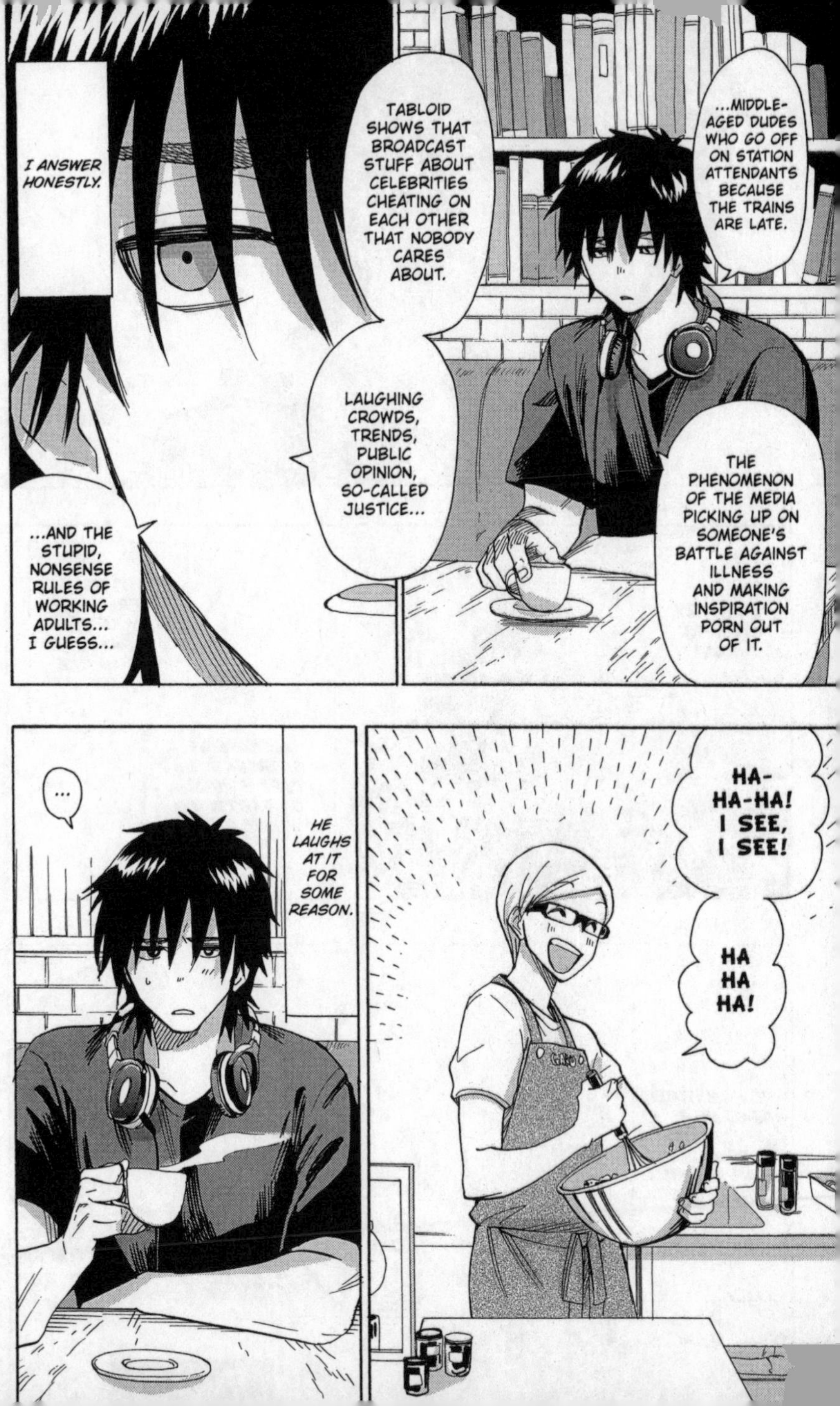
...MIDDLE-AGED DUDES WHO GO OFF ON STATION ATTENDANTS BECAUSE THE TRAINS ARE LATE.
TABLOID SHOWS THAT BROADCAST STUFF ABOUT CELEBRITIES CHEATING ON EACH OTHER THAT NOBODY CARES ABOUT.
THE PHENOMENON OF THE MEDIA PICKING UP ON SOMEONE'S BATTLE AGAINST ILLNESS AND MAKING INSPIRATION PORN OUT OF IT.
LAUGHING CROWDS, TRENDS, PUBLIC OPINION, SO-CALLED JUSTICE...
I ANSWER HONESTLY.
...AND THE STUPID, NONSENSE RULES OF WORKING ADULTS... I GUESS...
HA-HA-HA! I SEE, I SEE!
HA HA HA!
HE LAUGHS AT IT FOR SOME REASON.
...

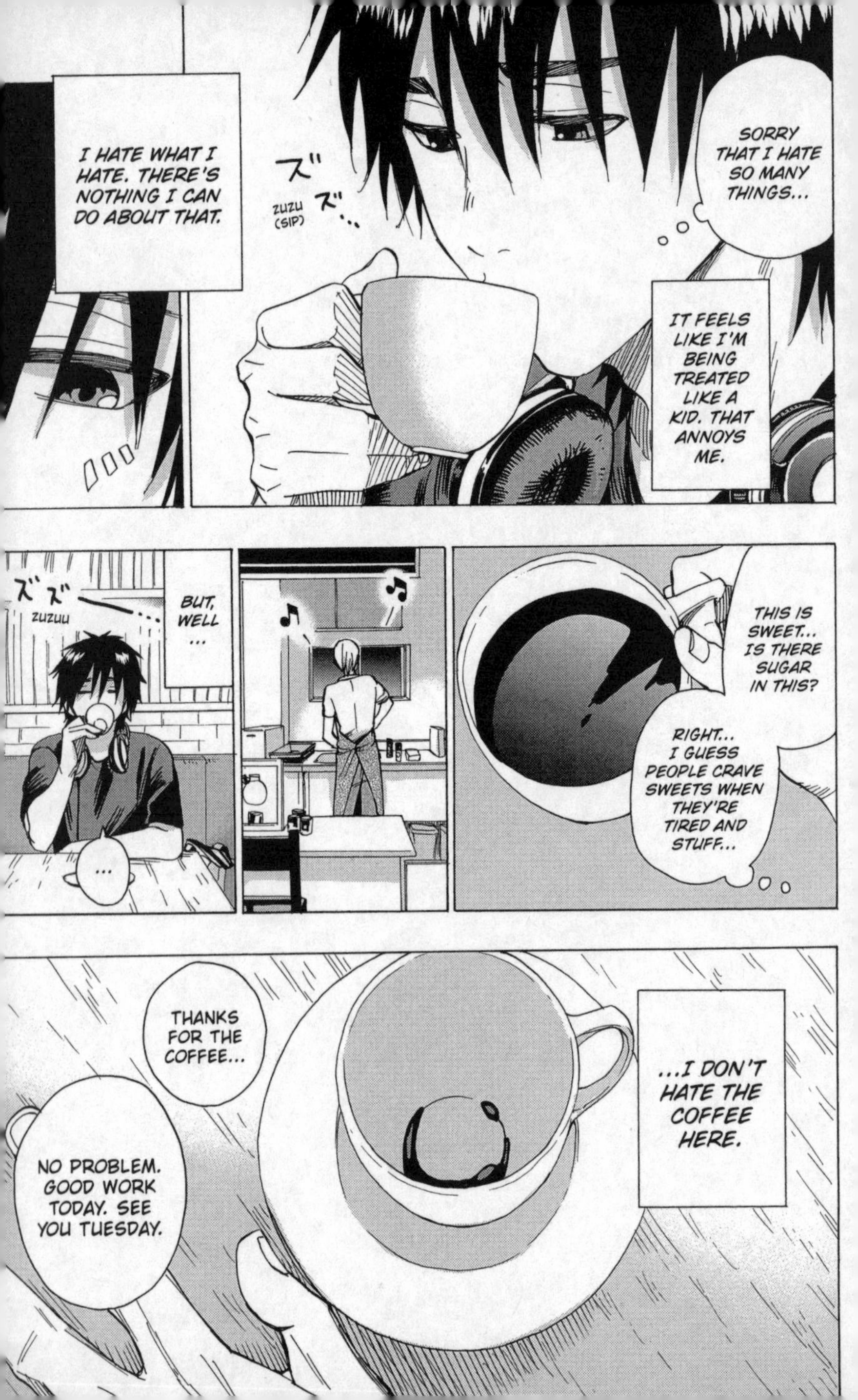
SORRY THAT I HATE SO MANY THINGS...
IT FEELS LIKE I'M BEING TREATED LIKE A KID. THAT ANNOYS ME.
ズズ...
ZUZU (SIP)
I HATE WHAT I HATE. THERE'S NOTHING I CAN DO ABOUT THAT.
THIS IS SWEET... IS THERE SUGAR IN THIS?
RIGHT... I GUESS PEOPLE CRAVE SWEETS WHEN THEY'RE TIRED AND STUFF...
BUT, WELL ...
ズズー...
ZUZUU
...
...I DON'T HATE THE COFFEE HERE.
THANKS FOR THE COFFEE...
NO PROBLEM. GOOD WORK TODAY. SEE YOU TUESDAY.

Days on Fes

SP 4

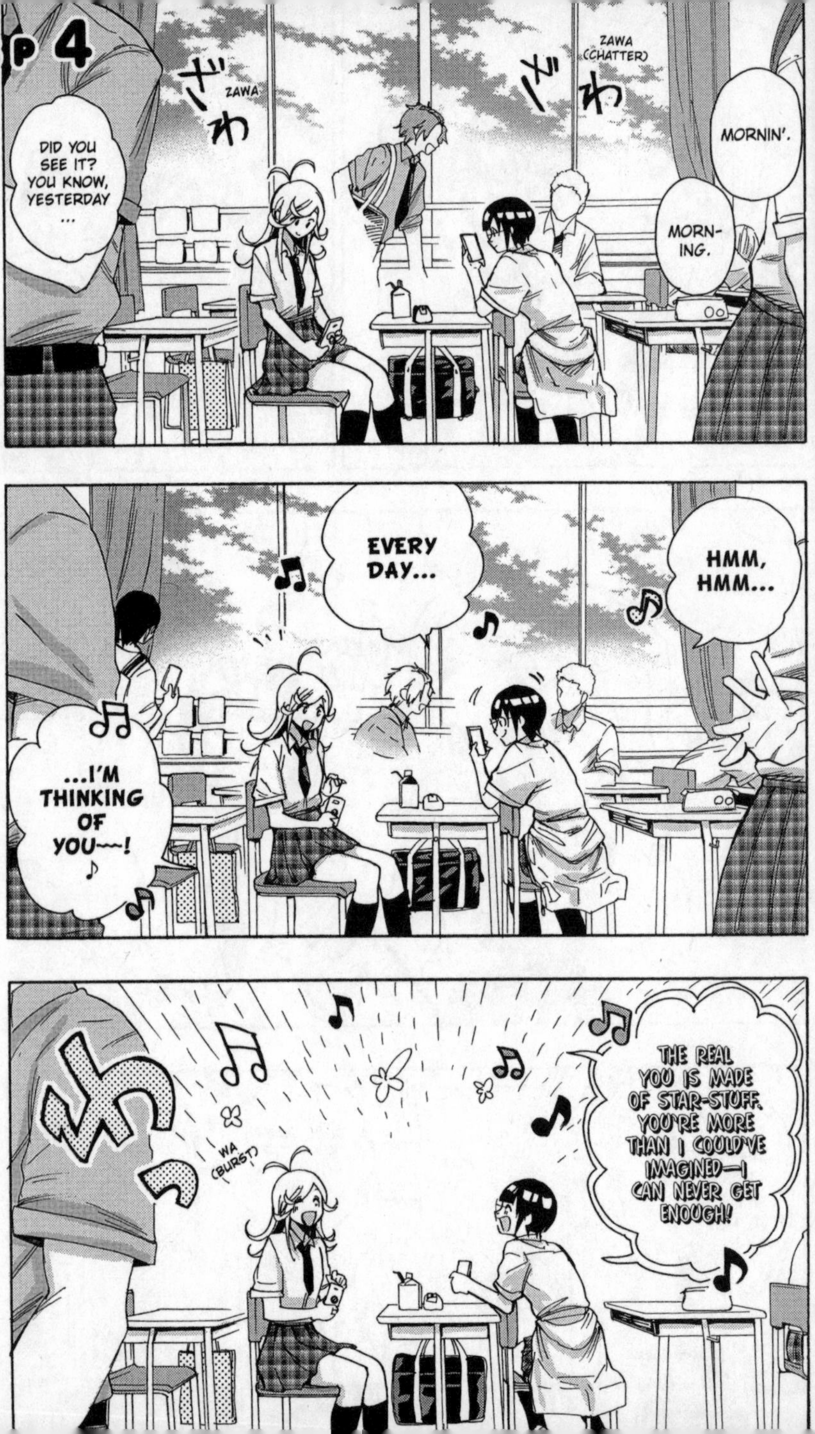
MORNIN'.
MORN-ING.
ZAWA (CHATTER)
ZAWA
DID YOU SEE IT? YOU KNOW, YESTERDAY ...
HMM, HMM...
EVERY DAY...
...I'M THINKING OF YOU~~~! ♪
THE REAL YOU IS MADE OF STAR-STUFF. YOU'RE MORE THAN I COULD'VE IMAGINED—I CAN NEVER GET ENOUGH!
WA (BURST)

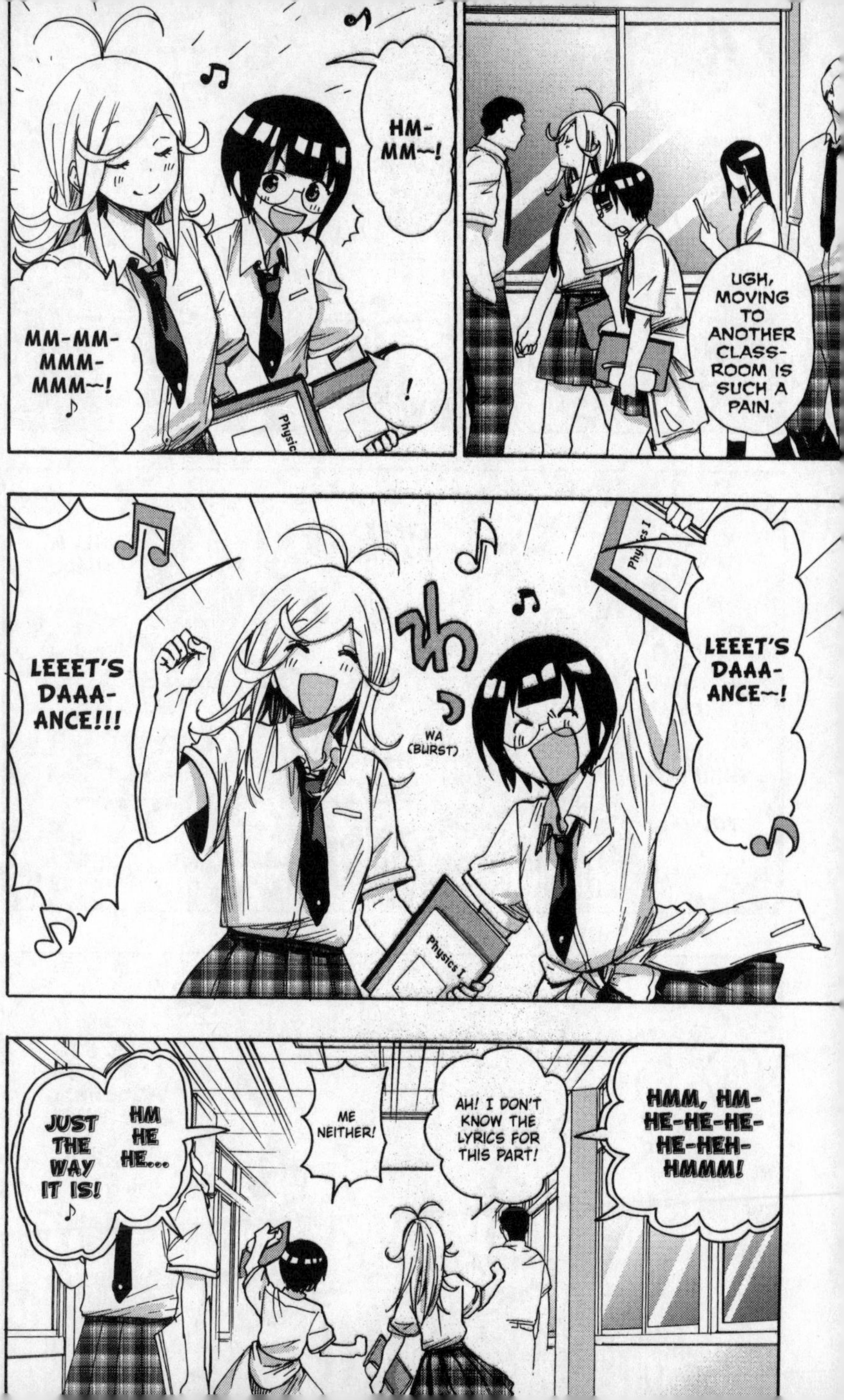
UGH, MOVING TO ANOTHER CLASS-ROOM IS SUCH A PAIN.
HM-MM~!
!
MM-MM-MMM-MMM~! ♪
Physics
LEEET'S DAAA-ANCE~!
WA (BURST)
LEEET'S DAAA-ANCE!!!
Physics I
Physics I
HMM, HM-HE-HE-HE-HE-HEH-HMMM!
AH! I DON'T KNOW THE LYRICS FOR THIS PART!
ME NEITHER!
HM HE HE...
JUST THE WAY IT IS! ♪

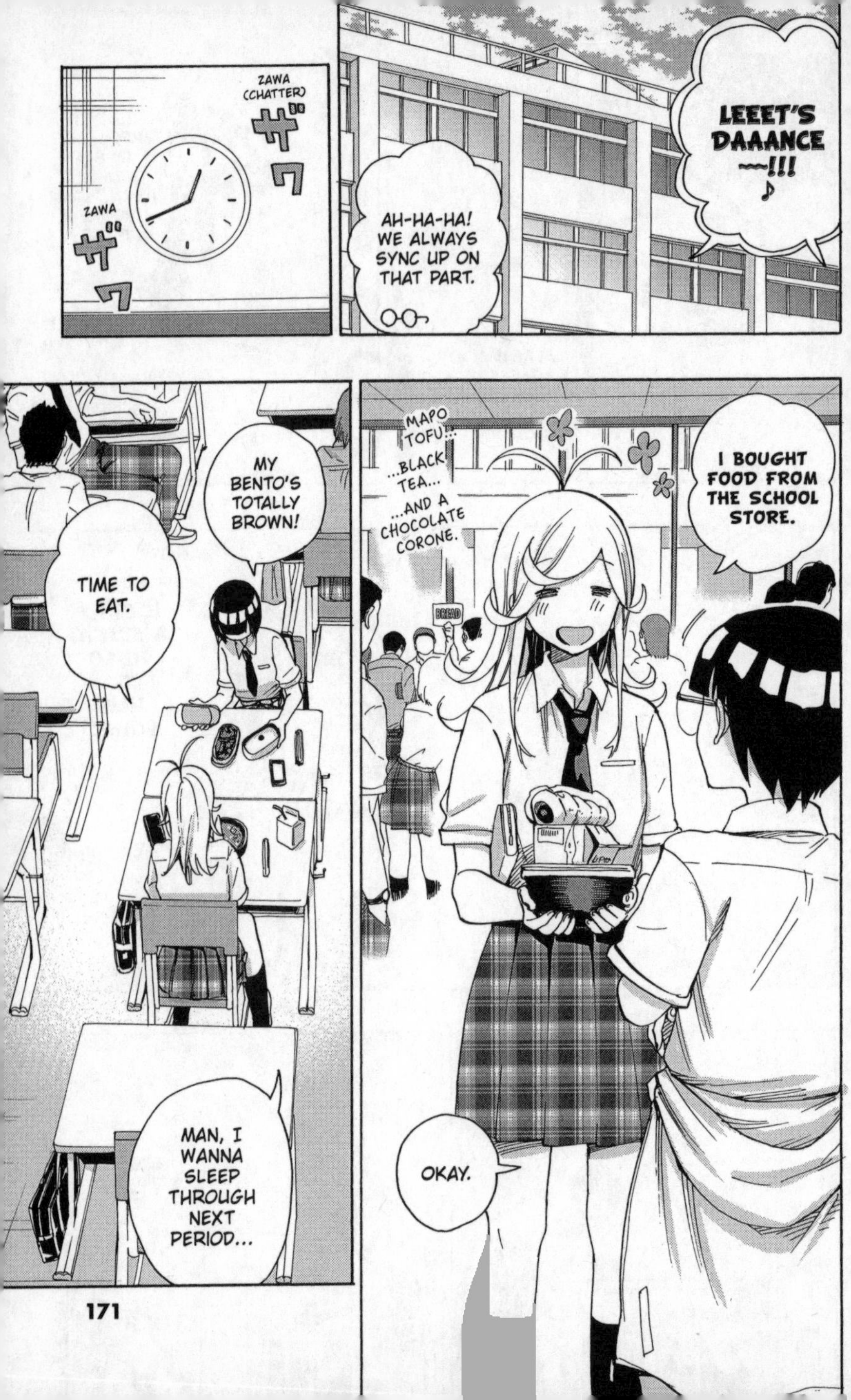
LEEET'S DAAANCE ~~!!! ♪
AH-HA-HA! WE ALWAYS SYNC UP ON THAT PART.
ZAWA (CHATTER)
ザワ
ZAWA
ザワ
I BOUGHT FOOD FROM THE SCHOOL STORE.
MAPO TOFU...
...BLACK TEA...
...AND A CHOCOLATE CORONE.
BREAD
OKAY.
MY BENTO'S TOTALLY BROWN!
TIME TO EAT.
MAN, I WANNA SLEEP THROUGH NEXT PERIOD...

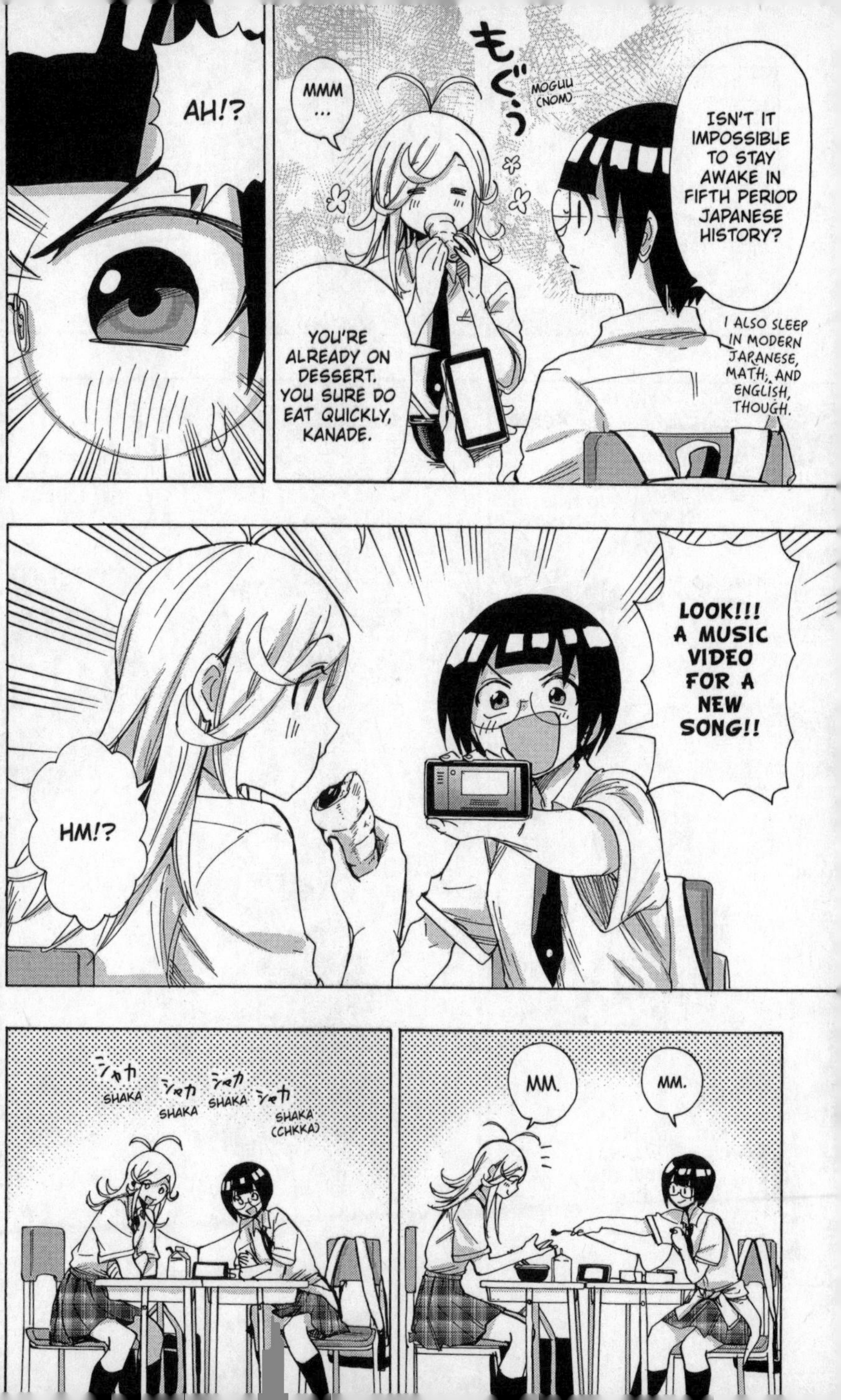
ISN'T IT IMPOSSIBLE TO STAY AWAKE IN FIFTH PERIOD JAPANESE HISTORY?
I ALSO SLEEP IN MODERN JAPANESE, MATH, AND ENGLISH, THOUGH.
もぐぅ
MOGUU (NOM)
MMM ...
YOU'RE ALREADY ON DESSERT. YOU SURE DO EAT QUICKLY, KANADE.
AH!?
LOOK!!! A MUSIC VIDEO FOR A NEW SONG!!
HM!?
MM.
MM.
シャカ
SHAKA
シャカ
SHAKA
シャカ
SHAKA
シャカ
SHAKA (CHKKA)

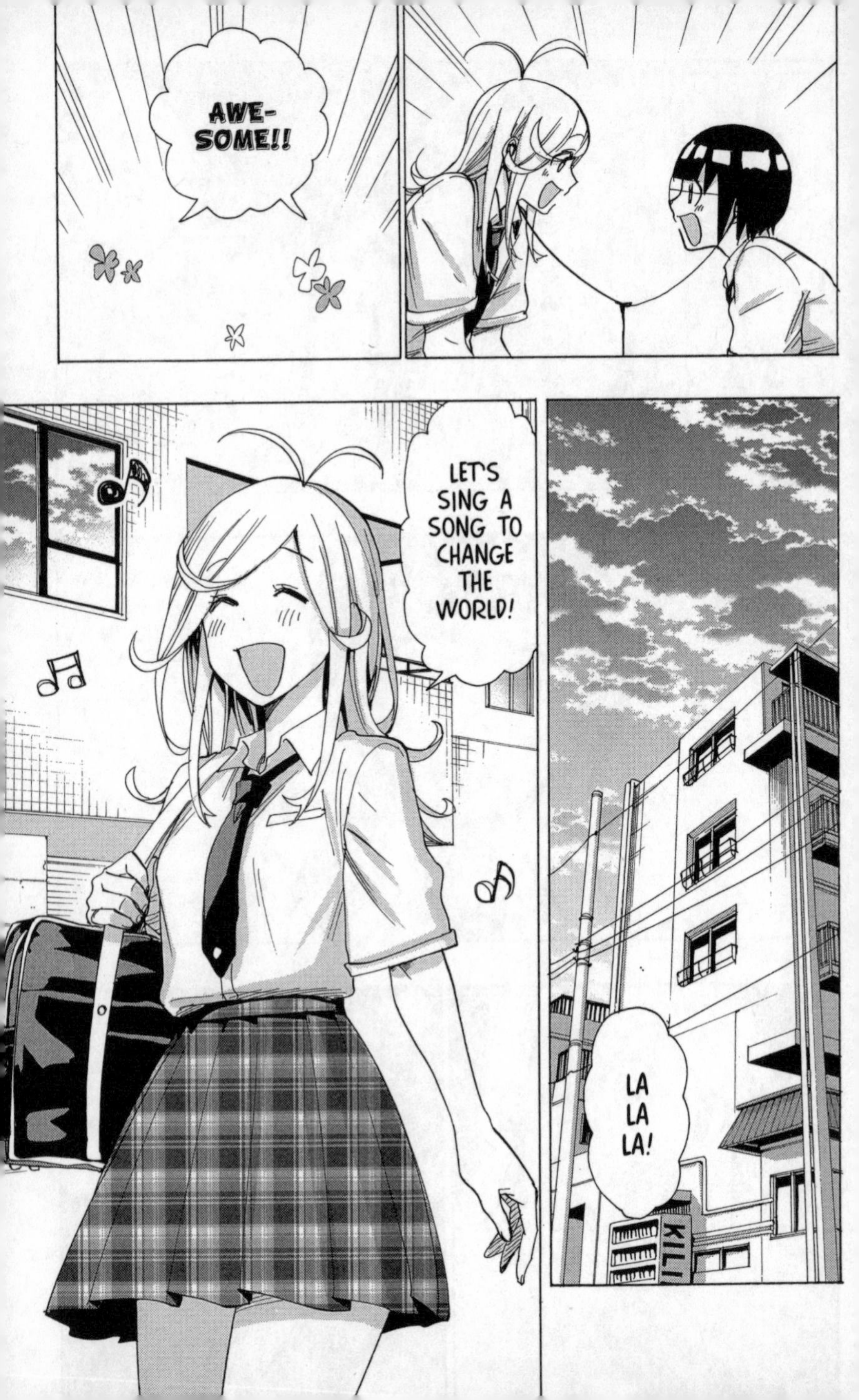
AWE-SOME!!
LA LA LA!
LET'S SING A SONG TO CHANGE THE WORLD!
KILI

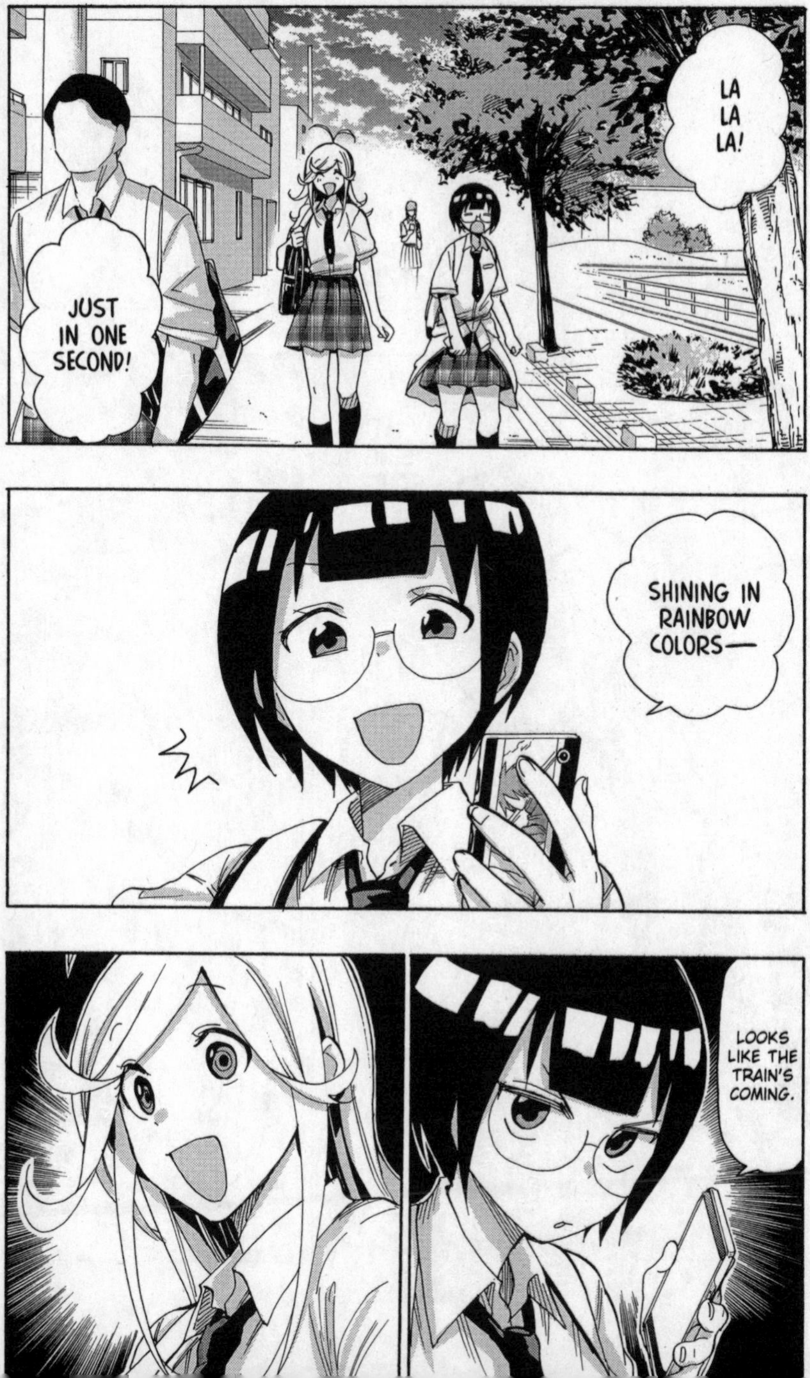
LA LA LA!
JUST IN ONE SECOND!
SHINING IN RAINBOW COLORS—
LOOKS LIKE THE TRAIN'S COMING.

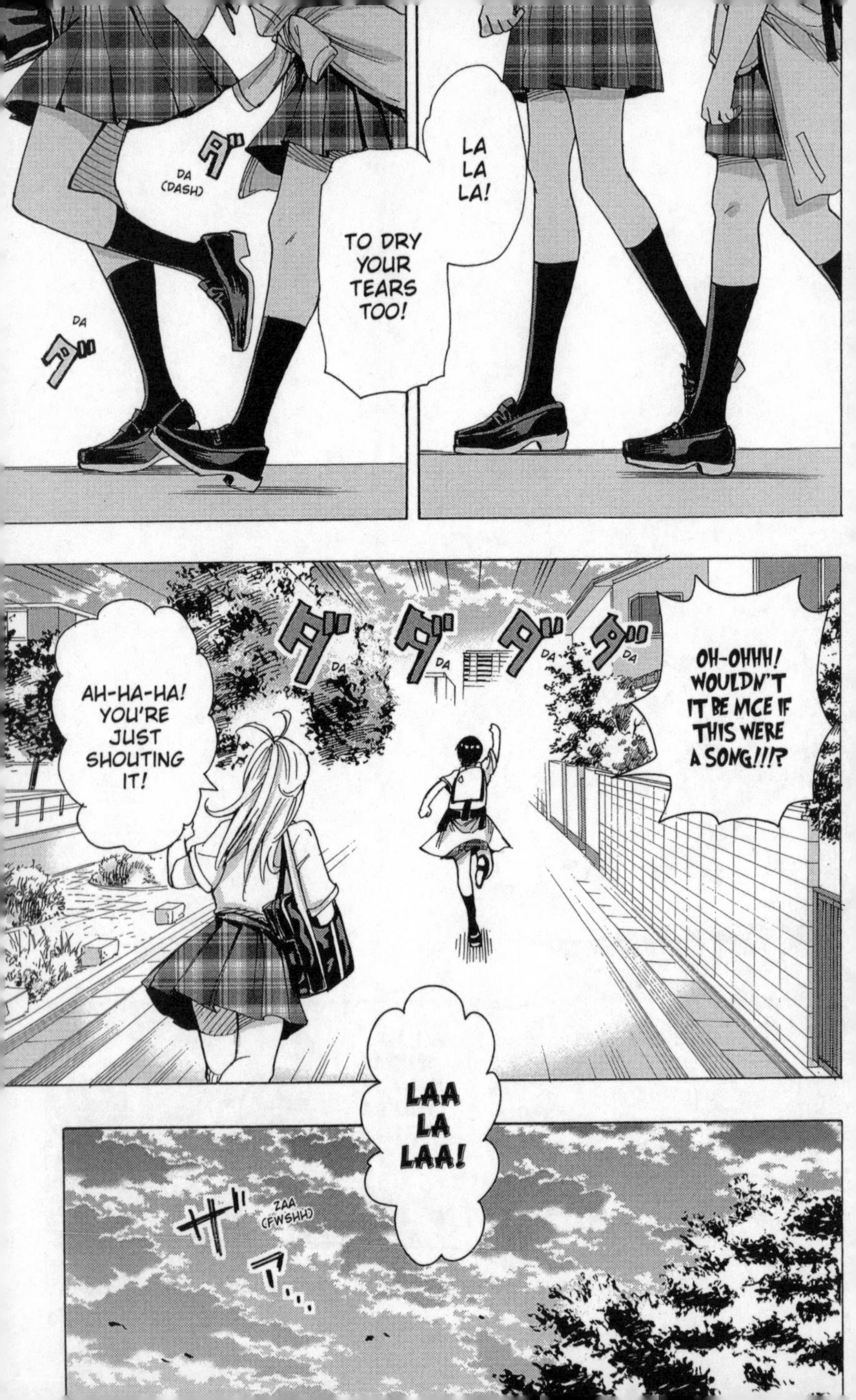
LA LA LA! TO DRY YOUR TEARS TOO!
DA (DASH)
DA
OH-OHHH! WOULDN'T IT BE NICE IF THIS WERE A SONG!!!?
DA
DA
DA
DA
AH-HA-HA! YOU'RE JUST SHOUTING IT!
LAA LA LAA!
ZAA (FWSHH)

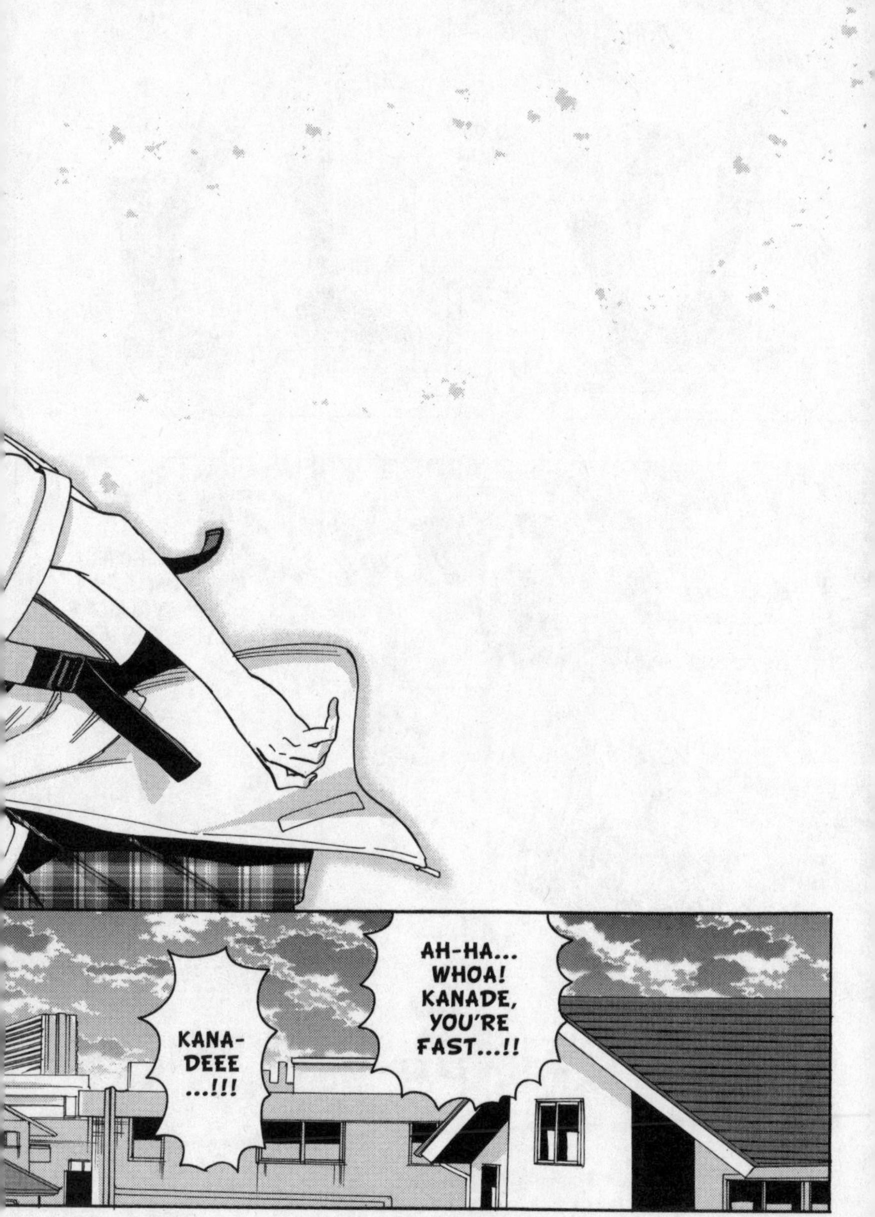
AH-HA... WHOA! KANADE, YOU'RE FAST...!!
KANA-DEEE ...!!!

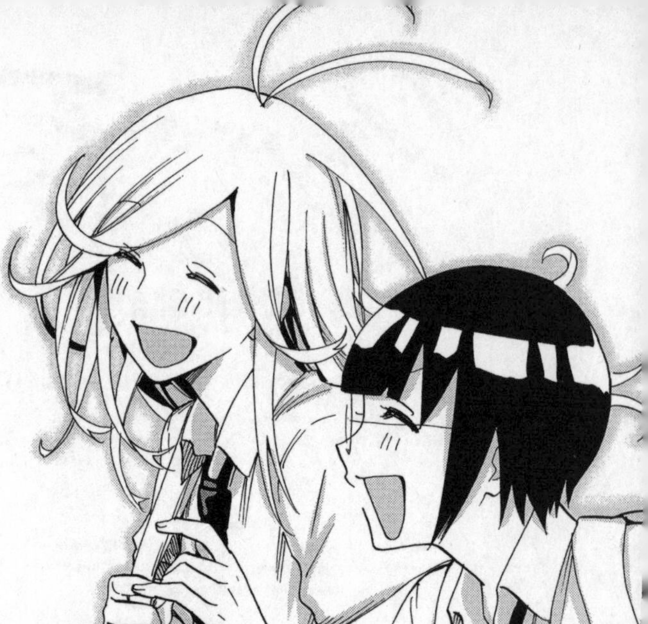

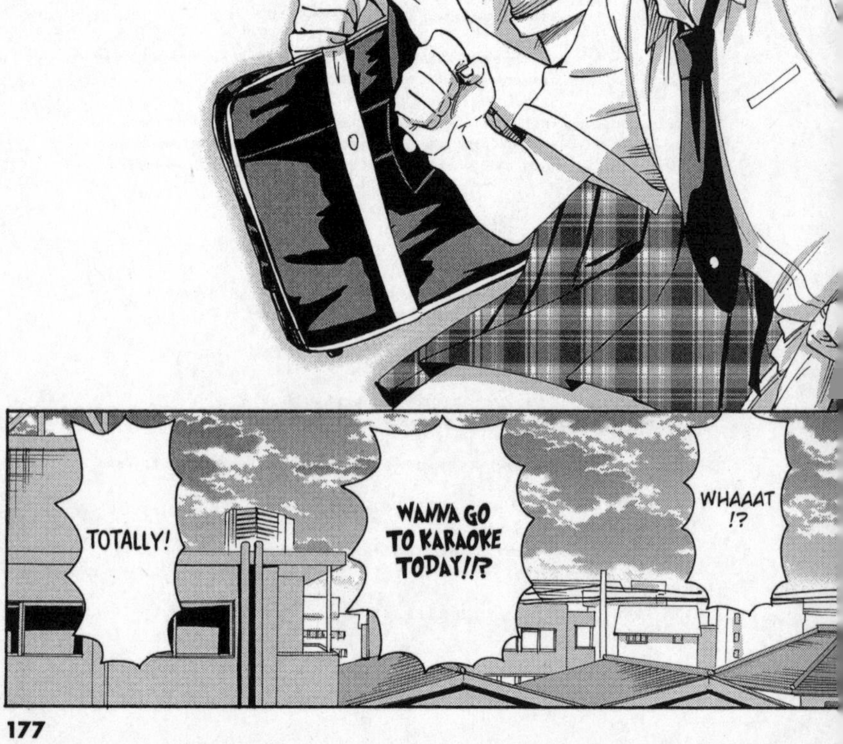
WHAAAT!?
WANNA GO TO KARAOKE TODAY!!?
TOTALLY!

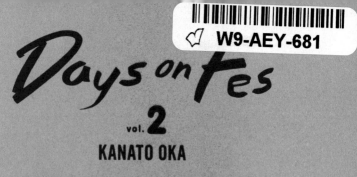

Days on Fes

vol. 2

KANATO OKA

TRANSLATION: AJANI OLOYE | LETTERING: ALEXIS ECKERMAN

DAYS ON FES Vol. 2
©Kanato Oka 2019
First published in Japan in 2019 by KADOKAWA CORPORATION, Tokyo.
English translation rights arranged with KADOKAWA CORPORATION, Tokyo through Tuttle-Mori Agency, Inc., Tokyo.

Yen Press
150 West 30th Street, 19th Floor
New York, NY 10001

Visit us at yenpress.com ♪ facebook.com/yenpress ♪ twitter.com/yenpress
yenpress.tumblr.com ♪ instagram.com/yenpress

First Yen Press Edition: June 2021

Library of Congress Control Number: 2020950221

ISBNs: 978-1-9753-1963-2 (paperback)
978-1-9753-1964-9 (ebook)

10 9 8 7 6 5 4 3 2 1

BVG

Printed in the United States of America